D1598664

A Civil War Captain
and His Lady

Love, Courtship, and Combat
From Fort Donelson through the Vicksburg Campaign

To Elizabeth
Hope you
Enjoy the
Book!

Gene Barr

SB
Savas Beatie
California

First Edition, first printing

Library of Congress Cataloging-in-Publication Data

Names: Barr, Gene, author.
Title: A Civil War Captain and His Lady: Love, Courtship, and Combat from Fort Donelson Through the Vicksburg Campaign / by Gene Barr.
Description: First edition | El Dorado Hills, California: Savas Beatie, 2016.
Includes bibliographical references and index.
Identifiers: LCCN 2016017915| ISBN 9781611212907 (hardcover: alk. paper) | ISBN 9781611212914 (ebk.)
Subjects: LCSH: Moore, Josiah, 1833-1897. | United States. Army. Illinois Infantry Regiment, 17th (1861-1866) | United States--History--Civil War, 1861-1865--Personal narratives. | Illinois--History--Civil War, 1861-1865--Personal narratives. |
Soldiers--Illinois--Peoria--Correspondence. | Peoria (Ill.)--Biography.
Classification: LCC E505.5 17th .B37 2016 | DDC 973.7/8092 [B] --dc23
LC record available at https://lccn.loc.gov/2016017915

SB

Published by
Savas Beatie LLC
989 Governor Drive, Suite 102
El Dorado Hills, CA 95762

Phone: 916-941-6896
(web) www.savasbeatie.com
(E-mail) sales@savasbeatie.com

MIX
Paper from
responsible sources
FSC® C011935

Savas Beatie titles are available at special discounts for bulk purchases in the United States by corporations, institutions, and other organizations. For more details, please contact Savas Beatie, P.O. Box 4527, El Dorado Hills, CA 95762, or you may e-mail us at sales@savasbeatie.com, or visit our website at www.savasbeatie.com for additional information.

Proudly published, printed, and warehoused in the United States of America.

To Mary, Lauren, Ryan, and Morgan . . .

Peoria, April 5th 1862.

Capt Moore.

Dear Friend,

With pleasure I devote the present in tracing a few lines to that ever dear friend, Now a Stranger, in this so called "Land of love and sunny Skies"

For Your Support, Encouragement, and Love

Vicksburg Battle Field
May 30th 1863

Miss Jennie E. Lindsay.

Esteemed Lady,

This is such a lovely moonlight evening Oh how I do wish that some one could help me enjoy its balmy southron breezes! But you say that your evening looked so peaceful. what a contrast I believe I would prefer the wish of dear Jennie — a cooler climate and warmer hearts would be much more desirable.

Josiah Moore

The first known uniformed image of Josiah, shown here as a captain, Company F, 17th Illinois Infantry, sometime in 1861.

David and Liz Djupe

Jane Elizabeth (Jennie) Lindsay

This photo is an enlargement of a cased tintype that Jennie sent to Josiah. He mentions in his March 24, 1862 letter to her that he came close to accidentally destroying it at Pittsburg Landing.

David and Liz Djupe

Table of Contents

Table of Contents (continued)

List of Maps

Photos have been placed through the text
for the convenience of the reader.

Preface

IN 1980, William Walton edited a fascinating collection of letters entitled *A Civil War Courtship: The Letters of Edwin Weller From Antietam to Atlanta.* The book featured correspondence written during the American Civil War by a young man named Edwin Weller of the 107th New York Infantry to a young lady from his hometown named Nettie Watkins. "What a pity," editor Walton wistfully exclaimed, "that Nettie's own letters to Edwin have not survived."[1]

It is indeed rare to have nearly all the letters written by both sides of a Civil War correspondence conducted over several years between anyone, let alone young lovers during the 1860s. Hard campaigning made it difficult for soldiers to save their mail from home. As one soldier wrote to his wife during the conflict, "I have to burn all of your letters because I have no way to keep them." Men were also concerned that enemy soldiers would read their private communications if they were killed or captured. "You kneed not be afraid of your letters," wrote another, "for I take good care of them and burn them as soon as I get a few of them."[2]

Several years ago, I was fortunate enough to acquire a rare mutual correspondence that provides the main framework for this book. The story

---

1   William Walton ed, *A Civil War Courtship: The Letters of Edwin Weller From Antietam to Atlanta,* (New York, NY, 1980), 5.

2   Steven J. Ramold, *Across the Divide: Union Soldiers View the Northern Home Front,* (New York and London, 2013) 52.

found within these pages is based around 75 letters penned by Josiah Moore, an Irish immigrant and college student who enlisted in the 17th Illinois Infantry in 1861, and a young woman named Jennie Lindsay who Josiah met while in training camp in Peoria, Illinois. The letters turned up in an unheated cabin, built about 1880, on Lake George in Rhinelander, Wisconsin. I bought the package of correspondence from a business colleague who had inherited the cabin and the items it contained. In addition to the letters, the collection included photographs of Josiah, Jennie, and their families, period images of the men with whom Josiah served, and other materials. More artifacts related to Josiah and Jennie turned up later, including a worn brown leather memorial book with clippings, telegrams, and other items related to Josiah's passing.

These letters set forth the story of the courtship between Josiah and Jennie. The romance began in the summer of 1861, as Americans were making plans to wage war on their fellow countrymen. Despite a significant difference in age, (Josiah was 27, Jennie just 19), the relationship blossomed during Josiah's military service. Both were quite literate, and their letters are full of day-to-day details, the kind of things a man away from home in the service would have wanted to know so he could feel connected to all that was normal and familiar and good. Another thing that makes these letters rare is that they are from the war's Western Theater (generally described as stretching west from the Appalachians to the Mississippi River), and accounts from that sector of the war are less common than those from the Eastern Theater.

Because both Josiah and Jennie wrote about so many subjects, their letters give us a unique window into this period in our nation's history as experienced by two people who lived through it. Their writings demonstrate the impact of religion on their views, and the impact of the war upon their religion. They offer a unique perspective on a Victorian-era courtship and also illuminate the politics of the home front—particularly as Northern Democrats gained a larger stage when the Union war effort stumbled in 1862 and early 1863. This put Jennie in a decidedly difficult position, for her father, John Lindsay, was a Peace Democrat (or more pejoratively, a Copperhead) and held a seat as a member of the Illinois state senate. Josiah's observations of the war, along with those of many of the men with whom he served, allow us to understand how the conflict changed—or better, hardened—these young men, and how their views of abolition, emancipation, and black people evolved over the course of their three years of service. One thing absent from Josiah's letters is any reflection about his homeland, Ireland. Given that he was an infant when he left for the United

States, added to the typical desire of immigrants to integrate themselves into the culture of their adopted land, this omission is not surprising.

Unfortunately, there is no published history of the 17th Illinois, a gap in the literature that made this project a bit more challenging, and also (hopefully) that much more valuable. But this is not intended to serve as a regimental history; whatever it is, it will have to suffice until someone fills that void. As part of the research for this project, I uncovered some previously unpublished information that hopefully adds to our understanding of the men and women of the period.

Regarding the letters themselves, I elected to keep all of the language in each of Josiah's and Jennie's letters intact except for some very minor punctuation issues. Even though some letters discuss the most mundane matters, the words were important to both of them, and particularly to the soldier in the field who longed for the most common gossip and minute details of what was going on at home. These letters were Josiah's lifeline to the outside world, and they sustained him through illness, injury, campaigning, battle, and unending bouts of boredom and loneliness.

The original copies of all the letters printed in the book are in my possession. I did all of the transcription myself, so any errors fall on me. In a few places, the words were illegible—not a surprise for letters that are more than 150 years old—and I have noted that in the copy. I did my best to footnote individuals or especially noteworthy matters, but decided not to overly do so because I wanted the book to be as readable and accessible as possible.

Rather than place the letters between Josiah and Jennie in strict chronological order, I decided to run them in the order in which Josiah would have received them. Sometimes Josiah sent two letters before he received one from Jennie, while her response might have been en route. I believe this structure allow readers to better see the value these communications had to the individuals involved, and they will make more sense.

Acknowledgments

THROUGHOUT the course of this project, I had the help of numerous old friends, new friends, and the assistance of many people I met in person, over the phone, and via email. All of them have contributed to my effort. To anyone I may have overlooked, just know that I know who you are, and you have my most heartfelt apologies and my enduring gratitude.

Dan DePalma, a friend for more than four decades, was insistent that I purchase this remarkable collection. As always, I am glad I listened to Dan. David Djupe, the great- grandson of Josiah and Jennie, was a tremendous help with details of the family history and provided some of the photos in this book. His enthusiasm and assistance is greatly appreciated. Unfortunately, David died in October of 2015. Dr. Randall Miller, a friend and my professor at St. Joseph's University, is truly a "historian's historian." He read multiple drafts and offered encouragement and tremendous ideas and suggestions that helped point me in the right direction. Many thanks to my former colleague Bob McVety and his wife, Pam, for thinking of me when looking for a new home for this collection. To Jeff Rankin and Dr. William Urban, I thank you for your assistance on my questions as well as providing so much important information about Monmouth College. Tom Best of Monmouth was a tremendous research source.

Thanks are due to all of the good people I met during my research trips to Illinois: Charles Frey, Karen Deller, and Sherri Schneider at Bradley University Special Collections, Carley Robison at Knox College in Galesburg, and particularly Linda Aylward and Joe Hutchinson, who were a tremendous help while I was in Peoria, and continued to answer my follow-up questions. Terry Winschel, the long-time chief historian at Vicksburg National Military Park and now recently retired, could not have been more accommodating during my trip to that magnificent battlefield and in my numerous follow up e-mails with questions about the campaign. To Jeff Giambrone, a wonderful source of knowledge about Vicksburg campaign, my thanks. A big thank you also to Diana Dretske at the Lake County Illinois Discovery Museum for searching through the Peats collection, which has added greatly to this book, and to Mary Michals, Roberta Fairburn, and Cheryl Schnirring for their help in getting what I needed from the Abraham Lincoln Presidential Library and Museum.

There were so many other people who helped along the way, often simply by making sure this particular story of American history was told. They include: Phil Rayburn (who invited me to his home in Galesburg); Jim Martin, the webmaster of the Civil War Message Board; Jim Huffman, Kevin Tucker, Bruce Allardice, Greg Biggs, Doug McGovern, and Jim McGhee; Mary DeCredico of the U.S. Naval Academy; John Sickles, Paul Djupe (David Djupe's son), Donald Andrew, John Pillers, Pat Granstra, Randy Fletcher, Matt Anderson, Greg Peterson, Chris Sullivan, Ron Coddington of *Military Images* magazine; Greg Schuller, Jim Jobe at Donelson and Shiloh NMP; Wayne Motts, CEO of the National Civil War Museum in Harrisburg, Pennsylvania; Art Miller of Lake Forest College; and Paul Gamble of Westminster. To Brad Quinlan, my old "pard" from the 21st Ohio, thanks for your suggestions, research, and friendship. My gratitude goes to academics such as Jim Oakes and Chandra Manning, who were willing to take time out of their schedules to answer details about their work.

A special note of recognition to those who helped me, but also unfortunately passed away: Chuck Moody, my former neighbor, retired Army officer, and a volunteer at the Military History Institute at Carlisle, PA, for his assistance at that wonderful facility; Al Neri, who assisted in the publishing process; and Rick Brown, who told me about his ancestor, killed on July 4, 1863, at Vicksburg. Rick passed away not long after our discussion.

Many people in addition to Randall Miller read my drafts and offered suggestions including Tom Previc, Laurel Belding and Will Guilliams, and particularly my daughter Lauren. Longtime friend Dan McDevitt not only read the manuscript but worked with me on the concepts that turned into Hal Jesperson's great maps. Thanks to Steve Snavely for his help on graphics, and the people at Capitol Copy.

Thanks to those who helped me through the process of securing a publisher, including Scott Mingus, Sr., Laurie Harper, Soni Dimond, Dan Lynch, Pete Shelley, Alan Crawford, and of course, Theodore P. Savas, managing director of Savas Beatie. Ted was willing to give an unpublished author a shot. Thanks also to others at Savas Beatie, including Sarah Keeney (marketing director), Renee Morehouse (media/marketing specialist), Yvette Lewis (Administrative Director), and Kailyn Jennings (editorial). It was a stroke of immense luck that Ted assigned Tom Huntington, a well-known Civil War author in his own right, to read my work and offer sound advice. Tom lives nearby, and his suggestions helped improve my manuscript.

To my attorneys at McNees Wallace and Nurick—thanks Mike Doctrow and Shawn Leppo for the quick turnaround on materials.

I would be remiss if I did not thank all the men and women who, like Josiah, served in this country's armed forces. Their number includes my father, who passed away in 1998, and my father-in-law, both of whom wore the uniform of the United States Army. To my mom and dad—thanks for so much, including that long ago trip to Gettysburg that helped fan my interest in American history in general, and in particular the Civil War period.

Finally, to my family, my wife, Mary, and children Lauren, Ryan, and Morgan—and our relatively new "son" Brian, thank you for the support during this long journey.

Prologue

S̶L̶A̶V̶E̶R̶Y̶ had been an especially confounding issue for the United States throughout the early history of the American republic. Various attempts to deal with this difficult subject had only delayed a final resolution. The 1860 election of Abraham Lincoln as president was just the latest flashpoint. Lincoln was the candidate of the relatively new Republican party, which included those who believed that slave labor was anathema to economic growth and those who saw it as a moral evil. In the South, where a slave population of almost four million people was an integral part of the economic and social fabric, Republicans were viewed as the enemy. Indeed, throughout his public life Lincoln had criticized slavery, which he called "an unqualified evil to the negro, the white man, and the State." However, Lincoln also stated that he had no interest in abolishing the practice where it currently existed, and even expressed concern that the growing movement to abolish slavery "tends rather to increase than abate the evils" by drawing many in the South closer together in opposition.[3]

By February 1, 1861, seven states (South Carolina, Florida, Georgia, Mississippi, Texas, Alabama, and Louisiana) had responded to Lincoln's election by seceding from the Union. On April 12, 1861, South Carolina troops fired on Fort Sumter, a Federal fort in Charleston Harbor. The actions initiated

---

3 James M. McPherson, *Battle Cry of Freedom: The Civil War Era* (New York, NY, 1988), 55, 229-232.

open hostilities between the new Confederacy and the United States government.

On April 15, President Lincoln issued a call for 75,000 militia to serve for 90 days to counter the rebellion. By June 1861, four more states (North Carolina, Virginia, Tennessee, and Arkansas) had joined the seven that had previously seceded. Following Lincoln's call for troops, tens of thousands of men in the North flocked to join up for what most assumed would be a short and glorious war. Men of the South, operating under the same mistaken assumption, swelled military organizations across the South.[4]

4   Margaret E. Wagner, Gary W. Gallagher, and Paul Finkelman, eds., *The Library of Congress Civil War Desk Reference* (New York, NY, 2002). 4-8.

Buttons and the regimental number from Josiah's uniform.
Author

One Man Moore

RESIDENTS of the small town of Monmouth, Illinois, crowded into the Warren County Courthouse on April 20, 1861. They had been attracted by an article in the previous day's edition of the local paper, the *Atlas*. "Freemen! Do You Hear the Call!" blared the headline. The article announced a meeting to form a military company in answer to President Abraham Lincoln's call for militia to put down the young rebellion. Many at the meeting were from Monmouth College, a Presbyterian institution that had been in the town since 1853. The school, which charged between $15 and $25 a year for tuition, was noteworthy in that it admitted females on the same term as males.[1]

The same wave of excitement that pulsed throughout the North after the firing on Fort Sumter also coursed through Monmouth, a town of just 2,500 people in west central Illinois about 25 miles from the Mississippi River. Eighty men of the town had already answered Lincoln's call. During the meeting, 19 more agreed to serve, leaving the new organization just one enlistee shy of the full company complement of 100. The secretary of the committee appointed to raise the company and oversee the welfare of the families who would leave behind called out that he needed "just one man more." One of the Monmouth students, Josiah Moore, slowly lifted his six-foot, four-inch frame from his seat,

---

1   Daniel Mayer and Jeffrey D. Rankin, *A Thousand Hearts Devotion: A History of Monmouth College* (Monmouth, IL, 2002), 18; *Circular and Catalogue of the Officers and Students of Monmouth College* (Monmouth, IL, 1861), 27.

stood for a moment, and then strode confidently to the front. "I am that man Moore," he proclaimed.[2]

According to local legend, Moore staged the dramatic moment by telling others in the room to wait until 99 men had enlisted so he could make his grand statement. Whether Moore possessed great timing or a tremendous sense of theatrics, his dramatic announcement had a significant impact on the other recruits. They elected Moore as captain of the company.[3]

Given the patriotic fervor of the times, it was difficult for the able-bodied young men of the North to resist the urge to participate in what many believed would be a short adventure against an out-manned enemy. The almost festive atmosphere of the opening days of the war was, in the words of one historian "something grotesque, almost poignant" when viewed against the slaughter of the next four years. "Very well, let's go it while we're young," wrote one journalist. "We never had a civil war before, you know . . . and now we've got one we're going to show the world that we can beat it at that as well as every thing else."

In those early days of the conflict, both sides tossed out boastful and bellicose statements. The *New York Times* promised that Confederate president Jefferson Davis and his cohorts "will be hung before the 4th of July," while Confederate Secretary of War Leroy Walker predicted the Rebel flag would "fly atop the Capitol in Washington before the first of May." The prevailing opinion on both sides was that the war would end quickly.[4]

The Civil War would be fought overwhelmingly with volunteers like those from Monmouth. Since Colonial days, Americans had distrusted the idea of a large standing army, viewing large military forces as more appropriate for monarchs. Horace Greeley, the influential editor of the *New York Tribune*, wrote that "we have no more need of a Standing Army than of an order of nobility." At the outbreak of the Civil War, the U.S. Regular Army comprised just over 16,000 men, including fewer than 1,100 officers. Previous military conflicts had relied on volunteers, sometimes drawn from state militias and often bodies of

2   Monmouth College, *Oracle*, Volume XV Number 34 (Monmouth, IL, May 30, 1911), 11.

3   Dr. William Urban, *Paper on William P. Rupp*, Department of History, Monmouth College, Monmouth, Illinois, 1-2.

4   Mark Wahlgren Summers, "The North and the Coming of the Civil War," in Gabor Boritt, ed., *Why the Civil War Came* (New York, NY, 1996), 180; Vincent Fraley, "Uniting for the Union," *Philadelphia Inquirer*, August 17, 2014, Section C1.

citizens with no military experience of any kind. Greeley and many others in the North firmly believed that these state militias would do just fine in the current war.[5]

What made these men from Monmouth, as well as others in the North, join the fight? Some enlisted for the promise of adventure. Some believed fervently that the war was necessary to end the evil of slavery (although other soldiers were both anti-abolitionist and strongly prejudiced against blacks). Most, though, joined because they believed "the Union" meant democracy, liberty, and free labor. It was, as one modern historian argued, "a bulwark against the forces of oligarchy personified in the American context by proud aristocrats from the slaveholding states." The commitment to the Union, he wrote, "functioned as a bonding agent among Americans who believed, as a citizenry and a nation under the Constitution, they were destined for greatness on the world stage." For those in the antebellum North, this view of American nationalism and Union "was bound up with the ideals of human betterment." By rebelling, the Southern states threatened this great and shining ideal. According to this view, the people in the South did not value free labor (even though many of the Union soldiers did not view blacks as citizens), and exploited poor whites.

Frank Peats, a 27-year-old from Rockford, Illinois, who would rise to the rank of major in the 17th Illinois Infantry and become one of Josiah Moore's friends and colleagues, explained his main reason for going to war when he wrote to a female acquaintance, Betsey (Bessie) Tew, in April 1861. His choice was a difficult one "between his love of kindred and duty to our country. You must not forget Bessie I claim the high prerogative, the title of an American citizen. Shall I not by remaining inactive render myself unworthy of so high a position?" In a valuable recollection written after the war, Peats asserted that nearly everyone in the North, "Republican and Democrat, Protestant and Catholic, worshiped at the one common altar of country." For men like Peats, preserving the Union meant preserving the concepts for which their forefathers had died during the American Revolution. "We fight because we love our

5   Allan C. Guelzo, *Gettysburg: The Last Invasion* (New York, NY, 2013), 10; Wagner, Gallagher, Finkelman, *The Library of Congress Civil War Desk Reference*, 367-369; Mark Boatner, III, *The Civil War Dictionary* (New York, NY, 1959) 495; Adam Goodheart, *1861: The Civil War Awakening* (New York, NY, 2011), 194.

government," explained one Yankee soldier, "and they [the South] fight because they hate it."[6]

To be sure, there were men who fought from a desire to destroy the institution of slavery and free those in bondage, although they were in a distinct minority, especially during the war's early years. This relatively small group shared a moral opposition to the forced servitude of human beings. Others opposed slavery from self-interest, believing the expansion of slavery into new territories limited their ability to acquire their share of those lands. Although there is widespread evidence that many Union soldiers realized the war was about slavery—that is, they believed the South was willing to destroy the Union to protect that institution—most were not enlisting to fight to end slavery, free the slave, or even improve the lot of blacks.

At the time, only 7,600 blacks lived in Illinois out of a population of 1.7 million, with the largest concentration residing in Chicago. As a result, many men of the 17th Illinois had little, if any, exposure to them. Prejudice against blacks, a feeling that they were second-class citizens at best, was a common sentiment in Northern armies. Even those opposed to the institution of slavery blamed both slaves and abolitionists for bringing on the war. According to one historian, "[T]he hostility of the average Union volunteer towards anti-slavery sentiment should not be exaggerated. If he had no love for trouble-making abolitionists and much antipathy towards blacks, he also had no fondness for slavery." Oliver O. Howard, who would become a senior commander in the Union armies (and the head of the Freedmen's Bureau after the war), proclaimed that hostility to abolition was "bitter and unmeasured."[7]

Among Yankee troops, even those born in other lands felt the desire to fight for "Union." "[T]his is my country as much as the man that was born on the soil," announced one Irish-born recruit, "and so it is with every man who comes to this country and becomes a citizen." To this immigrant, a Union loss meant "the hopes of millions fall and . . . the old cry will be sent from the aristocrats of Europe that such is the common end of all republics." During the

6 Gary W. Gallagher, *The Union War* (Cambridge, MA, 2011), 42-48; Letter from Frank Peats to Bessie Tews, April 18, 1861; Frank Peats, *Recollections of Forts Henry and Donelson*, 2, Frank Peats Collection, Lake County Discovery Museum, Wauconda, IL; Steven Woodworth, *While God is Marching On: The Religious World of Civil War Soldiers* (Lawrence, KS, 2001), 260.

7 Chandra Manning, *What This Cruel War Was Over: Soldiers, Slavery, and the Civil* War (New York, NY, 2008), 3, 4, 12, 13; Reid Mitchell, *Civil War Soldiers* (New York, NY, 1988), 13, 15; Gallagher, *The Union War*, 43; Guelzo, *Gettysburg: The Last Invasion*, 125.

four years of the war, 500,000 immigrants put on a blue uniform; 150,000 were Irish. For many of them, the Union "was synonymous with the republic—America's unique experiment in self-rule 'by the people'" that carried with it "a transcendent, mystical quality as the object of their patriotic devotion and civil religion." Failure of America's "Grand Experiment" meant, for men like the Irish recruit, a potential return to the tyranny and despotism from which they had fled Europe and other lands.[8]

The concerns of the young Irishman about the failure of the American experiment were more than just speculation. Henry John Temple, the prime minister of Britain and an aristocrat known as Lord Palmerston, believed the American struggle demonstrated the problems inherent in a democracy. "Power in the Hands of the Masses throws the Scum of the Community to the Surface and that Truth and Justice are Soon banished from the Land," he wrote. "[I]t seems your Republic is going to pieces," crowed a French official to a visitor from the United States, and predicted "a reign of terror, and then two or three monarchies" for the American republic. Another French official rejoiced at the news of war and hoped that both North and South would be "irretrievably ruined." The war, declared members of Germany's elite, was a "natural consequence of unlimited freedom."[9]

Many in Europe viewed the American nation as the height of hypocrisy. Early in the nineteenth century, Englishman Sydney Smith sneered at the idea of the United States calling itself a democracy. "Under which of the old tyrannical governments of Europe is every sixth man a slave, whom his fellow-creatures may buy and sell and torture?" he asked.[10]

Southerners had their own view of the causes of the war. They believed that God ordained slavery, and therefore any attack upon it had to be opposed. Many whites in the South spoke of the North's "tyranny" and claimed their Northern brethren were motivated by greed and desire. Like those in the North, Southerners claimed the mantles of both patriotism and religion. They believed they were the ones really fighting for liberty and independence, and compared

8 Gallagher, *The Union War*, 5; Adams, *Living Hell*, 16; Manning, *What This Cruel War Was Over*, 6.

9 Don H. Doyle, *The Cause of All Nations: An International History of the American Civil War* (New York, NY, 2015), 1, 41, 98, 99.

10 Guelzo, *Gettysburg: The Last Invasion*, xviii.

themselves to the people of Israel who sought to leave Egypt. Both sides felt justified in claiming the moral high ground.[11]

Unfortunately, nothing in any of Josiah's writings explicitly states why he enlisted. Interestingly, while attending preparatory school at Westminster (now Westminster College) in 1859 in New Wilmington, Pennsylvania, Josiah wrote a poem entitled "The Murder of John Brown." It was published in the December 1859 student newspaper. Brown was a strident abolitionist who led a bloody raid on the Federal arsenal at Harpers Ferry, Virginia (now West Virginia) in October 1859 with the aim of sparking a slave insurrection. A contingent of U. S. Marines under the command of Robert E. Lee retook the facility and captured Brown, who was hanged in December of that year. Josiah's poem was a scathing indictment of those involved with Brown's imprisonment and hanging. In his ode to Brown—a man detested throughout the South but hailed as a martyr by the anti-slavery movement—Josiah called him a "hero" whose life was taken by "cowards." In the same edition of the paper, the editors, while acknowledging "the sin of slavery" and advocating "all right means for the removal of this incubus," excoriated many in the abolitionist movement as people looking to simply "make political capital" while demonstrating "no real desire or intention of benefitting the slave." The editors labeled these people "insane enthusiasts." Despite his ode to Brown, Josiah displayed no significant level of abolitionist sentiment as the war progressed. Perhaps his ardor for the movement had cooled by 1861.[12]

The slavery question that had split the country also created schisms in other institutions, including organized religion. Despite a reluctance on the part of many Presbyterian clergy to enter a debate on an issue they believed could harm their overall evangelization mission, a segment of the church that came to be known as "New School Presbyterians" began to talk more openly about abolition by the 1850s. Many in the New School remained hesitant to agitate too much, for they recognized the issue's real threat to the Union. Things came to a head in May 1861 when the Presbyterian General Assembly met in Philadelphia shortly after war began. New School adherents attempted to press the issue against slavery. Southern church members, anticipating the conflict, largely

---

11 Manning, *What This Cruel War Was Over*, 138-139; George C. Rable, *God's Almost Chosen Peoples: A Religious History of the American Civil War* (Chapel Hill, NC, 2010), 274-276, 70.

12 Boatner, *The Civil War Dictionary*, 91; Westminster College, *Students Journal*, Volume 2, Number 12 (December 1859), Author's Collection.

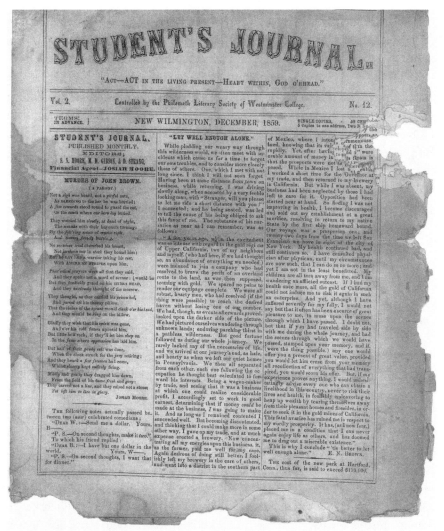

The *Student's Journal*, December 1859 (Westminster College, New Wilmington, PA.) Josiah's poem about the death of John Brown is visible in the left column. *Author*

avoided the meeting. The Old School members admitted the war was over slavery, but cited biblical passages to mean God supported the practice, and so insisted the North had no right to interfere. Being a Presbyterian institution, Monmouth College was roiled by the conflicts within the church.[13]

13 Rable, *God's Almost Chosen Peoples*, 15-16, 26, 35-37, 45, 57-59, 84.

The morning after the rally in the courthouse, the new recruits filed into Claycomb Hall, a large, imposing brick structure that still stands on the Monmouth square, to hear patriotic speeches. One of the speakers was David Wallace, the president of Monmouth College. He was anti-slavery but not outspokenly so, perhaps to avoid controversy at the school given the great divide in the Presbyterian Church at the time. Wallace took the opportunity to address his former students who had joined the Union Army, and "invoked the God of battles to be with them, to protect and assist them" in their upcoming campaigns.[14]

Of the 100 men who had volunteered for the company from Monmouth, 20 were students at the college. In 1861 the school had only 220 students, of whom 137 were male. By the end of the war, 232 Monmouth students had joined Union armies, including 81 of the 137 male students attending in 1861. Included in that number were 41 commissioned officers and one brigadier general. By 1863, not a single male of military age remained on campus. One out of eight of those who served died either in battle or from disease, a much more common killer of the Civil War soldier.[15]

The company's original muster sheet lists 105 men who volunteered for service. Many were later rejected for medical and other reasons. Because of the government ban on blacks serving in the military, all of the enlistees were white. The youngest was 18, and the oldest 45. Eight of the men were 30 or older. Nineteen of the original enlistees were six feet or taller. The shortest was 5 foot, 3 inches and the tallest, Josiah, stood 6 foot, 4 inches. Eight were married and just 15 listed their birthplace as Illinois. One of those was Josiah, who perhaps avoided noting his Irish birth due to the era's nativist tendencies. The recruits listed numerous occupations, with farmer being the most common (in fact, about half of all Union enlistees everywhere were farmers). There were accountants, laborers, teachers, blacksmiths, and one pugilist—Murry Claycomb, the nephew of the man responsible for Claycomb Hall. Only 14 men noted they were students, although some who were enrolled at Monmouth

---

14 Mayer and Rankin, *A Thousand Hearts Devotion*, 12; Dr. William Urban, "Monmouth College in the Civil War," *Journal of the Illinois State Historical Society* (February, 1978), 14; Monmouth College, *Oracle*, 11.

15 Monmouth College, *Oracle*, 5; Meyer and Rankin, *Thousand Hearts Devotion*, 18. The general was Abner Harding, a member of the board of trustees. He enlisted as a private in the 83rd Illinois and was later promoted to colonel and then brigadier general in March 1863, but had to resign a short time later because of deteriorating eyesight.

listed different occupations. One of them was future sergeant Robert Duncan, who stated he was a farmer. The enlistees also included one of the town physicians, John B. Stephenson, who joined as second sergeant at the age of 29.

Another young man who joined was 19-year-old James Earp, who described himself as "five feet, eight inches tall with fair complexion and blue eyes" and his occupation as "coach driver." Earp was born in Kentucky and lived for a time in Monmouth before leaving for Iowa with his family. His father, Nicholas, had served with a Monmouth volunteer unit during the Mexican War, and James returned to Monmouth to enlist in the Civil War. His brother Virgil served with the 83rd Illinois, and a half-brother, Newton, joined the 4th Iowa Cavalry. Two other brothers, Wyatt and Morgan, were too young for service in 1861. Both brothers would see their share of gunplay years later.[16]

Moore, the anointed captain of this new military organization, was a 27-year-old college junior who had enrolled at Monmouth in September 1860. The company's muster sheet describes him as having light hair, blue eyes, and a fair complexion. It's likely that few of the men in his company knew him. Until enrolling at the college, he had been a resident of Hanover, Illinois, a town to the northwest. He was born to Charles and Hannah Moore in 1833 in Ballybay, Ireland, in the county of Monaghan in the north-central part of the country. Ballybay, a Gaelic name that translates to "At the Mouth of the Ford of the Birches," was the center of a thriving linen industry that had fallen on hard times by the time of Josiah's birth. The Moore family left Ireland in 1834, fully a decade before the potato blight caused the death of a million Irish through disease and starvation and the emigration of a similar number. The Moores sailed from Ireland to Liverpool, and from there took the *Edwin* to Baltimore, where they arrived on August 20 that same year. From Baltimore, the family journeyed by wagon on the National Road to Washington County in western Pennsylvania. They lived there with friends until 1836, when they moved by water to Illinois to join Charles, who had left the previous fall to prepare land he had purchased. A log cabin 12 miles outside Galena, Illinois, was the Moore family's new home. At the time, Illinois sat on the western frontier of the young nation. American Indians were frequent visitors to the Moore home and farm.

---

16 James B. McPherson, *For Cause and Comrades: Why Men Fought in the Civil War* (New York, Oxford, 1997), 182; Original muster sheet of Company F, Author's Collection; Jeff Guinn, *The Last Gunfight* (New York, NY, 2011) 24-25. Wyatt Earp, of course, was the famous gambler, gunslinger, and sheriff engaged in the famous shootout at the O.K. Corral on October 26, 1881.

Tintype of Hannah Moore, mother of Josiah. *Author*

After settling in Illinois, Josiah's parents had five more children. Two children, Margaret and William, had been born before Josiah in Ireland, but both had died before their first birthdays. Charles became a founder of an active Presbyterian community in nearby Hanover. Josiah went to western Pennsylvania to attend preparatory school at Westminster, taught briefly in

Josiah Moore's Hanover home, believed to have been built in the 1840s. Josiah's father is on the front porch. His mother Hannah is barely visible on the porch to the right. *Author*

Illinois, and then enrolled at Monmouth. His younger brother William was enrolled in Monmouth's preparatory section at the outbreak of war, but it does not appear that he joined the military.[17]

The new enlistees named their company the Monmouth Union Guards and made the transition from civilian life to the military. Students traded their books on classics and theology for books on drill, and waited for the call to battle. Robert Duncan, another Monmouth student who served as a sergeant and company clerk, wrote that the men "are commencing to keep step and face right and left—they think there is considerable romance to a Soldiers life."[18]

17 James H. Murnane and Peadar Murnane, *At the Ford of the Birches* (Monaghan, Ireland, 1999), Foreword; David J. Hogan, et. al., *Irish American Chronicle* (New York, 2009), 88-90; S. J. Connolly, ed., *The Oxford Companion to Irish History* (Oxford, 1998), 228. Clarke, *History of McDonough County, Illinois* (Springfield, IL, 1885), 453-454; Judge David Matchett, address delivered at the United Presbyterian Church, Hanover, August 3, 1935, Author's Collection.

18 Duncan, Robert L, Sergeant, Company F clerk, *Log book of Company F, 17th Illinois Infantry*, Warren County, Illinois Historical Society (transcribed by Tom Best).

During the Civil War, it was typical for the bulk of a company of 100 men to come from the same town or general area. This meant that brother served with brother, father with son, co-worker with co-worker, and, in the case of the Monmouth Union Guards, student with fellow student. Serving for and with his community provided a tremendous motivating force for a soldier. Men from close-knit communities such as Monmouth knew they would be a focus of attention. People back home received reports of their conduct and actions, so the men in the ranks had a tremendous incentive to maintain a good name and record. In addition, officers knew that if they survived the war they would have to go home and live among the men they commanded, which tended to work against unfair or tyrannical behavior. On the other hand, it did not always lead to the highest ideals of military discipline.[19]

The men who enlisted in 1861 were strong believers in democratic ideals, and that extended to life in the military. Since neither the typical officers or enlisted men in these new units had much if any training, the men in the ranks tended to view themselves as equal to their officers. "Many of the men seem to think they should never be spoken to unless the remarks are prefaced by some words of deferential politeness," complained one Michigan officer. Southern soldiers shared this philosophy. A Confederate veteran remarked that each individual reserved the right to "decide some questions for himself [and] to the last he maintained the right of private judgment, and especially on the field of battle." The fact that Josiah was older than most men in the company—and towered over them—probably helped him maintain discipline.[20]

Selecting officers by election was another common practice. Sometimes a local merchant who financed the company or regiment was elected captain or colonel. Sometimes, as in the case of Josiah, a stirring action or speech gained support for a captaincy. As the war progressed, governors appointed the colonels of state volunteer regiments. In many cases, these were political appointees, and many rose to lofty heights without any formal military training. Daniel Sickles, for example, a former Democratic member of Congress from New York with no military experience, received an appointment as colonel and rose to command a corps in the Army of the Potomac. Within a year, Josiah and

---

19 Frances M. Clarke, *War Stories: Suffering and Sacrifice in the Civil War North* (Chicago, IL, 2011), 37.

20 Guelzo, *Gettysburg: The Last Invasion*, 11; Reid Mitchell, *The Vacant Chair: The Northern Soldier Leaves Home* (New York, NY, 1993), 21-25, 42-51.

A painting by John Thomson of the square in Monmouth, Illinois, in the 1860s. The building on the left is the original courthouse built in 1839 and the location of the recruiting rally in April 1861. It was replaced by a new courthouse in 1890. The building on the right is Claycomb Hall, where the new enlistees met the evening after volunteering for service. Claycomb Hall still stands. *Jeff Rankin, Monmouth College*

his men found themselves under the command of a general with a similar background. Trained military men showed little respect for these citizen soldiers and "political generals." In turn, politicians and civilians often distrusted the military class and felt formal military training was unnecessary for the task at hand.[21]

On Monday, April 29, the Monmouth Union Guards were called to assemble in Peoria, Illinois, about 50 miles away. There, they joined recruits swarming to the city from points throughout Illinois. They were the first troops from Monmouth to leave for the front, and "the entire city turned out to see their departure." Before the troops boarded the train to Peoria, Miss Kate Beach (Monmouth Class of 1861) addressed them with a poem that concluded:

And now, with aching hearts, and dark forebodings,
And many a smothered sigh
We bid you go! Oh, cherished friends and brothers,
God bless you all, good bye!

21 McPherson, *Battle Cry of Freedom*, 318; Boatner, *The Civil War Dictionary*, 760.

Send-offs like this took place in communities throughout the North and South and reinforced the belief of these new soldiers that they were not only fighting for a higher cause, but for the people back home. The feelings of "dark forebodings" Miss Beach noted would prove sadly prescient.[22]

---

22 Monmouth College, *Oracle* 11-12; Urban, *Monmouth College in the Civil War*, 15; Mitchell, *Vacant Chair*, 21-25.

CHAPTER 2

Students to Soldiers

PEORIA, the destination of the Monmouth Union Guards, was a city of 14,000 near the state's center. It would become an important training site during the war. Despite the thousands of recruits flowing into it and the tens of thousands who called Peoria their temporary home, support there for the Union cause was but lukewarm. Illinois bordered the slave states of Kentucky and Missouri, which stayed in the Union but supplied troops to both sides. Rebel sympathies were not as pronounced in Illinois, but many in the central part of the state were decidedly against abolition and opposed using force to keep the Southern states in the Union. More than 10 percent of Illinois's population were natives of Southern slave states and most had settled in the southern part of the state, while northern Illinois was mostly populated by arrivals from across the North. The result was high levels of anti-abolitionist and anti-war feelings in southern Illinois throughout the war.

In the legislature at Springfield, Democrats and Republicans wrangled during the opening days of the 1861 session. Party and philosophical differences colored debates over secession, abolition, and the matter of providing militia for future military action. Republicans had a 41 to 34 edge over the Democrats in the House, although they held the Senate by just one seat. The partisan divide reflected the divergence of opinion throughout Illinois.[1]

---

1 Ronald White, *A. Lincoln. A Biography* (New York, NY, 2009), 75; Jennifer L. Weber, *Copperheads: The Rise and Fall of Lincoln's Opponents in the North* (Oxford, 2006), 17; Russell McClintock, *Lincoln and the Decision for War* (Chapel Hill, NC, 2008), 126-127.

Illinois and Area
of Early Operations

0   miles   60
Hal Jespersen

Democrats controlled the elected offices around Peoria. In the 1860 presidential election, Republican Abraham Lincoln lost the presidential vote in Peoria County, albeit by narrow margins. It was one of just 24 counties in the North that Lincoln did not win. He lost the Peoria vote again in 1864. With very few exceptions, Democrats triumphed in national, state, and local races throughout the area during the war years.[2]

Somewhat ironically, Peoria provided the setting for one of Lincoln's most significant speeches. In October 1854, prominent citizens from the town had invited the former congressman, then practicing law but seeking a return to elected office, to visit Peoria and make some remarks. The speech provided some of the earliest indications of Lincoln's view on slavery. Lincoln told his Peoria audience that "no man is good enough to govern another man, without that other's consent," and said this was "the leading principle—the sheet anchor of American republicanism. When the white man governs himself that is self-government; but when he governs himself and also governs another man, that is more than self-government—that is despotism." Lincoln meant this to include both black and white Americans. "Few American politicians in 1854 ventured so boldly," wrote historian Lewis Lehrman.[3]

In 1862, Illinois Republican governor Richard Yates commented on the state's difficult internal situation in a revealing letter to Lyman Trumbull, a prominent Democrat who had sided with President Lincoln. "Secession is deeper and stronger here than you have any idea," reported Yates. "Its advocates are numerous and powerful and respectable." Some of these advocates believed that Illinois itself, or at least southern Illinois, should secede and join the South.[4]

Even with this strong secessionist sentiment, Peoria supplied 2,700 men for the Union, 241 of whom never returned home. While many of Peoria's citizens were ambivalent, at best, about the war effort, the city's central location and its site on the Illinois River made it an ideal training and assembly area for troops. Once the Civil War began, the city transformed its sprawling

2 George May, *Students History of Peoria County, Illinois* (Galesburg, IL, 1968), 92-94; McPherson, *Battle Cry of Freedom*, 232.

3 Lewis E. Lehrman, *Lincoln at Peoria: The Turning Point* (Mechanicsburg, PA, 2008), 57.

4 May, *Students History of Peoria County, Illinois*, 94; Weber, *Copperheads*, 28. Lyman would go on to co-author the Thirteenth Amendment to the United States Constitution.

Hamilton J. Herbert enlisted in April
of 1861 in Company F of the
17th Illinois Infantry.

Author

fairgrounds into a military camp
named Camp Mather, in honor of
Illinois's adjutant general,
Thomas Mather.[5]

When the boys from
Monmouth arrived in this city of
conflicted allegiances, the
romance of military life Robert
Duncan had written about while
back in Monmouth started to
dissipate. They reached Peoria on
the evening of April 29 to find
that no arrangements had been
made for their reception or
accommodations. The men were marched to the fairgrounds and "housed in
open cattle sheds without covering at night and only straw for bedding."
Unaccustomed to such conditions, many fell ill from the exposure and close
proximity of so many other men. An epidemic of measles swept the camp and
killed several young soldiers before they had fired a shot in anger. Ironically, it
was often the hardy backwoods country boys who were the most susceptible to
childhood diseases like measles and mumps (and some cases, smallpox), since
they had not been exposed to them the way men from cities had been. In due
course, a second wave of sickness, dysentery and diarrhea, struck. When the
men moved south into hotter and more humid climates, malaria would also take
a toll. The courage an individual expected to display in battle was of little help in
fighting these debilitating and so often deadly diseases.[6]

5   Newton Bateman, et. al., *Historical Encyclopedia of Illinois and History of Peoria County*, Vol 2
(Chicago, IL., 1902), 160.

6   Monmouth College, *Oracle*, 11; Duncan, Company log. George O. Smith, *A Brief History of
the 17th Illinois Volunteer Regiment,* Abraham Lincoln Presidential Library, Springfield, Illinois;
Gerald Linderman, *Embattled Courage: The Experience of Combat in the American Civil War* (New
York, NY, 1987), 115-116.

Once Monmouth folks heard about the sufferings of their hometown boys, they began a collection to buy "nice gray army blankets from Chicago," wrote Duncan. The city council appropriated $2,000 for clothing (the company's first uniform), which Duncan described as "gray pants and red and gray shirts." At this early stage, uniforms were not simply Union blue or Confederate gray. According to another member of the 17th Illinois, "A greater variety of hats and caps could be found in our western armies than in all the country beside."[7]

Some of the original 105 enlistees had been rejected for medical and other reasons, so the remaining 93 members of the Monmouth Union Guards were sworn into state and then Federal service on May 25, 1861. Captain John Pope of the Regular Army swore the men into Federal service. An 1842 graduate of the West Point, Pope was a distant relative of Lincoln's wife Mary. Two months earlier he had accompanied the president-elect from Illinois to Washington for his inauguration amid rumors of assassination plots. According to Sergeant Duncan, Pope demonstrated "the meanest cussing by note of any man I ever heard try it." Most of the Monmouth men agreed to serve for the duration of the war (officially a three-year term), but some enlisted for three months. Pope went after these short-timers, claimed Duncan, for he "commenced a momentary cussing for their benefit—it was very abusive—I could not have received such abuse."[8]

James S. Herbert enlisted in April of 1861 in Company F of the 17th Illinois Infantry. James was not related to Hamilton Herbert. *Author*

7 Peats, *Recollections*, 6.

8 Boatner, *Civil War Dictionary*, 659; Stashower, *The Hour of Peril*, 113, 160. (Shortly afterward, Pope was promoted to brigadier general of volunteers and experienced some success in Missouri before being sent east to command the Army of Virginia. The Confederates soundly thrashed him in the summer of 1862 at the Second Battle of Bull Run.)

Once inducted, the Monmouth Union Guards became Company F of the 17th Illinois Volunteer Infantry Regiment. On paper, a full regiment totaled 1,000 men, made up of 10 companies of 100 men each. Three to six regiments formed a brigade, two to six brigades formed a division, and two or more divisions a corps, with one or more corps organized as an army. These numbers and structures varied between the Union and Confederate armies and changed throughout the war.[9]

The commander of the new 17th Illinois was Col. Leonard F. Ross. A veteran of the Mexican War, Ross trained as a lawyer and served as a judge. Along with Company F, his regiment included nine other Illinois companies from seven different counties. Companies A and B were local, having been formed in the city and county of Peoria. The 1st Lieutenant of Company A, Abraham Ryan of Peoria, became a friend of Josiah's and later the regiment's adjutant. Ryan was one of the few men in the regiment with any kind of military experience, having served in a local militia group called the National Blues. The commander of that unit, John Bryner, would later become the colonel of the 47th Illinois.[10]

Now sworn into service, the 17th Illinois began its military training in earnest. According to Duncan, he and his comrades "drilled on the march each day from 7 a.m. to 11 a.m. and from 1 p.m. till I am heartily sick of such proceders." Duncan was hardly alone in his negative view of daily drill. Most recruits wanted to immediately sweep south and forcibly haul their wayward countrymen back into the Union. However, they first had to be molded into a cohesive fighting force. The military tactics of the time relied on linear warfare, with regiments and brigades advancing in a line one or more ranks deep. The men marched elbow-to-elbow with the ranks separated by only a short distance. Doing this correctly required a significant amount of training even before the men received weapons. It required endless hours of drill for a green soldier to learn how to move in concert with the man on his left and right and how to quickly shift from a marching column into line of battle.

Reveille was typically sounded around 5:00 a.m., followed by breakfast and other daily functions. Drill began shortly afterward, and became part of their regular routine throughout their service, curtailed only during active

---

9 Wagner, Gallagher, Finkelman, *Civil War Desk Reference*, 374-376.

10 Boatner, *Civil War Dictionary*, 709; Cloyd Bryner, *Bugle Echoes The Story of the Illinois 47th* (Springfield, IL, 1905), 11.

Abraham (or Abram) Ryan

Ryan served as the captain of Company A of the 17th Illinois Infantry and as the regiment's adjutant. This image was taken late in the war when he was the colonel of the 3rd Arkansas Cavalry. There is no photographer's backmark but the reverse is dated February 3, 1865 at Lewisburg, Arkansas, and inscribed "To my old comrade in arms, Capt. Josiah Moore 17th Ills Vols Monmouth Ills." *Author*

campaigning. Writing of his daily routine, one Pennsylvania soldier said, "The first thing is drill, then drill, then drill again. Then drill, drill, a little more drill. Then drill and lastly drill. Between drills, we drill and sometimes stop to eat a little and have a roll call." The men first learned the School of the Soldier—how to properly stand, face, salute, and so forth. From there, they advanced to marching and turning— first in small groups, and then in progressively larger units. Eventually, the soldiers received weapons and learned how to load and shoot a rifled musket, which had an effective range of about 300 yards. A veteran soldier could load and fire about three times a minute under ideal conditions.[11]

The monotony of camp was bad enough for the Monmouth boys, and their delayed pay only made matters worse. On May 30, 1861, Colonel Ross had to write a letter to Illinois's Governor Yates. "Can we get paid?" he begged. "Our men are very much in need of a little money." An attempt to break the tedium of drilling proved deadly for one individual in Camp Mather that summer. Maurice Dee of the 47th Illinois died when he put too much trust in a comrade's

---

11 Wiley, *Life of Billy Yank*, 45-54; McPherson, *Battle Cry of Freedom*, 472-477.

James L. Shaw enlisted as a musician in
Company F, 17th Illinois Infantry,
in April 1861.
Author

marksmanship. Dee placed a tin
cup on his head so his friend
could shoot it off. The man
missed the cup.[12]

The camps also provided a
breeding ground for intrigue and
rumor. Josiah wrote that "several
spies were apprehended while
passing the road outside the
camp," and noted a need to post
an extra guard by the spring "lest
some of the enemy should get in
and poison the well." Such stories were due to the normal skittishness found
amidst new troops, but they could also be traced to the recognition of the
uneasy coexistence between pro-Union and pro-Southern populations in
central Illinois.[13]

The Peoria location did have some benefits. According to Duncan, "The
ladies of the city favored us frequently with a smiling countenance encouraging
us in our death like work, also favouring us with delicacies more palatable than
Soldier's fair." One of these ladies caught the eye of Duncan's captain, Josiah.
The young lady was 19-year-old Jennie Lindsay, the daughter of one of Peoria's
more prominent citizens.

Nothing in Josiah's or Jennie's letters indicates how they first met. In the
spring of 1861, Jennie lived with her family on property adjacent to the camp,
but it is highly unlikely that she visited on her own. Customs of the time dictated
that men chaperoned women to shield them from "an impertinent glance" or

---

12 Duncan, company log; Letter from Colonel Leonard Ross to Governor Yates, Illinois State
Archives, Official Regimental Papers of the 17th Illinois; Bryner, *Bugle Echoes*, 14.

13 Josiah Moore, "*A History of the 17th Illinois*," Author's Collection; Cloyd Bryner, *Bugle Echoes*,
24.

"an unwelcome compliment." In addition, women would attend only functions considered "proper for their status." If Jennie and Josiah did meet in the camp, it is almost certain that Jennie was accompanied by her father and/or other citizens of the town. In addition, the Victorians had a prescribed method for introductions. It was considered vulgar to approach someone with whom you were unacquainted without being formally introduced. Lord Chesterfield, the author of behavior manuals of the time, wrote that "when a gentleman is to be first introduced to a lady, her permission must first be privately obtained by the introducer." Perhaps Josiah obtained an introduction through Abraham Ryan, the Peoria man who was one of his comrades and appeared to know the Lindsay family. Once properly introduced, the couple could exchange calling cards or *carte de visites*—paper photos about the size of a modern index card. With the woman's consent, the couple could begin formal correspondence, an important part of a nineteenth-century courtship.[14]

Jennie's father, John Lindsay, was born in 1818 in McConnellsburg, Pennsylvania, where his father, a veteran of the War of 1812, operated an inn. The elder Lindsay died in 1835, and the next year his wife and son moved to Peoria. Young John rose to prominence in his new surroundings. He became a member of the "Old Settlers Union," open only to those who arrived in Peoria prior to 1840, as well as an attorney and a member of the Peoria Board of Trade. He was one of the citizens who had invited Lincoln to speak in 1854, and he served for a single term as a Republican member of the Illinois House from 1858 to 1859. By 1860, John had amassed real estate holdings of $22,500 and a personal estate of about $10,000—amounts comparable today to $575,000 and $256,000, respectively.[15]

Lindsay married Sarah Belle Patton, another Pennsylvania native, in 1839. The couple had six children, five of whom were still living in 1861. (A son, James Columbus Lindsay, had died in 1852 at the age of four.) John and Sarah's oldest child, Maggie, born in 1840, had married George Updike in 1858. They moved to Chicago sometime between the 1860 census and July 1861. William Patton Lindsay, born in 1845, and John Thomas Lindsay Jr., born in 1851, lived

14 *Root's City Directory*, Peoria, 1860; Patricia L. Richard, "Listen Ladies One and All: Union Soldiers Yearn for the Society of Their Fair Cousins of the North," in Paul A. Cimbala and Randall M. Miller eds, *Union Soldiers and the Northern Home Front* (New York, NY, 2002), 148-149.

15 Ernest E. East, *Abraham Lincoln Sees Peoria: An Historical and Pictorial Record of Seventeen Visits From 1832 to 1858* (Peoria, IL, 1939), 24.

with their parents. Another son, James Andrew, known as "Andie," lived with Maggie and George in 1860 but probably returned home after Maggie moved to Chicago. The Lindsays also had two servants, 18-year-old Mary Galt and 16-year-old Peter Cady, both natives of Ireland. John's mother Jane still lived with them, as did six-year-old Sarah Barr, the daughter of John's younger sister Cynthia, who had died in 1859.[16]

We know very little about the 19-year-old Jennie. From the evidence of her letters to Josiah, she was obviously well educated, which is not a surprise given her father's social status. Her letters also show a maturity that belies her young age. We do know that Josiah and Jennie spent a good deal of time together until the 17th Illinois left Peoria. Josiah invited Jennie and her family to social functions hosted by the regiment's officers, including an event at Wood's Hotel in May 1861.[17]

After roughly six weeks at Camp Mather, orders finally arrived for the 17th regiment to leave Peoria. Before its departure, the regiment hosted a farewell party on June 14. The "party" committee was composed of Colonel Ross, Lt. Col. Enos P. Wood, Maj. Francis M. Smith, and Adj. Abraham H. Ryan. The Transcript Steam Printing House printed formal invitations. One was sent to "Mr. J. T. Lindsay and Family." Although no records remain of the event, it is easy to imagine that Jennie had a pleasant but sobering evening with her new friend in blue, knowing Josiah's time in Peoria was coming to a close and his return uncertain.[18]

The men of the regiment marched out of Camp Mather on June 17 to the boat landing at the foot of Main Street. Their destination was Alton, Illinois, a town on the Mississippi River about 125 miles below from Peoria and not far from St. Louis. There, the 17th Illinois was slated to receive additional training.[19]

Frank Peats, who was promoted to captain and now in command of Company B, wrote about the irony of the townspeople telling the men to take care of themselves when those men were soldiers "armed with instruments of death who were going out to meet men similarly armed and each to meet the

---

16 Eighth United States Census, 1860.

17 Original invitation in collection of the author.

18 Original invitation in collection of the author.

19 Illinois Adjutant General's Report for the 17th Illinois Infantry. wwwcivilwar.illinoisgen web.org/history/017.html.

other in deadly combat." A band playing "The Star Spangled Banner" and "The Girl I Left Behind Me" led the regiment to the boat landing. "The streets were lined with friends, wives, mothers, sisters, sweethearts, all wishing us God-speed and a safe return," wrote George Smith of Company F, an 18-year-old farmer from Monmouth.[20]

Almost a year and a half would pass before Jennie and Josiah would once again set eyes upon one another.

20 Peats, "Recollections," 3-4; George O. Smith, *A Brief History of the 17th Illinois Infantry;* Illinois Adjutant General's Report.

CHAPTER 3

"Little Egypt"

W HEN the 17th Illinois reached Alton, it marked the second time in a quarter-century the small town had hosted men on their way to war. In 1846, another group of Illinois men had passed through on their way to fight in the Mexican War. The town's citizens had cheered those soldiers, believing they were fulfilling America's "Manifest Destiny," the country's "inevitable" expansion to the Pacific Ocean. The belief that the territories the United States would acquire from Mexico would be open to slavery had made the earlier war even more attractive to the people of Alton, who were strongly anti-abolitionist.[1]

Alton had been sympathetic to the Southern cause for decades. In fact, blood had been spilled there over slavery as far back as 1837, when a mob murdered abolitionist Elijah Lovejoy over his efforts to publish an anti-slavery newspaper.[2]

If the men of the 17th regiment sensed ambiguous feelings for the war in Peoria, they found no ambiguity in Alton. This section of southwestern Illinois was widely known as "Egypt" or "Little Egypt." The term might have derived from a belief that the area was a fertile land of grain, much as Egypt had been for the Israelites, or people may have thought the land around the Mississippi River resembled Egypt around the Nile River. Whatever the name's origins, the

---

1 Amy S. Greenberg, *A Wicked War* (New York, NY, 2012), 135.

2 Lehrman. *Lincoln at Peoria*, 137.

Illinois Egypt was rural, poor, strongly Democratic, and anti-black. Its citizens did not look kindly on Union soldiers. Some counties in the region favored secession for themselves, and pushed to make Cairo, a town deep in southwest Illinois, an independent city. However, not all the local Democrats were Southern sympathizers. The Democratic congressman from the region, John McClernand, not only opposed secession but was in favor of using force to keep the Southern states in the union.[3]

A postwar letter from one of Josiah's colleagues, Benjamin Baldwin, described the atmosphere the men of the 17th encountered in Alton. Baldwin, who commanded Company B, said that when the 17th's Illinois reached town, the men "were surrounded by a rough crowd impeding our march as much as possible and trying to induce our boys to partake of their poisonous liquors." According to Baldwin, the locals harassed the pickets for some time. Once again, the men reached a new town without tents or sufficient arms. More more fell ill, including Baldwin, who subsequently resigned.[4]

Shortly after reaching Alton and settling in at Camp Pope, Josiah took the opportunity to send his first letter to Jennie.

Camp Pope, June 26, 1861
Miss Jennie Lindsay,

Dear Lady,

With pleasure I take this opportunity of sending a few lines as a testimony of remembrance.

Well Jennie (for that is thy name) perhaps you will say I might have remembered sooner but all I can say, I never forget, the only trouble being that my wandering condition tends to prevent to any great extant the "wielding of the pen" yet the mind keeps acting still in silent thought.

---

3 Ginette Aley and J. L. Anderson, "The Great National Struggle in the Heart of the Union: An Introduction," in Ginette Aley and J. L. Anderson, *Union Heartland: The Midwestern Home Front During the Civil War* (Carbondale, IL, 2013), 3; Jon Musgrave, "Welcome to New Egypt!," *American Weekend Magazine*, a supplement of various southern Illinois newspapers, January 6, 1996, listed in www.illinoishistory.com/egypt.htm; Weber, *Copperheads*, 23-24; Russell McClintock, *Lincoln and the Decision for War* (Chapel Hill, NC, 2008), 70, 266.

4 Letter from B. Baldwin to Frank Peats, May 4, 1883.

For the first few days we were tossed to and fro to such an extant that I found epistolary correspondence reduced to pencil and paper in lieu of pen and paper and very limited at that. We did not quarter in the old prison as was expected but took another "row of stumps" about two miles from town—I say stumps for its equal I never saw since I left the old classic hills of Penn. Our Col. has been looking up a better place, but as yet none has been found to please i.e. there are other three Col.s to suit all of whom have Regiments here in the Brigade.

We moved on yesterday for the 3rd time since we came and all inside less than ½ mile and for the first time I have had my place fixed up like living also for writing—but now I fear that I shall be as bad as ever for as Col. Turner[5] is commander of the Post pro tem, he has issued orders for about 2 hours of training per day. I have just returned from training since 4 ½ o'clock this morning. It is now 7. Our men were paid off yesterday, and in this forenoon they will get their uniforms, so they feel pretty well and I do too i.e. I like to see my men cheerful.

We have no instructions when we shall move from this place. When I finish this I shall go down to town for the first time except once when we passed through from the river—Oh Jennie I do not like this place and think I never shall leave. I have got acquainted with no persons as yet and from the general outlines I don't think I will—I have never yet seen a much harder specimen of the genus homo O perhaps I have become prejudicial from anticipating Egyptian peculiarities.

Well Jennie (I know self praise is not good) we have the best Regiment here i.e. we have the best reputation. Aint that good? We have had but very little drunkenness in camp for the last few days—discipline is becoming more thorough every day.

But Jennie I must close. I wrote to Tom Currie[6] some days since today I mail it. I send you a paper.

I must bid you goodbye, Jennie. I often think of the happy times at Camp Mather, nor do I expect to meet with such again even though a "southern clime" sounds very practical. My regards to all the Friends—Tell them that the 17th

5   Colonel Thomas Turner of the 15th Illinois Infantry. This and all other detail on names of Illinois soldiers mentioned in the letters are from the Illinois Secretary of State website; Illinois Civil War Muster and descriptive rolls database (www.ilsos.gov/isaveterans/civilMuster Search.do). Tom Currie is the husband of Jennie's cousin, Sarah (Weis) Currie. She married Tom in 1859. Based on the names of Peoria residents sprinkled liberally through the letters, Josiah evidently made a number of acquaintances while there.

6   Tom Currie was the husband of Jennie's cousin, Sarah (Weis) Currie. She married Tom in 1859. Based on the names of Peoria residents sprinkled liberally through Josiah's letters, it is evident he made a number of acquaintances during his time there.

Regiment has not forgotten the bright days of the past—I have not had a buggy ride since I left Peoria. I wish I had that "old white horse" and about a mile of Camp Mather parade ring. But I presume I need not wish now Jennie. Don't wait as long as I did. Please write soon and let me know how Peoria prospers, and may the sweetest blessings of heaven ever be thy boon is the sincere wish of your friend, Josiah Moore. I was going to put this in another i.e. Mrs. Currie, but didn't. Oh Jennie I almost forgot to tell you that I loved the program on the boat but I have not forgotten it. It was good company on the boat. I did not know where you were. When leaving the warf til after we had left. Then I found out.

Jennie to Josiah

Peoria July 11th \61
Capt. Moore,

Dear Friend,

Your long looked for letter came at last and right gladly was it welcomed by one whose thoughts often wander towards Alton and memory carries her back to the happy hours that are now numbered with the past—But twere vain to repine for the days that were but now are not. So much there is for us to accomplish in this busy world of strife to spend the precious moments of our short existence in needless repinings, but I would not if I could recall one single moment of my past life, for "every joy has had its corresponding sorrow" But it is only by contrast we enjoy the fleeting pleasures of this sinful World. If it were not for the clouds we would not fully appreciate the glorious beauty of the sunshine. It is when we have passed through the dark waters of affliction we are brought to realize the deep and fervent love of "Him who doeth all things well."

Peoria moves on as usual. It seemed quite deserted for a few days after the departure of the Regiment but it has since fallen into its old routine of July just as quietly as if it had never been disturbed with the cry of Stolen Fish chickens onions and all the other articles to numerous to mention. There has nothing of importance occured since your leaving. indeed the Local Editor of the Mirror became so devoid of news that out of pity for Him I one day while in the City induced the ponies to run away with me so He might have a terrible catastrophe to relate—kind was it not? but it was a kindness I think will not be repeated. I should have answered your letter sooner had I not left home the morning after receiving it for a short visit to

Canton in carriage and it proved a very tiresome ride but we were fully repaid for it by the kind entertainment of our friends while there.

I hope you are becoming more comfortably situated than you were when on first arriving.

It is with pleasure I hear their are others who know how to appreciate our model Regiment as well as we of Peoria but it could not be otherwise than good under the guidance of such Leaders but what a responsible position you occupy you Capt. Moore. As a professor of religion might wield a good influence over the hearts of many an erring one, your Heavenly Father has placed you in the midst of a class of men where but few revere their Maker. perhaps you think it the harder to do right so it is for often "when the spirit is willing the flesh is weak" but if you were constantly associated with the good your faith would never be put to the test. it is from Him above you must look for strength to do what is demanded of you, and remember "Christ came not into this World to call the righteous but the sinner to repentance" I know when we try to be good evil is often present with its many alluring pleasures but Beware of them they flatter but to disobey There is no real happiness save in doing good.

"Weary not of well doing" And in due time you will reap the reward of your efforts in the real glories of a brighter and better world. But I must bring this to a close as I know your patience has been exhausted long ere this. And I hope you will pardon this miserably written missive and take "the will for the deed" You know "practice makes perfect" and as I have made it a point never to answer letters (knowing my indifference to do so) I am therefore very far from being perfect.
I had again and again taken up pen and paper to write you and as many times laid them down but I at last concluded a poor letter better than none. I hope though you will "return good for evil" and answer soon. And may success attend your every effort at doing good And the peace of God, which the world gaveth not neither can it take away, be with you now and evermore is the true wish of

Jennie

P.S. Can not you try and get a little sick (I mean Home sick) so as to procure a leave of absence we would all be so glad to see you. Farewell for the present.

To date there has been no documentation found for the near-accident Jennie mentions, nor is there any evidence of a publication called the *Mirror*.

Alcohol, as made clear by Josiah's comments regarding the decline in "drunkenness," posed a problem for the regiment (as it did for many others on both sides). His comments about the citizens of Peoria also reflect the sense of community that men in the ranks found important.

Jennie, as dictated by the customs of the time, consented to receive formal correspondence from Josiah, despite the eight-year age difference between the couple. People attached great importance to written communication in the nineteenth century. It was a way in which "a respectable mid-nineteenth century woman might aspire to distinguish herself," as one historian put it. Jennie's apology for her "poor letter" was not surprising; people of the time believed letters were "evidence either of . . . good sense or . . . Folly . . . industry or carelessness . . . self-control or importance," and that proper letters had to provide information, generate interest, or lead to self-improvement. As will become evident, Jennie and Josiah kept these guidelines in mind throughout their extensive correspondence.[7]

As noted, the exchange of letters was an important part of Victorian courtship, but they were especially important for the soldier trying to survive so far away from loved ones. The letters served as a "lifeline between home and camp."[8]

Josiah to Jennie

Camp Pope Alton Ills.
July 17th 1861

Miss Jennie Lindsay:

Esteemed Friend,

I improve with pleasure the much prised opportunity of once more speaking *with my dear little friend Jennie.*
And now before I begin I must tell you Jennie that I shall not attempt a reply to that most worthy epistle of the 11th inst. that came to hand under that dear signature "Jennie," and my reason is, that the task is too much for this "sojer boy"—but I shall just talk a little as of "days gone by."

---

7   Drew Gilpin Faust, "Ours as Well as Men," in James McPherson and William J. Cooper, eds, *Writing the Civil War* (Columbia, SC, 1998), 237-238; Richard, *Listen Ladies One and All*, 150.

8   Ibid, 148.

Now Jennie when I say that I would not attempt such a reply as that precious missive requires, I do not thus only pretend to flatter you, but as I often told you that all the trials and privations of "sojer life" were fully compensated by meeting with such a friend as you. So, after reading and perusing the sacred folds of that precious epistle, I thought seriously for a few minutes and then concluded that I had received payment in full for all past sacrifices if not for a good share of those to come. Indeed, Jennie, only half is told when I say that that epistle shall be long preserved for the joy and gladness it has inspired, and also as a model of a letter from an Ills. Lady to an Ills. Volunteer, would that more such letters could be written, but I know one that can write them, and Oh, Jennie you can't imagine how sweet it is to sit down amid the turmoil and bustle of camp and through the medium of such an epistle ponder over the firm "bright moments" of the past—But the "tattoo" beats for lights out, so I must bid you "good night" sweet dreams attend thee.

I was going to write a partnership letter with the Adjutant but I thot that I better go on my own capital three ain't company.

Thursday July 18[9]
Good morning Jennie,

Well another day has returned and with it news. We have received "marching orders"—we are ordered to be ready to be ready to march by evening, as our orders are sealed our destination can only be guessed at, but I suppose that it will be some point in Missouri. I did think St. Louis or about 100 miles below but we may go up the Mo. [Missouri] river. I have but little compunction of conscience at leaving this semi barbarous Egypt.

Capt Davidson[10] is here and will go with our brigade. There has been a Mrs. Webb from Peoria paying us a visit.

But I had almost to tell you that some other folks have been expected here on a visit—you know—Oh I do wish so much that we could have staid here a while longer—then we would have had the pleasure of receiving visitors, but Jennie don't forget us when we move—tell Mr. Currie to not forget either. I saw his letter to Adjt. Ryan and I should have been glad to have seen about one or a dozen from Peoria, It would look so much like home.

---

9   This is the same letter. Josiah continued writing on the same page the following day.

10 Probably Captain Peter Davidson, 2nd Illinois Artillery, Battery L.

I also saw that letter from [illegible] *when it seems you had all had a good time I wish there had been one more there. Major Smith and Lady are here now. Lieut. Col. Wood has gone home on acc. of his health. Mrs. Cunningham from Monmouth has taken the position of principle nurse in the Hospital. I think she will give a new turn to Hospital affairs. Very much needed, I think she is a very excellent Lady. Oh, Jennie excuse me I must have wearied you, I shall apprise you of our destination as soon as possible.*

My best regards to all the friends—I am now well and hope that this may find Jennie enjoying life's sweetest blessings.

As ever: the same
"Sojer boy"
Josiah Moore

P.S. It would be of no use to get sick now, tho if I had staid here a little while I do not know but I should—[illegible]. *Is a good time coming—The drum beats for the striking of tents good by for a time. J.M.*

Jennie to Josiah

Peoria July 25th 1861
Capt. Moore

Dear Friend,

Through the mercy of Him who ruleth all things And holdeth our lives as it were in the hollow of his hand, I am once more permitted to hold sweet converse with you through the medium of pen and paper. A poor substitute indeed for the actual presence. But a medium of communication that ought in no wise to be depreciated.

Letters often come to us like angel visitants laden with loveing kindness and fraught with the sweet hope of meeting "On some future day" But alas "we know not what a day or hour may bring forth" Who can doubt the existence of a God, if in nothing else then in vailing from us the pages of the future. If we but knew in the starting out in life the many crosses we would have to endure I fear there would be but few who would accomplish their allotted duties. For every one must have their share of sorrow grief and disappointment in this world, but we must go on remembering that "wisdoms ways are ways of pleasantness and all her paths are paths of peace."

We had a grand fishing party on last week and contrary to the usual order of things we went to the water to fish. But as for the amount the ladies caught they might as well have fished in a clover field. The gentlemen were more successful on account of haveing a seine. Had you been there you would have met with some familiar faces—Mr and Mrs Weis, Mr and Mrs Currie, Mr. Speers and Sister,[11] Capt. Cromwell[12] and a few others and last but not least "The Old White Horse". You may be sure I gave him a slight] little nod of recognition in memory of the happy past. We had any amount of sport, but there was one at least who would have enjoyed it far better had there been one Moore there.

There is nothing talked about now but picnic, parties and telegraphic dispatch.

I suppose Capt. Bush is in his element since his arrival among his colored brethren "joy be with him."

I have a Lady Friend here visiting from Cincinnati. I received a letter from Sister Maggie[13] this morning saying she and a Friend of hers would be down from Chicago next week so there is no fear of my becoming lonesome. But still there is a missing one. On this day the Artillery left Peoria. Mr Currie, Sallie and I attended a picnic on our way home we thought we would call at Camp Mather and see the Company before they left but on arriving we found they had been gone half an hour. What a difference between this visit and the last one before you left. You cant imagine how dreary and deserted it looked. reminded me of the city of the dead. so lonely it seemed. But I must say farewell for time. And I pray God may preserve your life in the coming contest and may you never for a moment forget to whom you owe your existence. you dont know how much I want you should be a good man with a pure heart and true principles and may you never fail in the trust reposed in you is the prayer of

Jennie
P.S. I received your letter on the 22nd and a Waverley this morning. "I say unto you" write soon. J.E.L.

11 Probably Josiah's younger sister and her husband John Speer.

12 Captain John Cromwell of the 47th Illinois Infantry.

13 Maggie is Jennie's sister, born in 1840 and married to George Updike in 1858.

While Josiah's first letter contains little of consequence other than an opening written play in the courtship, Jennie's letter fulfills a task that women of the period believed to be a crucial responsibility—"to promote morality and work for men's salvation." Jennie has a dim view of the religious and moral inclinations of many of the men, and given the large number from Peoria she likely knew many of them. Her perspective was likely reinforced by the thefts she noted that occurred in Peoria while the 17th was in town. She conveys to Josiah what she believes is her responsibility—to encourage him to do good among men who would often not be inclined to do so.

Soldiers served to protect their communities, but were also expected to take the community's moral sense with them into the service. In many ways, Jennie's concerns were justified. One Illinois soldier claimed that while it was not impossible for a soldier to lead a Christian life, it was pretty difficult. If military life did not eliminate morality, it certainly seemed to reduce the shame soldiers felt over their transgressions. According to a soldier, "war is pretty sure to relax the morals of everybody it come in contact with." Many of the men were away from home for the first time and thus outside the influences of parents, siblings, clergy, and teachers who had held them to high moral standards. Under such conditions, it was all too easy to partake in drinking, gambling, swearing, and other similar behavior. Many younger soldiers adopted these habits because they felt it made them look tougher and more mature. The 20th Illinois, stationed at Alton with the 17th, for example, experienced gambling binges and drunken riots in the summer of 1861 before a man in the ranks had fired a shot at the enemy.[14]

As a more mature person who had spent time away from family while at school, Josiah might have had an easier time resisting the vices prevalent in army camp. There is also some evidence that more idealistic officers, such as Josiah, had a stronger sense of religion and commitment to the cause.[15]

Jennie's reference that the only topics of conversation were "picnic, parties, and telegraphic dispatches" indicates that daily life had changed little for many civilians in the North this early in the war. The first major battle of the war at

---

14 Clarke, *War Stories*, 100-110; Rable, *God's Almost Chosen Peoples*, 144; Woodworth, *While God is Marching On*, 184-188. Confederate soldiers felt the same temptations. One wrote to his wife, "[Y]ou wanted to know if I was trying to get religion or not. I have been trying and I intend to try all that I can, but I tell you it is a hard place here in camp." Bob Blaisdell editor, *Civil War Letters: From Home, Camp, and Battlefield* (Mineola, NY, 2012), 32.

15 Rable, *God's Almost Chosen Peoples*, 28.

Bull Run (Manassas), had been fought in northern Virginia not far outside Washington on July 21, just a few days before she her July 25 letter. The news of that battle, an embarrassing defeat for the Union, had not yet reached her. The first major engagement in the war's Western Theater would not take place until August at Wilson's Creek, Missouri. The 17th Illinois would not participate in that fight, but the regiment's baptism of fire would come soon enough.

1861 CHAPTER 4

First Blood

FEW states had been as prominent in the march toward civil war as Missouri, and as a result it witnessed significant personal bitterness, violence, and hardship. The wrangling over whether Missouri would enter the Union as a free or slave state had set neighbor against neighbor. About three-quarters of the men from Missouri who served in the Civil War did so under the Union banner, and guerilla warfare plagued the state throughout the war—and for years afterward. Men with pro-Southern sympathies, such as Bill Quantrill, Bill Anderson, and Frank and Jesse James, clashed with antagonists on the other side and kept the region in a state of near-constant bloodshed. Men of the cloth were not exempt from the violence. Union troops sometimes burned the churches of clergy unwilling to take an oath of loyalty, while Southern partisans attacked those they viewed as unsupportive of their cause.[1]

Missouri was one of the "border" states, a slave state that had not seceded. President Lincoln was determined to keep it in the Union. The governor, Claiborne Fox Jackson, was a staunch pro-slavery Democrat who favored secession. One of his opponents was Francis P. Blair, a state congressmen whose brother served as Lincoln's postmaster general and whose father was one of the president's closest advisors. At the outset of hostilities, Francis Blair moved quickly to safeguard the Federal government's arms and munitions by appointing Capt. Nathaniel Lyon to command the detachment at St. Louis,

1   Rable, *God's Almost Chosen Peoples*, 198-199.

which had the largest arsenal of any slave state. Governor Jackson continued to press the state legislature to join the Southern states in secession, even though a state convention in March 1861 had voted to remain in the Union. Jackson even managed to have the Confederacy ship him cannons for his militia. Lyon mobilized pro-Union militia, largely German-Americans, and some U.S. Regulars. In May, he surrounded Jackson's pro-secessionist militia on the outskirts of St. Louis and captured them without firing a shot. The next month, after rejecting entreaties for compromise from Jackson and Sterling Price, a Mexican War veteran and former governor, Lyon marched on the state capital at Jefferson City and drove out the largely pro-Southern legislature. A quorum of the state convention that had rejected secession earlier in 1861 reconvened, declared the offices of the governor and legislature vacant, and elected new individuals to those positions. Meanwhile, Jackson, who had been pushed out of the state almost entirely, re-formed the old legislature and passed an ordinance of secession. The Confederate state government accepted Missouri as the twelfth Confederate state, but shortly afterward Jackson and the pro-secession legislature were driven from the state and remained a "government in exile" for the rest of the long war.[2]

In July 1861, the Confederates routed the Union army at Bull Run (Manassas) and sent it tumbling back toward Washington. Lincoln urged his Western armies to move against Southern interests, "giving rather special attention to Missouri." To lead this effort, Lincoln appointed John C. Fremont as commander of the Western Department. Fremont, a topographical engineer who had become known as the "Pathfinder" for his explorations of the American West, had run for president as a Republican in 1856 and served as a U.S. Senator from California. He had the support of key Republicans, particularly the Blairs, who pushed Lincoln to give Fremont a meaningful command. Lincoln hoped Fremont could end the internecine warfare in Missouri and take the offensive against the Rebels. Unfortunately, Lincoln misjudged the Pathfinder's abilities. Fremont, wrote one historian, was "weak and unstable," and "inefficiency and failure marked every phase" of his actions in Missouri.[3]

Fremont reached St. Louis, the headquarters of the Western Department on July 25. On August 10, General Lyon, promoted from captain and now

---

2 McPherson, *Battle Cry of Freedom*, 290-293.

3 Ibid., 350-351. T. Harry Williams, *Lincoln and His Generals* (New York, 1952), 34-36.

under Fremont's command, moved out to confront his old nemesis Sterling Price at Wilson's Creek in southwest Missouri. The impetuous Lyon, outnumbered two to one and denied reinforcements by Fremont, attacked the Confederates. Wilson's Creek was a bitter defeat for the Federals. Casualties were about 1,300 on each side and included Lyon, who was killed. Coming on the heels of the Union debacle at Bull Run, the fight at Wilson's Creek added to the inauspicious start to the North's war efforts.[4]

Fremont assumed that the free hand Lincoln had given him on military affairs also applied to political issues. Three weeks after the Union defeat at Wilson's Creek, he issued a proclamation emancipating the slaves of Confederate activists in Missouri. Fremont did this not only to further suppress the rebellion in Missouri, but to also curry favor with the strong anti-slavery wing of the Republican Party. In addition, he issued a declaration of martial law and announced that he would summarily execute any guerilla caught behind Union lines. Lincoln had working hard to keep border states in the Union. Fremont's unilateral actions threatened that tenuous bond.[5]

Fremont's declaration against guerillas infuriated leaders such as M. Jeff Thompson, the former mayor of St. Joseph's, Missouri, and now a Southern partisan. Thompson issued his own proclamation, threatening to "hang, draw, and quarter one minion of said Abraham Lincoln" for every guerilla executed under Fremont's orders. His was no idle threat. Confederate guerrillas, called "bushwhackers" by the Federals, were skilled in long-range sharpshooting and routinely attacked Union patrols.[6]

Lincoln quietly asked Fremont to withdraw his order. Rather than accede to the wishes of his commander-in-chief, Fremont sent his wife to Washington in an effort to persuade the president that Fremont's course was correct, and to tell Lincoln that he would not rescind the proclamation without a public order. Lincoln issued the order the day after Mrs. Fremont left Washington. Shortly afterward, he also transferred the Pathfinder to a less prominent post.[7]

Captain Moore and his regiment found themselves tossed into this cauldron of sectional strife. The 17th Illinois did not fight at Wilson's Creek, but

4   McPherson, *Battle Cry of Freedom*, 351-353.

5   Ibid., 352-354.

6   Victor Hicken, *Illinois in the Civil War* (Champaign, IL, 1966), 15-16.

7   McPherson, *Battle Cry of Freedom*, 352-353.

it was part of the overall military force dispatched to keep Missouri in the Union. The regiment was part of the District of North Missouri, which was led by General Pope, the same man who had sworn the 17th into Federal service just two months earlier. Later in the year, the 17th would become part of the District of Southeastern Missouri and then the District of Cairo, both under the command of Ulysses S. Grant, another Illinois man.[8]

Starting on the day Josiah finished his letter of July 18, the 17th Illinois remained in near-constant motion as it responded to real or perceived threats in the war-torn state. On July 18, the regiment sailed from Alton to St. Charles, Missouri. On July 20, it was dispatched to Warrenton, and eight days later was on its way to St. Louis. On July 31, the command left St. Louis to begin garrison duty at Bird's Point, Missouri, an assignment that lasted about two weeks. From there the men trekked through various parts of the state in search of Jeff Thompson and his men.[9]

It wasn't until mid-August, while aboard a troop transport, that Josiah found time to write to Jennie.

Sulphur Springs Mo, 30 miles below St. Louis
Cabin of the Chancellor
Augt, 16th 1861

Well Jennie after just finishing the foregoing and ere it was sealed the order came "pack up" so we packed up. Hence the anticipated attack at Birds Point is "non est comatible."

We went on board the Boat at Birds Point on the night of the 14th inst. and arrived here this evening at dark. We had a very slow trip owing to the incapacity of the boat for such a number of men—all the 17th Regt. Some 4000 men have come from Birds Point with us. We are staying on the boat for the night, in the morning we shall disembark and take the interior of the state at which point we expect to form an army of about 15000 Union troops and then with heaven's fair smile

8   Frank J. Welcher, *The Union Army 1861-1865, Organization and Operations, Volume II: The Western Theater* (Bloomington, IN, 1993), 89, 155.

9   Illinois Adjutant General's Report.

freedom's cause will "forward march" even tho our noble Lyon has fallen. We will show them that there is still another in the way.

Genl Prentiss[10] takes command of the Ills boys—I should prefer "our Colonel"—Jennie he is one of the men whom soldiers delight to honor. He took charge of the fleet coming up the river and as our boat was slow, he beat us about 12 hours, but he came down to the wharf and met us and just as soon as the boat touched you should see our officers jump off—each one as it were eager to catch the first shake of the old familiar hand. But I must say that it is really delightful to enjoy the good feeling and warm sympathy that exists as ever throughout the whole Regt—officers and all. The more we are tossed and moved around, the closer the bonds of Union seems to be drawn. So much consolation to compensate for the sorrows of war.

Lieut Reynolds[11] Lady is here now. As I presume you are aware, Mrs Clemens has gone home—Excuse this extra.

My kind regards to Mr. & Mrs. Currie and all the old friends. Good night, pleasant dreams, not of war but of peace—

J.M.

I presume the groves of Camp Mather have taken off their gloom for a time since Cap Cromwell had returned. Thus the way of earth—one goes and another takes the place and the void is filled. Oh how I should like to visit that classic old camp, but it cannot be now—our work is forward to the battle cry. Oh, I told Cap Bush[12] that he had the best wishes of a lady, among "his cherished friends"—didnt say who.

Now Jennie, please dont forget the address 17th Regt Illinois Volunteers St. Louis Mo.

We are off Nov 5th good bye. J.M.

10 Benjamin Prentiss, former colonel of the 10th Illinois, was promoted to brigadier general on May 8, 1861.

11 2nd Lieutenant William Reynolds of Company A.

12 Captain Henry Bush of Company D.

One of Josiah's fellow officers described the 17th's new surroundings: "Across the Mississippi to our right is 'Bird's Point' in Missouri, until recently it was a great field of corn, now it is covered with the tents of our army. Across the Ohio to our left, thickly wooded," he added, "is an entrenched and fortified camp named Fort Holt."[13]

Almost a month later, Josiah find the time to write once more to Jennie:

Fort Holt, Ky Sept 11th /61

Miss Jennie

Esteemed Friend

With the bright scenes of "Auld lang syne" still in view I take my pencil—Oh what a painter! Well Jennie, I guess I can't paint, but, I presume it is no harm to feel just as tho I could.

Your dear epistle of the 28th ult[14], came to hand while we were yet parked at Jackson Mo, 10 miles W. of Girardeau and Jennie I need not say that "weary weeks" in Mo. on such a campaign as we accomplished will challenge any comparisons even with those that linger around the old classic hills and peaceful arbors of Peoria and I for the first time partialy felt the reality of a "stranger in a strange land" so Jennie you may guess that a message from the angel land and especially coming from the hand of one of its cherished inhabitants was well read.

As you spoke of "Old Camp Mather" it seemed as tho its once happy groves were again enjoyed as in days gone by not to speak of those dear evenings when old luna was wont to look so pleasantly. Oh "it seemed to me but yesterday, nor scarce so long ago."

I should like to visit the old camp and hear Miss Harris "cheer on" the patriotic few.

I presume Cap. Cromwell will enjoy himself as usual, I thought that Mr. Currie would have gone but I need a letter from him stating that he had not gone, still he didn't say that Sallie prevented him. I guess he wouldn't like to acknowledge

---

13 Peats, *Recollections*, 7.

14 The August 28 letter from Jennie is missing.

"womans sovereignity." Well Jennie, I think that it is a pretty good institution to be married, especially in war times, it is so calculated to keep a person out of danger.

I presume you've heard of our removal to Ky. We landed here on the morning of the 8th inst. (Sabbath)and in co, with Heckens Regt. were the first on the Ky. Shore opposite Cairo.

There are now about 6 Regts of infantry and 3 cos cavalry here the sappers and miners have cut down timber for a park and mounted 3 large guns. (34 pounders) to guard the river.

On yesterday morning a person gave us word that 800 rebel cavalry were parked 6 miles down the river. Heckens[15] Regt. and 6 cos. of ours started at 2 Oclock A.M. to surprise and take them. We surrounded the supposed camp about sun-rise, but to our surprise no cavalry were to be found. They had been there the day previous and cut down a Union flag, but soon left, our boys were eager for the fight and I shouldn't much like to have been the secesh to meet them when they found out that there was no game. They left home traveled 12 miles and did without breakfast—to noon—"the hungry bear is not to be fondled with"—the boys are mostly in good health, Abe is not so well, Col Ross is at home Mrs Reynolds is still with us. Major Smith is home sick I suppose he is waiting at the depot. I shall write to Mr. Currie pretty soon—Remember me to Mr & Mrs Currie and all the old friends and young ones too—Especially Jennie, and hoping that this hasty letter may find you in the sweet enjoyment of good health and happy friends.

I remain as ever, yours with pleasure

Soldier boy

P.S. View me with a critics eye? only, so that it is Jennie's eye. Now Jennie don't forget the length of 4 weeks in Ky. Address Cairo Ills. Our gun boats[16] made an

15 Frederick Hecker, colonel of the 24th Illinois.

16 Josiah's comment about gunboats was likely a reference to the periodic trips Union naval patrols made down the Mississippi River to test Rebel fortifications at Columbus, Kentucky, at the direction of the commander of the District of Southeast Missouri, General Grant. Nathaniel Chears Hughes, *The Battle of Belmont: Grant Strikes South* (Chapel Hill, NC, 1991), 25.

attack down the river but you can get the items of news in the Chicago papers better than I can give it as I have not yet rec'd an official statement. J.M.

Josiah's matter-of-fact letter strayed into the realm of marriage, one arena where war could create differences between single and married men. Even at this early stage of their relationship, it is clear Josiah and Jennie shared an attraction and a desire to reunite. However, other letters from the front demonstrate the anxiety to see loved ones was even more acute among married men separated from wives and children. Back home, the wives agonized over the possibility that their husbands might not survive. Some wives openly demanded their husbands leave the army and return home. As the war went on, the sentiments of an Ohio woman became more typical. "I would not feel so badly if I thought you felt very sorry to leave but you know you don't feel half about it as I do, do you?" she asked. "I am more a wife than a patriot & although I do care for my country, I care for you much more." For many women, the absence of husbands not only left an emotional vacancy, but made it truly difficult to provide for their families.[17]

Jennie to Josiah

Peoria Sept 21st 1861
Capt. Moore

Dear Friend,

 Your kind message of the 11th inst was read with much pleasure. Happy to hear that past scenes still have a place in memory I hope they may always have an abiding where neither time or place can erase them from off memorys fair pages.
 The Regt. seems to be endowed with a moving propensity we but just hear of your being stationed at one place when news comes of your removal elsewhere.

---

17 Megan McClintock, "The Impact of the Civil War on Nineteenth Century Marriages," in Paul Cimbala and Randall Miller, *Northern Home Front* (New York, NY, 2002), 396; Nina Silber, *Daughters of the Union: Northern Women Fight the Civil War* (Cambridge, MA, 2005), 14.

Col. Bryner's Regt.[18] has been encamped here the same length of time as that of the 17th but I can tell you they have met with a far different reception from what our Regt did while here. The only redeeming quality in the officers is their being nearly all good democrats and that you know is an indication of their having right good sense. The people in general give the Regt. credit for being a very quiet set of men "Honor to whom honor is due" but the reasons of that is they are principally from the country and dont know enough to make a noise. I suppose their mere approach to the City of Peoria perfectly awes them into silence.

Saturday Eve.

On yesterday afternoon while writing I was interrupted by the arrival of Mrs Currie accompanied by our little Adjutant. Oh but I was glad to see him but I was so disappointed that Somebody else wasnt with him you know who Mr Ryan looks very ill we are going to keep him here untill he gets well again We dont know what a great blessing health is untill we are afflicted. We went over to Camp Logan to see the dress parade. and from the Camp we went back home with Cousin Sallie to have tea.

The Regt left this morning on the Eastern Endenscon Road for parts unknown. Mr Currie Mr Speers and several other Peoria gentlemen and ladies went as far as Cherroa with them and returned on the Evening train. This has been another sad day to Peoria. When will there be an end to this parting. It seems so sad for those that have familyes to leave them. but their country calls them and they must obey they leave with saddened hearts with the expectation of a happy reunion but alas, their is many a one departs never more to return.

But God alone knows what is best for us and it is to him we must look for strength and guidance in our time of trouble. In prosperity we are to apt to forget to whom we own everything. And this God afflicts us so as to bring our souls in closer communion with him. But it is now going late so I must bid you good night. Take good care of yourself and try to do right in all things and you will meet your reward.

Yours ever, Jennie

---

18 Colonel John Bryner of the 47th Illinois Infantry.

Jennie's teasing of Josiah about the Democratic leanings of the 47th Illinois is a possible indication of partisan differences between the two, or at least between Josiah and her father, who had been a Republican office holder in Illinois but was now inclined to side with the Democrats. Although there is no indication Josiah had been politically active prior to the war, as the war progressed his letters indicated a growing disdain for the Northern Democrats. This faction became known as Peace Democrats, and opposed the war and Lincoln's prosecution of it. Many Northern women became increasingly active supporters of the war effort by speaking up for the Union, filling the gap left by the large numbers of Republican men who were serving in the military. The women left behind often had to defend the war effort against the Peace Democrats. With her father's leanings, it was likely very difficult for Jennie to become part of this female, pro-Union movement.[19]

However, the 17th regiment also contained a strong anti-abolition element. In August 1861, the regimental newspaper attacked the typical "northern fanatic" who, in the words of the writer, "gleefully accepted the suffering of war as long as the goal of abolition was attained."[20]

Jennie's letter also speaks of another theme that ran through their exchange—the thought that God sent the war as an affliction upon the land for its transgressions, in the hope that it will "bring our souls in closer communion with him." Many Americans in 1861 believed everything good and bad—storms, illness, harvests, or death—was a product of God's will. It is no surprise that Jennie detected divine intervention in the bloody conflict. There was growing sentiment in the North that the war was a punishment for tolerating slavery. Others believed God's rationale for the war remained unfathomable. Americans on both sides saw the conflict as part of some "unfolding providential story" whose end remained in doubt.[21]

After spending most of September building fortifications in Kentucky, the 17th Illinois departed for the swampy grounds around Cape Girardeau, a Mississippi River town in southeastern Missouri. Many of the men, including Josiah, fell ill from the miserable conditions at the camp and had to stay behind when the 17th and other units moved out to corral M. Jeff Thompson.

19 Faust, *Ours as Well as the Men*, 234.

20 Manning, *What This Cruel War Was Over*, 44.

21 Woodworth, *While God is Marching On*, 262-263; Rable, *God's Almost Chosen Peoples*, 2, 9.

According to the member of another regiment, "the 17th is in a pretty hard condition, nearly half of them sick and as a regiment pretty badly used up." In all, 26 men from Company F, including two officers and five non-commissioned officers, were unable to participate in the expedition against Thompson. They also missed the unit's first skirmish, which took place on October 21 at Fredericktown in south-central Missouri. Second Lieutenant Charles Williams commanded the company in Josiah's absence. The 17th was assigned as part of a Union force under the command of Col. Joseph Plummer. They caught up with Thompson at Fredericktown and routed his Missouri State Guard command.[22] There is evidence that some Union troops burned the homes of townspeople they believed had let them to walk into an ambush. This was not an uncommon practice in many of the border states, where Union troops often viewed themselves as avenging the atrocities committed against citizens who had remained loyal to the Union.[23]

Years later, Frank Peats recalled the words of the chaplain of the 20th Illinois when the 17th Regiment had moved into line: "Give them hell boys, the Lord is on our side." As Peats put it, "no sermon ever wrought a more profound conviction and I have ever since then been a warm supporter of short sermons."[24]

Josiah to Jennie

Cape Girardeau Mo.
Nov. 4th 1861

22 When General Thompson led about 1,500 men into southeastern Missouri, a pair of Union columns, one under Colonel Plummer of about the same number, and a second under Col. William P. Carlin with 3,000 men, were dispatched to track him down and defeat him. Thompson moved south of Fredericktown, but on the evening of October 21 turned and attacked. The Rebels lost 145 men (25 dead, 40 wounded, and 80 missing/captured) and an iron 12-pounder artillery piece, while Union casualties were seven killed and 60 wounded.

23 Mary E. Kellogg, *Army Life of an Illinois Soldier, Letters and Diaries of the late Charles W. Wills* (Washington, DC, 1906), 36; Duncan, Company log; Illinois Adjutant General's Report; Susannah J. Ural, *Don't Hurry Me Down to Hades: The Civil War in the Words of Those Who Lived It* (Oxford, England, 2013), 65; Ramold, *Across the Divide*, 30. Colonel Joseph Plummer was a career officer, graduate of West Point (1841) and was badly wounded at Wilson's Creek. He would be elevated to brigadier general in March of 1862, but die in Corinth, Mississippi one year after his injury from the lingering results of his wound and life in the field.

24 Peats, *Recollections,* 22-23.

Miss Jennie E Lindsay,
Esteemed lady,

After a long silence the echo returns to seek its native woods, so your humble servant after being tossed by land and by sea at the first sessation of his "little toils" accounts it a pleasure to enjoy the privilege of returning once more to hold converse with the dear folks at home.

Your kindly little missive of the 21st of Sept came duly to hand while I was lying sick at Fort Holt Ky. I read it with pleasure but was denied the pleasure of replying—I took fever and as I presumed it impossible that fever could keep me down over a week at most I staid in my quarters but soon found that I must yield. I went to the Hospital at Cairo where I was well cared for by our excellent lady Mrs Cunningham who had previously gone there to visit on some of our boys, in the mean time "our Regt" moved to the Cape and as soon as I could get round I became so lonesome that ere I was well I took boat and followed the boys. While at the Hospital father heard of my being sick and came to see me and to bring me home but I told him that I could not go for about a month, but now I guess it wil be another month ere that happy time comes round tho I am bound to go that's to O Col Ross says I may.

I have been here now three weeks stopping at the tavern and hence have not yet gone on duty. I had no idea that I would be so long recovering but perhaps it was well, for we are too often prone to forget that we are mortal—God does not afflict only for our good.

I think that I shall go on duty in a few days if I get no reverse. I regretted much that I was not able to go with the boys in their celebrated march to Fredricktown but they conquered and that was enough. A stronger power than numbers led them on to victory. I presume you have had the items from the papers before this, if not there has been an official report sent to the Monmouth journals for insertion, it is short but good from it—I think Jennie that you will learn that "our Regt' has gained the brightest laurels of the present campaign. Yes Jennie if the age of miracles was not past I should exclaim, truly a miracle! first—from the position and advantage of the enemy, the escape of our men from the advantages of the enemies ambuscade was most miraculous and then when has victory been more sanguine—for tho we have to lament the fall of a few of our brave fellows, yet how did so many escape the rifle fire of an enemy under cover not 100 yds distant sometimes 25 yds. Cos A, D, F, made the first charge and closed up within 25 yds of 800 rifles. They had to fall back but only one of my company was wounded. Cap Nortons[25] suffered a little more severely, but had none killed.[26]

Well Jennie it is getting late my candle is exhausted my paper is giving out—so I shall have to bid you good evening. May your dreaming moments cheer you on for the brighter morn.

J.M.

In all, the 17th Illinois lost four men killed or mortally wounded at Fredericktown, including Lt. John Jones, a Peoria man in Company K, and 25 wounded. The men of the 17th had finally "seen the elephant," a colloquial term for experiencing combat, and their attitude began to grate on other regiments. Most soldiers were anxious to see combat and demonstrate their bravery, and being kept out of a fight was not merely disappointing but deemed somehow dishonorable. "Don't it almost make you sick the way that 17th brag and blow about themselves" fumed Charles Wills of the 8th Illinois, a regiment that had yet to see action. "That affair at Fredricktown didn't amount to a thing. From the best information I can get, there was not to exceed 50 Rebels killed, and I'm not sure that many." According to Wills, "our boys are perfectly sick for a fight so they can be even with the 17th." Wills appeared to be particularly incensed that "the 17th doesn't deserve to be named the same days with us for drill or discipline with all their bragging."[27]

Wills might have had a cause for complaint. The men who had received their baptism of fire clearly felt a sense of accomplishment. One member of the

<hr>

25 Addison Norton of Company A.

26 The one man confirmed wounded in Josiah's company was James Earp (although some accounts list Cpl. John Shelly as being slightly wounded when he was grazed by a bullet). Earp was struck by a bullet that "passed from behind the shoulder through the joint coming out near the breast bone." This resulted in an "inability to raise and extend his left arm from the shoulder." Earp received a surgeon's discharge from Henry H. Penniman, the 17th's assistant surgeon. Pension file of James Earp at National Archives Research Administration (NARA), Washington, DC.

27 Kellogg, *Army Life of an Illinois Soldier*, 39, 44; McPherson, *For Cause and Comrades*, 30-33, 43-45.

17th who had fought in the small battle needled a comrade who had been left behind. "Oh you camp cook, you don't need to talk to me!" he teased.[28]

With the exception of a few forays to try and capture the elusive Rebel Thompson, for the rest of the year and through January of 1862 the men of the 17th Illinois remained at Cape Girardeau. The men who missed the fight at Fredericktown would "see the elephant" soon enough.

28 Smith, *A Brief History of the !7th Illinois.*

CHAPTER 5

"I Was Looking for You Every Day"

JOSIAH was still in war-torn Missouri when 1862 began, and he had yet to return to Peoria since his departure the previous July. Jennie took note of the fact that other officers from the 17th Infantry had returned home, but Josiah had not done so. In addition, he had written her but one letter since September 1861, although this was likely because of his illness and the regiment's travels, and not from a waning interest in his home front sweetheart. It was not uncommon for a soldier who was ill to avoid writing home about his sickness to keep from worrying family and friends. The lack of communication concerned Jennie and she likely felt slighted, despite acknowledging to Josiah that she had not written him for four months.

Jennie enlisted the assistance of her cousin, Sallie Currie (or perhaps her cousin volunteered), to reignite the spark between the two. Adjutant Ryan, perhaps intentionally, aggravated the situation between the couple. Ryan, who was an acquaintance of the Lindsay family before the war, also considered himself to be Jennie's suitor. Even Josiah knew of his intent. In his July 17, 1861, letter to Jennie, Josiah had joked about his plans to "write a partnership letter" with Ryan, but decided not to because "three ain't company."[1]

---

1 Steven J. Ramold, *Across the Divide: Union Soldiers View the Northern Home Front* (New York and London, 2013), 28.

Mrs. T. L. Currie to Josiah

Peoria January 3rd 1862
Capt. J. Moore
Dear Friend

At the urgent request of Mr. Currie, I have seated myself to pen an answer to your kind + interesting missive dated somewhere back in the old year. Thomas has intended answering it time + again but always something prevented—and now he is in Camp clerking for Quartermaster Currie that letter writing is utterly out of the question. however he will endeavor in a short time to write you.

He received a letter from Adjt Ryan last evening, but he mentioned none of you. I thought it very strange. I had almost forgotten to tell you that I am out at Jennies spending the day: She is sitting by me—waiting very anxiously for something—I hardly know what. Poor Jennie! she seems to feel so sad lately—for what reason I know not—She as well as myself was provoked because Mr. Ryan did not mention you in his letter.

Jennie says she deferred writing to you—thinking that perhaps you would be here any moment—and still you did not come—Now Capt. why dont you! What in the world is the matter! Have you forgotten your old friend! I will not harbor such a thought but perhaps you are sick: If so, you are certainly excusable. Remember your friends in Peoria will never forget you—wherever you are.

Cousin Jennie will write next week if you do not make your appearance. Thomas said last evening (oh what ink) that Col. Ingersoll's[2] regiment had received marching orders—I do not know whether Mr Currie will go on ?. If he does—poor me! What will I do? Jennie says I must come out and sympathize with her. All your old friends are well I believe.

Jennie's sister, Mrs. Updike is here visiting from Chicago. She is a sweet little woman. It seems like old times for us all to be together again. You must not forget to call and see us before going further out of the city when you come.

Thomas wishes to be remembered to you all. Please present also my kind regards to Ryan, Major Smith, Capt Bush + all the rest of my acquaintances—not forgetting your own good self. What do you think? Jennie sends her best love to one Capt Moore. Write very soon.

---

2 Colonel Robert Ingersoll of the 11th Illinois Cavalry.

I remain, ever your friend

Mrs T.L. Currie

The following letter is undated and indicates no location. However, Josiah wrote it some time after he received the letter from Mrs. Currie and before the letter from Jennie dated January 12, 1862, because he attempted to apologize for his lack of communication.

Josiah to Jennie

Good morning!

Well Jennie "Younder comes the powerful king of day" O and here is a little frost about the first in this place this fall tho, we have had very chilly weather so much so that several of the officers have taken rooms to sleep in. Mrs Reynolds has come to the tavern to stay. She gets along finely.

There is generally pretty good health now in the Regt. Col Ross was complaining a few evenings since of Rheumatism but went to a little dance and he says that he thinks it cured him, wasn,t that nice?

Lieut Robson[3] has returned in good health Cap Harding and Lieut Charter[4] have gone home on furlough, they intend visiting Peoria ere they return they have been quite sick.

We have been looking anxiously for Adjt Ryan for some time but I fear that his mind has become distracted from "grim visaged war" I just imagine how reluctant I should feel to think that the "time has come to leave" it seems as tho it would be "the saddest of the year" so I can hardly blame our little fellow for being sick a leetle over time. I hope however to see him restored soon to the circle of his friends. Mr. Bush was telling me that he was well cared for.

I have nothing much to say of the present destination of the 17th only that I have now gone on duty and the Regt. has orders to be ready at an hours warning to be on the march I expect to Bloomfield the point where Jef. Thompson took the

---

3   First Lieutenant George W. Robson, Company A, 17th Illinois Infantry.

4   Roderick R. Harding of Company E, and First Lieutenant John R. Charter of Company F, both of the 17th Illinois Infantry.

*stand after being whipped out at Fredricktown. I am not certain whether or not we
shall go tho Jef must be whipped again before he keeps quiet.*

*I see an account of Col Bryners Regt. being very sickly now Jennie you see that
our democrats cant stand these little toils. But I guess we wont disagree about this
matter as there are some good democrats.*

*I heard Jennie that you had a visit to Chicago. I hope that you have returned
in safety and that your visit to the "queen of the Lakes" was of the most agreeable
character.*

*Now Jennie you must not think my tardiness the result of forgetfulness for
indeed I thought often of the "bright past" there tho I enjoyed good health, I did not
write a letter for nearly six weeks. I have one now from Mrs Currie and I hardly
know how to begin to apologize for my long delay, but I cannot help it now and can
only say that having no "abiding place" you must all judge us as little as possible
with a "critic,s eye" Oh you must excuse my prosey letter you can easily see that I
am not yet quite compas mentis but hope soon to recover.*

*Then hoping that you may not forget the soldier boy and that this may find
you in the enjoyment of a dear home and happy friends in good health and a
participant of Heavens brightest favors.*

I remain, as ever yours

Josiah Moore

*P.S. I think the ladies of Peoria are very kind in sending Hospital stores tho I think
we have now about all we can carry on the march. Dr Tomkins and I had a game of
backgammon with a case sent in one of the boxes we enjoyed it hugely not knowing
what tender fingers had moved the sets before, at least it came from Peoria. J.M.*

Josiah's disappointment in not hearing from Jennie since the fall of 1861 is
quite apparent. Soldiers were desperate for word from home, family, and
friends. "You have no idea what a blessing letters from home are to the men in
camp," wrote one soldier in Virginia. "They make us better men, better
soldiers." The letters contained news from home—the kind of news that didn't
appear in newspapers. Letters were their connection to family and friends and
the communities for whom they fought. A soldier from Ohio wrote that "it is
the greatest comfort to a soldier to hear from home," while another said "it is
like seeing an old friend." Many viewed letters from home as virtually a military
necessity. "We don't need money down here, don't need anything but men,

muskets, ammunition, hard tack, bacon, and letters from home," wrote one soldier.[5]

The mail system was remarkably reliable and affordable—the postage for a letter was just three cents in the North and the only disruption in service tended to be when the army was on the move—so soldiers could feel abandoned when they received no letters from home.[6]

Jennie to Josiah

Peoria Jan. 12th 1862
Capt. Moore

Dear Friend

    Nearly four months have flown on the tardy wings of time since I last addressed a few lines to you. I had hoped to see you ere I wrote again But Alas! Hope is a sad deceiver Yet with all her faults we cherish her as our guiding star through many a dark and dreary hour bidding us look forward to a "brighter morn." Sometimes far away in the dim distance.

    I received your dear good letter a long long time ago and would have answered it without delay had I known where to direct to for you remember you were just on the eve of departure when you wrote me. And knew not how long you would be away I did not see your letter to Mr. Currie for a couple of week after he received it and I thought it useless to write then so instead of writing I looked for you But as you know dear Friend it was a look in vain. And now Capt. Moore the query is why dont you come. I think if you only knew how much your friends and how very much your Friend would like to see you you would come just to please them, and you know by imparting pleasure, to others we often catch a little glimpse of it ourselves.

    I was sorry to hear of your being ill poor boy. What a lonesome time you must have had of it—I guess many thoughts of Home Sweet home with a gentle mothers hand to soothe away pain glanced before your weary eyes.

    Cousin Sallie wrote to you last week and I suppose gave you all the news if there is such an article in Peoria.

---

5 Linderman, *Embattled Courage*, 94; Ramold, *Across the Divide*, 26.

6 Ibid., 26-27; Wagner, Gallagher, and Finkelman, *Civil War Desk Reference*, 710-711.

Sister Maggie came home New Years Eve and returned last Saturday it seems quite lonesome since shes been gone. She was very much disappointed at my not going back with her. I would have gone but I was looking for you every day and Oh So disappointed that you did not come.

I suppose the little adjutant keeps well since his return please remember me to him. and say to him I was very sorry I was not at home when he called to bid me good bye. I think I had the misfortune to offend Mr Ryan though not intentional by any means.

Well Capt. Moore, I guess you have grown wearied over this monotonous scribbling so I will close wishing you a very happy New Year. and may God bless you and preserve you from danger is the earnest wish of,

Jennie

P.S. I expect a verbal answer to this. Soon too dont forget to come.

In Josiah's handwriting at the end of the letter he had written: Recd Jan 22nd 1862.

Josiah to Jennie

Camp Fremont
Cape Girardeau Mo,
Jan 29th 1862

Miss Jennie E. Lindsay,
Esteemed lady,

Your dear favor of the 14th [probably meant the 12th] *inst came to hand in due time and tho the vision had passed and the dream almost ended yet the opening day brought charms of more sweet delight—hope long deferred gave way at last –the long looked for tiny messenger came laden with its treasure of thought –which I regret were not vive voce yet consoled not a little by resolving for a time the dreary present into the brighter scenes of a once happy past.*

And dear friend I am sorry that I was in any way the cause of your missing such a pleasant visit with your sister—but you could not be more disappointed that I was – Oh I can,t tell you all—of course I want to do my duty where ever I am but I be tempted sometimes to think that this is a little too much duty so Jennie I need scarcely tell you that it was no fault of mine that I did not make my visit about the holy days—I had the promise of a leave of absence then and never having asked one before I thought it would be all right but—stern fate under the heel of sterner war decreed it otherwise—I was very anxious to attend the literary performances of Monmouth College about that time and of course should have preferred having some others participate but "the vision is past" still there is no need to pine over departed glories, after the storm comes a calm and the greater the former the more sublime the latter; thus, hope remains our "guiding star."

Of course others got to go home but—O they are married, so you see the advantages of married people –I think it aint fair—What you think? I think so too.

I had a letter from Mrs Currie she spoke of being at your house & I presume from my reply she would think that I had the blues pretty badly but I have partially recovered since that.

I was out on a famous scouting expedition on last Sat, & Sunday we marched to Benton 17 miles stoped all night—and marched back again. That is all.

There is some talk of leaving this post entirely pretty soon—for parts unknown—but probably Ky—Col Ross & Cap Norton are going home for awhile.

Abe asked me, just the night before I received your letter, when I heard from Peoria? Of course I could answer nothing definite tho I think he suspected. O I almost forgot to give him that "kiss" (I believe it was excuse if mistaken) you sent him—but he is well and just as big an imp as ever.

I have not been on company duty since before Christmass, being appointed on a general court martial. We have had quite an interesting time and some pretty hard cases to try. but we are nearly through and I am not very sorry.
We have had a very pleasant time since our arrival at the Cape. The health of our men was never better and your humble servant has the pleasure of rejoicing with the rest and Jennie I believe I can apreciate to some extent the blessings of health since my little indisposition.

I have not heard from Lieut Hough[7] for some time is he recovering from his wound.

Well Jennie I presume I am imposing on good nature but I must talk a little about the weather—we have had no snow and but little frost till yesterday one of those sudden changes took place that has an equal only among one horse politicians in the morning all was bright and pleasant –at night all was snow and disagreeable

---

7 John Hough, a Peoria man who enlisted in Co. A but had been promoted to an officer in Company B.

there is now 6 or 8 inches of snow and more coming so I think we have a pretty fair show yes—for a southern sleigh ride wont you come and and try it—it will be so pleasant being so much warmer than you have it up north.

But my bed is made so I must retire wishing thee sweet dreams and pleasant sleep, I bid thee good night , only wishing that these words were "verbal".

Remember me to Mrs Currie and all the friends and accept my sincere thanks for your kind hope for my success & wellfare and your "happy new years wish" and hoping that you may be non the less happy by [illegible] and hoping to hear from thee soon.

Adieu-pro tempore.

Josiah Moore
Co. F. 17th Ills Regt, Cape Girardeau, Mo,

Excuse scribbling , please do, Please address as above & oblige yours truly J.M.

Once again the personal interplay of Josiah, Jennie, and Ryan manifested itself in Josiah's letter. However, the letter from Sallie Currie seems to have had the desired effect. Josiah's letters to Jennie began take a more personal tone.

Jennie to Josiah

Peoria Feb 8th 1862
Capt. Josiah Moore

Dear Absent Friend,

On learning today that Capt Norton intends leaving on Monday next to rejoin the Regt. I thought it a good opportunity to send a word or two to thee. I received your letter on last Evening And I need not say how disappointed I was that it was not you instead but disappointment seems to be the order of the day. The present looks dark and dreary with only a slight gleam of sunshine when Hope predominates over memory and whispering the sweet resolution of a future where sorrow and sadness will be unknown, and all will be peace and happiness.

I have not seen Mr. Hough since he returned home and have not heard from him lately.

Sallie Currie spent the day with us yesterday. She says she will answer your letter soon Mr Currie is going East next week to be gone a month I expect Sallie will break her heart with grief if he stays that long.

Well Capt Moore as my time has expired and my paper giveth out I will have to bid thee good night. We have just got news of your leaving the Cape and I have been wondering where our poor soldier boy is tonight. Would that we knew but in war times we have to learn "to [illegible] *and to wait."*

I will answer your letter next week and direct it to the Cape as I suppose your letters will be forwarded to you. Once again good night.

Yours ever,

Jennie

"Your Noble Boy is No More"

CONFEDERATE General Albert Sidney Johnston was an 1826 graduate of the United States Military Academy and a veteran of the Mexican War. When the Civil War broke out, many North and South considered him to be one of the best generals of either side and much was expected of him. Jefferson Davis, the Confederate president, was especially hopeful and appointed him to command the Western Military Department, a sprawling territory that stretched from the Appalachian range westward to the Ozarks. General Johnston counted on a string of river forts on the Cumberland and Tennessee Rivers, and especially Forts Henry and Donelson, to keep Union forces from advancing along these arteries deep into vital Confederate territory.[1]

The Union's Brig. Gen. Ulysses Simpson Grant commanded the military district at Cairo, Illinois. Grant was also a West Point graduate (Class of 1843) and veteran of the Mexican War. After the latter conflict, Captain Grant was posted on the west coast, where loneliness and the separation from his family caused him to turn to alcohol. He resigned from the army and returned east to try his luck at a variety of jobs, including helping to oversee the slaves on his father-in-law's farm in Missouri. Nothing seemed to work out. When war came in 1861, Grant was working as a clerk in his father's leather goods store in Galena, Illinois, not far from Josiah's home. Anxious to get into the fight to

---

1 Boatner, *Civil War Dictionary*, 440.

save the Union, Grant successfully secured the colonelcy of the 21st Illinois before being promoted to his current position.[2]

Grant, who would prove tenaciously aggressive throughout the war, believed the design and location of the two Confederate forts in northern Tennessee just below the Kentucky border—Fort Henry on the Tennessee River and Fort Donelson on the Cumberland—exposed them to capture. He received permission from Maj. Gen. Henry W. Halleck, the commander of the Department of Missouri and Grant's superior, to launch an expedition against the forts. The plan included working in conjunction with Admiral Andrew Foote, the commander of the Western Gunboat Flotilla. On February 2, 1862, the 17th Infantry, along with the other troops of Grant's command, boarded river steamers and embarked on the expedition. Fort Henry was the first target.[3]

As the Union vessels steamed up the Ohio River and then down the Tennessee, the Illinois men watched the green lands of their home state pass. Years later, Frank Peats wistfully described their leave from familiar lands as they viewed "the quiet pastoral scenes of meadow and woodland, of cosy cabins and thrifty orchards, troops of boys partially dressed in ventilated panteloons, that gazed upon us with wide wondering eyes and bashful girls whose youthful beauty was half concealed in poke bonnets and primitive gowns that were unvexed with tuck, pucker, or bustle." Peats also described what the journey was like aboard ship. "Our boat is crowded full," he wrote, "blankets are spread on deck, between decks and on the cabin floors. Officers can enjoy the privilege of occupying the state rooms a rare privilege when we discover that the little 4x7 state rooms are bereft of all beds, bedding and carpets. Even the little dainty Cleopatra lace curtains have been removed from the windows, inviting all the 'peeping Toms' of the regiment to make observation."[4]

The 17th, along with the 49th Illinois and two batteries of Missouri artillery were part of Col. William Morrison's 3rd Brigade, in Brig. Gen. John A. McClernand's 1st Division. McClernand was a Democratic congressman from southern Illinois, but he was also ardently pro-Union. A "political general" rather than a professional soldier, Lincoln had given McClernand his commission to help keep southern Illinois solidly aligned with the Union—to

---

2 Brooks D. Simpson, *Ulysses S. Grant: Triumph over Adversity 1822-186*5 (New York, NY, 2000), 71; Boatner, *Civil War Dictionary*, 352-353.

3 McPherson, *Battle Cry of Freedom*, 392-397; Boatner, *Civil War Dictionary*, 367.

4 Peats, *Recollections*, 9.

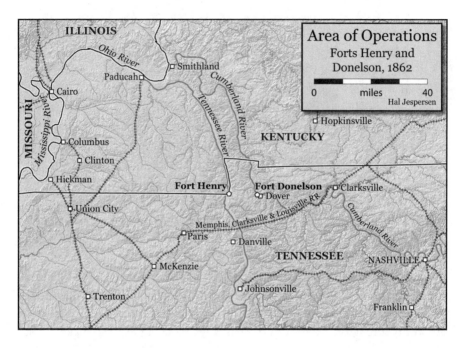

"keep Egypt right side up," as the president put it. McClernand had a difficult personality and has been described as "irascible, overly ambitious, flamboyantly patriotic, and polemic." As the war progressed he became increasingly alienated from the senior staff with whom he served, particularly military professionals such as Grant and William T. Sherman, later one of Grant's chief lieutenants.[5]

Escorted by seven gunboats, Grant's men reached Fort Henry on February 6. The fort was poorly constructed, flooded, and its guns improperly positioned when Foote's vessels made their appearance. The river warships reduced the fortification with heavy shelling. Some of the defenders surrendered, but about 2,500 fled as fast as they could scramble away, crossing the narrow neck of land separating the two rivers to reach Fort Donelson about 12 miles away. A Union infantry assault to take Henry proved unnecessary.[6]

McClernand's division waded ashore through waist-high water and deep mud and spent time investigating the fort's interior and examining the

5   Hicken, *Illinois in the Civil War*, 12-13, 162-164.

6   McPherson, *Battle Cry of Freedom*, 396-397. McClernand was difficult, but he was also a fighter. Grant despised him and would eventually sack him, but he would also give him important tasks, especially during the Vicksburg Campaign. McClernand proved to be one of the better Union political generals of the war.

A postwar image of Frank Peats, who joined the 17th Illinois in April of 1861 as captain of Company B. He would rise to the rank of major and command the regiment at Vicksburg.
Abraham Lincoln Presidential Library and Museum

prisoners. Frank Peats, who commanded Company B during the 17th Illinois' first major field campaign, was unimpressed with the Fort Henry captives, who "stand together in a straggling group and present a sorry appearance, clothed in misfit butternut homespun, unwashed and apparently hungry." Some Union soldiers picked through the abandoned enemy belongings. One member of the 17th Illinois recalled confiscating an eclectic list of items, including "two or three corkscrews, an antique cameo breast pin, half a pair of earrings, an Italian night robe trimmed with sable . . . two pieces of child's coral, part of a set of false teeth (somewhat worn), one dessert spoon with the initials Y. B. D. plainly engraved, six pages of a manuscript sermon entitled 'What Shall I do to be saved,' a lady's morning wrapper . . . one and a half pairs of high heeled shoes and one quilted Morrocco side saddle, just as momentoes you know." On February 11, Grant sent McClernand's division overland to invest Donelson.[7]

Josiah recalled after the war that the short sloppy march to Fort Donelson took place on "a beautiful moonlight night," with the weather so pleasant and the air so warm that the men decided to leave their gloves and overcoats behind them. On February 12, the Josiah and the rest of the Union soldiers caught their first glimpse of the outer ring of Fort Donelson, behind which rested a powerful garrison comprised of about 17,000 Confederates under the overall command of Brig. Gen. John B. Floyd. If the Union men had been excited

---

7 Peats, *Recollections*, 15-16.

about the prospect of a major battle, the strong outer earthworks mounted with heavy guns surely gave them pause.[8]

McClernand put his men into motion toward the Cumberland River to block reinforcements to the fort and prevent the troops inside from escaping. The move ran into a Confederate cavalry screen commanded by Lt. Col. Nathan Bedford Forrest. After some sparring, the Union troops pushed Forrest's men aside and established a position along Wynn's Ferry Road, about one mile from the fort's outer defenses. According to Peats, the unit advanced skirmishers to within range of the fort while the rest of McClernand's men strengthened their position. As nightfall approached, they scraped away "sticks, stones, and briars" to make places to sleep.[9]

The next day, February 13, McClernand continued shifting his troops east to complete the fort's encirclement, and his men came under fire from the Confederate batteries of Graves, Maney, and French. McClernand had orders from Grant not to bring on a general engagement, but the division commander was anxious for a fight, especially since the navy had done all the work and received all the glory from the the fall of Fort Henry. He ordered an assault to silence the Rebel guns, targeting a portion of the outer works held by Maney's Tennessee Battery and an infantry brigade commanded by Col. Adolphus Heiman. The Confederate brigade consisted mostly of Tennessee units defending their home state, with one regiment of Alabama troops. Morrison's brigade had only two regiments available, the 17th and 49th Illinois, but orders arrived to make the charge. At the last minute, McClernand ordered the 48th Illinois from W. H. L. Wallace's brigade to assist. The 17th Illinois took up a position in the center of the line. According to one eyewitness, the men were to "descend a hill entangled for two hundred yards with underbrush, climb an opposite ascent partly shorn of timber; and make way through an abatis of tree-tops." Even if the attack reached the fort, the entire garrison inside was available to reinforce the point of attack.[10]

---

8   Moore, *A History of the 17th Illinois.*

9   Peats, *Recollections,* 23.

10 Steven E. Woodworth, *Nothing but Victory: The Army of the Tennessee, 1861-1865* (New York, 2005), 87; James Jobe, "The Battles for Forts Henry and Donelson," in *Blue and Gray Magazine* Volume XXVIII, Number 4, (2011), 25-26; Peats, *Recollections,* 20-25. Lew Wallace, *Battles and Leaders of the Civil War. The Century War Book: People's Pictorial Edition* (New York, 1894), Vol 1, Number 3, 40-41. Lew Wallace (not to be confused with W. H. L. Wallace), would go on to pen the bestseller *Ben-Hur.*

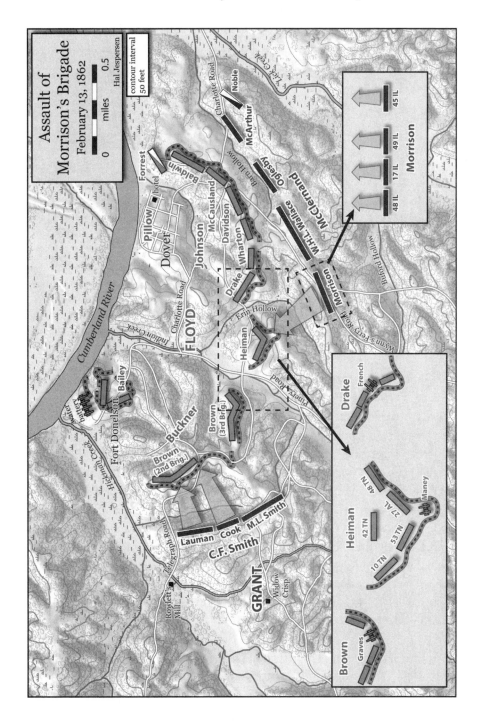

Assault of
Morrison's Brigade
February 13, 1862

Hal Jespersen

0   miles   0.5

contour interval
50 feet

"The Soldier in Our Civil War," by Frank Leslie depicts the "Gallant charge of the Seventeenth, Fortieth, Eighth, and Forty-Ninth Illinois regiments Led by Colonel Morrison, on the outworks of Fort Donelson February 13th, 1862," by Henry Lovie. *Frank Leslie*

Shortly before stepping off, Col. Isham Haynie of the 48th Illinois asserted that he was senior to Colonel Morrison and ought to command the assault. Morrison replied that he would command the brigade until the assault began, and would then relinquish leadership to Haynie.

Peats maintained that the Confederate artillery did not molest the Union assault line until "our little command of three colors started forward." At that point they were "saluted with shrapnel, shell, and canister." The three regiments moved down the hill, struggling to keep their alignment through the heavy underbrush and moving forward with "bowed heads as though buffeting a storm." They had to contend not only with the fire from Maney's battery, but from the supporting guns of Graves to their left and French to their right. In the valley between their jumping-off point and the fortifications, "Morrison reported to Haynie who neither accepted nor refused the command," but announced, "Let us take it together."[11]

By the time the assaulting column emerged from the tangled undergrowth, any sense of orderly formation was long-since gone. The serrated line of men in blue continued up the slope as best they could to within a short distance of the

11 Ibid., 40-41; Peats, *Recollections*, 24; Jobe, *The Battles for Fort Henry and Donelson*, 43.

Confederate line, when the five enemy regiments within small arms range opened fire. For about a quarter-hour the boys from Illinois traded shots across the smoke-filled field with the men inside the fort. One of the Confederate musket rounds knocked Colonel Morrison from his horse. Unable to capture the Rebel position, the Union men fell back down the hill.[12]

McClernand sent over another Illinois regiment, the 45th, which had no better luck. The men tried and failed a third time before withdrawing. According to one of Peats's poetic descriptions, a charge pushed forward toward the fortifications "only to fall back in broken fragments, than reform and again sweep forward, as the waves of a troubled sea whose foaming crest climbs the rock bound cliff only to fall back in glittering drops, to mingle again in unity of purpose." The Union wounded experienced a new terror when the battery fire ignited dry leaves on the ground and many helpless men burned to death, "their despairing cries for help adding a new horror to this pandemonium of hell," wrote Peats. The Confederate troops inside the fort, who just moments before had done everything in their power to kill the blue-coated men pouring out of the underbrush, jumped from their sheltered positions in an effort to drag as many of the wounded as possible to safety.[13]

This affair was no Fredericktown. The 17th and 49th Illinois regiments suffered 149 men killed or wounded. Haynie's command lost nine casualties. One source numbered the Confederate losses as 10 killed and 30 wounded, most of whom were artillerymen. McClernand described the failed attack as "one of the most brilliant and striking incidents" of the campaign, and claimed it would have been successful if the rest of the army and navy had provided support. Grant, of course, had told McClernand not to make an assault or bring on a general engagement before the resources to support such a thing were in place. Peats had an entirely different view of the charge, which he called "wanton, cruel, and heartless."[14]

---

12 Colonel Morrison was struck in the hip and knocked out of the battle and the war. Unable to take the field, he finally resigned in December 1863. He was replaced as brigade commander by Leonard Ross, the commander of the 17th Illinois, who was absent on the day of the battle.

13 Peats, *Recollections*, 20-25.

14 Wallace, *Battles and Leaders*, 41. Smith, *History of the 17th Illinois*; M.F. Force, *Campaigns of the Civil War: From Fort Henry to Corinth* (Edison, New Jersey, 2002), 42-43; Report of Brig. Gen. John A. McClernand, *The War of the Rebellion: A Compilation of the Official Records of the Union and Confederate Armies*, 128 Vols. (Washington, DC 1880-1901), Series 1, Volume 7, 173 (hereafter cited as *OR*. All references are to Series 1 unless otherwise noted); Peats, *Recollections*, 20-25.

A cold front arrived during the night, bringing with it snow, sleet, freezing rain, and temperatures that reportedly dropped to as low as 12 degrees. The survivors of the charge suffered terribly, for not only had they left some of the warm weather clothing behind, but Grant had banned fires in the Union camps to avoid giving away their positions and drawing enemy fire. Charles Smith of Josiah's company wrote to complain that the men went to bed on the bare ground without any tents and awoke covered in two inches of fresh snow. When he checked the guards that night, Josiah "found their hands frozen to their guns."[15]

Despite these miserable conditions, some of the men of the 17th found the strength and vigor to taunt the Rebels the next morning. "Hello Johnnie, who's dat knocking at de door?" they hollered. The men inside the fort replied in an equally feisty manner by inviting the attackers to "come over and see, you damned Yank."[16]

That day, February 14, Grant had Foote's gunboats attempt to repeat their success at Fort Henry by pounding Fort Donelson into submission. This fort, however, was well built and some of its guns were situated to fire down the river. The Federal warships were knocked back, and Foote was wounded in the effort. The Union infantrymen watched with keen disappointment as their hopes for a speedy victory were dashed.[17]

The cold and snow continued to bedevil the Yankees. Peats reported how some men in the 17th Illinois ignored the ban and built campfires to brew some coffee. A squad formed a small circle and built a fire on one side of a tree away from the fort, hoping to keep the flames hidden from the gunners inside. The effort didn't work and a ball from a Confederate rifle zipped through the kettle, spilling the precious brown liquid on the ground. As men scrambled to scoop what they could into their cups, an artillery shell burst overhead, scattering the men and drawing the attention of officers, who hurried over to rail against the violation of orders. One enlisted man lifted his cup to one of the officers. "Colonel, won't you take a drink?" he asked. "It's danged thin but its like you—'hot.'" To the dismay of the man who had offered it, the officer grabbed the cup and drained it dry. When the officer left, the soldier muttered, "[I]ts all

15 Woodworth, *Nothing But Victory*, 88-89.

16 Peats, *Recollections*, 26.

17 Ibid, 26-27.

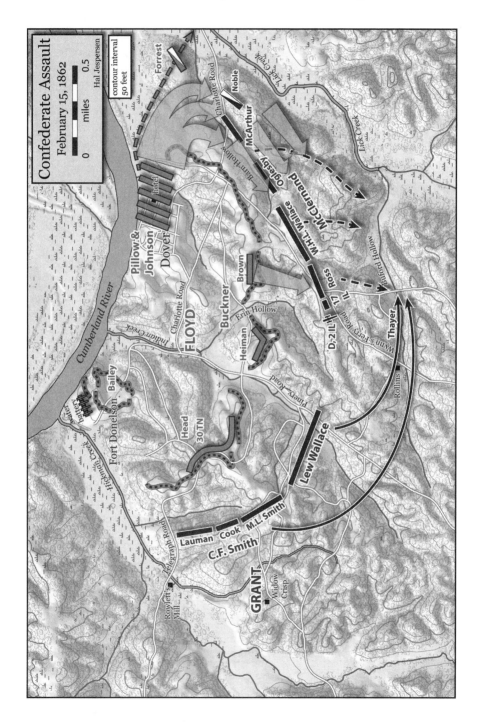

Confederate Assault
February 15, 1862

Hal Jespersen

0   miles   0.5

contour interval
50 feet

Colonel Leonard F. Ross, the first colonel of the 17th Illinois. He was promoted to brigadier general in April 1862. This image was captured that year in St. Louis. *Abraham Lincoln Presidential Library and Museum*

well enough to talk about having confidence in your officers, but I'm hanged if I haven't lost all confidence in that feller."[18]

As daylight crept over the frozen ground on the morning of February 15, the men of the 17th Illinois found themselves on the far left of McClernand's divisional line, which held the right side of Grant's investing army. Only the guns of Battery D, 2nd Illinois, were arrayed beyond them. The right flank of Lew Wallace's division (in position on McClernand's left) was almost a mile away. The killing ground of the previous day, where so many men of the unit had fallen, remained a no-man's land in front. The Confederates, still assailed by Foote's gunboats and increasingly constricted by Grant's noose of infantry and artillery, were planning to open the river road on Grant's far right flank in an effort to escape to Nashville. Shortly after dawn, five brigades of Brig. Gen. Bushrod Johnson's division, along with Forrest's cavalry, rolled out of the fort and attacked the Yankees. The effort brushed aside a contingent of Federal cavalry and crashed against John McArthur's brigade of mostly Illinois troops. McArthur's men held for a while, but eventually the Rebel assault shoved them backward. Rebel artillery pounded McClernand's line from the front, and the enemy infantry advance threatened him from the right and rear. Three additional regiments from the fort stormed against the front of Lew Wallace's brigade on the right side of Morrison's brigade (now commanded by Ross). The sudden attack

18 Ibid., 27-28.

shoved McClernand's entire division out of position and folded part of it back upon itself.

Peats was with his company in an advanced skirmish position when he spotted Confederates in their rear and a heavy line of gray infantry in their front. The enemy infantry demanded their surrender. According to Peats, they "profanely called us Yankees, with a prefix and an affix that would shock all ears polite." As Peats put it, he made the decision to "advance backwards." After some searching, the skirmishers found the rest of the regiment in the new position where it had been driven and reorganized.[19]

McClernand sent couriers flying in a desperate search for assistance. Lew Wallace sent some troops from his division to help stymie further Rebel progress. The assault gave the Confederate defenders a brief window to make good their improbably escape. Inexplicably, after tearing a large hole in the Yankee right wing, Brig. Gen. Gideon Pillow ordered his troops to halt their advance and return to the fort for baggage before setting out for Nashville. By that time, Grant was busy bringing up reinforcements to restore his lines and bottle up the Confederates. The small brigade now led by Leonard Ross, consisting of the 17th and 49th Illinois regiments, joined with other units of McClernand's and Lew Wallace's divisions and moved forward against the Rebels. On the far left of the Union line, which Grant believed must have been stripped thin, Brig. Gen. Charles Smith's division went over to the attack. All that remained there was a lone Tennessee regiment. Smith's men overwhelmed the Tennesseans and occupied the outer works before stopping. The gray troops who had pushed back the Yankee right returned to their defenses, once again pinned inside the fort.

Confederate officers met that night to debate surrender. Those present included brigadier generals John Floyd, Simon Buckner, Gideon Pillow, and Bushrod Johnson. Forrest, who commanded the cavalry that had opposed the 17th during the fight's opening action, determined not to give up. He called his men together. "Boys," he explained, "these people are talking about surrendering, and I am going out of this place before they do or bust hell wide open!" Floyd and Pillow also managed to find a route out of the fort for themselves, leaving Generals Buckner and Johnson to deal with Grant. (Johnson, too, escaped after the fort surrendered.)

19 Jobe, *The Battles for Fort Henry and Donelson*, 45-48; Peats, *Recollections*, 28-31.

On Sunday, February 16, white flags fluttered above Fort Donelson and Buckner sent Grant a request for surrender terms. The generals knew each other from their days at West Point and time together during the Mexican War. Buckner had even helped Grant financially before the war. If he hoped for lenient terms from his old friend, he was disappointed. Grant demanded "unconditional surrender," and added that if he failed to comply, he would "move immediately upon your works." Buckner called Grant's terms "ungenerous and unchivalrous," but had no choice other than capitulation. The surrender of the fort and its garrison gave the Union 12,000 to 15,000 prisoners, 20,000 small arms, 48 pieces of artillery, 17 heavy guns, 2,000 to 4,000 horses, and large quantities of commissary stores.[20]

When the Yankees arrived in the fort, Josiah discovered the enemy had "torn up old carpets and clad themselves in all kinds of rags to protect themselves from the cold." When the men of Grant's army marched past the disheveled and dispirited prisoners, Frank Peats recalled, an Irishman of the 17th Illinois discovered another son of Erin clad in gray. "What the devil are yees doing here?" he demanded.

"Foiten," came the reply.

"Foiten for what?" asked the Yankee.

"Fur glory."

"How much glory did yees git yer damn fools?" shot back the blue-clad Irishman. According to Peats, "Blue and gray both roared with laughter"[21]

*   *   *

Jennie's letter of February 8, 1862, arrived when Josiah was in the battle line at Donelson. He wrote back after the fighting ended.

Fort Donelson Tennessee
February 22nd 1862

Miss Jennie E. Lindsay,

---

20 Jobe, "The Battles for Fort Henry and Donelson," 45-49; Benjamin F. Cooling, "Forts Henry and Donelson," in *Blue and Gray*, Volume IX, Issue 3, (1992), 52.

21 Peats, *Recollections*, 37.

Esteemed Lady,

The "poor soldier boy" is here, the storm has passed and I improve the first opportunity of making known my whereabouts.

Well Jennie it is a dark day that has no sunshine and tho "disappointment" rules the day yet for once disappointment came as a pleasant messenger to your humble servant on last Sabbath morning, as you have no doubt heard of the Fort Donelson battle I need not say much the old 17th had its share, for 3 days and nights we were incessantly exposed to the rebel fire—shell, grape, canister & leaden hail by day—storm rain & snow by night all combined to exhibit in the most vivid colors the true "horrors of war."

Col Ross, Lt. Col Wood, Cap Norton, & Dr Kellogg[22] all arrived on the afternoon of Saturday the 18th inst being the third day of our engagement—we had then fallen back a short distance to give place to some fresh troops but on the arrival of our commander our Regt took new life and fixed for the contest anew—Col Ross lead us forward to support other advancing forces but as the enemy disappeared behind their breast works, we after remaining there till dark fell back to get a nights rest but Oh what a nights rest—not that of the criminal conscience stricken, no, but that of the wearied soldier drenched in rain for we had no tents and but little covering since we left Fort Henry about daylight we were called on to prepare for the solemn contest of the day for this day (Sabbath) had been fixed to give the decisive blow to the infernal crew—I was pondering over the past (for I had loosed one of my most noble men the morning previous a fellow classmate) when Cap Norton called my name delivered me a paper and left.

I was in no plight to read newspapers but from the fact of it coming from Peoria I first examined and then suspected and then came the pleasant "disappointment" for Oh what a dear little package that was – it seemed like sunshine amid the storm—the horrors of the past 3 days yielded to the welcome "intruder" and sorrow was wiped away, while thus exulting over that happy moment the report came that Fort Donelson had surrendered and I thot it must be a dream, that was too much joy for one hour but the fact was real for as our

22 Lucius D. Kellogg was the surgeon of the 17th Illinois Infantry.

Regiment was in the Brigade more directly engaged we had the honor of first entering the fort—this was a very strong place and tho many of our noble freemen have fallen in the conflict yet it is a great victory.

Oh Jennie it was a sorrowful sight to pass over the battle field on Sabbath, hundreds lay dead side by side and Oh the contrast, true american soldiers here and a few rods beyond the vile rebel each sleeping the sleep that knows no waking.

Capt Swarthout formerly of Peoria fell mortally wounded on Saturday I spoke to him not 20 minutes previous, he was a fine fellow, my company lost one killed[23] (by a shell) and four wounded I did not receive a scratch tho I do not feel very well since, but were ready for Nashville as I think that is the next point (110 miles up the Cumberland river).

Well I must have wearied you Jennie you have all this in the papers ere this – I keep that dear little memento of Sabbath morning noteriety as my daily companion to cheer on through these darksome days my only regret being that the "intruder" had not been the original—Remember me to Mrs Currie and all the dear old friends of Peoria and in view of a brighter day I bid thee most worthy lady, a kind adieu (pro tempore).

Josiah Moore (I am still waiting for those letters)

P.S. Excuse blots and scribling for this is a sorry place to write. J.M.
Please address: 17th Ills. Regt. Co. F via St Louis Mo I think this is the surest way

The man killed "by a shell," Pvt. Clark Kendall, was killed at 7:00 a.m. on February 15 when an artillery projectile carried away the top of his head. According to Sergeant Duncan's log book, Kendall was "[b]uried near the center of the north line of the graveyard near Dover Tenn. Head board marked with name." Kendall, who enlisted at the age of 18, was the first Monmouth College student killed in the war. His body was one of the hundreds that lay in the fields after the fight for Donelson. Unfortunately, in 1862 there was no organized system of communication that existed to inform families of the fate of their loved ones. After initial reports of a terrific battle, people back home

---

23 Private Clark Kendall.

would anxiously wait for news and, in the absence of a letter from the front, scanned the casualty lists of killed and wounded that often appeared in hometown newspapers. Typically, the job of notifying a family with news of a fallen member was taken up by one of the soldier's comrades or his commanding officer. In Kendall's case, that sad task fell to Josiah.[24]

On February 21, Josiah composed the following letter to Kendall's parents, which eventually appeared in the March 28, 1862, edition of the Monmouth *Atlas*:

Letter from Capt. Moore
Fort Donelson, Tennessee
February 21st, 1862

Mr. and Mrs. Kendall:

Dear Friends:

I improve the first opportunity of writing you a few lines, and though at other times the task would have been pleasant, yet on such an occasion, it is most painful, yet duty requires that I conceal not the fact. My request then is, that you prepare for the worst. Your noble boy—Clark A. Kendall—is no more. Comment is not necessary. The stroke is a hard one, and bereaved friends, you have your sympathizers. Clark was beloved by all. The loss of a brother could not have made me more sad. In him my highest hopes were centered. But God's ways are not as ours. He doeth all things well. It then becomes our duty, though sad and solemn, to bow in humble reference and say, not our will but thine, O God, be done. Clark's work on earth is finished; but I trust he has left the blood—stained hosts of earth to join the blood washed army of the redeemed in glory. Dear Christian friends, though we may weep that the silver cord is broken, yet we do no sorrow as those who have no hope.

[The next dozen or so lines are illegible.]

---

24 Drew Gilpin Faust, *This Republic of Suffering: Death and the American Civil War* (New York, NY, 2008), 14.

I hope that by trusting in a friend that sticketh closer than a brother, you may be enabled to best the present shock with Christian resignation. I am not old but have tasted some of the sorrows of this present evil world; yet I have never drank a more bitter draught than the subject of this epistle calls me to indite. A fellow class mate, a fellow soldier, and last but not least, I trust, a fellow soldier of the cross, constitute a three fold cord of friendship, than which, except the parental ties of endearment few are more sacred.

A few items, (though I presume you have heard ere this) Clark was killed on Saturday morning of the 15th inst, about 7 o'clock, by a four pound shell shot from the enemies' batteries. The shell carried away the entire top of his head, killing him instantly. Sergeant Duncan, Corp. Clark, J.C. Weede and G. Matchett stood close by—none were hurt. Matchett had his coat torn and himself shocked badly, but not hurt otherwise. We saw brother Frank immediately afterward. He requested that we send the corpse home. We were forced by the enemy to leave our position that night, so we carried the body over two miles to our camp. In the morning, news came of the surrender. We were marched through the fort and after being stationed we had the body brought to our camp, with the hope of being able to get up some sort of a coffin that would bear transportation. Sergeant McClanahan worked hard nearly a day, but without any success. No tools could be found, and as the weather was becoming warm, our only alternative for the present was to bury him. He is buried in a grave yard close to a little town called Dover, that is included inside of the enemies breastworks. We had a board marked with his name as well as we could, and I think it will not be interfered with. I was to see it today. It is easily found. If I had any assurance of remaining here for some time, I would send to Cairo for a metalic case but I believe we have orders now to move, and I have no chance. Our destination I do not know. The war clouds are gathering thick and fast. God only knows what the result shall be; but we have the assurance that all things work together for good to them that are called, according to his purpose. There are fiery trials—the people have sinned and the land mourneth. O, may we as a nation be enabled to break off by righteousness and bow before the footstool of the most High.

Dear friends, anything that I can do for you, shall be done with greatest of pleasure. I shall speak to the Orderly, that he may also write you a little. Excuse my random letter. I should have written sooner, but I had no means. We stood these days and nights on the battle field; often exposed to the enemies fire. We were almost exhausted—the only wonder is that any escaped. The wounded are doing well and we are all fast recruiting.

That God may enable each of you to look beyond this dark world to the brighter land, is the sincere hope and prayer of your sorrowing friend.

Josiah Moore

In their letters home, soldiers typically omitted the more gruesome details of a soldier's death, or asked male recipients not to show the letter to the women of the family. Josiah graphic description of Kendall's death perhaps was intended to assure the family that he had died bravely for a noble cause. His wish that Kendall's parents endure with "Christian resignation" is typical of the time. Josiah and many other Christians of that era believed that bearing the loss of a loved one with dignity while suffering with nobility brought one closer to God. A contemporary historian notes the importance of "well borne suffering" by soldiers as "evidence of the justice of their cause." Josiah was asking the family to adopt that same "well borne suffering" as a testament to their son. Unfortunately for Josiah, he would have cause to pen similar letters over the months to come.[25]

Josiah's graphic description illustrates again the crucial role that officers played in the lives of their men. Many soldiers had never left home before they entered military service. Previously, a mother or sister had taken care of their basic needs. In the absence of women, officers typically fulfilled that role. They oversaw the safety of the men, made sure they were keeping themselves clean and healthy, and served as mentors and consolers. This role of consolation was one of the most important "feminine" duties the captain of a company assumed. As the man who had led his men away from Monmouth, it was Josiah's duty to explain to families such as the Kendalls why their sons would not return. In fact, it is fair to say the captain of the company filled the traditional nineteenth-century roles of both mother and father. He oversaw their needs, enforced discipline, and somewhat ironically, issued orders that often led to their deaths. Enlisted men were aware of how their company commanders treated them, and they approved those who prioritized their

25 Ramold, *Across the Divide*, 4, 28; Clarke, *War Stories*, 16—19, 54.

welfare. Men also wanted their leaders to be morally upright. By all accounts Josiah won the approval and respect of his men. He also complimented his company in his letters back home, something that people in the community took note of and appreciated.[26]

A letter from the mother of Sgt. Joshua Allen of the 17th Illinois' Company B provides yet another example of the lingering agony family members endured back home. Mrs. Allen sent the letter to Frank Peats after she heard rumors that her son had been killed in the Fort Donelson fighting. "Will you be so very kind as to take the trouble to write and let an anxious mother know if he is dead?" she pleaded. Before she could mail it, however, the Allen family received confirmation of their son's death. His mother added a postscript to the letter: "Will you write me and let me know if there is any possibility of me getting his body? We hear that it was buried on the battlefield. Is his grave marked by anything? If you can find his body and send it to Hartford (Connecticut) you will confer an unlimited favor on his mother."[27]

In addition to the notification of death, families yearned for details of how their loved ones lived and died. They wanted to know if they had been good soldiers and good people, and if they had experienced what people in the nineteenth century called a "Good Death," which meant dying bravely and willingly giving up one's soul to God. We find an example of this in another letter Peats received, this one from the family of John Pendleton, another sergeant in his company:[28]

Captain, while the whole Nation, North has been filled with ecstasy at the late victory won at Fort Donelson by the 'brave sons and youths of our land' many hearts at the same time have been filled with mourning for their dear ones that fell in defence of the Old Stars and Stripes. I too had an only brother fall on the 15th of Feb. one on whom all of my pride, hope, and anxiety was placed. Will you allow me to ask me what kind of life he lived in camp? Or did you ever hear him say he was ready to die at any moment? Were you near him at his late moments so that you could hear what his last words were? Captain, I ask these questions as none others

26 Mitchell, *The Vacant Chair*, 82—84; Ibid., 42—51.

27 Letter to Frank Peats from Mrs. Robert Allen, March 4, 1862.

28 Faust, *This Republic of Suffering*, 6.

can ask unless they feel the anxiety that a sister does when she finds her only brother and idol has been torn from her."[29]

This with respect,

Rose Pendleton

Rose Pendleton also asked for her brother's personal effects, including a picture of her he had carried in his knapsack. Peats reported that both Joshua Allen and John Pendleton were killed on February 15 and found clutching their rifles, "their faces upturned with open eyes looking through the calm bright sunlight of the Sabbath." Unfortunately, the enemy had taken the items Rose requested be returned.[30]

More than a quarter-century after the battle, Peats recalled that the "saddest duty that falls to the lot of a soldier—gather up the dead," and he remembered retrieving the bodies of these two young men "just standing upon the threshold of manhood." "Will the infirmities of age so dim the vision, that our eyes will lose the reflected image of a soldier's funeral? Will our ears ever become so deaf that we will forget the sound of the muffled drum and the three mournful volleys that have echoed above the grave of a fallen comrade?" Peats wondered.[31]

A visitor to Fort Donelson a month after the battle discovered indications of just how ferocious the fighting had been. "Frozen pools of blood were visible on every hand, and I picked up over twenty hats with bullet holes in them and pieces of skull, hair, and blood sticking to them inside," he wrote. "The dead were buried from two to two and a half feet deep; the rebels didn't bury that deep and some had their feet protruding from the graves."[32]

Grant's army numbered about 25,000 men and lost about 500 killed and another 2,100 wounded. Smith's brief history of the 17th Illinois claimed the regiment lost 14 killed, 58 wounded, and seven captured during the Fort Donelson operations. According to the *Official Records*, however, 13 enlisted

29 Letter to Frank Peats from Rose Pendleton, March 9, 1862.

30 "Inventory of the Effects of Deceased Soldiers" for John Pendleton. Peats Collection.

31 Peats, *Recollections*, 37.

32 Hicken, *Illinois in the Civil War*, 42.

men were killed (one in Company F, Clark Kendall), five officers and 57 enlisted men wounded, and six enlisted men missing. Confederate strength was about 16,200, and of that number 327 were killed, 1,127 wounded, and 12,392 captured.[33]

Many in the Confederate ranks reexamined some commonly held beliefs after Fort Donelson. "I had been taught by demagogues and politicians to believe that I could whip a 'cowpen full' of common Yankees," confessed a Mississippi soldier. "I lived and acted under this delusion till Gen. Grant and his army met us at Fort Donelson. I soon found that the Yankees could shoot as far and as accurately as I could, and from then until the end of the war I was fully of the opinion that the United States Army was fully prepared to give me all the fight I wanted."[34]

Desperate for positive war news after the debacles of Bull Run, Ball's Bluff, and Wilson's Creek, as well as the Army of the Potomac's continued inactivity, the people of the North were jubilant when news of the fall of Forts Henry and Donelson reached them. Newspapers trumpeted victor U. S. Grant as "Unconditional Surrender" Grant, and President Lincoln promoted him to major general, making him the highest ranking officer in the Western Theater after Henry Halleck. The twin victories were critical turning points in the war in the West. The successes opened broad avenues of invasion into the deep South and eliminated about one-third of Albert S. Johnston's command in the Kentucky-Tennessee theater. Of the remaining enemy troops under Johnston's control, about one-half were organized around Nashville with the balance much farther north at Columbus, Kentucky.[35]

The 17th Illinois remained in the vicinity of Fort Donelson until March 4. Six days later Jennie wrote another letter to Josiah.

Peoria, March 10 1862

Capt. Moore

33 Smith, *A Brief History of the 17ᵗʰ Illinois Volunteer Regiment*; Kendal D. Gott, *Where the South Lost the War: An Analysis of the Fort Henry-Fort Donelson Campaign, February 1862* (Mechanicsburg, PA, 2003), 284–85, 288.

34 Jeff Giambrone, Blog: Mississippians in the Army of Tennessee, www.mississippi confed erates.wordpress.com/2011/09/01/mississippians—in-the-army-of-tennessee; Statement of George E. Estes, 2nd Lieutenant, 14th Mississippi.

35 McPherson, *Battle Cry of Freedom*, 405; Smith, *History of the 17th Illinois*.

Dear Friend,

I received your dear kind letter on last Thursday and was so thankful to hear of your safety. The first news we had of the battle was on Sabbath the 16th Oh that day of fearful suspense I would wish that we might never realize another such of it were not too impossible to hope for, for alas I fear it is but the commencement of many [illegible] *busy with her thousand tongues telling of the dreadful conflict then raging and adding fuel to the flame by exaggerating everything that came within her reach It were impossible to give half the accounts that were told. One time the 17th Regt were all killed then again they had not left Fort Henry. So passed Sunday no one knowing what to believe But all hoping that our Father in Heaven would be merciful and give unto us the victory and forever crush this wicked rebellion.*

Monday morning dawned upon many an anxious heart. all longing to hear the news yet dreading lest it might be such as to forever banish the sunlight from the lonely heart made desolate on hearing that the loved one has gone gone without a parting word or look to cheer them on through lifes dreary pilgrimage.

About noon we received a dispatch telling of the surrender of the Fort. The people were perfectly wild with joy, truly it was a great victory and we all rejoiced on that day not knowing what sad tidings the morrow might bring. On Tuesday morning as dispatch came from Capt Norton saying the officers of the 17th were all safe. I say blessed be the hand that sent that message.

I have been staying with Cousin Sarah while Mr Currie was in New York. The Regt left while he was gone his brother took his place to keep it for him but I guess as Sarah is so much opposed to his leaving home he will give it up. Your old Friend Mr Young has gone with the Regt so poor Mollie is left a widow She is keeping house on the bluff. They have a very pleasant little home and seem to live very happily.

The week after the battle they had it reported that the 17th Regt were on their way to Peoria with one thousand prisoners to be stationed at Camp Mather. But this child felt that was one of the joys too good to be true. The Peorians were looking daily for your arrival but as you are aware they looked in vain.

I suppose you have received my letter ere this time it was mailed on the 17th day of Feb and directed to Gireudeau.

Well as it is growing dark and this uninteresting epistle must be in the office
tonight I will have to say farewell hoping many happy days are yet in store for thee .

Please write soon
 Jennie
P.S. I know it is wrong to cherish a feeling of envy but I do envy this letter. JEL

Jennie's letter demonstrates the anxiety those at home experienced after hearing reports of a major battle they feared might have involved their loved ones. Unsubstantiated rumors of disaster crushed morale at home, while talk of victory sent jubilation sweeping through the community. Meanwhile, soldiers' families could do nothing but sit and wait with apprehension until more definite news arrived.

*   *   *

Grant's victorious command had to deal with the military material it captured at Fort Donelson, and faced here in the Donelson aftermath another problem for the first time: slaves in the field. Confederates soldiers, particularly officers, often took their slaves to war with them, and the victorious Union forces now had to deal with the slaves of surrendered Rebel soldiers. On February 27, Lt. Col. Enos Wood, now in command of the 17th Illinois after Leonard Ross was advanced to brigade command to replace the wounded Morrison, issued an order directing officers to "report . . . all slaves in their possession that were taken at the Capture of Fort Donelson. Company Commanders will be held accountable for all violations of this order." Captain Peats and Lt. Jones, also of Company B, "engaged [a black youth] at Fort Henry to carry our blankets and rations."[36]

The treatment of captured and runaway slaves had posed problems for the military from the outset of the war. The typical Union soldier, neither an abolitionist nor a believer in the equality of the races, nonetheless understood that slavery lay at the root of the bloody conflict. Those who were ardent abolitionists protected runaways from their masters who came to claim them,

---

36 Order book for Company K, 17th Illinois, May 1861-July 1862; Regimental Order No. 55, Abraham Lincoln Presidential Library and Museum; Peats, *Recollections*, 33.

and any Northern soldiers who might want to mistreat them. But these soldiers were in the minority. Many others routinely used derogatory and demeaning terms to describe the slaves they encountered. Some treated them as sources of amusement and played practical jokes on them—or worse. Since soldiers saw slavery as the cause of the war, they viewed slaves as both culprit and victim. Some Union officers returned runaway slaves to their masters. Others, most notably Union General Benjamin Butler, did not. Just one month into the war, for example, Butler, who was then at Fort Monroe in Virginia, announced that he would keep escaped slaves as "contrabands of war." As far as he was concerned slavery had caused the war, and only its destruction could end it. Butler felt justified in not returning them. Through the second half of 1861, many more men in blue came to see things about the same way. As one Wisconsin soldier saw it, the war was "abolitionizing the whole army."[37]

In order to clarify the status of freed and escaped slaves, Congress passed the First Confiscation Act in August 1861. It gave the Union army the right to take any slaves engaged in overt acts of support for the Confederate effort, such as building entrenchments. In practice, though, any slaves who entered Union lines voluntarily or were left behind when their masters fled were considered emancipated. As one historian pointed out, military emancipation and state abolition were two different policies pursued by Republicans along parallel lines throughout the war.

The Second Confiscation Act, enacted in July 1862, went even further. This law officially emancipated every slave who entered Union lines on their own volition, freed slaves who had been "abandoned" by their masters in the face of incursion by the Yankee armies, and finally ended the bonds of slavery for all those slaves living in areas that were currently occupied by northern armies, whether their masters remained or not. The act also gave Lincoln the discretion to further broaden the scope of emancipation by granting the president the power to end slavery in all areas still in rebellion and, for the first time, to allow blacks to wear Union blue. Lincoln would soon use this power to transform the war effort.[38]

---

37 Manning, *What This Cruel War Was Over*, 43-45; Mitchell, *Civil War Soldiers*, 122-125.

38 James Oakes, *Freedom National: The Destruction of Slavery* (New York, London, 2013), xiii, 224-225, 226-229.

"Place of Peace"

FOLLOWING the victory at Fort Donelson, Gen. Henry Halleck, the Western Theater's overall commander and General Grant's superior, determined to march on the northern Mississippi town of Corinth, a major logistical hub where the main north-south and east-west railroads in the Mississippi Valley connected. Halleck (dubbed "Old Brains") was an 1839 graduate of West Point and noted military scholar appointed a major general in 1861. He took over for John Fremont when Lincoln pushed the "Pathfinder" aside after his failures in Missouri. Halleck had not yet demonstrated conclusively that he was unfit for field duty, but he had proven himself to be a capable administrator.[1]

On March 4, 1862, the 17th Illinois joined the other troops of Grant's command for the march from Fort Donelson to the Tennessee River. From there, the men traveled by steamer to Savannah, Tennessee, where they arrived on March 14. The fleet that carried Grant's command included 89 passenger boats and a half-dozen gunboats.[2]

The Illini of the 17th made a brief foray to the town of Pinhook 20 miles south of Savannah, where they destroyed a flour mill and "distributed 150 sacks to the poor in the vicinity." On March 19, the Illinois men were loaded aboard transports and deposited three days later at Pittsburg Landing, Tennessee,

---

1   McPherson, *Battle Cry of Freedom*, 406; Boatner, *Civil War Dictionary*, 367.

2   Moore, *History of the 17th Illinois*.

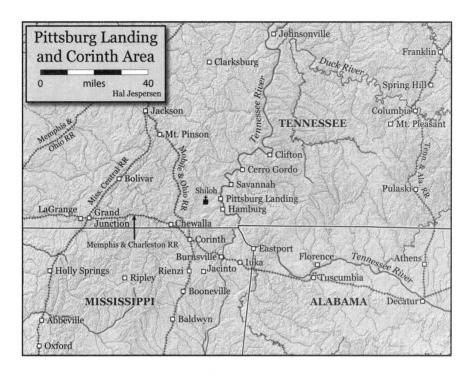

about 20 miles north of Corinth, Mississippi. They disembarked not far from the small wooden Shiloh Methodist Episcopal Church. The name was taken from a Hebrew expression meaning "place of peace."[3]

Halleck's master plan involved marching Don Carlos Buell's 35,000-man Army of the Ohio to Pittsburg Landing to join forces with Grant. From that point, Halleck intended to push the combined 75,000 men southwest into northern Mississippi and capture Corinth. The Confederate high command fully recognized the need to defend the important Mississippi road and rail hub. General Albert S. Johnston pulled troops from various Tennessee and Mississippi locations and assembled the collection around Corinth in an effort to do just that.[4]

Shortly after arriving at Pittsburg Landing, Josiah took the time to write a long and detailed letter to Jennie.

3   Ibid.; Winston Groom, *Shiloh 1862*, (Washington, DC, 2012) 142; Edward Cunningham, edited by Gary D. Joiner and Timothy B. Smith, *Shiloh and the Western Campaign of 1862* (New York, NY, 2007), 86.

4   McPherson, *Battle Cry of Freedom*, 406.

Camp McClernand Tenn
Pittsburgh Landing March 24th 1862
Miss J. E. Lindsay

Esteemed friend,

After an unwilling silence I return once more to the pleasant task of speaking with the dear friends at home.

By the context you will see that we still keep moving which is by no means a very pleasant disposition so far as it concerneth the subscriber, being naturaly inclined to like an occasional missive from the land of civilization.

Dear Jennie I recd, your of the 15th ult⁵ while I was at Fort Donelson but we had orders then to move and accordingly took out line of march to strike the Tenn. River five miles above Fort Henry and as we have been driving to and fro ever since we have neither had a chance to send or get news—one item, however, in your epistle makes me more especialy regret that this reply should be protracted so long, yet, dear lady you must take the "will for the deed" – I refer to that "message" to a certain gentleman of our number – you think I was "mistaken"—no that was not quite it—and now Jennie you will permit me to apologize for whatever misrepresentation I may have given to your message for such an idea never yet entered my head—your letter was all right—but at the time of answering it I was at the Cape and being pretty well I felt too mischievous to do anything right but I assure you that tho I did make the statement of which you speak yet I certainly intended to construct it so that you might doubt its correctness and regard it only as a joke I regret that I did not think in time that jokes are too often made at the expense of other folks but as crime consists more in the intention than in the action I need not weary you with apologies as I know you will not judge too hard when you know the circumstances—at the same time Jennie so far as my experience would dictate I think that such winged messengers of joy would not be unwelcome visitants even in the distant wilds of strife and war, but the "land of song" this "sunny South" is unworthy of such joy—you ask what I think of this, would be, bright genial clime, of course the switzer loves his native hills, the caucasian rejoices in his mountain fastnesses & the nigger driver may love niggerdom but as for me give me priariedom—I would just about as soon see one good prairie fire in Ills as Gen'l Grants grand transport fleet on the Tenn river I believe the sublimity

---

of the former would be loosed in the smoke of the latter—till I believe that there are happy homes in the south and perhaps habit might change my taste, I think it is a most beautiful climate and sometimes I think that if our northern & southern institutions could be made agreeable and get "Yankee enterprise" initiated this land might be made the Eden of the world but for the present you need not feel jealous of "ye land of cotton."

But the Orderly just now brings me another of those dear little missives of the 12th inst it was 12 days on the road. I am pleased to hear of your wellfare I presume that if I could have visited Peoria about the 17th or 18th ult I could have finely enjoyed their excitement over our victory but it seems strange that so many of the new papers could have made such mistakes in recounting the Regts that were engaged. I saw two or three statements when the Regts on our right and left were spoken of while ours was unmentioned –one of the N.Y. Pictorials, however, gave the 17th a pretty fair show.[6]

As to our going to Ills, with prisoners I don,t know how the story started I believe I first saw it in one of the Chicago papers—I only wish it had been true but Jennie I have almost given up all idea of getting any leave of absence till the war is a little better settled than it now is.

We have some big work ahead now what the result may be is only known to the supreme ruler in him our help is found he can make the night shine as day. with his favor we can conquer— beneath his frown earth melts away.

Our Camp is on the river and within 10 miles of the Miss, & Ala line there are over 60,000 U.S. troops her now and more coming—Buel is crossing away above with 60,000 more while I understand that Genl Pope is quickly progressing towards Memphis with 40,000, now as the enemy have their position on the rail road 12 and 20 miles above him. I think that after a little we will have them so completely invested that their only resort will be to do as they have done before i.e. run—still if they don,t run and we don't run there must of necessity be some fighting.

Some of our troops are rather tired out especially those of Fort Donelson but others are in fine health & spirits.

We remained several days at Savanah Tenn. a small vilage of 200 inhabitants. I find very many fine loyal citizens in Tenn, many more than we found

---

6 Josiah's reference to the "N.Y. Pictorial" was likely an engraving by Frank Leslie called depicting the 17th's Illinois' assault on February 13, 1862, at Fort Donelson.

in Mo, and I believe that if the people of Tenn. were now permitted to vote on the union that they would come back with a large majority.

I shall send this letter part of the way by one of my men that is going home. My health is still as good as usual I feel as tho I am specialy favored as we have not half of our officers fit for duty. But my prosey letter must have wearied you excuse its tediousness and random composition fit—emblem of the turmoil and noise of large army.

With many thanks for your kind regards for my wellfare and hoping that your joy may be none the less diminished but made brighter and happier as you pass along the sunny shores of time ever beloved by the good & great.

I bid you a kind good night.

J. Moore

Please don't forget the anxious lookout for a reply 2 weeks hence J.M. Oh I wish I were a letter_there_there

P.S. Oh Jennie I almost forgot to tell you my misfortune—I came nearly destroying a certain little miniature on last evening but the principle plate being iron the picture was not injured as badly as I supposed the glass broke across one corner and I fixed it so that I think it will still preserve the picture. I would not like to loose it when so far from the original as at present. J. M.

Josiah's comments about a "message" that had been delivered "to a certain gentleman of our number" was likely a reference that Abraham Ryan continued to interfere in the relationship. Josiah attempted to convince Jennie that a statement he had made (and we do not know what it was) had been taken out of context by the person who delivered it.

Josiah's derogatory comment about blacks is an interesting contrast with the strong identification he felt with John Brown just two years earlier. Slurs about blacks were common in mid-19th Century America. A letter penned by Sgt. George Turner, a New England soldier, to his father in June 1862 offers a typical example. Turner wrote about a Sunday service he attended led by Massachusetts abolitionists, where "there was so much talk about the confounded niggers that I came out disgusted and by the way if any one comes to you asking for contributions for the niggers, tell them you have a son in the army who needs your help more than they do. The niggers are used much better than the soldiers, and there is not a soldier who does not hate the sight of a nigger." Too often, Union soldiers viewed blacks as simple entertainment, servants, or objects of ridicule. Even those whites who supported abolition often had a difficult time envisioning blacks as their social equals. Turner's views, and those of other soldiers, evolved over the course of the war once they saw the military benefit of ending slavery and granting blacks the ability to join the Union army. Only a small percentage of Union soldiers supported abolition at the start of the conflict, but the level of support grew, especially when the soldiers realized that ending slavery meant depriving the South of an important resource. Black troops also eventually earned respect for their fighting abilities.[7]

Josiah's "Yankee enterprise" comments echo a common theme in the letters of many Union soldiers who developed a feeling of moral superiority over the people they encountered as they moved deeper into the Confederacy. Most Northerners believed free labor markets gave men an equal opportunity to "engage in politics and the marketplace." In their eyes, Southern society rejected this concept and, as a result, had become immoral, self-indulgent, and backward.[8]

Jennie to Josiah

Peoria April 5 1862
Capt Moore

Dear Friend,

*   With pleasure I devote the present in trying [illegible] a few lines too that ever dear friend, now a stranger, in the so called hand of love and Sunny Skies but at the present time more appropriately [illegible]. The place of desolation and strife. Truly nothing so desolates the heart, and land, as the grim monster war. The true representative of the Evil One, and, but this prelude to numberless evils that follow closely in his wake, Sent at a fitting time to allure men to destruction. War, may be pardonable among heathen nations when they have never been taught the Rule of love and obedience too that Higher Power, But, in a Christian land where*

---

7   David Cecere, "Carrying the Home Front to War: Soldiers, Race, and New England Culture during the Civil War," Cimbala and Miller, *Union Soldiers and the Northern Home Front*, 293—323.

8   Clarke, *War Stories*, 22, 131.

all have felt Gods loving kindness and tender mercy, It seems a poor [illegible] to make for all his goodness, to be ever governed more by an evil passion than his holy word.

I hope the day is not far distant when the angel of peace will spread her wings over our troubled country and proclaim that long looked for day of peace and then dear friend will be at liberty to return to your own loved "prairiedom". then too witness one of those grand illuminations namely a "good prairie fire" or, which I think you would like much better a few large houses on fire judging from the "pleasure" you manifested on a certain accident.

I sincerely hope the rebels will have common sense enough to run when they are attacked at Corinth and continue running until they land in the Gulf of Mexico where they will be at liberty to run their temple of rebeldom unmolested by the Yankees.

We are now having beautiful weather and the heart is made glad at the return of the pleasant spring days and we can better appreciate them after a long an dreary winter.

Well, Capt Moore, me thinks I hear you exclaim after perusing this epistle, Well Jennie, not a very entertaining correspondent, But all I ask dear friend, is for you to be [illegible] if possible and I'll try too improve.

I thank you dear friend for those flowers you sent I would like to make you a like return but you know April in this region is not honored with floral offerings.

As a token of remembrance, you will find impressed upon these leaves what you wanted to [illegible] me of sending to another but which I prefer sending to you. I will now bid thee good night hoping to hear good news from (illegible) soon.

I remain, as ever yours

Jennie E. Lindsay

Jennie's views blaming the war on the devil ("the Evil One") contrast with her earlier letter of March 10, 1862, when she called for efforts that would "forever crush this wicked rebellion." By April her opinion had evolved from hoping for the destruction of the Rebel armies to simply somehow obtaining peace. Her evolution on this issue could be an indication of her father's influence. As 1862 progressed, her father found himself siding more with the growing peace movement within the Northern Democratic party, an affiliation that would have significant political ramifications later in the war.

Bloody Sunday

A T Corinth, Albert Sidney Johnston's command was bolstered by the arrival of Gen. P. G. T. Beauregard. An 1838 graduate of the U.S. Military Academy and former superintendent of West Point, Beauregard led the troops that attacked Fort Sumter in April 1861. The Louisiana creole went on to enjoy the fruits of a hard-fought victory on the plains of Manassas in northern Virginia just three months later. Now, less than a year later in northern Mississippi, he and Johnston had to find a way to reverse the South's string of setbacks in the Western Theater. Both determined that the best chance to do so was by destroying Grant's army before Buell's Army of the Ohio could link up with it. If that was allowed to happen, the Union command would likely be too strong to effectively resist. "We must do something, or die in the attempt, otherwise all will be shortly lost," was how Beauregard described it.[1]

Grant believed the defeats at Forts Henry and Donelson and the subsequent retreat out of Tennessee had demoralized the Confederates. There was truth in this, but the Rebels remained a dangerous enemy. The optimism blinded Grant and many of his subordinates to the threat of a Confederate offensive. As a result, the Union army camped at Pittsburg Landing was ill-prepared to meet an attack, and many of Grant's troops, particularly those under brigadier generals William Sherman and Benjamin Prentiss, had never seen combat.

---

1 Boatner, *Civil War Dictionary*, 55; McPherson, *Battle Cry of Freedom*, 406.

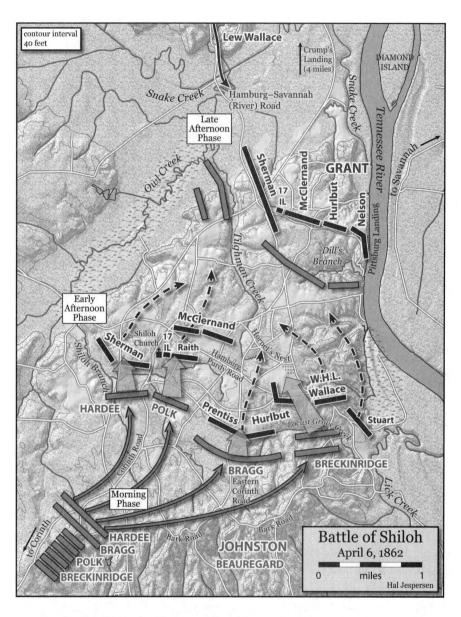

On April 6, 1862, the Union soldiers bivouacked along the Tennessee River reveled in the beautiful spring weather. "Trees are budding through all the forests and some that bear flowers are an airy cloud of pink and white which truly look beautiful," wrote Willie Shepherd of the 1st Illinois Light Artillery. Another Illini man would describe the momentous day as "one of those beautiful soft spring mornings that seem to come far too seldom in a lifetime."

For far too many Americans, whether dressed in blue and butternut-gray, that lovely Sunday would be the last morning of their short lives.[2]

That morning, Prentiss's men held the center of Grant's line and were positioned farther south than any others, while Sherman's division was on his right, west and a bit north of Prentiss. John McClernand's divisional camps, which included the 17th Illinois, were about 600 yards behind Sherman and Prentiss. Although some Yankee troops had detected Rebels moving in the woods beyond the Federal picket line and reported that fact, few Union commanders believed they comprised anything but advance enemy pickets. In fact, Johnston and Beauregard had marched the Confederate army back into Tennessee and deployed it for an offensive. When it struck that morning on April 6 at Shiloh, the result was one of the greatest surprise attacks in American history. The assault poured out of the woods and caught most of the Union army by complete surprise. The first Union soldiers struck by the surging Rebels were the raw troops under Prentiss and Sherman.[3]

Colonel Ross had been granted leave because of the death of his wife, so the 17th Illinois was under the command of Lt. Col. Enos Wood when the enemy attacked. The regiment, still in McClernand's division, was now part of Col. Julius Raith's 3rd Brigade. Born in Germany in 1819, Raith reached the United States in 1836, fought in the Mexican War, and helped form the 43rd Illinois and became its colonel in 1861. Raith assumed command of the brigade just that morning when Col. James S. Reardon reported that he was too ill to lead it. Josiah's friend Abraham Ryan, now the brigade adjutant, was explaining some of the new responsibilities of brigade command to Raith when scattered gunfire erupted about dawn beyond Sherman's camp off to the south. Colonel Wood later admitted that he dismissed these early shots as nothing but inconsequential firing from the pickets.[4]

A short time later, as the fighting escalated and it became clear a major action was underway, McClernand formed his division into line of battle. Sherman's officers, meanwhile, desperately attempted to rally their men, one of

---

2 Ural, *Don't Hurry Me Down to Hades*, 65; Woodworth, *Nothing But Victory*, 155.

3 McPherson, *Battle Cry of Freedom*, 408; Woodworth, *Nothing But Victory*, 168.

4 Cunningham, *Shiloh and the Western Campaign of 1862*, 174; James Grant Wilson, *Biographical Sketches of Illinois Officers Engaged In the War Against the Rebellion of 1861*, 43. (As listed on the Civil War Notebook Blogspot.) Woodworth, *Nothing But Victory*, 166. In addition to the 17th Illinois, Raith's brigade consisted of the 29th, 43rd, and 49th Illinois regiments and Carmichael's company of Illinois cavalry.

Capt. William Lorimer
Born in Perth, Scotland in 1840,
Company I's captain described some of
the retreating troops at Shiloh as a
"mob . . . without organization."

*Abraham Lincoln Presidential Library
and Museum*

whom sought assistance from a member of the 17th. Lieutenant Ephraim C. Dawes, the adjutant of the 53rd Ohio, part of Jesse Hildebrand's brigade, approached Pvt. William Voris of Josiah's company. Dawes knew Voris from before the war and also knew that Voris was a veteran of the fighting at Fredericktown and Fort Donelson. Dawes pleaded with him to help calm his frightened Buckeyes. Voris readily agreed to do whatever he could. While handing out extra ammunition, Voris instructed the raw Ohio soldiers that all would be well, and they should "keep cool, shoot slow, and aim low." Before rejoining his own regiment, Voris added one more bit of advice. "Why, it's just like shooting squirrels," he claimed, "only these squirrels have guns, that's all."[5]

The 17th Illinois formed on the right side of Raith's brigade line. About 8:00 a.m., the division was finally ordered to move forward and support the embattled troops fighting under Sherman and Prentiss. They advanced only a short distance when much of Sherman's shattered division came tumbling back in disorder. One member of the 17th described the onrush of terrified Union men as a "mob [that] passed through our lines without organization." Voris's earlier encouragement to the Ohio men failed. The 53rd Ohio fired but two volleys before its colonel panicked and shouted, "Fall back and save yourselves!" The triumphant Confederates surged through the abandoned

---

5 OR 10, pt. 1, 264-265. Both the *Official Records* and a later recounting of this incident in Catton's *This Hallowed Ground* refer to "A. C. Voris of the 17th." There was only one "Voris" in the entire 17th Illinois, and that was William M. Voris of Josiah Moore's Company F.

camps of Sherman and Prentiss and headed for McClernand's division and Raith's brigade.[6]

From the 17th's line, Wood reported that he could see the enemy advance, but that the fire from the Union line seemed to slowed the Rebel surge. He also watched helplessly as the Rebels almost directly in his front captured a section of Union artillery. Lieutenant Alexander Davis of Company K grabbed a musket from one of the men and fired, downing the color bearer who had planted the Rebel colors on the guns. Outnumbered and outflanked, the 17th and the rest of the brigade received orders to fall back a short distance and align with the remnants of Sherman's division. After helping support another battery, which allowed the guns to safely withdraw, the 17th fell back with the rest of McClernand's division. At one point Wood reported that his regiment found itself "20 or 30 yards in advance" of the main line. The 17th continued to slowly retire, but the men were by this time running short of ammunition. Wood, who lost his horse early in the engagement and was now commanding on foot, ordered the regiment to retire and resupply around noon.[7]

During the withdrawal, Raith took a minié ball through the thigh and was left on the field during the confused withdrawal. Wood, who was in temporary command of the regiment because of Ross's absence, suddenly found himself commanding the brigade. Major Francis Smith took over for Wood at the head of the 17th Illinois. Unfortunately for Raith, he was left where he fell all night in a steady rain before being recovered the next day when the reinforced Union army advanced and recaptured the area. Surgeons amputated Raith's leg, but blood loss, exposure, and infection proved too much. Raith, whose wife had died in 1859, would soon follow her to the grave. He left behind two orphaned sons.[8]

On the left-center of the Union line, soldiers under Generals Prentiss and W. H. L. Wallace fought a hard holding action in an area called the "Hornets Nest," a testament to the intensity of the fight. Prentiss and a large number of his men were eventually captured when the Confederates surrounded and overwhelmed the position; Wallace fell with a mortal wound. The collapse of the Union right forced McClernand's division and the remnants of Sherman's

6   OR 10, 141-142; William Lorimer paper, in the collection of the Vicksburg National Military Park; Bruce Catton, *Grant Moves South* (New York, NY, 1960), 228.

7   OR 10, pt. 141-142.

8   Ibid., 144.

command to fall back from their line around Shiloh Church. Throughout much of that morning McClernand's men engaged in a back-and-forth battle. According to one eyewitness, "The ground was lost and won more than once, but each ebb and flow of the struggle left the Union side in a worse condition." McClernand and his men retreated first to the crossroads of the Hamburg-Purdy Road and the Corinth Road, and then back near the Hamburg-Savannah Road. At one point, McClernand was forced to face about one-half his command to the south and the remaining units to the west to counter Confederate attacks. According to McClernand, his division occupied six different battle positions before the fighting ended that night.[9]

Ambrose Bierce, who would be deeply influenced by the Civil War and go on to become a famous writer of the macabre, fought at Shiloh Monday, April 7, with the 9th Indiana, part of Col. William Hazen's command of Buell's Army of the Ohio. His view of the confused nature of battle in general was held by most of those who fought on the first day. "A few inaudible commands from an invisible leader had placed us in order of battle," recalled Bierce. "But where was the enemy? What protected our right? Who lay upon our left? Was there really anything in front?" Bierce's insightful observations reflected the perspective of the common soldier in any major engagement. He had no idea of the grand tactical scheme, and his viewpoint was limited to only what he could see to his front. The powder smoke from rifled muskets and artillery often shrunk that distance to a handful of yards. As one soldier put it, a battlefield is "the lonesomest place which men share together."[10]

By the end of the day, the roughly 40,000 men of Johnston's army had pushed Grant's 36,000 back into a tight arc around Pittsburg Landing on the river. Thousands of tired and dispirited Union troops huddled along the Tennessee banks. Bierce claimed some panicked men stormed transport ships attempting to land reinforcements. "This abominable mob had to be kept off with bayonets," he wrote. Fortunately for Grant, gunboats on the Tennessee lobbed artillery rounds that helped convince the Confederates to end their attacks that early evening, and Buell arrived with his army later that night. With his left anchored on the river under the protective cover of the gunboats, and

9 Cunningham, *Shiloh and the Western Campaign of 1862*, 241-242; General Don Carlos Buell, *Battles and Leaders of the Civil War*, Century Series (New York, 1894) Vol 1, No 4, 58.

10 Ural, *Don't Hurry Me Down to Hades*, 69; Guelzo, *Gettysburg:The Last Invasion*, 276.

his right extended with reinforcements, Grant prepared to renew the fight on April 7 as soon as it was light enough to do so.[11]

The 17th Illinois would fight on without Enos Wood. At the end of the day, Wood left the field with what he called a severe "ague chill." William McClanahan of Josiah's Company F, another Monmouth College student, wrote home that Wood had broken down in tears and exclaimed that he "never expected to see the time when the 17th would be drove to do what she had just done—when he saw the mere fragment of a regiment that he loved as dearly as any man could." McClanahan blamed the nervous breakdown on Wood's "feeble state of health."[12]

Many Confederates took advantage of the shelter the retreating Yankees had left behind and spent the night in their camps, most thinking they had won a grand victory and that Grant would surely retreat that night. Albert Sidney Johnston was not among them. The general whom President Jefferson Davis described as "the greatest soldier, the ablest man, civil or military, Confederate or Federal," was dead. A rifle ball had severed an artery in Johnston's lower leg, and the general bled to death. General Beauregard, who assumed command that afternoon, believed he had won a tremendous victory and spent the night in General Sherman's captured tent.[13]

Assigned to picket duty in the regiment's front, George Smith of Josiah's company described that Sabbath night as the longest he had ever experienced:

I will never forget the cries of distress of the wounded who lay on the battle- field that night. They called for mother, sister, wife, sweetheart, but the most piteous plea was for water. One would be praying and another singing. Some one started the old hymn 'Jesus Lover of my Soul,' singing the first verse. Another sang the second, another the third and still another the fourth. This continued until sometime during the night when it began to rain; then the cries for water ceases. We hoped that many were refreshed. As the wounded lay between the battle lines we could not help them.[14]

---

11 Michael C.C. Adams, *Living Hell: The Dark Side of the Civil War* (Baltimore, MD, 2014), 117.

12 Letter from William McClanahan in the April 18, 1862 edition of the Monmouth Atlas.

13 Cunningham, *Shiloh and the Western Campaign of 1862*, 323; Stacy Allen, "Shiloh!," *Blue and Gray Magazine*, Volume XIV, Issue 3(February 1997), 64; McPherson, *Battle Cry of Freedom*, 394, 412.

14 Smith, *History of the 17th*.

Sergeant Robert L. Duncan
Duncan enlisted in Company F in
April of 1861 and was wounded at
Shiloh when shrapnel tore into his
hand. As company clerk, Duncan kept
an invaluable log of the company's
activities. This photo was taken by E.
S. Cleveland's Art Gallery in
Monmouth, Illinois. *Author*

Determined to reverse his fortunes, Grant sent his army into the attack the next morning. Now it was the Confederates's turn to be surprised. The fighting was fierce, but the thousands of fresh Union soldiers turned the tide and shoved Beauregard's exhausted army southward. By the afternoon, Grant had pushed the Rebel troops back to roughly their starting position the previous day. Beauregard recognized the futility of further action and ordered the army to retreat toward Corinth.[15]

The 17th Illinois fought again on this second day. According to Josiah, the regiment at one point moved so far in advance of the main line that it was ordered to halt. William McClanahan, "either failing to hear the order, or in his enthusiasm determined to press the enemy to the wall, had charged out two or three rods ahead of the line, singlehanded and alone, till I had to send a comrade to bring him back," recalled the Illinois captain.[16]

The Union soldiers regained the ground where they had camped the day before. "I found a Confederate soldier of the 5th Mississippi dead in my bed," wrote George Smith. "From him I got the big knife that I have." According to A. J. Vanauken of Company K, "[O]ur tents were completely riddled with balls holes," while Captain G. W. Robson counted 164 bullet holes in a tent belonging to members of Company E. One of the regiment's companies reported firing 5,700 rounds during the two days. Considering that a veteran

15 McPherson, *Battle Cry of Freedom*, 412-413.

16 Monmouth College, *Oracle*, 40.

company numbered significantly fewer than 100 men, the number spoke volumes about the intensity of the fighting.[17]

Despite his second-day success, Grant's debacle on the first day generated extensive criticism. "There was no more preparation by General Grant for the attack than if he had been on a Fourth of July frolic," argued Horace Greeley in his *New York Tribune*. Some accused Grant of being drunk, a charge that would dog Grant throughout the war. In a reminiscence after the war, Josiah defended his commander from those charges. According to Josiah, he was "within a few rods of Grant [on the first day] at about 10 and saw no signs of such." Grant's star, which had shone so brightly after the capture of Forts Henry and Donelson, lost some of its luster after the news of his apparent surprise at Shiloh and the subsequent casualties he suffered there.[18]

The carnage of that single battle was simply staggering. The Union lost about 13,000 men killed, wounded, and captured, while the Confederates lost nearly 11,000. McClernand's division suffered 285 killed, 1,372 wounded, and 85 missing. Raith's brigade also suffered heavily, with 96 killed, 392 wounded, and 46 missing. The 17th Illinois, which went into the battle with about 350 men, lost 13 men killed, five officers and 57 men injured, and six men unaccounted for and presumed captured, or nearly 22%. Josiah's company had two men killed and seven wounded, including Sergeant Duncan, the company clerk, who was wounded in the hand by shrapnel. The 17th lost its regimental flag, along with numerous papers and documents and the official books of Company F. According to Peats, his company alone lost 15 rifled muskets along with other accouterments when the Rebels overran the camp. The enemy also took or destroyed the company's books and papers.[19]

17 AJ Vanauken, *To the Beat of the Long Roll: The Diary of A. J. Vanauken, Co. K, 17th Illinois Volunteers, 1861-1863*, Abram Vanauken papers in the collection of the Abraham Lincoln Presidential Library; Diary of George Robson, Captain, Company A, 17th Illinois Infantry, Illinois Archives, Springfield, IL; Abstract of Materials expended or consumed in Company B, Frank Peats collection.

18 John F. Marszalek, *Sherman: A Soldier's Passion for Order* (New York, NY, 1993), 183; Woodworth, *Nothing But Victory*, 198.

19 Report of Maj. Gen. John A. McClernand, in *OR* 10 113-114, 123. One of the Confederate dead was Sam Todd, Abraham Lincoln's brother-in-law. Sam was Mary Lincoln's brother and had joined a Louisiana infantry unit just a handful of weeks earlier. Ural, *Don't Hurry Me Down to Hades*, 69; Robert Colville, *Jottings from Dixie*, Knox College Library; Official regimental records in Illinois Archives; Peats, Official Report of May 4, 1864.

*   *   *

Given all there was to do after the massive slaughter, it was more than two weeks before Josiah could find the time to sit down and write Jennie.

Pittsburg Landing Tenn.
April 22nd 1862
Miss Jennie,

Dear Friend,

Again the storm cloud has passed and again the joyous sunshine illuminates the darksome scene.

Dear Jennie your kind favor of the 5th inst came duly to hand several days since and I should have replied sooner but for the consequences of the late battle these I need not enumerate as I presume you have the results long ere this.

This is the first pleasant day that we have had for some time and about the first opportunity that I have had of musing over the past without interruption. I was much pleased to hear from you. it seems Jennie that your dear missives always come at a happy time—Just in time to cheer the drooping spirits and dear lady let me assure you that it is not only pleasant but "interesting" to hear from dear friends on such occasions as it has been our fortune lately to pass through.

You seem Jennie to think that war is far from being consistent with the Institutions of a country like ours and no doubt your imagination can picture a partial reality but dear lady the Battle Field of Pittsburg Tenn, must be seen on the 8th inst the day after the fearful conflict so as to form any real idea of the ghastly horrors of grim visaged war.

As usual the old 17th had the pleasure of sharing in the battle from its commencement till its close and hence have a share of the sorrows of the reverses of Sabbath and the joys of Monday,s sanguine victory.

Oh Jennie Sabbath was a sad day my feelings on that day I can never forget. I still had hope but Oh what a dark cloud hovered round, almost too dark for the eye of faith to pierce—panic stricken our lines fell back and back till all seemed lost—But God was merciful his sabbath was not to be desicrated, he arose in his might and monday, joyous Monday ushered in a new area, at least, in my existence. but tho we came off victorious yet Oh what a sight our camp presented after the battle—our quarters (camp of the 17th) was strewn with friend & foe some wounded and writhing in pain or quietly sleeping in the cold embrace of the King of terrors—but the scene is past—it seems like a dream and Oh forbid that it ever should be reenacted even tho it be a dream.

The casualties of the 17th amount to 14 killed & 120 wounded this was a large proportion considering that our whole number on the field at the opening contact was only 350. Our Regt Jennie is far from being as large now as when it used to parade in "Camp Mather" many of our brave comrads have fallen in the wake of the fell destroyer—the worthy sacrifice of a most worthy cause.

But it is hoped that a merciful God in his good pleasure may soon remove his afflicting hand and that the present lesson may learn us as a nation that there is a God and that he reigns.

But I must close as I have already imposed too much on good nature. It has rained almost all the time since the battle, roads very bad, some talk of a forward move on Corinth. heard today that the rebels were again advancing, also that they were evacuating and going south, only reports.

My health is still very good and for some wise ends known only to my Great Benefactor I have for so far escaped the fury of the foe may it be my happy lot to be equally shielded from the enemy of souls—I believe that my Country will yet be saved even tho it be "by fire."

Ever hoping to hear from you often and that this may find you in the sweet enjoyment of heaven,s choicest blessings I bid thee esteemed lady good night.

Josiah Moore
Pittsburgh Landing Tenn.

Those tiny leaflets recall some bright days of the past, that are in wide contrast with the present—only for the idea of being a soldier I believe I should feel home—sick—I fear that person to whom you were about to send them will feel jealous on learning the facts, wont I feel bad? J.M.

Josiah spared Jennie many of the details of the Shiloh fight. Many soldiers were careful with what they shared with loved ones back home. In a related example, an officer in another Illinois unit, Maj. James Connolly of the 123rd Illinois, chided his wife when she asked him for details of battle. "In your last letter you seem to think I don't give you enough description of battles, armies, scenery, etc.," he wrote. "If you were as tired of battles and armies as I am you wouldn't care to spend much time on them for they are very unpleasant things to be in and one does not like to reproduce memories of unpleasant things." Young artilleryman Willie Shepherd struggled with his thoughts after the battle. "I cannot describe the fury of the engagement during the two days—and very much doubt the ability of anyone to do so," he wrote. Shepherd had a vision of the killing field that was similar to Josiah's: "The only true idea of this horrible fight could be gained by a sight of the field on which we fought for two days. Dead and wounded soldiers by hundreds, Federals, and rebel, side by side. . . . The horrible sights we were obliged to behold on every side were enough to chill the blood of the most vile murderer. Fredricktown, Belmont, and Donelson—cannot be compared with it. God grant that we may never be called to see the lightest of it again."[20]

Both Josiah and his comrade Abraham Ryan received official recognition for their efforts at Shiloh. As acting assistant adjutant general of the brigade, Ryan prepared the official report. Among those he cited was Capt. Josiah Moore, "who distinguished himself by daring bravery on the battlefield." General McClernand made a positive note of Ryan's contributions during the two-day fight.[21]

What made men remain steadfast in the face of such an onslaught of shot and shell? We know that most joined to save the Union and had gone off to war to protect and represent their various communities. But was ideology enough? The inspiration of the women back home certainly helped. They were the "key to domesticity and its virtues, key to the homes and community," notes one historian. "Women provided the moral influence." The words of another historian would have resonated with Josiah and many others who were away from home and loved ones. "A woman's love," he wrote, "was a stimulus that, often by admonition, sometimes by inspiration, would propel the soldier's combat performance, as he might put it, above self," However, on the battlefield, with death all around, the men in line beside you—the friend, co-worker, fellow student, or even a son or brother—provided the

---

20 Earl J. Hess, "Tell Me What the Sensations Are: The Northern Home Front Learns about Combat," in Cimbala and Miller, *Union Soldiers and the Northern Home Front*, 123; Ural, *Don't Hurry Me Down to Hades*, 69.

21 OR 10, 140, 121.

encouragement to move forward. While the desire to preserve the Union and protect the community might have led men into line of battle, the need to prove to themselves and their comrades that they were not cowards was what kept them there. If a man failed the test, word would get back and make for a difficult homecoming.[22]

Ferdinand Oelert was a member of Josiah's company killed at Shiloh. Oelert, a native of Germany, had been court-martialed in December of 1861 and found guilty of leaving the company for five days. His sentence was a public reprimand and the loss of one-half of his pay for six months. The sentence was handed down by the court on April 2, 1862, but the regiment did not receive the information until after the battle.[23]

Another man from Company F, Murry Claycomb, was court-martialed around the same time. Claycomb was the company's only pugilist, and his fighting nature, fueled by alcohol, landed him in front of the military court. Court-martial records indicate that on November 19, 1861, Claycomb "became grossly intoxicated and while in this condition did become boisterous and use abusive and reproachful words toward General Grant his superior officer." Claycomb was also charged with being "grossly intoxicated on or about 12/5/61" and failing to accompany his regiment on an expedition to Benton, Missouri. Finally, Claycomb was accused of leveling his rifle and cocking it at an officer of the regiment during an argument over the ownership of an overcoat. Claycomb was found guilty of the charges and forced to "forfeit all his pay and allowances due him from the United States, have half his head shaved, and be drummed out of the service at the point of the bayonet to the tune of the 'Rogue's March.'" Claycomb was given a dishonorable discharge dated April 2, 1862. Like Oelert, Claycomb fought at Shiloh without having yet been informed of his sentence. Later, during the war's final year, Claycomb enlisted in an Illinois cavalry unit, perhaps helped by a letter of recommendation from Josiah.[24]

The horrors of Shiloh had a lingering effect on Colonel Wood. According to that officer, he was "spitting blood and matter when he mounted his horse on April 6," and that "he was given up by the army physicians while lying at the

---

22 Mitchell, *Vacant Chair*, 74; Linderman, *Embattled Courage*, 80-81, 95; McPherson, *Cause and Comrades*, 72.

23 Court Martial records of Ferdinand Oelert, NARA.

24 Court Martial records of Murry Claycomb, NARA.

Colonel Addison Norton joined as the captain of Company A in 1861, and rose to colonel and command of the 17th Illinois. This image was taken by "Thurlow" in Peoria.

Abraham Lincoln Presidential Library and Museum

point of death from a swamp fever," but recovered. The breakdown he experienced at the end of the first day had an adverse impact on his reputation, and he was denied leave to recuperate. Wood implored Governor Yates to appoint him colonel of the 17th when Ross received promotion to brigadier general. "My whole heart is in this war," he wrote to Yates. His entreaty fell on deaf ears, however, and Wood finally resigned.[25]

With the colonelcy of the 17th open, Illinois politics came into play. Yates moved to appoint Francis Smith, the regiment's major. Smith, who had started the war as the captain of Company E, was from the strongly abolitionist town of Galesburg, Illinois. On July 10, Ross sent a letter to Yates asking him to appoint Addison Norton as colonel and Smith as lieutenant colonel. Norton had commanded Company A, but had been serving as assistant adjutant general on McClernand's staff. Yates replied that he had promised the commission to Smith and "his Galesburg friends." McClernand joined Ross in urging Yates to appoint Norton. Smith got wind of this maneuvering and complained in a letter to Yates that the crux of the matter was really a "Democrat v. Republican issue," and "the regiment is democrat from the chief officer on down." In the

---

25 Letter from Lt. Col Wood to Gov. Yates, May 14, 1862, 17th Illinois Regimental Papers, Illinois Archives.

Captain George W. Robson
Robson served initially as the first lieutenant
of Company A, and then as the captain of
Company B. He survived the early April
carnage and left a graphic description
of the 17th's camp after Shiloh.

Author

end, Yates yielded to the popular Ross and the political strength of the Democrat McClernand. Norton received his coveted appointment.[26]

The official reports of the battle also demonstrated the growing conflict between McClernand and Grant. McClernand sent his report, dated April 14, 1862, directly to President Lincoln. Without mentioning Grant by name, the report was critical of his commanding officer. "It was a great mistake that we did not pursue him [Beauregard and the Confederate army]" Monday night and Tuesday," argued McClernand. Grant filed his report ten days later and dismissed McClernand's as "faulty" because it was incorrectly critical of other combatants and inaccurate in much of its detail. McClernand also made similar statements after Fort Donelson and had disregarded orders in the opening of that battle. If Grant was unsure before, he no longer was: This political general was going to be an ongoing problem.[27]

On May 9, Jennie responded to Josiah's letter from Pittsburg Landing.

Peoria May 9th 1862

Dear Friend,

I received a message a few days since, which I have likened [illegible] one of those bright and beautiful Sunbeams, breaking in upon the darkness, and

26 Letter from Major Francis Smith to Gov. Yates; Letter from Ross to Yates, July 10, 1862; Letter from Yates to Ross, July 18,1862; 17th Illinois Regimental Papers, Illinois Archives.

27 *OR*, Series I, Volume 10 Chapter XXII, 113-114; Simpson, *Ulysses S. Grant—Triumph Over Adversity, 1822-1865*, 140.

gladdening the weary heart—with its warmth and beauty, but like (illegible)all other joys, too few and far between.

Just one year ago last Monday you entered "Camp Mathers happy glories" for the first time I thought perhaps your memory might prove treacherous so I would just remind you of the fact. Alas many a poor soldier boy entered those groves on that day, with heart beating, high with hope and patriotism and casting a lingering thought upon home and kindred. Who would oft look for his coming in vain. For the Good Being had marked him for his own, and he is now "sleeping his last sleep" and the loved ones are left alone to mourn over the dear departed. Yet He doeth all things well and afflicts only for our good, but how hard for the rebellious heart to say, Oh "Father thy will, not mine, be done." As I traverse the halls of memory and review the past I can scarcely remember a sorrow but what I now see was some good. So It always is, yet a month ago on receiving the news of the late battle and of the great loss of life, and not knowing for a whole week whether you were numbered among the living or dead me heart told me how hard it would be too born beneath the afflicting hand if thy life had been taken, but God in his mercy hath shielded you so far. And I hope if it seemeth good in his sight, he may preserve your life through this rebellion that you may become one of those good workers in his vineyard, and wear an immortal crown of glory for another world where it shall be said unto the "Well done thou good and faithful servant."

[The next sheet appears to be a continuation of the same letter.]

Did you now feel sorry to loose Col Ross. I never heard who took his place I saw through the paper that Maj Smith was Lieut Col, and Mr. Ryan had command of Co. A so many officers resigning makes quite a change in the Regt. But you still have enough brave men left to man the helm and guide the ship safely into the harber called peace. Which I sincerely hope is not many miles distant. We all feel very proud of our 17th Regt and surely you deserve to be honored for you have acted nobly in every engagement. We knew of so much sickness at Pittsburg. I am so glad you keep well but mind now if you get sick again you must come right home where you will be well taken of. I almost wish you would get just little sick so you would come, even luna seems lonely without you, for she looks not half so smiling as she was want to look in the days of "Auld Lang Syne."

We are having very pleasant weather. The trees are being clothed anew and all things look so fresh and beautiful. The birds are sending forth their sweet wild warblings in praise to the great Being who called them into life, and putting to shame the indifference of man, to the Creator of all things. I think May the loveliest month of the year I would it were always May.

Well dear friend if I did not know what a dear patient little boy you were I should ask pardon for the length of this non interesting epistle but then you can read it at your leisure, but please dont take your leisure to reply. I know you would not if you knew what pleasure it gives me to hear from you. I now bid you a kind good night with many bright hopes for your future and speedy return to your peaceful home as it were in times gone by.

Ever yours

Jennie

Once again Jennie makes it clear that she was much more concerned with Josiah's physical and spiritual welfare—specifically her desire that he serve God and become "one of those good workers in his vineyard"—than ultimate victory.

Shiloh triggered a wave of religious reflection across the country, North and South. In the words of one historian, religious faith during the war was both "wind and weathervane—a driving force and a sensitive gauge" that shaped thinking but also reflected attitudes. Civilians and soldiers alike scrutinized every military development for some message from God. Each side sought Biblical passages to support its position. After the Union victories at Forts Henry and Donelson, the U.S. Secretary of War Edwin Stanton remarked, "We owe our recent victories to the Spirit of the Lord, that moved our soldiers to rush into battle, and filled the hearts of our enemies with dismay." After those same battles, Confederate President Davis proclaimed February 28, 1862, as a day of "fasting, humiliation, and prayer." This was not because he believed slavery was sinful, but because prayer and humility would compensate for the daily transgressions of individuals. Many people believed God parceled out victories and defeats based on the quality and quantity of prayer and fasting. If Stanton's comments painted God as a divine field general, Davis made him appear like a Divine Accountant, doling out victories with guidance from some sort of ledger book.[28]

Josiah took note of the blasphemous nature of the Confederates' Sabbath attack, and many in the North believed that was a factor in the Confederate defeat. Confederates who fought the battle hoped God would forgive their transgression of attacking on a Sunday, for it was deemed necessary to "achieve our independence and liberty." One Union soldier claimed that by fighting the battle, he was acting "in the performance of the noblest duty—except the worship of God that a man is ever permitted to perform here upon earth."[29]

Grant believed his victory at Fort Donelson would soon bring the war to a close. After Shiloh, he "gave up all idea of saving the Union except by complete conquest." Corinth was the next obvious Federal target. General Halleck stepped in to command an assembled force of more than 100,000 men that included the armies of Grant, Buell, and John Pope, and moved cautiously toward the vital railroad junction. Beauregard, his Rebel army reinforced and reorganized, faced Halleck's sloth-like advance with perhaps 65,000 men. Outnumbered, short of supplies, and with thousands of ill soldiers, Beauregard evacuated Corinth on May 29 before Halleck could surround the town.[30]

The 17th Illinois took part in the advance on Corinth. On May 6, 1862, Josiah was in charge of a detail of 75-80 men corduroying roads and bridges. He later wrote about an incident that occurred during the operation:

> An amusing episode here occurred—our men got the poles and logs cut and laid on the road but had not yet put the brush and earth on to complete the work when a Qr. Master came with a large supply train saying he was sent post haste for ammunition, supplies etc. and on attempting to run his six mule teams on to the unfinished road (the bark being loose on the poles it would all peel off and tear the road to pieces if used before ballasted as above) I turned the leaders of the 1st team off into the swamp and the second also. By this time the quartermaster himself came at me with the butt of a

---

28 Rable, *God's Almost Chosen Peoples*, 7, 148, 153; Manning, *What This Cruel War Was Over*, 141-143.

29 Woodworth, *While God is Marching On*, 80, 105.

30 Ulysses S. Grant, *Personal Memoirs of U.S. Grant* (New York, NY, 1885), 368; McPherson, *Battle Cry of Freedom*, 414-417.

"black snake" but I reached up, caught him by the collar pulled him off his horse put my knee on him while I directed my men to keep the teams off the track"[31]

*   *   *

After Beauregard withdrew from Corinth, the men of the 17th were sent first to Bethel, Tennessee, and then marched to another camp near Jackson. Not surprisingly, the locals gave their visitors a cold reception. The soldiers showed an equal disdain for the locals. In his brief history of the 17th Illinois Josiah wrote in 1868 for one of the reunions, he quoted another member of the regiment: "We remained [in Jackson] for nearly a month, hugely enjoying the balmy southern climate made thrice congenial by the noble bearing of sneering women and insolent men strutting around with as much sangfroid as a little tad in its first pants." Words virtually identical to these also appear in Sergeant Duncan's company log book.

Though the Yankees received a rude reception from the white locals, the slaves in southern Tennessee and northern Mississippi had a very different reaction to the Union advance. As the Yankees moved toward Corinth, slave owners in the area fled. Their former slaves moved in the opposite direction— toward the liberating force. John Eaton, a chaplain in the 27th Ohio, recalled that they "flocked in vast numbers—an army in themselves." Some came alone, and some with their families. Many were shoeless and their bloody feet fed the soil. As Eaton put it, the exodus was like "the oncoming of cities." This phenomenon was not new to Tennessee in 1862. "Where the army of the Union goes, there slavery ceases forever," explained a Wisconsin soldier.[32]

Josiah to Jennie

Bethel Tenn

June 7th 1862

Miss Jennie E. Lindsay,

---

31 Corduroying a road involved placing branches and tree trunks on the soil to make the road more passable. A blacksnake was a whip. In personal papers of Josiah Moore, now in collection of the author.

32 Bruce Levine, *The Fall of the House of Dixie* (New York, NY, 2013), 102-103.

Dear Friend,

Your dear epistle of the 9th ult, came duly to hand after and long and anxious lookout and I need not attempts to describe to you the pleasure it afforded to look back beyond our then trouble and anxious position to where wars and rumors of wars were only known in the abstract in other words to visit the joyous scenes of dear old Camp Mather.

I am now writing on a box in front of my tent and as you are aware the sun shines here in the South I have had a kind of little summer house put up covered with green bushes Oh it is such a pretty place you should just be here to see how nicely men can keep house. However don,t understand that they are superior to the ladies for as Beauregard says with regard to the falling back of his army, our keeping house "is a military necessity," and I for one would have no objections to its speedy removal.

Well Jennie I presume ere this reaches you, you will have all the items of the "anticipated Corinth Battle" –for four long weeks we moved forward anxiously and cautiously as tho the destiny of nations rested on a single maneauver and when all is ready, as we thought, to close the net, to our great surprise the bird had flown—gone to its sunny clime –yet as the plumage is reported to be of a rather inferior quality we are rather indisposed to shed many tears over the premature loss; still we have some hopes that even yet we may be able to coy the timid creatures.

I was on picket duty two days & nights previous to the time when the rebels left, and I believed I had one of the most interesting times that I have had since I came to the war. (Camp Mather excepted).

On the 28th ult our forces advanced in front of our works and towards the enemy for the purpose as we understood of making our final attack after marching about one mile we reached our picket lines sharp firing soon opened all along the picket lines 10 or 12 miles in extent several shots from the artillery being exchanged yet no general engagement ensuing—opposite our Division (McClernand Comd,ing) a R.R. formed the line, our guards and those of the rebels being less than 100 yds apart our part of the lines had been rather quiet through the day—toward evening Genr,l Ross took a notion of occupying a house on a hill.[33]

On the opposite side of the R.R. and held by the Rebel guards—he ordered a cannon to be placed in ambush and bearing on the rebel guard post, and then sent your humble servant with Cos "A" & "F" a very impudent undertaking in ordinary times but war has its peculiarities and its orders must be obeyed. I moved forward to the R.R. halted and sent word to the rebels to leave tho I did not know whether they would obey my orders or not—after a few minutes we crossed over deployed as skirmishers and advanced, up a ridge through brush—wood, across a fence and soon found ourselves close by the house—all was suspense for a few moments for we did not know but 10,000 might be ready to meet us not with outstretched arms of peace but of war, we gained the hight however and took position just in time to see the rebels become invisable on the opposite hill.

After a short while one of them appeared with a white flag I went to ascertain his desire. he proved to be from Louisiana and Capt of the rebel guard he was quite sociable and if it would not seem absurd I would consider him a gentleman— he wished to have some understanding regarding our general duties and we finaly concluded on the following—that our men should not shoot at each other while on duty and if a superior force advanced from either side we should give timely warning so that if either wished to peaceably yield we could do so and retire without firing—when I reported this arrangement to our Com,ders they laughed quite heartily at such an amicable adjustment of war—we passed the night as indifferently as tho no enemy were near.

The morning of the 29th dawned all was calm and serene as tho nature awaited with solemn anxiety the pending struggle –slight skirmishing soon began often extending along the whole line and again entirely ceasing on assuming a sharp contrast at one point thus the day passed still our forces kept closing on the rebel lines, I had several interviews with my rebel friend who like the infidel about his religion, seemed quite anxious about what I thought would be the result of this

---

33 Sergeant Duncan's company log book confirmed the encounter with "cooperating Confederates." Duncan noted, "On May 28th, in conjunction with Company A we crossed the Mobile and Ohio Railroad and took possession of a house occupied as a rebel picket post. Agreed with the rebels that our pickets should not fire on each other while on duty." According to Duncan's log, the 17th was "advancing on Corinth" from April 29 through June 4.

war &c, &c of course I referred him to their success for the last six months and left him to soliloquize –I think I did not ease his conscience very much, that night Colonel Ross sent me over about 300 men with spades &c to fortify we pulled down the houses and worked all night at intervals through the night we could hear heavy trains moving out from Corinth and a good deal of suspicion was created but no news came till morning when our first intimation of an evacuation was the smoke of the burning Ware Houses and occational explosion of Powder, Pope,s forces soon took up the pursuit joined by other Nyes Division—we remained (i.e. McClernands forces) in camp till the 4th inst. when we marched for this point ((25 miles distant) Bethel) on the R.R. leading to Columbus on the Miss,; and 18 miles West of Savanah Tenn.

We occupy the site of a rebel camp but the folks are not at home—we may remain here a few days and then go to Bolivar on Miss Central R.R. our troops are in fine spirits and this seems to be a fine part of the country the people are tired of the war and deserters pass us every day returning home, they report the C.S.A. played out, well I must stop this prosey stuff as "endurance" sometimes ceases to be a virtue, But Oh Jennie I almost forgot I presume you heard of the 17th having a lady Major.[34] Aint that a good joke? A few days since a young man wrote from the East enquiring if it was "really so—that the 17th Ills Regt had a lady major?" The 17th is becoming notorious! Genr,l Ross has gone home again I think my time should soon come. Your plan Jennie was very amusing but I dont like to risk it, it might work too well. We have no Col, yet, some speak of Maj Norton (formerly Capt Norton) but I think that would not be fair for Lt Col, Smith.

Hoping that this may find thee enjoying the dear old scenes of home and its sweet delights, ever the worthy participant of Heavens choicest smiles, and

---

34 The "lady Major" was Belle Reynolds, the wife of Lt. William Reynolds of Company A, a druggist from Peoria. Mrs. Reynolds joined her husband in camp in August 1861. At Shiloh, she moved with the demoralized men as they fell back to Pittsburg Landing. She spent the next week tending the wounded there and shared her stories of the battle and its aftermath with passengers aboard a ship returning to Peoria including Illinois governor Richard Yates. When a listener remarked that Belle deserved a commission more than most of the men in field, Yates agreed and asked for a blank commission form. He asked her the rank of her husband and, adding that he believed in "giving the women the best of it," appointed her a major. She was the only woman commissioned during the war. Lori Tuttle, "Major Belle Reynolds of Peoria," *Illinois History Magazine* (February 1994), an online project of the Northern Illinois University Libraries. www.lib.niu.edu.

Lieutenant William Reynolds and wife Belle,
the "Lady Major," in an undated image. *Author*

*wishing that this may afford even a feeble return for your last dearest letter I bid
thee esteemed lady a kind goodnight.*

Josiah Moore

*P.S. Oh Jennie I almost forgot to tell you of our luxuries—I had Black berries,
green peas & new potatoes all for dinner, so we are ahead aint we? I wish you could
go help us gather berries in this pretty sunny clime. Inclosed you will find a "rebel
paper." I got it in Corinth, quite a number came into our hands after the rebels left,
I have to sent it thus sealed to keep the Post Master from stealing it.*

CHAPTER 9

"Land of Barbarism"

IN late summer of 1862, Henry Halleck was still Grant's superior, but he had demonstrated conclusively that he was not a suitable commander in the field. President Lincoln called Halleck to Washington, D.C. to serve as his general-in-chief. After the painfully slow advance to capture Corinth, Halleck decided to abandon major offensive operations in the West to consolidate and hold the ground that had been won. This meant protecting railroads and supply lines. "Old Brains" also advised Grant to "clean out west Tennessee and north Mississippi of all organized enemies." As for the civilians who continued to make life difficult for Union soldiers, Halleck told Grant, "Handle that class without gloves and take their property for public use." Halleck was turning over the hard-won initiative to the Confederacy.[1]

Meanwhile, unhappy with Beauregard and upset with his decision to take leave without permission, Jefferson Davis had appointed one of his corps commanders, Gen. Braxton Bragg, to assume command of the Confederate Army of Mississippi. In a bold move, Bragg left about 32,000 men in northern Mississippi to hold Grant back, and took 34,000 more on a circuitous route to invade Kentucky. The move, together with other smaller Rebel thrusts into the state, failed. Kentucky's citizens did not rally to the Southern banner, the Confederate command remained divided, and a lack of supplies and a reliable logistical lifeline made remaining that far north impossible. After a sharp fight against General Buell at Perryville, Bragg retreated back into Tennessee.[2]

The Confederates remaining in northern Mississippi tried to advance into middle Tennessee to recapture some of the territory they had lost and help Bragg's Kentucky effort. Confederate Maj. Gen. Sterling Price retook the Mississippi town of Iuka, but was driven from the place on September 19. He joined his Army of West with Maj. Gen. Earl Van Dorn's Army of West Tennessee and they unsuccessfully attempted to capture Corinth, where Union forces under Grant tried to trap the combined armies. A sharp battle was fought on October 3-4, but the Southern forces managed to slip away.[3]

*   *   *

From June until October of 1862, the 17th Illinois was part of the force detailed to keep the rail and supply lines safe from the Confederates. According to Sergeant Duncan's log, the regiment spent a good part of its time guarding various posts and chasing small Rebel parties around Middle Tennessee. The Illinois regiment was part of the force intended to trap Sterling Price at Iuka, but he slipped away before Union forces arrived.

Josiah to Jennie

Bolivar Tenn
August 4th 1862
Miss Jennie

Dear Lady,
Be, not surprised I had not forgotten-Well Jennie you will no doubt think that something strange has happened, no nothing more than ordinary.
Now then you must be patient while I tell you my story-could I but lay aside this dull medium for a better I think I could make my case much more satisfactory i.e. to one side at least.

---

2   For an even-handed, high-level treatment of the 1862 Kentucky Campaign, see Earl J. Hess, *Braxton Bragg: The Most Hated Man of the Confederacy* (Chapel Hill, NC, 2016), 58-73 (advance review galley viewed May 2016).

3   McPherson, *Battle Cry of Freedom*, 512-524.

Your[4] epistle of June 18th came in due time and was perused as usual with much pleasure. I was also pleased to hear from our dear little friend Mattie. I can almost imagine that I see Jennie & Mattie promenading along those dear old walks that once were so joyous, or while away in gentle song the mellow moonlight evening just such bright evenings as were wont to come, like angel visitants, over a year ago—Oh I often think that there will be other evenings more brilliant still.

Well dear Jennie I should have replied sooner but till now I have been unable to make a full reply that "good likeness" could not easily be found you know we soldiers enjoy but few of the sights of civilization away down here in this land of barbarism the natives don't seem to have any such institutions as picture gallerys – one of our 17th boys started one here a few days since but Jennie when I went to try it I almost backed out, just think of a soldier who for over a year has lived in the woods only once and a while hearing from the confines of civilization scarcely ever seeing a spark of that divine institution that makes man what he is, going to have a picture taken well such an idea not to speak of the picture I think would very well suit a comic almanac—still I thought it would not do for a soldier to be scared especialy at his own shadow—and now Jennie you have the result—my dear why draw such a long breath? I couldn,t help it I tried to look just as white as possible but then I think the glass was green.

Well Jennie since I last wrote many strange items have transpired in our Countries destiny I had hoped that ere this the bloody conflict would have closed, but where are we? The desired goal seems to be as distant and more desperate than ever! Now don't think that I despair my hope of success has not loosed a single radiant. I believe that our cause is just and that God will prosper the right. Yet what a sad scene does our poor weeping prostrate country present at the present time—but trials make friends more firm and sorrow only makes the cup of joy more full—God knows what is best for us not only as a nation but as a people we must wait his good time and way.

"Our Regt" spent a few weeks at Jackson 27 miles North of here—two or three weeks since we moved down here and as we are now on about the front lines we are kept pretty busy. for some time after coming here we looked for an attack every day.

I had my company out 10 miles south on the R.R. guarding it while the cars could assist our troops that had gone a little too far in the advance, to fall back to this station we got all away safely only 100 bales of cotton this the rebels burned

---

4   The page is torn here and a word is missing.

just as our troops left. The rebels also followed up the line of rail way and burned a station (Depot and 80 bales of cotton) within 1 ½ miles of where I was stationed. This was coming pretty close and for 2 or 3 days I hardly knew how soon I might go up but we finely got safely back to camp tho we have not had much rest as we have strongly suspected an attack still affairs appear more favorable now. Gen,l Ross is comding and he has 5 forts nearly completed—300 negroes[5] have been to work for over 2 weeks we also took 2000 or 3000 bales of cotton to build temporary works – At present I think the enemy have turned their course towards Chattanooga

Well I presume Jennie that you are tired of this long story I had not forgotten but I had hoped that ere this I could have been able to bid an honorable adieu to the old 17th as it's affairs look too gloomy, now more than ever every freeman is needed at his post. I scarcely know what to do, other than look on the brighter side—it seems that those who are of but little use or rather nuisances in the service can get any privileges they want, go or stay as it suits them while those who can do duty get their share these are men whose object seems to be to be absent when needed and spend the rest of their time seeking for office and I and sorry to say that there are Illinoisans who should blush over such facts.

Now Jennie you will excuse my delay and I shall try and do better and hoping to hear from you soon and that this may find you in the enjoyment of good health amid the joys of dear friends & peaceful home I bid thee dear Lady a kind good night

J Moore

P.S. I had tho't of attending a "fair" this fall but I fear that the connections cannot be made however I wish you all success and hope that it may be pleasant occasion—But dear Lady if we cannot go the fair we shall just think fair and that well be some consolation, As above J.M.

Oh Jennie we have such nice peeches I wish I could treat you to some I know you would like them even tho secesh but we make them take the oath—this is the greatest peech district I ever saw.

---

5   These were likely former slaves who had been freed by the advance of the Union forces and were now working to help the Federals.

I must write Mattie a letter soon I have not forgotten her kindness towards us while strangers Jennie I think she is such an excellent Lady so cheerful and kind may her friends be worthy of her.[6] J.M.

Oh Jennie I almost forgot to thank you for that compliment to Mr Hough especially since it so much concerned myself I only hope that I may be ever worthy the admiration of such worthy friends.

Excuse such letter folding.

This August 4 letter evinces that Josiah's enthusiasm and optimism about the war was flagging. His hope that the conflict would end soon, especially after the victories at Fort Donelson and Shiloh, was obviously not going to happen. He also believed the war was progressing according to God's plan, but he was torn between his strong desire to come home and his sentiment that "every freeman is needed at his post." Jennie's constant urging that he return home, of course, created conflicting emotions that would have weighed heavily upon him.

Josiah to Jennie

Bolivar Tenn,
August 8, 1862

Well Jennie we have just voted on that Constitution, and what? You might guess the old 17th killed it deader than ever we should rather have voted some means of closing this war still it is some relief when we hear that "they are about to draft up North" That pleases the boys to think of the crokers[7] being brought out. Enclosed find a copy of our Union Banner, excuse this little extra and with that "little package" now sent off accept the best wishes of.

Yours truly, J.M.

---

6 Josiah often mentioned to Jennie that he received letters from others in Peoria, but it appears that he did not keep any of them except for the January 3, 1862, letter from Mrs. Currie. It was difficult for men in the field to preserve letters from home.

7 "Croakers" was a contemporary term for pessimists. Paul Dickson, *War Slang* (New York, NY, 1994), 7.

The "Constitution" Josiah mentioned was an attempt by some Illinois Peace Democrats to draft a new state constitution that would have stripped the governor of much of his power, re-drawn congressional and state legislative district lines to benefit Democrats, and barred African-Americans from settling in the state. Historian James McPherson defined the Peace Democrats, known to their detractors as "Copperheads," as that portion of the Northern Democratic party that "opposed the transformation of the civil war into a total war—a war to destroy the old South instead of to restore the Union." The Peace Democrats' opposition was stiffened by the growing casualties and Washington's imposition of a draft, passed in July 1862. The draft law allowed men to find substitutes or pay their way out of the service, which caused significant resentment among Irish and German immigrants and others in the poor and working classes. As Josiah pointed out, the Illinois voters, including the troops in the field, rejected the proposed constitution, but the draft and the lack of military progress for the North increased Copperhead support.[8]

Following the passage of the Second Confiscation Act in July 1862, Lincoln made plans to broaden emancipation's reach. Before the war, Lincoln had declared he had no intention of eliminating slavery where it existed, but now he saw that ending slavery and the free labor it supplied to the Southern war effort was necessary to win the conflict. Lacking a significant battlefield victory, Lincoln put his plans on hold, fearing that an announcement would appear desperate rather than courageous or enlightened. He penned a draft of an executive order that freed the slaves in the states still in rebellion, and included a provision to recruit blacks into the Union Army—but set it aside. When George McClellan blunted General Lee's invasion of Maryland at the Battle of Antietam on September 17, 1862, Lincoln finally had his opportunity to release it to the nation.[9]

On September 22, Lincoln announced his Emancipation Proclamation, which would free slaves in areas still in rebellion on January 1, 1863. While it did not apply to border states, the action struck at what many increasingly recognized as a "tower of strength to the Confederacy." Lincoln said that while he was conducting the war for "the sole purpose of restoring the Union," he acknowledged that "no human power can subdue this rebellion without using the Emancipation lever as I have done." Lincoln focused on reuniting the

8   McPherson, *Battle Cry of Freedom*, 492-494; Weber, *Copperheads*, 48-51.

9   Boatner, *Civil War Dictionary*, 265; Oakes, *Freedom National*, 302-307.

country, not because he was ambivalent about slavery, but because he realized that if reunification failed, then most slaves would be living in a foreign country where he had no influence. If he did succeed in reuniting the country, it would be, as one historian said, a "hollow victory" unless slavery was abolished. For Lincoln, "emancipation, however great a righting of a historic wrong, would be meaningless unless it was set within the larger question of democracy's survival." He understood that the European ruling class held the American experiment in contempt, and he was determined to prove that "popular government is not an absurdity." Making the war about freeing the slaves, of course, would also make it much more difficult for Europe to come in on the side of the Confederacy.[10]

The Emancipation Proclamation further emboldened the Peace Democrats, who intended to take advantage of the sentiments typified by a soldier in the 95th Illinois who wrote, "I certainly hope that they may lay down their arms before the first of Jan in order to keep the Niggers where they belong." Another Yankee put it this way: "When we cease to fight for the Union and begin to fight for Negro equality I am ready to lay down arms and will." Many Union soldiers shared those views, and many others worried that emancipation would trigger a flood of cheap labor and hurt their job prospects when they returned home.[11]

A sizable and growing number in the Union armies, however, had come to agree with their commander-in-chief that emancipation was more a pragmatic move to end the war than a moral action. "I think the President has struck the blow in the right time, " explained one soldier, while another announced it the "only remedy, and all know it will have a tendency to terminate the war shortly and permit us to return to better and more desirable vocations." Another Illinois soldier wrote that he and his comrades "like the Negro no better now that we did then but we hate his master worse and I tell you when Old Abe carries out his Proclamation he kills this Rebellion and not before. I am henceforth an Abolitionist and I intend to practice what I preach."[12]

While many Northern troops realized they did not have to change their negative view of blacks to support emancipation, others began to see blacks in a

---

10 McPherson, *Battle Cry of Freedom*, 354; Gallagher, *The Union War*, 75; Guelzo, *Gettysburg: The Last Invasion*, xviii, 480.

11 Mitchell, *Civil War Soldiers*, 126-128.

12 Hicken, *Illinois in the Civil War*, 130-131; Manning, *What This Cruel War Was Over*, 93.

much more sympathetic light. As the Union armies moved south, the men in the ranks were confronted with the harsh realities of slavery—the lack of individual liberty they took for granted, and the deliberate breaking apart of families and the physical and sexual abuse that accompanied it. One historian wrote that many Union soldiers became convinced "the immoral and blighting institution of slavery was antithetical to republican government, and that any republican government that tried to accommodate slavery was doomed to eventual failure."

Ironically, there were Union soldiers who found that their bigotry against blacks led them to support emancipation. In some parts of the South, the Northerners found slaves whose complexions were almost as white as their own as the result of sexual relations between white male slave owners and their female slaves. Many Northern troops came to believe that slavery must be inherently evil if it led to such immoral activity.

Southerners, of course, were outraged by Lincoln's action, and derived smug satisfaction in the belief that the true goal of Lincoln and the North all along had been to end slavery and destroy Southern society, not preserve the Union as initially announced.[13]

Lincoln's proclamation did, in fact, provide more ammunition for the Northern Peace Democrats for their opposition to the administration and its policies. With an eye toward the November 1862 elections, the Peace Democrats agitated in towns across the North. The men of the 17th took note of this rising tide of Copperheadism, and most were not happy about it. Lieutenant Edmund Robbins of the 17th Illinois' Company D was one of them. "Nothing would please our boys better than a campaign against those who are seeking to prolong the war by raising discontent in the army & weakening the hands of our rulers," Robbins wrote his parents in the fall of 1862. "They would burn their fences to cook rations by, carry off their stock and rummage their houses for money or silver plate & curse them for d——d rebel sons of b——s if they dared to open their heads. Tell your so called Democratic neighbor that it is in their power to bring upon themselves all the miseries and horrors felt by the border states by a factions of opposition to the U.S. Government." This was

13 Ibid., 51, 106.

certainly a change from the sentiment expressed in the regiment's paper less than a year earlier, which expressed disdain for the abolitionist movement.[14]

Unfortunately, some of the Union soldiers occupying Tennessee channeled their frustration with the war effort and the politics at home into a war on the civilian population. Robbins claimed that when the 17th Illinois left Bolivar, "several houses were burned down." He blamed the "worst men" in the unit for the deprivations. Some did much worse. "Ask some father of a family how he would like to have his house invaded by a couple of ruffians and after he himself was tied hand and foot to see his wife & two daughters ravished before his eyes & his house plundered," Robbins wrote to his parents. "If the army breeds just such men it was exemplified by two men of our regt. a few days since who deserted as soon as they found they were suspected and have not been heard from since. . . . I have often felt ashamed of the conduct of my companions in burning houses and destroying property but have not always been able to prevent it."[15]

Many Union soldiers blamed Southern women for the war. Josiah mentioned the "sneering women" of Jackson, Tennessee, and his fellow soldiers believed the constant harangues and insults directed at them by such "she-devils" meant they were a proper target of the war effort. Writing from Jackson, the colonel of the 4th Illinois Cavalry noted, "If we have to stay here all summer, somebody must come down and see us. They can help convert these obstinate ladies. We can easily whip the men but the ladies have the advantage of us decidedly." Another Union officer in Tennessee took a decidedly harsher and cruder approach in trying to "convert these obstinate ladies." He told the women of the town that if they didn't prepare a meal for the 600 soldiers of his command, he would "turn his men loose upon them and he would not be responsible for anything they might do." One byproduct of the harsh treatment

---

14 Letter in pension file of Edmund Robbins, NARA

15 This mistreatment of civilians was contradictory to the example Grant set. On one occasion the general spotted one of his soldiers chasing a women and her daughter while brandishing a musket. Grant grabbed the weapon and brained the soldier with it. Grant couldn't stop all such behavior by himself. Some 600 Union soldiers were court-martialed during the war for the rape of black and white civilians. Simpson, *Grant*, 149; James Marten, *Civil War America: Voices from the Home Front* (New York, NY, 2003), 55.

of Southern civilians was the way it worried men serving in the Rebel armies. Many understandably deserted to go home to protect their families.[16]

Brutality against civilians was one result of soldiers becoming more coarse, or "hardened" to war. One Union officer noted that as the war progressed and his men witnessed the brutality of combat, they became "not so good as they were once; they drink harder and swear more and gamble deeper." His explanation was that when "homicide is habitually indulged in, it leads to immorality." An Iowa soldier agreed: "War is hell broke loose and benumbs all the tender feelings in men and makes of them brutes." Another wrote that the descent into immorality "looks gradual from the top but how fast they seem to go as everything seems to hurry on the downward grade." He noted that many fine, upstanding men he knew in civilian life who "four months ago would not use a profane word can now out swear many others." One observer noted the "roving, uncertain life of a soldier has a tendency to harden and demoralize most men. . . . The restraints of home, family, and society are not felt."[17]

When Frank Peats wrote about scrounging for souvenirs at Fort Henry, he complained that such activity

> afflicted the body corporate of our whole army, it pervaded the atmosphere of all ranks, it affected no distinction of age, sex, or previous condition—The royal edict, 'Thou shalt not steal,' was suspended like 'Joshua's' sun until the carnage of war was ended—The farmer boy and the city boy seem to have been inoculated at the same time—The young reprobate who played marbles and hop scotch on Sunday and the Y.M.C.A. boy were co-partners in plunder and spoils. The wretched quartermaster and commissary for whose moral training no one desires to be held responsible, would appropriate to his own use whatsoever pleased his fancy that was not more bulky than a piano or a billiard table.[18]

Henry Penniman, the 17th's assistant surgeon, documented his own concerns about what he saw in camp, and was convinced the 17th was not impervious to this coarsening process. "War is a dreadful evil," he confirmed, "and the army is a school of bad morals; about nine-tenths of the troops

---

16   Leo Kaiser, "Letters from the Front," in *Journal of the Illinois Historical Society,* Volume LVI, Number 21 (Summer 1963), 52; Mitchell, *The Vacant Chair,* 100-103, 36-37.

17   Woodworth, *While God Is Marching On,* 184-185, 188-189.

18   Peats, *Recollections,* 15-16. Peats claimed that even the regimental chaplain was not above picking up a few items lying about the fort.

entering the army irreligious, become worse and worse. A great crowd of men, without the restraints of society, and no influence from women," he concluded, "become very vulgar in language, coarse in their jokes, and almost blasphemous in their profanity."[19]

One historian defined hardening as "a subtle process that culminated in the detachment of the soldier from prewar ideals." Soldiers became both physically and culturally separated from home and began to adopt behaviors they never would have considered in civilian life. Veteran soldiers told new recruits that "unless a man can drink, lie, steal, and swear he is not fit for a soldier." Hardening was a defense mechanism that allowed soldiers to cope with their experiences. One Union officer wrote of using the corpses of his own men as a seat and a table for a meal. Charles Wills, the man from the 8th Illinois who so desperately wanted to fight late in 1861, wrote, "The army is becoming awfully depraved. . . . [I]f we don't degenerate into a nation of thieves, t'will not be for a lack of the example set by a fair sized portion of the army." The most obvious manifestation of this process was the way many men reveled in the act of killing the enemy.[20]

It is not unrealistic to think that for the troops in the Western armies, the hardening process began in earnest after Shiloh. One soldier who experienced his first combat there came upon a dead Confederate lying on his back with outstretched arms. The man reached down and ripped a button off the Rebel's coat for a souvenir.

The paradox of the soldier at war was that in order to defend the community from which he came, he had to abandon many of the community's morals. "My virtues and vice must correspond to that of my fellows; I must lie to rebels, steal from rebels, and kill rebels" wrote one Northern soldier. Some men believed (or certainly hoped) that their, true, moral selves were simply "lying dormant" during the war. Others experienced self-loathing over what they had become. As the war progressed, there was a growing gulf between those at home and the soldier, because the soldier often advocated actions that were outside the bounds of proper behavior for civilians, such as theft and destruction of property, in the cause of saving the Union. When those at home questioned the necessity of such actions, it led the men in the ranks to believe

19   Blaisdell, *Civil War Letters*, 128.

20   Mitchell, *Vacant Chair*, 7; Ramold, *Across the Divide*, 8-11; Woodworth, *While God is Marching On*, 186.

those at home no longer understood them, or again, did not support their efforts.[21]

Religion provided one bulwark against this "coarsening." Men who were truly devout, such as Josiah, were a "significant, though in many ways powerful, minority in the Union and Confederate ranks." Religious belief was a great help for men facing their fear of death and the trials of war.[22]

Jennie to Josiah

Peoria August 19th 1862

Dear Friend

Within the last two months I have learned, well the bitter lesson of disappointment, "Hope deferred more fully realized than ever. I did think "something strange had happened" when so many weeks passed and still no missive from the dear soldier boy. I knew it was not on account of sickness for I heard through several persons of your being well, and—but I'll think I'll not tell you of the rest; for you know it hath been said "Man is like [illegible]."

So you see dear friend I dont want you too do any more than your share so I'll not tempt you by repeating the many good things I've heard of you, I at last concluded you were getting so brave that you wouldn't deign so [illegible] a little coward like myself. I found I had judged you wrongly when I received your dear kind letter, and better still that dear dear likeness, not half so welcome as the original would have been yet I feel this one can be shared much better than the other. Oh, how I would love to see you but I know it is as you say every freeman is needed at his post and it is a shame to see the many that neglect their duty and pretend of sickness at home and a great many other excuses just too get away from danger. It does seem hard that the good should have all the burden too bear yet they have the happiness of feeling that they are doing right which if far more too the noble minded than ought else.

Things have changed since the first part of Summer than [illegible] began to brighten and the universal opinion was, that the war would be ended by the first of September, but I fear that day of peace is far more distant than ever, the people

---

21 Ramold, *Across the Divide*, 1-3; Mitchell, *Vacant Chair*, 7-10, 35-37; Linderman, *Embattled Courage*, 240-244.

22 Rable, *God's Almost Chosen Peoples*, 8-9.

seem to be just awakened to the real dangers of the cause. That call for 600,000 men[23] *and the fear of drafting has aroused their patriotism wonderfully, they come into Peoria by the hundreds we now have four regiments here. I would that the rule had been made a year ago and we would have been far nearer the termination of this dreadful war. You would have been amused had you been here on the day the last call for men were made I tell you the cowards trembled for their precious lives they seemed to feel as though they were already drafted. It provokes me so to hear a man say he would go if he could leave his business, all the harm I can wish is that his business would leave him. I hope they will draft just to get such men.*

The opinion now is that they will not have to in Illinois but it is hard to tell. But dearest friend I am glad too think that all do not go for fear of being drafted. They say when their country needs men so much as to talk of drafting then every man should go so I say and if they can't put an end to this rebellion then let the women go and just give the rebels a talking too and bring them to their senses poor benighted people I really feel sorry for them for they are surely marking their own ruin. it seems as though God [illegible] *just left them too their evil passion. I hope they may be soon delivered from the promptings of the evil one and repent before it is too late. God alone can see what is to be the end of this rebellion. All we can do is to hope for the bitter God of darkness* [illegible] *light.*

I feel that there are still brighter days in store for us and we will remain here to appreciate them when they do come but my dear friend I know you are weary of this I must close, hoping God will give his angels charge over thee to keep thee in the right path. Let us put our trust in him and he will deliver us in time of danger.

Yours ever,
Jennie

PS. Brother Andrew has enlisted, we have opposed his doing so on account of his being so young but he says he thinks it his duty to go and that it is better for him to leave than some married man, the dear boy it's hard to have him leave and yet I feel that God can protect him as well in the camp and on the field of battle as at home. I pray that he may be kept from the many temptations that will surround him. I think the time has come for us to make any sacrifice for our Country for what is life worth to us if our Country is lost.

---

23   President Lincoln's call was for an additional 300,00 men, not 600,000 as Jennie wrote.

It is really surprising to see the many old and infirm men this war has brought to light, men, whom we thought but a short time ago men but they have suddenly discovered their age to be that of forty five they have ceased to use hair dye and I fear the dentist will go to ruin for loss of business. They have just realized that old age is honorable.

Capt Moore of one of the old Regts has been elected Col. of one of the Regts now in Peoria. The name sounds very familiar did ever you hear it? You remember Mr. Ballance ? He has command of a Regt.

I have been away from home for the last nine weeks and have not seen Mattie Culter since my return but I think of paying my respects on the morning. I know she will be glad to hear from you as you are quite favored. I suppose you heard of Capt. Harding's marriage he seems to be in favor of the union. Now dear friend do please write soon. J.E.L.

Jennie's letter highlights the disillusionment many in the North felt as the war dragged on and the casualties mounted. The Peace Democrats capitalized on this sense of disappointment.

In April 1862, the Confederate government initiated the first draft in American history. Three months later in July, Lincoln called for 300,000 more volunteers. The U.S. Congress followed that by passing a militia law, which defined "militia" as all able-bodied men between the ages of 18 and 45. The obligation to raise Lincoln's 300,000 men fell to the states. If a state failed to raise its required number, the members of that militia could be forced into the service. The policy met with some violent reaction, particularly among Irish and German immigrants and in areas of the Midwest antipathetic to abolition and the war. It also led to more support for Peace Democrats. Lincoln and Congress expanded the draft even further a few months later with the Enrollment Act, passed in March 1863.[24]

Jennie's letter explains the effect the Militia Act had on the able-bodied men of Peoria who had not volunteered for service. She excoriated them as cowards who tried to make themselves appear physically unable to serve. Her 18-year-old brother Andrew ("Andie") escaped her condemnation because he

---

24 Wagner, Gallagher, and Finkelman, *Civil War Desk Reference*, 17; McPherson, *Battle Cry of Freedom*, 292-294, 600-601.

had enlisted in the 77th Illinois, but the family had opposed his enlistment because they believed him too young to serve.[25]

The reversal of military fortune for the Union armies discouraged Jennie, just as as it had so many others across the North. The short and glorious war so many people had anticipated 18 months earlier had become a prolonged and unpredictable carnival of blood and death whose end remained out of sight and the victor still in doubt.

Josiah to Jennie

Bolivar, Tenn
Oct 7th, 1862
Miss Jennie E. Lindsay,

Esteemed lady,

Having a few moments that I venture to call my own I will improve to the best advantage i.e. by leaving the scenes of this beautiful moon-light eve away down in Dixie and going back (Alas only in imagination) to brighter visions when all was joy.

I hardly know where to begin my story, several long weeks have passed since your kind favour of August 22nd came to hand tho scarcely an interval uninterrupted by the battle cry nor does the programme seem to change and I presume if it were not for a little lazy spell yours most obdtly would not be allowed this evenings respite but would be far on the road in pursuit of our timid friends of the Sunny South.

You have no doubt had the items of the Iuka battle[26] and perhaps wondered why we did,nt catch the veritable Price, well he did,nt wait till the 17th came up, that is all I know— we had quite a trip it is nearly 240 miles the route we took but we arrived about 3 hours too late to meet our friends, they were quite well entertained however i.e. they seemed very well satisfied to retire tho they don't seem satisfied to stay retired—fighting has now been progressing for several days

---

25 Eighteen-year-old men made up the largest single age group in the service during the first year of the war. In fact, more than 10,000 youths under the age of 18 served in the Union Army. Before the war was over, Jennie's brother William, who was born in December 1845, would enlist in the 53rd Illinois. Linderman, *Embattled Courage*, 26.

26 September 19, 1862, in northern Mississippi.

the first attack was made by the rebels on Corinth, 3 or 4 days since,[27] *at one time (tho I understand our forces permitted it on purpose) the rebels had almost gained possession of the place but by a desperate charge our forces drove the rebels out and have been driving them ever since—the Federal loss is very heavy and also the rebel. Two of our Brig Generals*[28] *killed at least. Oglesby*[29] *is supposed to have died ere this from wounds received—the rebels retreated this way and the forces here were ordered out under Ord & Hurlburt*[30] *who came up with the rebels and fought them nearly all day yesterday (Sabbath) completely routing the enemy. Late yesterday an order came for two or three Regts to march from here to prevent the rebels from bridging a certain little stream in their retreat. The 17th went along they marched 18 miles last night and the last I heard this evening the rebels were still retreating closely pursued by the forces from Corinth under Rosencrans*[31] *and those from here under Hurlburt, Ord being wounded. Ross went out with the 17th and the other forces that went to prevent the enemy from crossing the river but as the rebels have not attempted to cross but are retreating on the other side. I presume that Ross will join in the route—If all prospers as present indications tend it will be a glorious triumph for our cause, for it seems that the rebels had made every calculation to drive the Federals from this part and to do this they have mustered every man. If they fail as fail they must their failure is most disastrous to them—I only hope that our hopes may be more than realized and that this may be the beginning of brighter days indeed dear friend it almost makes me feel well when I anticipate the results of the next few weeks—for I know that our troops cannot fail to drive the rebels from Ky if they half try, and in such an event the rebellion will be sorely oppressed out here in the West.*

Well dear lady, you will ask why I am not along. Well I would only I didn't to, or rather did,nt feel like going, a little home sick I suppose. Yes , but it will all be

27 The battle of Corinth was fought October 3-4, 1862.

28 In fact, only one general was killed. Pleasant Adam Hackleman was mortally wounded on October 3 when a ball struck him in the neck, severed his esophagus, and exited near his spine. Jack D. Welsh, *Medical Histories of the Union Generals* (Kent State, 1996), 145.

29 Richard J. Oglesby was shot through the lungs on October 3, 1862, but managed to survive. He would be elected governor of Illinois in 1864. Welsh, *Medical Histories of the Union Generals*, 242-243.

30 Edward O. C. Ord and Stephen A. Hurlbut.

31 Maj. Gen. William S. Rosecrans, commander of the Union Army of the Mississippi.

right I think in a few days Indeed I should not be much afraid of old Price now did he come in here to fight, tho I couldn,t follow him very well did he undertake to run. Just now Adjt. Reynolds has arrived from the Regt which he says, after pursuing 30 miles, is now returning having given up the chase.

I presume you heard of Major Cromwell of the 47th being captured at Iuka. I've heard nothing from him since.

I suppose ere this Jennie that the troops have all left Peoria and that you have bid goodbye to your brother, but I hope that "good bye" may not prove as sad as too many parting words of sisters & brothers have proven since the advent of this bloody strife. There is a power that can preserve nor is a mothers love or sisters prayers forgotten, may the Great Arbiter of nations soon be pleased to rebuke the raging storm and a nation redeemed and purified by made worthy the smiles of heavens King.

Well Jennie I have told a long story and I fear not very interesting but you will please take the will for the deed for could I lay aside this medium for another more direct it would be very pleasant for one at least. In replying please don,t imitate my tardiness. Oh I thing that if I were at home I could write almost every day, you see Jennie how selfish I am, good night pleasant dreams.

J. Moore

PS My compliments to Miss Culter[32] and tell her that Lieut (Orderly Srgt when we were at Peoria) W.S. McClanahan has been very sick for a few days his first sickness since entering the service. He is fast recovering however and I think will soon be again able for the rebels which he hates heart and soul. Did I say soul, yes, I hardly think they have any. J.M.

Find enclosed a secesh letter I got it among some secesh baggage at Iuka. The remarks are union. Well it is too bad to use a letter so but I couldn,t help it tho I tried. They may get some of mine still I shall keep clear if possible. They never got one yet.

Jennie to Josiah

Peoria Oct, 13th 1862

32 Miss Culter" is Martha Culter, a 24-year-old resident of Peoria and a neighbor of Thomas and Sallie Currie.

Capt Josiah Moore,

Dear Friend,

Having just received your kind letter of the 7th inst I hasten to reply in other words I intend returning good for evil by answering before "several long weeks" shall have passed. I thought as you were not well a few lines from home would not be unacceptable poor as they are. You say dear friend if you were at home you could write almost every day. Oh how I wish you were there for I am sure nothing would give me more pleasure than to hear from so dear a friend every day. I have the will and the time to do likewise but I'm sorry to say the gift of letter writing has been denied me, and such poor letters are not worth receiving.

All the Regts but one have left Peoria and I believe it leaves this week, two were sent to Louisville and were in that last battle in Kentucky. four were sent to Covington, Ky. Our Regt among this number. Peorians have two Regts now, the 17th and 77th The Col, Lt. Col, Maj,and Adj are from Peoria your old friend Mr Hough is Adj. Capt Price of the 8th Missouri Col and Mr Wells Lt. Col, They were encamped in Peoria 8 weeks. There were two Regts occupied "Old Camp Mather." I was over once while Col Irons Regt were there, it looks rather worse for the wear. The encampment at the Pottery is much pleasanter and they have nice barracks and a good drill ground. There were quite a number from the 17th in the different Regts encamped here. Capt Harding had a company in the 102nd he expected to be elected Lt Col., but was disappointed. Capt Rose is fifth sergeant in one of the companys of the 112th Regt. The first Lt. in the Company that Brother's in was a private in Capt Norton's Co. perhaps you remember him [illegible] Woodruff. he is such a good officer indeed Andie has been fortunate in having all good officers Capt McCullough is a good Christian man you don't know what a consolation it is to have him go under the influence of a Christian if go he must. Capt McCullough is a brother to the minister of the United Presbyterian Church in Peoria. His Co. thinks so much of him and I think they have good reason to, for he is well worthy of their respect if there were more such officers, that trusted in God more than in themselves, the omnipotent ruler would have given peace unto us long ere this.

Oh how we miss the dear one from our family circle, living in the country. We were more dependent and both being lovers of home we always miss the absent one. I hope God will preserve him from temptation and evil and spare his life unto us yet a while.

I'm sorry to hear of your being sick, yet there is one consolation you can't fight and I think homes the place for sick boys, don't you? (I wonder if "John" got to the "meeting" hope he did.)

Friend I will now say farewell for a while

Jennie E. Lindsay

P.S. I thought perhaps you would like to see the likeness of our soldier boy, but please don't show it to the girls in meeting write soon J.E.L.

Jennie was clearly conflicted as she tried to support Josiah in a cause she believed was just, yet she couldn't help but encourage him to come home. Despite her misgivings about Andie going into the service, she was comforted by the fact that his company commander was a "good Christian man."

The growing casualty lists, combined with the draft and the Emancipation Proclamation, swayed enough votes to give the Democrats major gains in the November elections. Democrats also captured the Illinois legislature. Jennie's father, John T. Lindsay, who had changed parties from Republican to Democratic, was one of those swept into office by that rising peace tide. He would be sworn in as a member of the Illinois State Senate in January 1863.

Lindsay had been active in local politics as a member of the Whig party in the 1840s and served in the Illinois House as a Republican in 1857-58. In November 1860, he ran unsuccessfully as a Republican in the general election. The *Peoria Daily Transcript*, the town's Republican paper, condemned Lindsay for deserting the Republicans for the Democrats "when he failed to secure a renomination at the hands of the former party." The *Daily Transcript* would continue to find Lindsay a tempting political target.[33]

Jennie to Josiah

Peoria Nov 1st 1862
Capt. Moore,

Dear Friend,

As I am having a slight attack of the Blues, I thought I could not better drive the unwelcome presence from me than in living over again in imagination those happy bygone hours with the thought that "joys that were tasted may sometimes

33 Weber, *Copperheads*, 68-69.

Gilman Smith, who joined the 17th Illinois and Company F in September of 1862, would transfer to the 8th Illinois in 1864 and finish his enlistment with that regiment. *Author*

return" while a still small voice whispers come again bright days of hope and pleasure gone . Oh that they may come again soon and be all the brighter from being so long darkened, but "He doth all things well" and only sends as clouds that we may love the sunshine all the more.

Mattie Culter spent several days with us last week. we had a pleasant time as usual, with many a chat of old times and absent friends. Mattie is as lively as ever. She wishes to be remembered to you, says she is going to write soon.

Capt Ryan is now paying Peoria a visit. he seems to be one of the favored ones, he honored us with a call last Monday. he is looking well. I wish I could have a real proof of our "soldier boy" looking so, but I suppose that is one of the impossibilities.

I do wish you could come home, just to see what a welcome you would receive. I tell you dear friend I've about come to the conclusion that the end of this war is far away in the dim distance if there be an end which I very much doubt unless the millennium comes soon. If I were a good Christian nothing would give me more pleasure than to look for such an event to come to pass. Sad alone knoweth what is to be and all things earthly find when he will it other wise. But we surely deserve our present chastisement for we have all gone sadly astray and have even been too boastful of our Country, forgetful of Him, who gave us the blessing. I do hope if ever we get our Union back again we will be more thankful for God's good gifts and try to be a better people. Why cant we be good instead of being so wicked. I'm sure the only way to be happy is to be good.

Maj. Cromwell has been in Peoria for a couple of weeks but has now returned to his Regt he did not look as though he had received very bad treatment from the rebles while a prisoner.

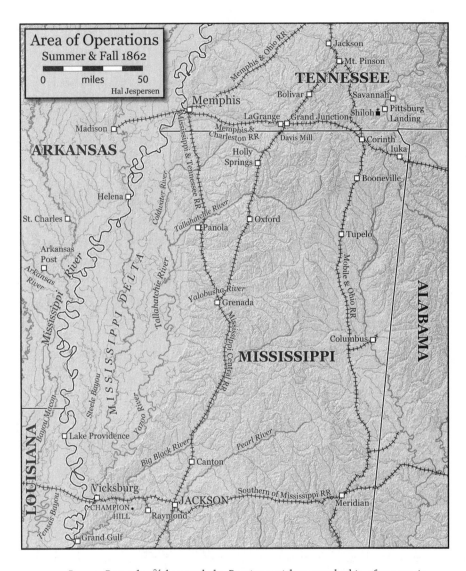

Area of Operations
Summer & Fall 1862

0   miles   50
Hal Jespersen

TENNESSEE

Jackson
Mt. Pinson
Memphis
Bolivar
Savannah
LaGrange   Grand Junction   Shiloh   Pittsburg
Madison   Memphis & Charleston RR   Davis Mill   Landing
Corinth
Iuka
ARKANSAS   Holly
Springs
Booneville
Helena
St. Charles   Oxford
Panola
Tupelo
Arkansas
Post
Arkansas
River
Grenada
Yalobusha River
Columbus
MISSISSIPPI
Lake Providence
Canton
Big Black River   Pearl River
LOUISIANA   Vicksburg   JACKSON   Southern of Mississippi RR   Meridian
CHAMPION   Raymond
HILL
Grand Gulf

ALABAMA

*Parson Brownlow[34] honored the Peorians with a speech this afternoon in
Pauleys Hall. I think his language more befitting a politician than a parson.*

34 Parson Brownlow was William Gannaway Brownlow, a former Methodist minister from
Tennessee who was strongly pro-slavery, but opposed secession. He became a Unionist leader
in eastern Tennessee, published a pro-Union newspaper, and was imprisoned for a time by the
Confederates. He later became the governor of Tennessee and a U.S. Senator. Boatner, *Civil
War Dictionary*, 93.

A ten-cent fractional currency note issued by the Mississippi and Tennessee Railroad Company on February 20, 1862, from Grenada, Mississippi. The Mississippi and Tennessee Railroad ran south from Memphis, Tennessee to Grenada, Mississippi, where it connected with the Mississippi Central Railroad. *Author*

"Having many things to write unto you, I would not writh with paper and ink" but I trust I shall soon see you "and speak face to face that our joy may be full."

Well dearest friend if you see [illegible] that displeases you in this unworthy epistle I pray you will pardon the writer and charge it to the "blues," I bid you a kind good night with many a wish for your safety.

Jennie
Do please write soon.

Jennie's description of Abraham Ryan, who was again back in Peoria, as "one of the favored ones" almost certainly refers to the fact that Ryan was back home and so many others, including her dear Josiah, were not. She also continues make it clear that the war was a "chastisement" of the people for having "all gone sadly astray." The nation had become unwilling to recognize the grace and gifts of God, and in her view had become too arrogant and self-reliant as a people.[35]

Josiah to Jennie

Camp 17th U.S. Vol, Inf,try of Ills, La Grange Tenn.
Nov, 13th 1862

35 Rable, *God's Almost Chosen People*, 7.

Miss Jennie E. Lindsay,

My dear lady,

With much pleasure I improve the few golden moments of leisure that it is my fortune to enjoy, this evening down here in Dixie, after the 9 O,clock P.M. "Roll Call" when all is partial quiet.

Strange scene! Tho present in body yet absent in spirit, even in this still hour when the sable curtains of evening gather round and close from view the outer world the imagination like the imprisoned bird seeks its ethereal clime, nor does it fail to hover round in sweet delight the enchanted grounds made joyous by the "bright days of hope and pleasure gone."

Two of those dear little messengers that like angels from the "better land" deign to visit the scenes of mortal woe, have come and with them the past recalled. You can scarcely imagine dear friend what joys and hopes, doubts and fears a "soldier boy" realizes on perusing the record of the past traced by dear friends at home nor is the anxiety decreased by the anticipation of the "welcome" in store for the future return. Sometimes I almost doubt whether my heart is in the cause or not, indeed I suspect that when it gets me busy it tries "to steal a while away" I know I would if I could but don,t mistake me I can never recognize a southern confederacy.

Well Jennie as yet I have not shown that picture to the "folks at meetin". Such opportunities are rather scarce down here in this "sunny land." I think Andrew looks quite soldier-like. I am glad that it has been his fortune to serve with "good officers" for I can assure you that I can appreciate such even for asociates not speaking egoistically either—I presume that by this time all the troops have left Peoria. The 103rd came here several days since, Lt. Col Wright was formerly Capt. of Co C of our Regt, and Maj Willison, 1st Lieut in Co H. A pretty good premium on non-combativeness in the past but if future developments prove favourable why all right.

Yours of the 1st inst came duly to hand and was a very pleasant surprise for I had received the one previous only a few days before but it was none the less welcome. I received it in the evening after a hard days march and tho I had to read it by the light of the camp fire. It was not passed slightly over and Jennie tho you requested me if I found anything in it to "displease," to charge it to the "blues" yet so far from this I think Jennie I must give the "blues" credit for one of your best, tho experience admonishes me to wish you more joy than the blues can impart. I should think that our excellent little friend Mattie could assist you by her lively disposition, in chasing such "dull cares away" however Jennie I believe I would be none the looser by making an even trade i.e. provided you should wish to dispose of yours.

Capt. Ryan was at my quarters yesterday to see me but I was not present and did not see him. I should have been pleased to hear directly from "Gods Country" (such we call the North) especially the City of the Lake. The Captain had quite a visit and I presume he enjoyed it accordingly. General Ross has now command of another Divison i.e. his old one in which we are in under Logan.

I saw some of the 47th yesterday. They have a Capt. Williams of the Regular Army appointed as Col, Cromwell will now be Lt. Col. tho he has not yet returned.

Well Jennie I presume you will all be looking for and expecting some serious work in this part but it is hard telling what the future contains. Grants Army is mostly all here now and it was expected that the rebels would make a stand at Holly Springs 14 miles South but it seems that they have now left the Springs and retired 12 miles beyond. Our army now occupies the Springs. Marched there today, but I think the intention is to follow-up as far at least as Jackson Miss unless the rebels fight sooner. I never saw our men so little concerned about a battle. They seem to think that our advance would be certain victory and hence they are eager for the work.

We expected to remain at Bolivar as provost guards and did remain for nearly a week after the other troops left but some of the Generals got uneasy because the 17th was not on hand and here we are now. We had quite a fine place at Bolivar almost fixed up for winter but it was no use. The men are generally healthy and would about as soon fight as eat hard crackers. Yesterday we had the first rain that has fallen for 2 or 3 months. It was very welcome indeed for it was awful work moving a large army over such dusty roads. The weather is quite pleasant tho the nights are quite cool, good blankets are very comfortable articles now.

This is a very fine region of country some splendid fields of cotton which as you are aware is now very valuable but the owners cant get it picked as the darkies have nearly all run away.[36] I never saw such work men women and children all on the run. What the result will be God only knows. Our country seems engulfed in one of wildest revolutions but such are often necessary for a nations purification. I long for peace but I would scorn to compromise a single principle of our nations honor,

---

36   This casual reference that slaves on local plantations were leaving in droves demonstrated one practical effect of the Union occupation of Southern lands: military emancipation.

no never. God would never forgive us, but Jennie I must have wearied you with my prosey letter. You must excuse. Please write often.

    My health is now very good and hoping that this may find you in the sweet enjoyment of heavens richest blessings I bid thee Dear friend a kind good night.

J. Moore
Remember me to Mattie and—Oh well I dont know who else, just as you think Jennie. Goodnight, J.M.

God was on the side of the North as far as Josiah was concerned, and the war needed to be prosecuted to the end. Still, it is obvious he was tired of life in the field.

*   *   *

By this point in the fall of 1862, the 17th Illinois and large portions of the Union Army of the Tennessee had begun congregating around LaGrange, Tennessee, a major staging area in the southwestern part of the state for additional incursions into Mississippi. According to Henry Forbes of the 7th Illinois Cavalry, LaGrange was "a neat little place of about a thousand people. The yards were beautifully improved, filled with evergreens and rare shrubberies. A fine College building crowned a gentle eminence to the east of the town and Seminary for Ladies looked across to it from the north."[37]

The town would not remain handsome for long. Foraging and destruction of private property became widespread; the war had taken a vicious turn. Charles Wills, formerly of the 8th Illinois and now an officer with the raw 103rd Illinois, wrote on November 7 about his march from Bolivar, Tennessee. "I think there is not a house left or rail unburned and 'twas all done on our trip down," he said. The hardening process was accelerating.

Despite their inexperience, the men of the 103rd Illinois became quite adept at finding food in the countryside. Wills wrote of an early December expedition to a point south of Holly Springs, Mississippi, and that the items his company "found" included "150 pounds of flour, a hog, a beef, two and

37 Hicken, *Illinois in the Civil War*, 154-155; Letter from Henry Forbes to Nettie Forbes, January 24, 1863. Forbes Collection, University of Illinois Library, Illinois History and Lincoln Collection. See www.tnvacation.com/civil-war/place/288/la-grange-union-supply-base.

one-half bushels of sweet potatoes, chickens, ducks, milk, honey, and apples." Wills claimed he allowed his men to take only "eatables," but seemed to have little trouble justifying the foraging. He thought it "right, and can find no arguments for any other side of the question." In short order, the 103rd and other regiments cleaned out the surrounding area. "Chickens, fences, swine etc are entirely unseeable and unfindable within 15 miles of where our camp has been this week," boasted Wills, who even took two freed slaves as his servants while stationed in the LaGrange area.[38]

Another green Illinois unit, the 124th, was also assigned to duty in LaGrange. Like those in the 103rd, the men of the 124th also quickly learned the ways of the army. On one of their first marches, the 124th soldiers lured half a dozen calves into their ranks and covered them with blankets and overcoats to keep them hidden from their officers until they could butcher them for their evening meal. One private in the 124th summarized his view of foraging this way: "Hang all the officers who won't let us steal from the rebel property. I will steal it whenever I get a chance." He wrote of one particularly destructive evening where the unit, "stole lots of niggers, killed six cattle, and burned the fence around the college—all in one night. It was one of the most jovial nights I ever experienced." Many officers turned a blind eye to the foraging and destruction or were spectacularly unsuccessful in preventing it. For regiments like the 103rd and 124th, the hardening process had not taken long to set in.[39]

Henry Forbes of the 7th Illinois Cavalry had left LaGrange in the fall. When he returned in January 1863, the bucolic town he had described was long gone. "All is vulgar destruction now," he lamented. Henry's brother Stephen, who succeeded him as captain of the 7th Illinois Cavalry, was one of the last soldiers to leave the town in 1863. He left this moving and extraordinarily gripping description of LaGrange:

> long lines of dark, empty houses that looked through the open doors and windows as if they were opening their mouths to show the blackness and confusion of their interiors,

---

38 Wills, *Army Life of an Illinois Soldier*, 129-137, 141-142, 161-163. One thing that disturbed Wills was when some of the men decided to "steal from the negroes (which is lower business than I ever thought it possible for a white man to be guilty of), and many of them are learning to hate the Yankees as much as our 'Southern Brethren' do."

39 Hicken, 82; Richard L. Howard, *History of the 124th Regiment Illinois Infantry Volunteers, Otherwise Known as the "Hundred and Two Dozen" From August, 1862 to August 1865* (Springfield, IL), 30.

with no living thing moving, save one solitary refugee woman, worn and dreary, who sat in the doorway of a large house without a window or door, gazing down the street quietly as if nothing under heaven could especially interest her, and three little black children playing slowly on the sidewalk, made me feel as if I was moving along the veins of some dead body looking in at the holes where were once the eyes, and into the great shell where seethed the brain, and this dark cavity where throbbed the heart, now all dry and pulseless and black.

Captain Forbes turned his horse and set his spurs, leaving the now-dead town of LaGrange behind him.[40]

The Union Army lost control of Holly Springs just a few weeks later when Confederate General Van Dorn, now in command of Rebel cavalry, looped around Grant's army and captured the town and destroyed its large stores of supplies on December 20. The Holly Springs raid ended one of Grant's many efforts to capture the Confederate Mississippi river bastion at Vicksburg.[41]

Jennie to Josiah

Peoria Nov 19th 1862
Capt. Josiah Moore

Dearest Friend,

The shades of evening have fallen and "Night, God's silent worshipper" has come to dwell with us for a while. The silent hours seem propitious for thine or as the heart loves to steal away from things present to those more distant. neath the soothing influence of their hours the weary one finds [illegible] *from the sorrow that are past bright of the* [illegible] *hopeful future rise up before us making the heart long for something better.*

Your kind message of the 13th inst. arrived safely. To say that it was welcome would but half express the pleasure it gave. I only regret they come so seldom.

Mr Currie's Father and Mother have come [illegible] *to spend the winter with them. The old gentleman preached for us on last Sabbath. He reminds one of the*

---

40 Stephen Forbes journal, October 18, 1864, Abraham Lincoln Presidential Library.

41 Woodworth, *Nothing But Victory*, 264-265

Vicar of Wakefield. It is a real pleasure to converse with him he is so good. I hope it will be a benefit to his son having him with them.

I've not seen Mattie Culter for over a month. I'm going in to fulfill a long promised visit to Mrs Young next week. I will then meet Mattie more often. I've formed such a habit of staying at home that it has become almost a task to visit. I rather my friends would come to see me. That I consider a pleasure, for I love "Home Sweet Home."

Jackson seems to be the place of interest now it looks as though we were going to have a battle there if we do I hope the 17th will not get there until its over. I think you deserve to rest, but you have proved so brave, and the Generals know how to appreciate such a Regt. and like to have them on hand when there's prospect of battle.

We received a letter from Brother last evening. They were just leaving Louisville for Memphis. They have done some walking from Covington to Lexington, stayed there for about a week then walked to Louisville, who wouldn't be a soldier, but with all the hardships they seem to like it, those that come home are always anxious to return they are so used to excitement that a quiet life does not please them. I expect when the war is over (if such an event shall ever come to pass) you will all be for joining the Regular service.

We are having beautiful weather now it has not rained for three days and that is something unusual for I believe it has rained about five days out of every week since last June.

Peoria is still honored by the presence of soldiers. There are two cavalry Regts here I believe they are to remain during the winter.

Well, dear friend, I know you have long ere this tired of my miserable attempt to interest you. Oh that I could speak with thee, but vain it is to wish for that which is impossible. Hoping many bright and joyous hours are in store for thee in "God's Country I bid thee my dearest friend a kind good night, good night.

Jennie Lindsay
Take good care of yourself and please write soon, Jennie

Josiah was detached to Peoria on December 14, 1862, to arrest deserters. His November 13 letter did not mention his visit. Perhaps he had no time to inform Jennie that he was coming, or perhaps he wished to surprise her. To his delight, Josiah set eyes upon Jennie for the first time since he left in July 1861.

1863 CHAPTER 10

"Let Us Get Vicksburg"

In the early days of the war, the venerable general-in-chief of the U.S. Army and former hero of the Mexican War, Winfield Scott, designed a plan to end the nascent rebellion. Scott, who was then 75 years old, suggested blockading the Southern states to stop the flow of munitions and other supplies and to prevent the South from sending cotton overseas to finance its war effort. He also proposed sending an expedition down the Mississippi River to capture the city of Vicksburg, Mississippi, sever the states of the Trans-Mississippi from the rest of the Confederacy, and regain control of the mighty Mississippi.

Critics, who wanted a more aggressive plan to win the war, derisively called Scott's strategy the Anaconda Plan, after the snake that slow strangles its victims. Many in the North believed that only a quick invasion of the seceded states would end the rebellion; others hinted that Scott's plan was part of a treasonous reluctance on the part of the general-in-chief to invade his native Virginia.[1]

Vicksburg, a town of 4,600 people (including 1,400 slaves), sat high on bluffs 200 feet above the Mississippi. In January 1863, after almost two years of bloody conflict, the town remained firmly in Confederate hands and its guns controlled the river's vital traffic. Northern cities upriver that had depended upon commerce from river transportation suffered as a result. The 1862 grain

---

1 McPherson, *Battle Cry of Freedom*, 333-334. In fact, Scott's plan proved prescient, and the Union war strategy evolved along the lines he proposed.

harvest in the Midwest had broken all records, but the inability to move the product south to the Gulf of Mexico and beyond crippled the Midwestern agricultural community. Pressure on the Lincoln administration to take Vicksburg and open the river increased. Lincoln fully understood the need to take Vicksburg from both a military and an economic perspective. "Let us get Vicksburg and all that country is ours," the president confirmed. "The war can never be brought to a close until that key is in our pocket." General Halleck agreed, adding that control of the Mississippi was "worth to us forty Richmonds."[2]

The South, too, had long recognized Vicksburg's importance. Confederate President Davis, himself a Mississippi native, called it "the nailhead that held the South's two halves together." It, together with Port Hudson about 100 miles farther south, prevented free Union use of the river and severely hampered the Union war effort.[3]

In the fall of 1862, Davis reorganized his command structure in the Tennessee-Mississippi theater and installed Gen. Joseph Johnston as head of the sprawling Department of the West. Johnston had been wounded just outside Richmond at the Battle of Seven Pines on May 31, 1862, and Davis used the opportunity to elevate Gen. Robert E. Lee to take command of the army in his place. Johnston nursed a number of grudges against Davis for a variety of reasons, including his denial of his proper military seniority at the beginning of the war.[4]

Davis also selected Lt. Gen. John Pemberton to lead the defense of Vicksburg. A Philadelphia native, Pemberton gained entry into Southern society when he married a wife from Virginia. Ironically, the campaign for Vicksburg would pit a native of the North against Ulysses Grant, a man whose wife's family held slaves and who himself had, at one point, owned a slave.[5]

President Davis was concerned about his native Mississippi and Vicksburg during the winter of 1862-63 and seriously considered shifting troops from

---

2 Terrence J. Winschel, *Triumph and Defeat:The Vicksburg Campaign* (New York, NY, 1994), 2-3; R. Douglas Hurt, "Agricultural Power of the Midwest" in Aley and Anderson, *Union Heartland-The Midwestern Home Front During the Civil War*, 71-77.

3 Winschel, *Triumph and Defeat*, 90.

4 Boatner, *Civil War Dictionary*, 441.

5 William L. Shea and Terrence J. Winschel, *Vicksburg is the Key* (Lincoln, NE, 2003), 36; Simpson, *Ulysses S. Grant*, 71-72.

Lee's army west to support Vicksburg. Lee balked at the suggestion, and later argued (successfully) for the reinforcement of his own army to move north into Pennsylvania as the best way to help relieve the growing pressure against Vicksburg. His raid north would end unsuccessfully at Gettysburg.[6]

When Pemberton reached Vicksburg, he found that work was well underway in an effort to make the city impregnable to attack. Once completed, the Vicksburg line stretched for eight miles, anchored on the Mississippi River above and below the city. It included nine earthen forts and extensive trenches and rifle pits, all placed with particular attention to where the Southern Railroad of Mississippi and various roads crossed the lines. Trees were cut down to leave a clear field of fire, and artillery studded the line. Pemberton had roughly 30,000 troops to garrison the defenses and operate against any Union force that moved against him. Swampy ground surrounded most of the city and made maneuvering difficult for any large body of troops. Only the eastern side, where the railroad ran between the city and the state capital at Jackson, invited approach by the enemy.[7]

In late 1862, the Union made its own series of command changes. General Grant was elevated to command the newly created Army of the Tennessee, an army that consisted of four corps: Sherman led the XV, McClernand the XIII, Stephen Hurlbut the XVI, and James B. McPherson the XVII. The latter commander, McPherson, was an 1853 graduate of West Point and a personal favorite of both Grant and Sherman. He had rocketed through the ranks, rising from lieutenant to major general in a little more than a year. Josiah and his men would serve under McPherson in Brig. Gen. John D. Stevenson's brigade, Maj Gen. John A. Logan's division, XVII Corps.[8]

After the action at Corinth, Grant began to plot his attempt to capture Vicksburg. The Union campaign against Vicksburg had begun in 1862, when Union troops under Gen. Thomas Williams attempted to dig a canal across the base of DeSoto Point on the opposite side of the river. The goal was to create a navigable waterway that would bypass the city's array of commanding gun

---

6   Edwin B. Coddington, *The Gettysburg Campaign: A Study in Command* (New York, NY, 1968), 5.

7   Shea and Winschel, *Vicksburg Is The Key*, 37.

8   Woodworth, *Nothing But Victory*, 245-246, 264. Boatner, *Civil War Dictionary*, 538. The other regiments in the brigade included the 8th and 81st Illinois, 7th Missouri, and 32nd Ohio regiments.

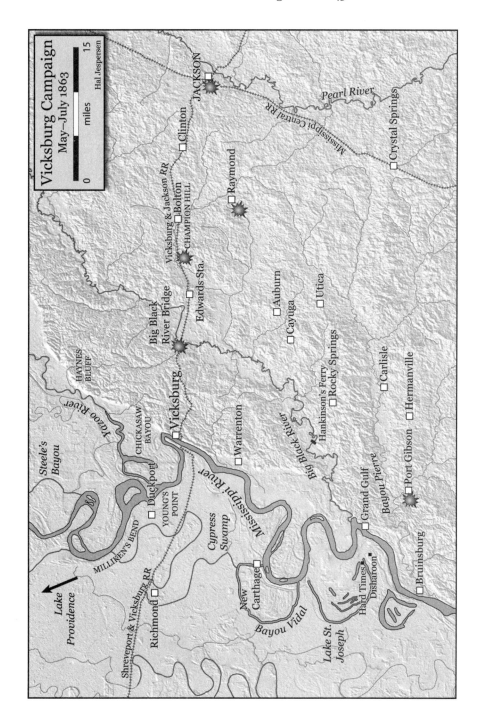

Vicksburg Campaign
May–July 1863

miles
0   15
Hal Jespersen

emplacements and allow the Union navy to move downriver. In addition to the Union soldiers on the project, Williams used "between 1,100 and 1,200 negroes, gathered from neighboring plantations by armed parties." Disease, along with heat, took its toll on the men and work ceased.[9]

Later in 1862, Grant decided to take his troops overland through northern Mississippi and attack Vicksburg from that direction. He instructed Sherman to take his men to Memphis and then move downriver to Vicksburg. The strategy was to attack simultaneously from two directions. Unfortunately for Grant, in late December 1862, Confederate General Van Dorn (as previously described) slipped around his flank and destroyed his supply base at Holly Springs, Mississippi, forcing Grant to call off his part of the attack. Unaware of Grant's withdrawal, Sherman landed north of the city at Chickasaw Bayou and attacked Vicksburg's entrenched defenders. His troops included Jennie's brother "Andie" Lindsay and the men of the 77th Illinois, who found themselves engaged in their first battle. Fortunately for the regiment, they were posted on the far right of Sherman's line and saw little action. The rest of Sherman's men were not so lucky. Thrown against the Rebel defenses, they were thrown back with heavy loss. The Federals suffered about 1,800 casualties while the Rebels lost perhaps 200. Sherman succinctly described his campaign in a letter to General Halleck: "I reached Vicksburg at the appointed time, landed, assaulted and failed." Sherman's men, including Andie Lindsay and the 77th, withdrew to the Louisiana side of the river at Milliken's Bend.[10]

General McClernand, in charge of the Union XII Corps, believed orders from Washington gave him command of Sherman's troops. He took them and moved against Fort Hindman, a Confederate position at Arkansas Post. McClernand hoped to remove this threat to Federal supply and communication lines. Working in conjunction with the gunboats under David D. Porter, McClernand captured the fort on January 11, 1863. Andie made it through this

9   Shea and Winschel, *Vicksburg Is The Key*, 22. The "canal" was one of Grant's attempts to bypass the strong defensive works at Vicksburg. The wet winter had made virtually all the roads in the area impassable, rendering any move south on the Louisiana side of the river impossible. Grant knew an amphibious assault against Vicksburg was likely beyond the capability of his army and almost certainly suicidal. An attempt to dash his troop transports down the river and past the city's guns was considered highly risky. Consequently, Grant cast about to find a water route that would get him around the city and land his men on the Mississippi side of the river. Smith, *History of the 17th Illinois;* Jeff Giambrone, *Illustrated Guide to the Vicksburg Campaign* (Jackson, MS 2011), 41-44.

10 Ibid., 52-55.

battle as well, only to be struck down by an illness (most likely malaria). More than one million Union soldiers would contract malaria, and the disease would kill 10,000 of them. Complications from the disease would plague Andie for the rest of his life.[11]

Tension between McClernand, the political general, and other professional officers, notably Grant and Sherman, increased during this period. Lincoln had promised McClernand an independent command, and the ambitious Democrat had raised troops for that purpose, but Grant proved superior at bureaucratic maneuvering and made sure McClernand remained subordinate to him as a corps commander within his army. McClernand's resentment at what he deemed ill-treatment simmered throughout the campaign.[12]

While Sherman's troops were engaged at Chickasaw Bayou and Arkansas Post, the 17th Illinois was foraging and guarding rail lines in the northern Mississippi area that included the towns of Davis Mills, Holly Springs, Abbeville, and Oxford. After Van Dorn's raid and Grant's retreat, the regiment was recalled with the rest of the army to Memphis to regroup for another attempt at Vicksburg. Once Grant consolidated his troops and came up with a new plan, he put the XIII, XV, and XVII Corps on transports and shipped them south. Hurlbut's men stayed behind in western Tennessee. Grant landed his troops on the Louisiana side of the river opposite Vicksburg and from that point evaluated his best options.[13]

* * *

Josiah's regiment began moving to Memphis without him, for Josiah was still on assignment arresting deserters in Peoria. His first few letters of the new year describe his attempts to catch up with his regiment and its journey to begin the next campaign to subdue the Confederacy.

Cabin of the Jeannie Deans
Memphis Tenn,
8 P.M. Jan 15th 1863

11 Adams, *Living Hell*, 49.

12 McPherson, *Battle Cry of Freedom*, 577-578.

13 Woodworth, *Nothing But Victory*, 286.

Dear Friend,

Having arrived safely at this place I have again taken my pen to address thee a few lines. When I wrote my last I put it in the office on the Boat expecting that there would be a chance to send it from some point on the way down but on going to the office this evening I found the letter had not gone and so I have opened it to add some more.

Shortly after writing the forgoing I met a soldier on board, a Lieut of Co. C. 77th Ills, he gave me good news—I was glad to meet him but sorry that I had not met him previous to writing, still it did not matter so much after all since the letter failed to get away. The Lieut was through all the fight i.e. was with the Regt. he said that the Regt, had no hard engagement tho it was in several little skirmishes. he said they had none either killed or wounded and tho I asked him if he knew Andrew which he answered negatively, yet I presume he is all right.

The Lieut also gave me some other good news, in place of 7,000 killed and wounded as per reports of reliable newspapers, he says that 1,500 will cover all losses.[14]

To night we have the news that a detachment from our fleet have captured a rebel garrison on the Arkansas river, supposed to be about 5,000 prisoners, 11 guns and a large amount of stores.[15] So far so good. now dear Jennie what else shall I say, well I am as well as can be expected but dear me I am so lonesome, a day seems a lifetime, Jennie could you suggest some plan of having them move forward more quickly? please tell me, now don't forget.

Our trip down the river was rather monotonous you need not laugh Jennie—any person would tire, I know of nothing that would interest you—only that it has snowed. it commenced last evening Jan 14th and snowed and stormed so that our boat had to give up running for the night and as it is not safe to stay near shore on account of guerrillas. The boat tried to anchor in mid stream but the wind blew so hard that the anchor dragged and finely snapped the line and let the boat adrift, it struck the shore quite heavily but fortunately only broke one of the wheels a little. we had to lie by the shore all night and I need not say that there were

14   Josiah is referencing Sherman's defeat at Chickasaw Bayou fought December 26-29, 1862.

15   The Battle of Arkansas Post, January 9-11, 1863.

some scared folks cotton buyers etc. The guerrillas did not come however and we to
day went on our way rejoicing. it has snowed nearly all day, snow 10 inches deep
such as storm has not been seen here for many years. I presume you have good
sleighing now, tho you no doubt will prefer walking. Well dear Jennie you will
excuse my wandering letter. remember me to all the friends and with my love to
thee dear lady.

Goodnight

J. Moore

P.S. Gen,rl Grant is now here and most of his army either here or on the way tho I
have not yet ascertained the whereabouts of the 17th unless it is at Lagrange. The
R.R. is all right, so by tomorrow I expect to see the boys. good by J.M.

Josiah missed little of a positive note by avoiding the posting in Memphis. A member of the 15th Illinois wrote from Memphis: "Too many of the boys were becoming too dissipated to attend to their ordinary duties. So foul had the pestilential breath of the city become that decent ladies were not seen on the streets. The city itself was beautiful but it harbored more vice and was more steeped in degradation and filth than any city I had yet seen but we will draw a veil over this scene." During the occupation of the city, Union authorities even had to take action against the local Methodist church after the pastor delivered homilies with decidedly pro-Southern views.[16]

Josiah to Jennie

Hd,qrs, 17th Ills, Vol, Infantry
Memphis, Tenn.
Jan 17th 1863

Well Dear Jennie,

16 Woodworth, *While God is Marching On*, 186, 201.

I fear I shall never get this finished, but I shall keep trying.

I was about to take the cars for Lagrange when I received information that the Regt. was in town, so I started and found them camped in the Navy yard close by the wharf, a very pleasant surprise indeed. I found the boys all well and very nicely fixed in houses, a very fine retreat in such stormy weather, but such visions do not last. Shortly after my arrival our Regt. got orders to report to Genr,l McClernand at Napoleon Ark, Hd,Qrs of Shermans fleet. I think we shall leave about tomorrow, tho I am not certain, the weather is rather cold for an army to move, but war knows no law—only to command. 3 or 4 boatloads of the rebel prisoners arrived here yesterday. I believe they will be sent North wont that be too bad Jennie! I think it is almost cold enough her now, tho ere this I presume you know what cold is. Well Jennie you must excuse this letter I shall try and do better the next time. I am sorry that is has been so long delayed, tho I shall look anxiously and even now expect one, is in coming Jennie, good by now don't forget the soldier boy.
J. Moore

Josiah to Jennie

Cabin of the Steamer "Superior"
Ark, shore 40 miles above Napoleon
Jan, 21st 1863

My Dear Jennie,

The fleet having put a shore for the night and as there is a boat from below on her way up, by which I may have an opportunity of sending this letter sheet in the morning, I speak with thee.

Well Jennie you don,t know how tired I am geting "home sick" I suppose! I feel I were getting about fifty miles from no place.

It is now over a week since I bid thee "good night" and yet no dear words have come to change the dreary scene and I presume that under the circumstances I shall have to content my self as best I can, but in my solitude I can contemplate the happy past and in this silent review it will be joy beyond measure to know that they miss me at home.

You said that you did not care so much for "news from the army" well Jennie I presume that by this you would rather that I should particularize of course I should not be egotistic, but for so far I have been prospering as usual, we did not leave Memphis as soon as I expected tho we were on the boat and lay in the harbor, last night we lay up about 40 miles above Helena. we have the 17th and 11th Ills. & two companies of the 16th Wis. On this boat of course we are crowded considerably and tho the officers have rather good quarters yet the men, as is usual on a boat, have rather rough times owing to the weather which has been quite rainy. Today for the first has been warm and pleasant, of course when my men are comfortable I feel better but a colder climate and a warmer heart would make me feel just a well. There are no ladies on board only two old maids and hence you see our company is rather onesided as is the fate of soldiers generally.

By tomorrow we expect to reach Napoleon beyond here I am not posted as to our movements, I may have the pleasure of meeting the 77th pretty soon I presume Jennie would like to meet it also, tho I should prefer to see her meet them in Peoria or some other civilized place.

Well Jennie I presume by this time you have rec,d my last little package I was almost ashamed of such a mixture but Jennie you will please excuse considering the circumstances. I shall have to address this as the last and untill I receive other instructions.

I saw by the Springfield papers that the Chicago Hotel had invited the "State House folks" to visit the "Queen of the Lakes" so by this time I presume you,ve seen some of them which will keep you from being home sick.

Well dear lady I must close for tonight, please write often, now don't forget. wishing thee good health and the sweet enjoyment of the company of good and dear friends. I bid thee dear lady a kind good night.
Sweet dreams,

J. Moore
Please don,t forget that little miniature or photograph.

It is interesting to note how much military information Josiah included in his letter, which indicates how little the military was censoring the letters back home. General Sherman, who had been appointed military governor of Memphis, adopted his own method of censorship by capping off a long-running feud with the media by having several reporters arrested—not only for printing military secrets, but for having the temerity to disagree with him. Sherman also had the correspondent for the *New York Herald* successfully court-martialed, for he believed information provided in the reporter's stories wound up in the hands of the enemy and helped them.[17]

Josiah to Jennie

Cabin of the Superior
Mouth of the Yazoo. 12 miles above Vicksburg
Jan, 24th 1863

My Dear Jennie,

As it is only now that I have an opportunity of mailing this I have concluded to tell you some more news. you have no objections Jennie? Well I saw Andrew yesterday evening a short while after we reached this point. he found out that we had come and he said that he would feel at home if he could only see the old 17th so he was not long finding us. he and his cousin staid with me last night. I need not tell you Jennie that I was glad to see them, tho I would not have known Andrew he is considerably changed tho he looks well and says that he feels well they have been traveling round considerably and have a great many sick I shall go to see them at my earliest opportunity.

Our men are now engaged on the canal for passing Vicksburg if this proves successful it will leave Vicksburg out in the cold, and if the river continues to rise I think it will be all right. The river rose 3 feet last night, a few days will tell the story. perhaps this will not reach you before the results of this expedition. The weather is quite warm no frost whatever, tho it rained some last night which makes some mud. but if our canal is successful we can stand a little rain. water rain is more agreeable than leaden, but the mail is about to close so I must bid thee

---

17   John Marszalek, *Sherman: A Soldier's Passion for Order*, 159, 189, 198, 211-213.

Jennie goodby. I shall write again soon, anxiously looking for a reply, excuse this style my regards to George & Maggie.

Goodby

J. Moore

The 17th Illinois went ashore at Young's Point, Louisiana, on January 25, 1863, and remained there but a brief time before being sent to Lake Providence on February 1.

Grant's effort to dig a canal and bypass the guns of Vicksburg was a continuation of the project General Williams had earlier started in 1862. It was no more successful the second time. Other projects included attempts to maneuver naval vessels and troops through the waterways north of the city, and an effort to cut a water route through the labyrinth of Louisiana's bayous and waterways and emerge below Vicksburg.

General McPherson's XVII Corps, which included the 17th Illinois, assumed responsibility for the Lake Providence canal. Lake Providence was 40 miles from Vicksburg as the crow flies, but 75 miles upriver by water due to the Mississippi's serpentine course. The six-mile long lake had been created when the river changed course and the former riverbed silted up at both ends. The canal project began in February 1863. Once again freed slaves—more than 1,000 by one estimate—were put to work for the arduous task along with many Union soldiers. At this point Grant considered the canal to be "the most practicable route for turning Vicksburg."[18]

The men of the Army of the Tennessee settled in on their assigned duties. For most of them, it was a depressing and unpleasant winter.

18 McPherson, *Battle Cry of Freedom*, 586-587; Woodworth, *Nothing But Victory*, 298-299; Edwin Cole Bearss, *The Vicksburg Campaign: Vicksburg Is The Key* (Dayton, OH 1985, 1991), 469.

CHAPTER 11

"A Vast Cemetery"

THE ongoing campaign to take the important river bastion at Vicksburg was not only hard on those at the front, but increased the stress on those manning the home front, as evidenced by Jennie's first letter of 1863 to Josiah.

Chicago Jan 21st 1863
Dear Capt Moore,

I received your kind letter on last evening I can't tell you how glad I was to hear from you. It seemed an age since you left me. The moments drag so wearily when we are sad and lonely, to great a contrast in thinking of those "happy bygone hours" with the present dark and gloomy cares. I was in hope you would be left that evening but when [illegible] came and no Capt Moore, then alas but this child was disappointed I felt the clouds had really returned I sought consolation in your precious gift the weary heart found rest.

The morning after you left the first thing I heard was the rain on the roof and as I listened to its patter I thought of the dear absent one now so far from me. My heart kept whispering Oh would I were with thee but the dream had passed, it rained for several days after you left then we had quite a heavy snow and good sleighing for about three days. I did not have the pleasure of a ride but I tried walking in the snow not from choice but from actual necessity. By the by I must tell you what a pleasant surprise we had last Saturday morning. Just after breakfast who should walk in but my dear father, how glad we were to see him he heard by some means that I was sick, so came up to take me home but I told him I thought I wouldn't go yet. In the afternoon we went up to my Aunts, missed the car and had to walk all the way there through the snow. You know what a long distance it is. when I got home I was so tired it cured me for walking I'll not try it very soon again.

I've not heard directly from Andie, but we heard through a gentleman just from the Regt that Andie was well which we have great reason to be thankful for. Oh how I wish this dreadful war was over.

We received those pictures of "one little boy", and what seems strange we weren't scared at all. I think they are so good. I thought you were never going to send them. I wanted one ever so much. I will have one taken next week if I can. I would have gone down sooner but the weather has been so unpleasant that we have not been down street since you left. It rained very hard yesterday and last evening. We have had but one cold day within the last week. I feel better this week than I have since I came to Chicago until today my head feels so dizzy I can scarcely write. It seems strange for I've not trusted a chap since you left, I am real sorry this is such a miserable [illegible] but it cant be helped I would have it other wise if I could yet I trust your dear kind heart will pass the imperfections by. Well dearest friend as it is growing late I will have to bid thee good night.

Jennie

George and Maggie wish to be remembered, now do please write soon and often. The only pleasure I have is to hear from the dear absent one. I hope our dream may be soon again realized. Once again I bid thee good night trusting God will protect thee and keep thee from harm, I remain, Yours truly

Jennie

Please address in care of George W. Updike Chicago Ill. I shall look for a letter very soon, now dont disappoint me. good night J.E.L.

Jennie's concern for Andie was well founded. His regiment, the 77th Illinois, was posted at Young's Point just a short distance upriver from

Vicksburg at the site of one of Grant's canal efforts. The 77th was bivouacked in a low-lying cornfield soaked by standing water, with a nearby levee towering 10 to 15 feet above the men's heads. They remained there from January 22 through March 9, with the river continuing to rise until it was nearly to the top of the levee. The wet miserable conditions led to major health problems. One soldier of the 77th described seeing three or four corpses laid out in front of the regimental hospital each day. The dead could not be buried in the swamp, so they were placed in the levees instead. An Ohio soldier described the levees as a "vast cemetery stretching for miles along the river." The 30th Iowa, one of the other regiments working on a canal project, lost 40 men to disease in a just a 60-day period.[1]

The 17th Illinois stayed only briefly at Young's Point before being sent farther upriver to Lake Providence. The camp at Lake Providence was in sharp contrast to the one occupied by Andie's 77th. Sergeant Duncan's company log described it as "a beautiful looking place" located in "a nice green meadow." The men camped in cotton fields just south of the lake, about one-half mile from the Mississippi. Peach trees were already in blossom. A Wisconsin soldier of the XVII Corps called Lake Providence "[a]s pretty a lake as ever was made," although on one occasion, as Josiah had feared, the river overflowed the banks and the men had to board their troop transports until the water receded. Artist Henri Lovie, who did sketches for *Frank Leslie's Illustrated Newspaper*, was with the troops. He wrote that on both sides of the lake "immense cotton fields stretch away" with "beautiful residences surrounded by elaborate gardens full of Southern shrubbery. . . . The soldiers are encamped all along the lake, and are in splendid spirits and condition. Not one of them thinks of getting sick in such a place as this, where they can have all sorts of amusement. Fishing is excellent, and ducks and geese are plenty. The foraging parties," he continued, "come back laden with turkeys and chickens, and the appetites of the soldiers are sharpened by games of football, etc. on the flat fields."[2]

Josiah to Jennie

Providence La.

Feb 14th 1863. Sat. Eve. 8,O'clock

---

1 Woodworth, *Nothing But Victory*, 293-294; David F. Bastian, *Grant's Canal: The Union's Attempt to Bypass Vicksburg* (Shippensburg, PA 1995) 64, 66..

2 Woodworth, *Nothing But Victory*, 299; Bearss, *The Vicksburg Campaign*, 475.

My dear Jennie,

Another happy moment has come, again I seem to speak with thee—Oh would that It were without paper or ink. then would this dream be realized—but no!no! dear lady it cannot be, then pleasure without pain would be realized and thus violate philosophy,s immutable course.

Well dear Jennie I have just returned this afternoon from a 3 days scouting excursion. I feel pretty tired, but have mostly forgotten it all—for judge of my most joyous surprise when on my arrival at quarters I received the dear little missive with the more than suspicious Chicago post mark. yes dear friend it was the hope of this that even soothed the weariness of many a tedious mile while yet on my journey, for you see I still hope for the best and I knew that my Jennie would not disappoint me. th,o the mail is now so irregular that no deffinite calculation can be made of its arrival. your letter was written Jan, 24th and only now came to hand, but still dear lady, it comes none the less welcome and with its other joys it adds the additional of being the first i.e. the first letter that I have received this year. Just think, February half gone and my first letter of /63 received today: would you be surprised if I should wish the gates of the cruel Jannus closed—But dear lady I must not complain, my King knows what is for the best, his will and not mine be done beneath his care we need not fear any storm,s angry wail.

I was glad to hear Jennie, of your health improving and congratulate you on your pleasant surprise th,o I somewhat expected it, but it seems that your father wanted to spoil your visit—wouldn,t that spite Maggie. Oh I think I can see her begging. Well Jennie so you have concluded to quit walking. Oh dear I wish I could tell Maggie something—I should request her to ask Jennie to take a walk—it would be such a good joke. I am sorry dear lady that the sleighing passed without your enjoying any of its priviledges , if the stay of certain one had been a little protracted I can assure you I should have known with whom the fault lay. have you been at any more "big meetings" when seats were scarce etc or been down the Avenue when horses make "fast time" since then—been to Mr Harsha's Church—I wish I could go there tomorrow but I presume I must fight old Mr Devil where I am so let him come we have still a little brimstone left.

But Jennie I must tell of our scout. on Tuesday last I took out a squad of 16 foraging I went to the left about 10 miles another squad of 80 took the right and proceeded about 9 miles when they encountered a strong force of rebels (of about 300) which after a sharp fight our men routed the entire force capturing 25 and wounding 7 or 8.[3] one of our srgts was killed and the Captain severely wounded he was of the 1st Kansas. tho several of the men were from our Regt one of Co A. was wounded, my squad entirely escaped and I hardly know how for we were at one time to the rear of the enemy, had they found us we would not have made a mouthful but we all returned safely. Then the whole Regt was ordered out which with the 1st Kansas have been prowling through these swamps ever since but no enemy to be found. We lived quite highly we made rich old plantations suffer, i.e. their chickens, hogs, sweet potatoes etc. most of the people have left, and left all, houses are deserted and the finest furniture commited to the merciless soldier. at one house we had the pleasure of some good music from a rebel piano that some of the boys pressed into service it seemed to be a very fine instrument. No person has any idea of the horrors of this war but those who feel its direct results, but the end is not yet. my candle is drooping good night sweet dreams.

15th inst.

Well how fares it with my dear Jennie to day? well I hope. please excuse my sabbath writing, you know the claims of a soldier and sick person are much alike in that either are liable to overstep their proper bounds as to their claims of right, but the temptation was too great I had to finish my letter , you won't be displeased?

It rained mostly all night and as our camp is behind the levee and hence below the river at its present stage, I lay awake several hours expecting every minute to be overflowed but happily we were not disturbed, tho when I contrasted the "patter of

---

3   The skirmish Josiah described was at Old River, Louisiana. An account in the Peoria paper described the action as 50 federals, including some from the 17th Illinois, in a skirmish with 300 men of the 3rd Louisiana Cavalry. Union infantry detachments included the 1st Kansas (Colored) Infantry, 16th Wisconsin, as well as the 17th and 95th Illinois. The paper claimed the Federals took one Confederate officer and 48 enlisted men prisoners. Union losses included one man killed (as Josiah noted), and several wounded, included one from the 17th's Co. A men. *Peoria Daily Transcript*, February 19, 1863.

the rain" on my roof and that of yours, I could not but recall the sweet idea "Oh that I were with thee!" but dear friend tho absent in body yet not in spirit, but few moments pass without living over again those bright hours of the past. I hope soon to return made more dear and precious from being tried.

We are still working at the levee i.e. opening it. I think it will be opened now in a few days. It is expected that boats can then pass into Lake Providence from thence through Bayous to Red river and get out several hundred miles below Vicksburg, these are prospects what the results may be I cannot say. I only hope that something may soon be done.

My health is still quite good excepting a slight cold and hope that this may find dear Jennie even better. and dear lady I can assure you that I have even now another "pardon" for the defects of another dear letter from you. would that I had such sweet work for every day. I shall look for that other gift soon now Jennie don't forget. My highest regards to George & Maggie. Tell George that when I return I shall beat him at a game of chess. I almost hate to give this up but I guess I must so wishing thee dearest Jennie heaven,s sweetest blessings I bid thee a kind adieu.

J. Moore Miss J.E. Lindsay, Chicago Ills.

P.S. I believe this is my third since I left Chicago. I believe my second was written from opposite Vicksburg and after I had seen Andrew, since then I have not heard from him. we left about the 27th ult I saw him one day previous. he came and staid with me one night in camp. he complained of not being very well but feared nothing serious. I was sorry on leaving there since occasionaly seeing him seemed to recall something lost now please write soon. sooner soonest goodby J.M.

Enclosed find some peach blossoms, first of the season, plucked from a tree on the battlefield Feb. 12th 1863 only now I am mailing this Feb. 17th first opportunity. so for the present and for only a short while, I hope, I must say goodbye. J.M.

The diseases of the Louisiana swamps were a greater threat to Grant's army than Rebel bullets. As the dismal winter wore on, the chorus of disaffected and disenchanted voices from the Union soldiers, as expressed in their letters home, reached a crescendo. Newspapers with Southern sympathies railed against the seeming stalemate that saw Union boys dying in fetid swamps. One historian compared this period to the Continental Army's trial at Valley Forge during the winter of 1777-78. Frank Peats, now the major of the 17th, confessed to his wife that he had no confidence in the "blundering star of Grant," and had "long since confessed to the humiliating fact that the generalship of the rebel army excelled that of our own. . . . I am disgusted with the army and wish I was out of it."[4]

This feeling of unease, even despair, was accentuated by a lack of success in the war's Eastern Theater, where the Union war machine had also stalled. Major General George McClellan, commander of the Army of the Potomac, failed in his attempt to capture Richmond in early 1862. General John Pope, the man who had sworn the 17th Illinois into Federal service, met with a humiliating defeat at Second Bull Run that August. The next month, September, McClellan stopped Lee's Army of Northern Virginia at Antietam, but failed to catch and destroy it before it could safely re-cross the Potomac River. The Antietam battle would prove to be the bloodiest day of the war, with more than 22,000 Americans killed, wounded, or captured.

In December, Maj. Gen. Ambrose Burnside, McClellan's replacement as commander of the Army of the Potomac, oversaw 1862's final bloodbath in Virginia at Fredericksburg. Almost 13,000 men were left dead or wounded, with Lee's losses coming in around 5,000 from all causes. Only the Union victory at Murfreesboro, Tennessee, in late December 1862 and the first day of January 1863 provided a glimmer of hope for the Union cause. Frank Peats's despairing sentiments were echoed throughout the Federal service. Thousands of officers resigned and went home. In Grant's army, even relatively minor items that could improve a soldier's lot fell short. Sergeant Duncan noted in his log that February that no mail had been received for a full month.[5]

The patient Grant was becoming frustrated by his failures cut alternate paths around Vicksburg or take it overland from the north. He could not afford too many additional delays given the toll that disease and apathy were taking on his army.

Many men reacted angrily when people back home wrote and asked about the war's progress or inquired when the armies would go on the offensive. One soldier, writing home to a friend, explained, "[L]et some of those who cry so

---

4 Woodworth, *Nothing But Victory*, 313; Frank Peats letter to wife, January 4, 1863.

5 Boatner, *Civil War Dictionary*, 21, 313, 507, 632-634; Philip Katcher, *The Civil War Day by Day* (New York, NY, 2010), 79; William Marvel, *Lincoln's Darkest Year: The War in 1862* (Boston, MA, 2008), 334.

much for an advance, enlist, shoulder a knapsack etc. & wade through the mud which at this season of the year is thick here . . . & we will see whether these cries will not grow fainter & fainter. It is a very nice thing for those who remain at home & have all the modern conveniences to cry advance, advance—it doesn't cost them any trouble." Another soldier wished for some of the able-bodied men to join the cause. "It would do me good though to see some of our Stay at Home patriots down in Dixie for a few months," he groused.[6]

McClellan's limited success at Antietam, as noted earlier, had given President Lincoln enough of a military victory to issue the Emancipation Proclamation, which freed all those slaves in areas still in active rebellion against the Union as of January 1, 1863. Clearly such an action had limited practical effect in many areas, but it did infuriate many in the Confederacy. Southern newspapers greeted the idea of arming blacks with horror. The *Mobile Register and Advertiser* was appalled by the thought that "our sons" would potentially encounter "their own slaves on the field." Because of this new policy, the paper encouraged "war to the knife." The *Richmond Examiner* called it the "most startling political crime . . . yet known in American history."[7]

Many in the abolitionist movement were disappointed and even angered by the proclamation's limited scope. Slaves in the border states who heard reports of the proclamation could not understand why it did not apply to them. Annie Davis, a slave in Bel Air, Maryland, wrote plaintively to Lincoln in the spring of 1864, "It is my Desire to be free. To go to see my people on the eastern shore. My mistress won't let me. You will please let me know if we are free. And what I can do. I write to you for advice. Please send me word this week. Or as soon as possible, and oblige."[8]

Lincoln's order fundamentally changed the focus of the war. It kept Britain, which had been providing military and other supplies to the South, from siding with the Confederacy. Britain had already abolished slavery, and once Lincoln officially made emancipation part of the war effort, it could not be seen backing an effort to preserve that abominable institution.[9]

---

6 Ramold, *Across the Divide*, 16.

7 Levine, *Fall of the House of Dixie*, 137-138.

8 A'Lelia Bundles, "The rrepressible desire to be free," *Philadelphia Inquirer* January 14, 2013, Section A14.

9 H. W. Brands, *The Man Who Saved The Union: Ulysses Grant in War and Peace* (New York, NY, 2012), 480.

Many in the Union armies remained divided by Lincoln's bold move. Not surprisingly, given the state's makeup, Illinois troops had varied reactions. "I am not in favor of freeing the negroes and leaving them to run free and mingle among us," wrote one soldier. Another penned, "I do despise and hate an Abolitionist almost as bad as a secess." Charles Wills of the 8th Illinois, the man who had spoken so jealously and disparagingly of the 17th Illinois after their boasting from having engaged in battle at Fredericktown, wrote, "Now I don't care a damn for the darkies and know that they are better off with their masters 50 times over than with us."[10]

There is ample evidence that the Emancipation Proclamation contributed to the army's morale problem for those in or close to border states. A number of officers resigned over the order, while hundreds of enlisted men attempted to do so. In the spring of 1863, Grant disbanded the 109th Illinois, a regiment from the southern ("Little Egypt") part of Illinois. More than 230 men in the regiment had deserted in reaction to the war's general progress, the Emancipation Proclamation, and their own poor performance in the clash with Van Dorn at Holly Springs. Grant's order stated that the officers of the unit had proved themselves "utterly incompetent." He discharged everyone but the officers and men of Company K, who were transferred to the 11th Illinois. The men who were drummed out of the service returned home to a warm welcome from the residents of "Little Egypt." The local paper, the strongly Democratic *Jonesboro Gazette*, proclaimed, "They are in good health and fine spirits and are perfectly satisfied of the fact that fighting to free the nigger is in no wise a desirable task." Federal troops would shut down the newspaper in May 1863.[11]

Other newspapers aligned with the Peace Democrats advised northern workers to organize against emancipated slaves, whom they said intended to cause "your impoverishment and annihilation." Democratic politicians attempted to rally support for their attacks against Lincoln. They threatened that "scenes bloodier than the world has yet witnessed" would occur as slaves streamed north to take the jobs of whites, all "in the name of philanthropy."

10 Kellogg, *Army Life of an Illinois Soldier*, 83.

11 McPherson, *For Cause and Comrades*, 123; Levine, *Fall of the House of Dixie*, 126; Frederick H. Dyer, *A Compendium of the War of the Rebellion* (New York, NY, 1959), 1093. George E. Parks, "One Story of the 109th Illinois Volunteer Infantry Regiment," in *Journal of the Illinois State Historical Society* (Summer 1963),Volume LVI, Number 2, 285, 295-296.

This discord would reach its zenith later that year when bloody rioting raged in the streets of New York City.[12]

For others, though, President Lincoln's action had the opposite effect. For obvious reasons, the proclamation cheered those who opposed slavery as an immoral practice, even if they were disappointed by the order's somewhat limited nature. People who did not share that moral perspective on slavery were satisfied that the removal of the South's pool of free labor would hasten the war's end. One Illinoisan who wrote from Memphis in early 1863 was elated that at last the war was imbued with a more specific purpose. Another member of the 7th Illinois wrote, "Among the soldiers, the proclamation is just the thing because it is the only remedy, and all know it will have a tendency to terminate the war shortly and permit us to return to better and more desirable vocations." An Illinois officer stated, "I have not met a soldier but that is in favor of closing the war as speedily as possible; and they all believe that the institution of slavery once out of the way, that war would be closed."[13]

There is nothing in any of Josiah's letters to Jennie to indicate his views on the Emancipation Proclamation. If he did favor it, he may have kept silent on the matter because he knew his views differed from those of Jennie's father.

Josiah to Jennie

Providence, La
March 1st 1863
Miss Jennie,

Dear Lady,

With a light heart I can seat myself by my desk, on this delightfull evening and speak with thee, dear friend I need not tell you that "good tidings" has come yes, would that it were the original.

---

12 Levine, *Fall of the House of Dixie*, 125-126; McPherson, *Battle Cry of Freedom*, 609-610.

13 Hicken, *Illinois in the Civil War*, 130-132.

Your dear letter of the 9th ult[14] came this morning, and I can only say that "hope deferred was more than ever "pleasure obtained" and I was glad that it came when it did for it arrived just in time to prevent me mailing one that I wrote last evening prefaced "Dear friend you need not be told that I have the "blues" for if you have patience you will doubtless fully realize the fact ere you peruse this wandering scroll."

Indeed my dear Jennie I believe that I can fully sympathize with thee now in your lonliness never before did I look so anxious for a letter I believed that you would not disappoint me but there the mail has been so tardy that it seems an age has passed since I rec,d your last.

But if dear Jennie is now well, all is well unless this cruel absence which will also be well if it "ends well." the shorter the better.

I shall not flatter you by saying that your picture is very good by this I mean very natural but as I am ordered on board the Stmr, "Crescent City" tomorrow morning with my company to go on some reconnaissance I shall take it along and thus manifest my esteem in a practical manner. what does dear Jennie say? do you think there is any danger of it being captured? well if such should be the case more than it will have to go along i.e. it will have company. it is now on the desk by me and I think it would just as soon as not take a pleasure excursion. Oh that it were the original, but dear friend if the original does not go personaly it shall in sweet remembrance. I see you patronised our old Galena artist Mr Hesler I used to consider him pretty good tho, I forgot about him being in Chicago when I got my work done. he however seems to maintain his old reputation—well he had a good subject—that is half the battle you know.

When George is away you and Maggie can come over to my house and while away your time. poor lonely little creatures I would,nt be lonely for anything—Oh dear, lonly in the Queen City of the Lakes!—why if I were there I should never think of loneliness, but here am I in Dixie the land of the rose i.e. of the negros. Just think of it, the sweet smelling shrub, ye little fishes! "Oh that I could take the wings of the morning" etc.

---

14 Either this date is incorrect or another of Jennie's letters is missing.

I presume Jennie that you have been mistaken as to the Div. in which we now are. when you speak of Gen,l Logans,[15] his Div. arrived here last week but we have been (and still are) in McArthurs [16]Div. ever since we left Memphis.

I would gladly comply with your request regarding Andie but there is not much prospect of our often meeting Ive not heard from him since we left there but I shall write to him pretty soon for I would like to hear from him.

We are still camped at Providence, La. and as yet hear nothing of a permanent move. the levee can now be opened in a few days but our lower fleet has been very unfortunate in losing two of their best gun boats[17] I have no idea of the program now. this news added to my "blues" yesterday evening.

I presume you've heard of the gallant defense of old Fort Donelson by the 83rd [Illinois] you see I am proud of it because the 83rd is from my old city but I must regret the fall of some dear friends of whom two or three were class or schoolmates.[18] Thus one by one they seem to fall the most noble of our land. one fell at Arkansas Post and several have fallen in the Army of the Potomac. I now look back in sadness over my college days when I recount the brave noble hearted fellows who have sacrificed all for that love borne to their dear country—"fatal love" I say because it prompted them to go forth in the defense of the best government ever given to man while there are so many heartless wretches who seem not to care whether our country "sink or swim live or die" I often feel as tho it were madness thus to cast pearls before swine, but I trust that there is a God with whom justice sleeps not forever, but my dearest Jennie (would that I could say so in

15 Illinois native John A. Logan, was one of the best of the many political generals.

16 Brig. Gen. John McArthur, a native of Scotland who immigrated to Chicago as a young man and become an able Union general in charge of a division in the Western Theater.

17 *The Queen of the West* and *Indianola* were sent to disrupt Confederate river traffic between Vicksburg and Port Hudson. The former ran aground and was captured by the Confederates, while *Indianola* was sunk. Shea and Winschel, *Vicksburg is the Key,* 64-67.

18 Josiah's reference to the defense of Fort Donelson refers to an assault against the fort by Confederates under cavalry generals Nathan B. Forrest and Joseph Wheeler. Donelson had been occupied by the Union since its fall in February 1862 and garrisoned by the 83rd Illinois, with Abner Harding of Monmouth in command. One of the Union officers mortally wounded was 68-year-old John McClanahan, a captain in the 83rd Illinois who was a trustee at the college back home. He was the father of 17 kids, including William McClanahan, who was serving as the second lieutenant of Josiah's Company F. Monmouth College, *Oracle,* 15-16.

reality) please excuse my desultory letter. My regards to George and Maggie and to Jennie the sweet enjoyment of heavens dearest blessings.

Pleasant dreams good night

Josiah Moore

P.S. I wrote my last about 10 days since. now dont forget the "wanderer" I shall look for a letter very soon are you getting tired to the city? when do you expect to return home? how are you enjoying yourself? Etc Excuse my inquisitiveness. you often say Jennie that you dont care for war news infering that you would rather have news more personal and this, is why I ask such questions. I would rather have the smallest items concerning your own dear self than the most important news of the great city. you see that I cannot help but be a little selfish but I know that I have a dear kind friend that will pardon. a short adieu J.M.

A blind eye was not turned to all theft. Major Peats had four men of the regiment tied up by their hands for stealing, although it is uncertain whether they took items from civilians, the army, or their fellow comrades.[19]

Jennie to Josiah

Chicago Feb 28th 1863

Dear Capt. Moore,

Another sunbeam has come to gladden the lonely heart, Oh how precious this dear missive that tell us of the welfare of him who is so far away. Your letter was two weeks coming it seemed like an age since I last heard from thee. I am always so anxious about you if I dont hear often. I fear something is wrong.

Just think we've not been to church since you were here it has either rained or snowed every sabbath, Maggie and I were going to hear Mr Harsha on last sabbath but alas the snow deprived us of the pleasure. I was real sorry, as I have a sleight partiality for Mr Hersha because he is somebody's friend.

19 Blaisdell, *Civil War Letters*, 108.

Maggie is now quite happy as George has got home again. He was gone nearly two weeks but she said it seemed like two years to her, it was real lonesome without him and someone else.

We were "down the Avenue" at a large party about three weeks ago and I had to ride and strange to say I found it very pleasant. I think I'm getting used to it so when you come home we will ride in preference to "walking." So you need not let the thoughts of having to walk keep you away poor boy how tired you used to get.

My health is better now than it has been for the last year. I think my visit has been a great benefit to me besides being very pleasant. Especially the first week yes dearest friend I love to live over again those happy hours and if it were not for the star of hope which giveth unto one a promise of their being soon again realized then present hours would indeed pass sad and weary.

I think I shall go home in two or three weeks. My dear Mother is getting impatient she thinks I've been gone long enough. I'm going to take Maggie with me but I guess we can't keep her long for she can't leave George. I think shes very foolish dont you?

I've not been to a "big meeting" since you left, but we talk some of attending one on Tuesday evening next. I wish you could be here to go with us. We are going to make sure of "seats" this time by engaging them before hand.

We are having all kinds of weather rain one day snow the next but we have had very few cold days. Such weather as we are now having makes it very unpleasant walking.

Aren't you getting most tired of camp life if I were you I wouldn't stay any longer I'd say good bye to the boys and come home. I am afraid I'm getting to patriotic. Well it is enough to make a person loose all patriotism to see the way matters are carried on the love of gain seems to predominate.

I was very glad to receive your photograph but have since come to the conclusion that I prefer the original so you will please send it immediately. now don't forget.

I'm so sorry you are not near Andie now we had a letter from him a couple of weeks ago he said he was well. I do hope he won,t get sick. Well my dearest friend as my time has expired I will have to say good bye hoping to hear from you soon sooner.

I remain Yours ever

Jennie

    Maggie always gives me a minute to write to you in she thinks I ought to devote all my time to her, but when I get home it will be otherwise. George and Maggie wish to be remembered, farewell, J.E.L.

    Be a good boy and come home soon for somebody wants to see you ever so much (I wish I were a letter there), JEL

With rare exceptions, such as Lee's invasion of central Pennsylvania in 1863 and the burning of Chambersburg, Pennsylvania, in 1864, few citizens of Northern states had to worry about enemy troops marching down the streets of their towns. Although Jennie suffered anxiety because her sweetheart and brother were in military service, the Civil War was not as integral to her daily life as it was for so many women, black and white, across the South. Jennie and many other women in the North carried on with their daily lives, in many ways, just as they did before the war. As one historian described it, for many in the North it was "almost as if the war was being fought in a foreign country."[20]

This was clearly not true for all Northern women. One Illinois woman wrote to a farm newspaper in February 1862, "I doubt if there were as many women and little boys hauling grain to the market, and chopping wood, and driving teams, as now." A 14-year-old Michigan girl noted, "I was the principal support of our family, and life became a strenuous and tragic affair." Understandably, this news of hard times at home, when communicated through letters to men away in the service, disturbed the soldiers, who could do little to assist.[21]

There was much discussion in the North about the differing impact the war had on working women versus those in the upper classes. Many women and girls, often fueled by economic necessity, went to work in the nation's arsenals, rolling ammunition cartridges and making other needed items. The women were often mistreated and sometimes suffered tragedy, such as when the

20 Hess, *"Tell Me What the Sensations Are,"* 120; Faust, *"Ours as Well as that of the Men,"* 239.

21 Ginette Aley, "Inescapable Realities: Rural Midwestern Women and Families during the Civil War," in Aley and Anderson, *Union Heartland*, 127-129; Ramold, *Across the Divide*, 3.

Pittsburgh Arsenal exploded in 1862, killing dozens of women and girls (some as young as 10).[22]

Calls were made for upper-class women of the North to make some sacrifices for the war effort. Many responded by volunteering for relief efforts, such as sending blankets, socks, and shirts to the men in the ranks, or serving in one of the many hospitals. Peoria saw the formation of various groups, many started by women, to support the war. The Peoria Ladies Assistance Society redirected their efforts as the Ladies' and Soldiers' Aid Society. Other women's groups began sewing and knitting items for the soldiers and collected hospital supplies. In June 1863, ladies of Peoria formed a chapter of the Women's National Loyal League to provide additional service and support to their men in uniform. Jennie made no mention in any of her letters of participation in any of these activities. It could be that, because of her father's political stands, she felt unwelcome or awkward participating in such volunteer efforts.[23]

Josiah to Jennie

Providence La.
March 16th 1863

My Dear Jennie,

Another bright beam has come to cheer the darksome way of the wandering soldier boy, another happy moment calls me to thy side while I would gladly peruse thy dear message of the 28th ult, that came on the 14th inst, would that I could lay aside this tardy medium. Oh how cruel! Yes cruel that I cannot greet thee as two months ago, but perhaps tis well life cannot all be sunshine. yet I should not complain when the recipient of such a dear letter as yours of the 28th ult. But dearest Jennie there is no substitute, without thee all is void –this dear missive—that precious miniature all point to the one dearest original perhaps I speak too strongly yet it is only a partial sketch of daily experience. it brings joy

---

22 Judith Giesberg, *Army at Home: Women and the Civil War on the Northern Home Front* (Chapel Hill, NC, 2009), 68-75.

23 Silber, *Daughters of the Union,* 156-157, 162-163; Clarke, *War Stories,* 103; May, *Students History of Peoria,* 88.

beyond measure even to live over the happy hours spent with thee in times gone by. how much dearer would the reality be? But Jennie you will consider me selfish unless I cease speaking of my own personal feelings. of course there is another to be consulted, and right gladly would I do so did the joyous moment offer, the sooner the better.[24] Well dear lady perhaps you will say of me as you have of Maggie i.e. that I am "very foolish" well if she was justifiable, and I know you wont deny that, how much more am I & Oh a great deal more, I think so at least.

I was glad to hear of your good health and that your visit was having the desired effect of improving your health, now Jennie you must not get sick any more for you dont know how much I was concerned for you when I was up there tho it gave me much pleasure to see a decided improvement before I left. yet I think your photograph is not as healthy looking as your other picture of a year ago, however I think that if you stay awhile with Maggie she will cure you she seems so cheerful but she must give you more than "a minute" to "write" else some person else will get sick. you must tell her that I cannot allow her to have all your time, would,nt that be pretty work? Well my dear Jennie as it was late when I commenced this letter I guess I shall not finish it to night. sweet sweet dreams good night good night.

J.M.

Just now I hear a cheer the levee is opened and I hear the old Mississippi rushing madly through the crevasse.[25] What the end will be God only knows. for over two months the water will keep rising, already hundreds of families white and black are surrounded on all sides and cannot escape the raging flood. we may not have to move camp for several days. who can count the cost of war?

---

24 This is the seventh letter Josiah had sent Jennie since his return to the regiment from his leave in Peoria. It is not unreasonable to conclude that this relatively high volume, together with the personal thrust meant the two had discussed marriage while he was on leave. Indeed, his comment about "another to be consulted" likely refers to his asking permission of John Lindsay for Jennie's hand.

25 Josiah's letter described the cutting of the levee on the night of the May 16, an action the Yankees hoped would allow them to navigate Louisiana's waterways and come out below Vicksburg. The plan did work, although by that time Grant had grown tired of waiting and had decided on another option to continue the campaign against the town. Bearss, *The Vicksburg Campaign*, 477-478.

March 17th
My dear friend,

Good morning and how fares it now with my dear Jennie? I hope well after her "pleasant dreams." I did not rise very early but I shall try and improve my limited time to the best advantage. the morning is pleasant, tho the morning sun has not yet succeeded in puting to flight the hazy atmosphere that hangs like a curtain around our encampment. our camp is close by the levee and the river is about seven feet higher than our camping ground, and within five feet of the top of the levee. a fleet of boats is now at the landing and General Logans Div. has embarked. as yet I know not its destination unless it be the Yazoo pass to reinforce Gnr,l Ross. the birds are singing grass growing and every indication points to the beauteous spring tho grim visaged war seems as tho it fain would frown down every smile of nature or of man.

The health of the troops at this post is excellent. a few hours work would turn the river into the Lake but our Comdr,s do not seem to be yet ready and as there is every probability of the river flooding the entire country and our camps also when the levee is opened it may not be done for some time. back 8 or 10 miles from the river the land is already flooded by cuting the levee 25 miles above. Gnr,l McArthur,s Div. is still here tho how long we may stay I know not.

I heard day before yesterday from 'Andie.' A Rev Henderson from Ills one of our U.P. ministers has been visiting us for several days. last week he went below and visited Capt McCollough and his boys. Mr Henderson reports all quite well he say Andie. they i.e. the troops opposite Vicksburg have mostly moved up to a place called "Millikens Bend" 10 miles, I believe, above their original camp which was overflowed by the high water.

Oh Jennie I must tell you that I had a very pleasant boat ride on Lake Providence last week. Most of our Division officers participated. our craft was the little propeller drawn over dry land from the river to the Lake some time since. we had a fine band of music which lent enchantment to the scene, in my opinion however we lacked the chief element of excellence—we had no ladies— so you see every rose must have its thorns but as the scenery around the Lake is beautiful, not sublime for there are no "craggy peaks," and our company was rather select we had a very pleasant trip. you should just see some of the fine plantations and princely dwellings that are daily being laid waste in this vicinity.

The trip I mentioned in my last was to accompany a surveying party up the river when the levees are now cut. we were absent only a day.

Well Jennie please excuse my wandering scrawl, already I fear I have imposed too much on good nature and I fear that I have not left room to send the "original" but dear friend I think you will have less trouble without it. if I were a letter then I should write no letter, but I must bid thee dearest friend a kind adieu My regards to George & Maggie and Jennie the sweetest joys of earth. Please write soon.

As ever yours, Sincerely

Josiah Moore

P.S. On the eve of my boat ride I plucked some flowers from the campus of a Mr Seller,s plantation where Maj Genrl McPherson makes his headquarters. I believe I cannot name the flowers. they are only to show that even there a dear friend was not forgotten I have also an early Magnolia but I scarcely know how to send it. it is so large. I shall try enclosing it in a news paper. be a good girl and go to church. thank you for your compliment to Mr Harsha to know him is to esteem him. Now dear lady if you write often I shall try and be a "good boy" you know I need encouragement don,t forget, good bye. J.M.

Mail continued to be a welcome connection to home during the 17th Illinois' time in Louisiana. Dr. Penniman, the outfit's assistant surgeon, described the scene in the regimental camp at Lake Providence when mail arrived. "The orderly of each company . . . receives the mail for his company," Penniman said, and "takes it to the tent of his company and calls out 'Boys come out for your mail' and then comes a rush."[26]

---

26 Blaisdell, *Civil War Letters*, 108.

Josiah to Jennie

Providence La
March 22nd 1863
Miss J.E. Lindsay

Much Esteemed Lady,

   Ere this I may presume to congratulate you on your safe return to your "sweet home" when you arrival will make many heads truly glad tho doubtless "Maggie & Co" would be almost selfish enough to deny you the happy retreat. but you spoke of having her along so I can almost imagine dear Jennie enjoying herself at the expense of poor little disconsolate Maggie. aint it too cruel to laugh at one when homesick? but such is the world, each one must have their turn, for "In Adam's fall we sinned all." [illegible]

   Well dearest friend our welcome epistle of the 11th inst[27] came duely to hand day before yesterday, bearing the joyous news of your continued improvement in good health, hence I dare say you do not regret your visit to the "Queen of the Lakes"-unless it be the "first part" tho my regret would be that the last had not been as the first aint I selfish? But You know a "soldier boy" must have a margin for allowances, tho absent yet dearest friend thou art not forgotten. to know that thou art happy is enough. but I must bid thee goodnight sweet dreams and a happy rest.
J. Moore

Good Evening, 23rd

   Well how is dear Jennie now enjoying the new delights of her dear home? Would that I could peep through the mystic vail of cruel separation and participate, even for a moment, in the joyous scene. But here I am all alone in my glory, now dont be "envious" "tattoo" has sounded (8 PM.) all is quiet except now and then the balmy evening air wafts to my ears the gentle sound of music from some distant fairy house, thus many of the boys now while away their anxious evenings. But

---

27 This letter from Jennie is also missing.

those plaintive notes often tell but too plainly where the "wanderer" lives. and tho your humble servant dont join the chorus yet like the Arab "he folds his tent and gently steals away". I wish some one was here to beat me on a game of chess. but I presume dear Jennie is tired so I shall.[28]

Than the mere amusement of gentlemen, tho dear Jennie my experience does not permit me to judge of such items. of course I believe that God has made all his work,s harmonious.

Oh dear friend I wish you could see the pretty bouquet that I have on my desk. I wish so much that I could send it to you. it would be such a rarity now up North. I collected it when on that trip mentioned in my last. we only crossed the river and spent part of one day on some plantations looking after and procuring —[29]

The desire of wives, girlfriends, and families that their men behave while soldiering was a strong one. Women of the time implored their men to "lead a truly Christian life" while in the service and avoid temptations. That included swearing, gambling, theft, and sexual indiscretions. The ready availability of women in the South, both white and black, tempted many Union soldiers and caused a surge in venereal disease among the troops. About 8% of Civil War soldiers suffered from some form of venereal disease. Northern military leaders were so concerned about the problem that in at least two cases—the occupations of Nashville and Memphis—military officials regulated the practice of prostitution in the hopes of limiting the spread of disease.[30]

28 The bottom half of page 3 looks to have been deliberately cut away. The letter continues on top of page 4.

29 Unfortunately, the bottom half of page 4 of this letter is missing because of the deliberate cut mentioned earlier. It is uncertain what would have caused Jennie, or someone, to cut away a significant portion of the letter. It is possible that it was related to Josiah's mention of the "fairy house," a term for which I could find no definition. It could be that it was a local tavern or even a brothel. Prostitutes of the time were sometimes called "fancy girls," which might lead someone to call the establishment a "fancy house," but Josiah definitely used the term "fairy house." Perhaps Josiah identified some of those frequenting the "fairy house," or mentioned some improper behavior that occurred on the plantations, and thought better of it after the war and cut out that section once he returned home. Or, for the same reason, Jennie might have destroyed that part of the letter to make sure local families never mistakenly read it.

30 Webb Garrison, *The Encyclopedia of Civil War Usage* (Nashville, TN, 2001), 75; Mitchell, *Civil War Soldiers,* 81; Woodworth, *While God is Marching On,* 186; Silber, *Daughters of the Union,* 105-108.

In many of his letters Josiah wrote about various aspects of the plantations he encountered. The bottom lands along the river in Mississippi and Louisiana were home to some of the wealthiest people in the United States, people who had made their profit in cotton and sugar on the backs of slave laborers. Federal occupation of lands in the lower Mississippi in early 1862 resulted in more than 150,000 slaves falling into Union lands. The Union invaders brought with them widespread emancipation at the point of the bayonet.[31]

Jennie to Josiah

Peoria April 3rd 1863
Dear Capt. Moore,

Here am I at home once more. Oh how I do wish you could be here too. it seems as though I must see you. It is to pleasant to be with the dear ones at home yet no pleasure is complete without thee. I find my self constantly wishing for the presence of some person. I'll not tell who yet I am sure tis, for somebody, and don't I get cross at this cruel, cruel war.

Maggie and I did really get to church on last sabbath. wasn't I a "good girl" though. I went because you told me to. I trust you will give me credit for obedience. please don't forget I almost forgot to tell you we went to the Hersha Church. While there I was reminded of another time in the same place yet how different everything seemed without thy presence Oh how I miss you not only then but always.

My health is very good at present. Mother was quite delighted to see me looking so much better. She says she would be almost willing to leave me go again my visit did me so much good. Poor Maggie, I'm afraid she will be lonely for a while. I wanted her to come home with me and she promised to at one time then she concluded to wait until summer so George could to too. She can't leave him. Maggie loves us but she loves her husband better strange isn't it. I received those flowers

---

31 Oakes, *Freedom National*, 219.

you sent in your dear letter. I thank you for your kind remembrance. I count them among my treasures for such they are coming from thy hand.

I arrived home on Tuesday last. I had just been gone three months. I've not seen Sarah Currie or Mattie Culter since I got home. I want to see them very much but I really feel just like a person who doesent like to "walk" that is a little lazy.

We are having beautiful weather now it begins to look like spring and I'm sure I am not sorry for I'm heartly tired of rain. We are so anxious about Andie now we had a letter from an uncle of ours who is now with him saying he was sick poor dear boy how I do wish we had him home. We thought when he enlisted he could never stand the hardships of a soldier for the heat exposure always made him sick but he wanted to go so much that we thought he might try it and we have been encouraged about his health for he has always written that he was so well, but I think he will now have to give up. Father went to Springfield on last evening and I think he will go from there for Andie Oh if we can only get him home. but I guess my dear friend you are tired of this scribble so I have to say good night, pleasant dreams. O that I could speak with thee it would be joy indeed. You musn't get sick now or I shall get crosser than ever at this awful war, but once again dearest friend I bid thee a kind good night, good night.

I am yours as ever
Jennie

Please write soon, J.E.L.

I do beg of you my dear friend not to read this letter with a critics eye as you will surely get sick, JEL

The following letter is but a fragment of the original Josiah wrote to Jennie. Unfortunately, there is no date or place indicated, although it was almost certainly written while Josiah was at Lake Providence.

Josiah to Jennie

. . . must also soon move. The water is now within six inches of my tent floor. we call the body of water between the river and Lake "Yankee River" I guess the secesh

wont like such a name but let them change it. No boats have yet gone through. Several of our men (5 or 6) have been drowned while crossing in skiffs. The town is nearly all submerged or burned , some scamp fired the M.E. Church to day. When will this war end? The South began this war to get their rights and I think it is getting them with a vengeance. If it is innocent I think God must be unjust. But this is not probable. Our hope then should be that God will yet delight to bless our nation with a purer holier government than we have ever before enjoyed.

Major Peats leaves for the North tomorrow on business[32] and as all our field officers are absent I presume that I and the old 17th will have our own times.

Well my dearest Jennie please excuse my random letter. I have just improved each moment as I could. I have been interrupted several times but never forgot the object most dear.

Now my dear lady if you promise to write soon I shall be ever so much pleased to "pardon the defects" of your last. Aint that fair? It will be such hard work. O dear I wish I could have some one to help me, but then this dear little "picture" might then be "envious" so I guess I had better wait for a more convenient season e.g. another visit.

But I must have already wearied you. For this I beg your kind indulgence and to spite me please write me a long letter in reply. Please dont forget.

With reluctance I once more bid thee my dearest friend a kind good night and steal a parting—kiss.

May heavens sweetest joys be ever thine.

Adieu, as ever

J. Moore

P.S. Dearest friend please excuse my "impertinence" for as you said of those fugitive little grass seeds coming South, so I thot that this letter might carry North the emblem of affections highest regard. If it should [illegible] please mark it as an error of the head and not of the heart. Goodbye for a short time only. J.M.

---

32 Military records list Peats as being absent from April 6, but it appears he returned by May, so it seems reasonable to assume this letter was written in early April.

Josiah to Jennie

Providence La.
April 13th 1863

Miss J.E. Lindsay,

My dear friend,

Would that I could comply with thy dear "wish" and meet thee this evening at thy own dear home. I feel very lonesome. strange aint it? when I have a whole Regt. for company. Oh beg your pardon dear lady—too much of a sameness.

I do not often wish for the presence of "some person" just as I would not wish angels to leave the abodes of bliss, tho I might wish to be with them. Just so, how I long to steal awhile away and spend it every moment with thee. This evening—just now—then, Oh then how joyous we could be. little parting sorrows would all be forgotten and then "All would note heaven's while Josiah had part." But it seems a dream, Oh Jennie I know it is too bad, tho perhaps all for the better.

Your dearest missive of the 3rd inst came on saturday. I looked for it very anxiously tho it came in due time but Jennie a week seems along time, an age, to be without a dear letter from such dear friend. it seems as tho I should hear from you every day, aint I selfish? perhaps I get more letters now than I deserve. Just as dear Jennie says but I know full well that my dearest friend is too good to weary in well doing. I am not afraid. she is such a dear "obedient good girl" Oh dear, and, now she wants me to give her credit for going to church But dear Jennie you did not give me the text how shall I know. I would rather be an eyewitness it would do me so much more good.

So dear lady you did not bring Maggie along after all. I thot that would be the way. She is too cunning to be flattered away. aint it too bad that people forget their dear old home so soon, a stranger preferred above all others. perhaps Jennie will not agree.

I was much pleased to hear of your continued good health. I should be much pleased to call some pleasant evening and see you and talk over old times and enjoy new ones.

I had not heard from Andie for some time till you wrote I hope he has recovered. you spoke of your father coming for him, I have not as yet heard from Mr Lindsay whether or not he came but if he came I should not feel very well pleased if he did not give us a call by the way.

A Messers Hansel and Boup called to see me one morning before I had opened my eyes on an evil world, and hand me a letter from Tom Currie but written by Mrs Currie. you had not got home then Mr Hansel said Mr Currie had sent me something but he could not find it. but if he found it after reaching the camps below he would send it back. so on last Saturday it came—what do you think? a good bottle of old bourbon—so now Jennie if you please just step in and have something to drink. I wish it was native.

Lt. McClanahan has returned. he called on Mattie Culter on his way back. he also heard that you had got home, of course that was my share of the news.

I presume you have heard of the last orders from the War Dept. ordering the arming of the negroes. two or three Regts are about to be raised at this point. they are already officered by our best men. What do you think of that Jennie? aint that good? I dont care who fights, but I must stop. I hope that this may find my dearest Jennie well and sweetly enjoying her dear home and dear friends the latter I envy excuse me. my health is still excellent. sweetly sleep, pleasant dreams and now dearest friend a kind good night, a kiss.

as ever
J. Moore

Please write soon J.M.

P.S. I did not read you last with a "critic,s eye" aint I obedient? wont you please send me another now please don't forget goodbye for only a short time.
P.S. Col. Norton, Lt. Col. Smith & Major Peats are all at home now aint we blest with field officers? J.M.

Josiah's comment about feeling lonely even though he had "a whole regiment for company" was not unusual and a feeling shared by many others. "I sometimes get so lonely when surrounded by thousands," wrote another soldier. This feeling was likely accentuated by the loss of comrades who had been killed, died of disease, or who had been discharged from the service.[33]

In his previous letter, Josiah referred to "the arming of the negroes," an acknowledgment that Lincoln had moved forward on another piece of the Emancipation Proclamation: the formal introduction of blacks into the military as combat troops. Lincoln laid out his plans in a March 26, 1863, letter to Andrew Johnson, the military governor of Tennessee who would serve as Lincoln's vice president during his shortened second term. "The colored population is the great available and yet unavailed of force for restoring the Union," explained the president. "The bare sight of fifty thousand armed and drilled black soldiers upon the banks of the Mississippi would end the rebellion at once; and who doubts that we can present that sight if we but take hold in earnest?"[34]

In the spring of 1863, General Halleck directed Brig. Gen. Lorenzo Thomas, the adjutant general of the U.S. Army, to implement Lincoln's plan by drilling thousands of black recruits for service in the Union. While at Lake Providence, General Thomas addressed many of the men of Grant's army, including the 17th Illinois.[35] Josiah's letter describing this address appeared in the April 13, 1863, edition of the Monmouth *Atlas*:

Never was a more jubilant day among our troops than when the General announced his mission to the assembled soldiery. "By the power vested in me," said he "I come to arm the negro." . . . [E]yes flashed with wonder and amazement. Silence for a time pervaded the astonished, gaping throng. . . . Had they seen a vision? No, it was a reality. There stood the solid columns of soldiery, clad in familiar blue—there, upon the balcony of some chivalrous Southern planter's gorgeous palace, once "his castle" stood the venerable speaker, closely pressed by men of high estate—the day made beautiful by a fine mellow southern sunlight, the camps and tents of the troops stretching away in the distance like flitting phantoms in a fairy land-a reality, yes, a reality. . . . How quickly fashions change!

---

33 Linderman, *Embattled Courage*, 247.

34 William Marvel, *The Great Task Remaining* (New York, NY, 2010), 183-184.

35 Smith, *History of the 17th*.

It was not fashionable last year for negroes to be free, much less to fight. How passing strange! It is now fashionable!

We dare not, we would not free the negro, much less arm him," said Jeff Davis and his minions, a few of whom are said to be up north, despite its "cursed government," rather than share with their southern friends the great boon of ye C.S.A. (Confed. States of Africa.) Now, let Jeff Davis and copperheads wiggle. The slave is not only free, but about to be armed, and I hope yet to see the day when Jeff will ornament the end of a rope, while "colored gemen" wait on him with sharp sticks.

The colored people seem to be much pleased at the idea of becoming soldiers, and I believe will do well, if properly managed, and I will not be surprised if they fight well; but one object of arming them is to keep them from their masters, and hence keep them from raising produce. I believe the scheme will prove a glorious success, and it takes well with the army, of course. Some always advocated the doctrine, but even the disaffected say that "stopping bullets is not so pleasant but that they would allow even negroes to enjoy their share." Of course copperheads would rather stop them themselves than allow the poor negro such "privileges."

This was Josiah's most public statement to date on the issue of emancipation and the creation of black fighting units—the first on his view of slavery and blacks since his 1859 poem about the hanging of John Brown. There is no question that Josiah strongly supported arming blacks. He also hinted at his views on emancipation with his comment that it is now "fashionable" for "negroes to be free."

This was not the first attempt to allow blacks to engage in combat. As early as April 1862, Maj. Gen. David Hunter took steps to arm a regiment of freed slaves in South Carolina. In August 1862, anti-slavery advocates in Kansas organized blacks into military organizations, but the men were not accepted into Federal service and fought as irregulars.[36]

Arguably, Lincoln's decision to allow blacks to join the army earned the support of many men in the ranks. Even though most Union soldiers did not join the war as "abolitionists," people who believed in the immorality of slavery, a large number—possibly a majority by this point of the war—had become

36 Levine, *Fall of the House of Dixie*, 136.

"emancipationists," as one modern historian described them. Soldiers had seen the value of denying slave labor to their enemies, and they came to see that adding another large source of armed men would help them end the rebellion. To be sure, many were won over by the moral argument as they came to understand that the Union they fought to save should stand for something, namely freedom for all. "I believe in my soul that God allowed this war for the very purpose of clearing out the evil and punishing us as a nation for allowing it," was how one Illinois soldier put it.[37]

Many in the ranks took a pragmatic rather than a moral view of both the proclamation and the creation of black regiments. "The necessity of Emancipation," explained a soldier of the 48th Illinois, "is forced upon us by the inevitable events of war . . . and the only road out of this war is by blows aimed at the heart of the Rebellion." An officer of the 123rd Illinois who described himself as a "conservative young Democrat" wrote, "While I am in the field I am an abolitionist; my government has decided to wipe out slavery, and I am for the government and its policy whether right or wrong, so long as its flag is confronted by the hostile guns of slavery." For this Democratic officer, the Union mattered more than the issue of abolition.[38]

Many men fighting for the Union had no trouble reconciling their racist views with their support for emancipation. They never accepted that blacks had a right to be free, but accepted the freedom of former slaves as a consequence of the moves to end slavery that would help end the war. In fact, some held such a dim view of blacks that they did not believe slavery was needed to keep them in a subordinate position.[39]

Charles Wills of the 8th Illinois, who professed a strong prejudice against blacks early in the war, now said he "took to emancipation readily." Even those who may not have been emancipationists adopted the kind of pragmatic view that Josiah mentioned when he said that, at a minimum, arming the former slaves would keep them from their former masters and prevent them "from raising produce." "Is he [the former slave] any better than we are?" asked one soldier. "Is it committing a sin to set him up for a mark to be shot at any more

37 Manning, *What This Cruel War Was Over*, 85, 94.

38 Gallagher, *The Union War*, 103.

39 Mitchell, *Civil War Soldiers*, 128; Manning, *What This Cruel War Was Over*, 92.

than us? I say arm them; put them in the front rank if need be. I would as soon have one of them killed on the battle-field as to have my brother or father."[40]

Lincoln's action certainly had the desired effect on a number of the slave owners in the area where the 17th Illinois was camped. Writing in March 1863, Kate Stone, a Louisiana woman whose family had 150 slaves on a plantation near Lake Providence, seemed most concerned about the sight of armed and uniformed blacks. In her view, they were a "dreadful menace to the few remaining citizens. The country seems possessed by demons, black and white." One Union soldier reveled in such Southern anxieties. "It does me good to see the old master look upon his slave with fear when he gets a musket in his hands," he said.[41]

The area plantations continued to be a tempting target for the Union army into April. Kate Stone complained about Union soldiers who "moved off every portable thing—furniture, provisions etc." After the war, Josiah wrote about a foraging expedition conducted by the 17th regiment. The soldiers had loaded several boats with "horses, mules, cattle, hogs, negroes, meat, meal, corn, chickens, turkeys." He noted that the "last articles rather disappeared with the Regt. at the landing."[42]

The presence of freed blacks also indicated the ongoing emancipation of slaves. Some of these former slaves ended up in the "employ" of the 17th and other units. General Order 73 of the United States Adjutant General's office, issued March 24, 1863, allowed the army to employ former slaves as company "undercooks" at 10 dollars per month but with three dollars deducted every month for clothing. Every company of the 17th, save Company G, took a handful of former slaves as cooks.[43]

By the end of the war, black soldiers made up about 10 percent of the Union forces. Josiah's optimistic view of the fighting abilities of the new black troops would be borne out in many battles, and the courage and bravery these former slaves demonstrated helped reverse the negative sentiments of many

40 Ramold, *Across the Divide*, 57-61, 74-75.

41 Susannah Ural, *Don't Hurry Me Down to Hades*, 116; Ramold, *Across the Divide*, 75.

42 Moore, *History of the 17th Illinois*.

43 Ural, *Don't Hurry Me Down to Hades*, 116; Moore, *History of the 17th Illinois*. Company G's aversion to the practice may have been due to the influence of Eureka College, a school in the regiment's home of Woodford County founded by abolitionists and one that maintained a strong opposition to slavery. www.eureka.edu/discover/our-history.

Union soldiers. A number of men from the 17th, including Abraham Ryan, Robert M. Campbell of Josiah's Company F, and Lt. Edmund Robbins, would even be commissioned as officers in newly formed black regiments. Unfortunately, blacks were still not deemed the equal of whites by the army, and these new black regiments were almost exclusively led by white officers.[44]

Ironically, while Josiah was exulting in the announcement that blacks would now be allowed to join the struggle, Jennie's father was increasingly making a name for himself as one of the "Copperheads" Josiah had reviled in his communication to the Monmouth paper.

The Copperhead movement evolved during the Civil War in three basic phases. The first came with secession and the outset of war, when those who opposed armed conflict to keep the Southern states in the Union opposed Lincoln's actions to raise troops. The second phase began in 1862 after it became apparent that the war would not be a quick and relatively bloodless one. The third phase came in reaction to Lincoln's issuance of the Emancipation Proclamation, which elicited strong anti-Union reactions in many parts of the North, including southern and central Illinois. In early 1863, Lincoln said he feared Copperhead activities, which he called "the fire in the rear," even more than the Confederate armies in the field.[45]

Lindsay's election as Peoria's new state senator—a Whig turned Republican turned Democrat—was clearly a part of this third phase. Lindsay quickly became a favorite target of the Peoria *Daily Transcript*, which excoriated him regularly in its pages.

One month after Lincoln issued the Emancipation Proclamation, the Democratic-controlled legislature in Illinois passed a resolution condemning the proclamation. The resolution claimed Lincoln's order was "as unwarrantable in military as in civil law" and was a "giant usurpation, at once converting the war . . . into the crusade for the sudden, unconditional, and violent liberation of 3,000,000 negro slaves." Further, they claimed Lincoln's action invited "servile insurrection as an element in this emancipation crusade."[46]

---

44 Mitchell, *Civil War Soldiers*, 194; Manning, *What This Cruel War Was Over*, 123-125; McPherson, *Battle Cry of Freedom*, 565.

45 Marvel, *The Great Task Remaining*, 74; Weber, *Copperheads*, 7-8, 66-67; Wagner, Gallagher, Finkelman, *Library of Congress Civil War Desk Reference*, 152.

46 Ramold, *Across the Divide*, 56-61.

Following its abortive move in 1862 to redraw the state constitution, the legislature prepared a vote barring blacks from settling in Illinois. Additionally, the Democratic legislature planned to make revocation of the Emancipation Proclamation the price of Illinois's continued support for the war effort. Although Lindsay was not a part of the legislature in 1862, he joined in the condemnation of the proclamation shortly after he was sworn in. In early 1863, Lindsay firmly established himself as a Peace Democrat when he railed on the floor of the Illinois Senate, "If Hell were boiled down to the consistency of a pint of liquid fire and the whole contents poured down the throat of Abraham Lincoln, the dose would be altogether too good for him."[47]

Governor Yates described the Illinois legislature in 1863 as "a wild, rampant, revolutionary body." The governor received Lincoln's approval to station four armed regiments in the capital city of Springfield as a precaution. In return, the majority Democrats moved to deny Governor Yates the ability to manage the war effort. A Republican member of the Senate claimed on the floor that "there are traitors and secessionists at heart in this Senate," and they are 'killing my neighbors' boys now fighting in the field. I go for hanging them." Yates's response to the Democrats was to invoke an obscure prerogative of his office and adjourn the legislature. The governor successfully rallied public sentiment to his side by claiming all this activity was part of the Copperhead movement.[48]

Copperhead sentiment spread to numerous places in the Midwest. The unofficial leader of the movement was Clement Vallandigham, a Federal congressman from Ohio who blamed the war not on the South's reaction to Lincoln's election, but on abolitionism. Vallandigham believed the "price of the Union" was the acceptance of slavery. Even the University of Michigan, which had strongly supported the war effort in 1861, displayed sympathy for the Peace Democrats. In 1863, a number of students traveled to Windsor, Canada, to hear Vallandigham speak. Later, a crowd of about 300 students paraded through the town of Ann Arbor cheering for Vallandigham, their support likely influenced by opposition to issues such as conscription.

47 *Transactions of the Illinois State Historical Society*, Number 16 85; May, *Students History of Peoria County,* Illinois, 94-95.

48 David Donald, *Lincoln* (New York, NY, 1995), 419; Brooks D. Simpson, *The Civil War:the Third Year Told by Those Who Lived It* (New York, NY, 2013), 39-41; McPherson, *Battle Cry of Freedom*, 595; White, *A. Lincoln*, 555; Ramold, *Across the Divide*, 117.

Given this turmoil, it was not a surprise the men in the ranks began to question the level of support from the home front. Up until this point in the war they had welcomed letters from home. Now the mail sometimes created anxiety and anger when the news from home discussed the growing discord. While soldiers viewed those who avoided service as cowards, they considered Peace Democrats to be outright traitors. An army surgeon from Connecticut wrote to his wife and encouraged her to speak out against those demonstrating anti-war tendencies, and even advised her to "spit upon those who manifest them if indeed they are worthy to be spit upon by their respectable female acquaintances."[49]

Civilians might favor public discussion on issues such as conscription and emancipation, but for soldiers the issues were decided. Anything short of complete support for the Lincoln administration was unacceptable. The fighting men had come to believe that the president's policies would end the war sooner, so most in the ranks supported him. They believed Lincoln knew what it would take to get them home quicker and truly believed he had their best interests at heart. Indeed, many came to support abolition because Lincoln did. His actions on emancipation and arming blacks inextricably bound Lincoln to the men serving in the field.[50]

Some on the home front took extreme measures to counter the Copperhead threat. A few Midwest newspapers deemed sympathetic to the Southern cause were threatened or attacked. In Peoria, military authorities prevented distribution of the *Demokrat*, the Democratic counterpoint to the *Daily Transcript*, to the men because it was critical of the war effort.[51]

With most of the Union men absent from Northern cities because they were serving in the military (or already in their graves) it often fell to the women back home to defend the war against the Peace Democrats. Jennie had both a sweetheart and a brother in the Union Army, so it would have been natural for her to have assumed that role. However, her father's very public activities on behalf of the Peace Democrats put Jennie in an awkward situation. Still, there is no outright evidence that John Lindsay's political ideology created any strain

---

49 Mitchell, *The Vacant Chair*, 33; Silber, *Daughters of the Union*, 131.

50 Ramold, *Across the Divide*, 5-6; Manning, *What This Cruel War Was Over*, 13-14, 100-102.

51 Brett Barker, "Limiting Dissent in the Midwest: Ohio Republicans' Attacks on the Democratic Press," in Aley and Anderson, *Union Heartland*, 169-183; Ramold, *Across the Divide*, 22.

between he and Josiah, and Josiah's indirect condemnation of Senator Lindsay's political statements seems not to have created any issues between him and Jennie. This is not as surprising as it may first appear, since soldiers typically exempted family members from criticism on these issues. Josiah was smart enough to avoid writing anything he was certain would threaten his successful courtship of Jennie.[52]

Lindsay's speech against President Lincoln was not the only indication of the senator's anti-abolitionist leanings. On February 4, 1863, the *Transcript* quoted Senator Lindsay saying "the introduction of negroes into Illinois would kill off the abolitionists." On February 9, the paper noted that Lindsay had been "censored for his attitude against the war in the Legislature." Later that month, the *Transcript* noted that Lindsay was going to give a speech at a gathering of "Peoria Copperheads." In June 1863, the paper reported that Lindsay offered a resolution in the Senate "expressing gratitude to Judge Drummond for his timely aid to the Copperheads and rebels of Chicago." Lindsay continued his peace sentiments at least into the fall of 1863. In October, he was one of the chief speakers at the Copperhead demonstration at Galesburg.

Josiah to Jennie

Providence, La.
April 21st 1863

Miss Jennie E. Lindsay,

My dear friend,

> *You can scarcely imagine what joy it gives to be allowed the happy privilege of once more addressing thee. Oh would that I could lay aside this tardy medium and enjoy for at least one short evening the sweet company of that dear one whose presence alone can make happy. Then dear lady I could tell thee my story and be satisfied with one for an audience.*

---

52 Silber, *Daughters of the Union*, 135; Mitchell, *The Vacant Chair*, 34.

But dear friend, I presume that I must be subject to the "powers that be" and take comfort in the words that "hope deferred is pleasure obtained." war you know cannot always last "there is a calm for those who weep."

About this time last evening (9 P.M.) the mail arrived—news to me joyous but anxious—I was beginning to feel very lonesome always so when absent from dear Jennie but especialy so when nearly two long weeks had passed and my dear friend still unheard from. I expected a dear little missive and I almost felt confident that it would come—I was not disappointed, would that I could repay such a dear kind friend, but to such an one, I know full well, that it will be recompense enough to know that she has made glad the heart of at least one poor disconsolate "soldier boy". Oh how cheering to read and ponder over the few sweet moments of the past—to trace those familiar words penned by the own dear hand—such momentoes Oh how precious! Like the oasis in a desert land, dull care quickly flees away, and I would quit this shadowy vale and spend the setting day with dearest Jennie at her "sweet sweet home."

Now dear lady I must tell you that your kind letter gave me no little anxiety where you informed me that your father had left for S[53]—and from there intended to visit the army in Co. with the Governor. you know I said that I should feel slighted if he did not call to see this little family. But what do you think, before opening my eyes, on this cruel world, this morning an orderly announced to me that the Governor and his friends waited outside to see me—well for a moment I felt as tho I had been captured, but as resignation is a christian grace I concluded to submit to my fate in the best manner possible, of course the "army toilet" is easily dispatched and the reception room soon in readiness. but to my inexpressible joy it was your father accompanied by Ex Gov. Wood in place of Gov Yates who not rising quite so early they had left on the boat. when seeing Mr Lindsay I almost felt like seeing some one else. It almost made me homesick. I believe I had not seen your father since we left Peoria. He looks quite as well as ever. after a few minutes we started for the boat where joined by the Gov. and some other of the friends we took a walk to Genr,l McArthur's[54] whom we also found in bed. staid a few minutes and then all returned to the boat. The Gov. wished to stay longer and see the troops[55] but the boat was on time (had only an hour) and could not stay. and as your father wanted to see Andie of course he was anxious to keep moving. They all promised to spend more time on their return. they will see some of the novelties of war to night at the lower fleet as I understand that several boats are to run the blockade tonight. when the last boats ran past Vicksburg the cannonading waked our entire camps in this vicinity tho seventy five miles from the scene of action this is a splendid night for such work it is very dark and a little rainy. Your father will no doubt have some interesting news for his dear daughter Jennie when he returns. I hope it may all be good especially as it regards Andie. he speaks of having him detailed in the Quartermaster Dept. that I think, would suit Andie very well for he is too young and slender to brave the ills of Camp life. perhaps he may get Andie a furlough, you I know would like this , well then I hope he may get one. If we detain him a little on his way, you will not be angry Jennie, you are at home and you will not be lonesome.

When I last wrote I expected to move soon but the Genr,l said today that we might yet remain for some time tho mostly all the troops are now below. Col Norton Lt. Col. Smith & Major Peats are still absent. I expect them soon but we are old enough to take care of ourselves I suppose.

---

54 Brig. Gen. John McArthur, a native of Scotland who immigrated to Chicago as a young man and become an able Union general in charge of a division in the Western Theater.

55 Governor Yates paid a visit to the army that spring of 1863 because of an invitation extended to him by General McClernand, who wanted the governor to see the difficulties he was experiencing in the field. Given the problems the governor was having with the Democratic legislature, he valued his relationship with a prominent Democrat like McClernand. The relationship between Grant and McClernand, as well as between McClernand and many other professionally trained commanders, had deteriorated to the extent that McClernand was actively circulating rumors that Grant had a drinking problem. Yates wanted to see for himself the truth about the command turmoil within Grant's army. Governor Yates' choice of Senator Lindsay as his traveling partner is curious given Lindsay's political leanings and the rancor that existed between Yates and the Democratic members of the Illinois legislature. It could be that Yates thought the trip would give him the opportunity to develop some type of relationship with Lindsay and perhaps dampen his Copperhead leanings. Jack Nortrup, "Richard Yates: A Personal Glimpse of the Illinois' Soldiers Friend," in *Journal of the Illinois State Historical Society,* Volume LVI, Number 2 (Summer 1963), 130-131; Hicken, *Illinois in the Civil War,* 162-166.

"Well my dearest friend." Oh how I would like to see you enjoying the pleasure of sweet "content" i.e. if the presence of the one you mention could thus make happy for in the enjoyment of such a privilege I assure you that none could be more happy than I. would that I could accept your kind invitation during the meeting of the Gen. Assembly, but it will be sweet to know that they miss me at home, even tho it be by only one. on my next visit I hope to comply with your request and not "disappoint" any of the friends. Please tell Miss Mattie to blame me Oh no, you for going away. I couldn't help it could I?

You must be tired of this prosey letter so my dearest friend please excuse too much imposition on good nature and pay me back with a long letter very soon.

By the divine blessing my health is still excellent. may dearest Jennie ever enjoy those rich heavenly blessings that shall make her ever truly happy is the highest hope of her ever. Admiring friend

J. Moore
P.S. I shall write to Mr Currie soon of course I had to write to Jennie first. that aint any harm is it? I presume Master Willie is the most important personage of the trinity. aint they foolish? Your last dear missive was written on the 9th and mailed on the 13th so the post mark showed. goodnight sweet sweet dreams as ever J.M.

Shortly before leaving for his trip with Governor Yates, Lindsay's stand on the war earned him a tongue lashing from a Union officer. Colonel Robert Ingersoll of the 11th Illinois Cavalry was captured in the fall of 1862 and sent home to await parole (an exchange of prisoners). Ingersoll, who had been a Democrat before the war and a former law partner of Lindsay's, was at the rail depot preparing to return to the regiment when he encountered the senator and W. W. O'Brien, a member of the Illinois State House from Peoria. The *Daily Transcript* reported, with probably no little glee, that when Ingersoll met Lindsay and O'Brien, he gave them a "Scotch Blessing" and told them that "the guerillas of Tennessee, Kentucky, and Arkansas were just as good Democrats as they."[56]

Unbeknownst to Lindsay, his visit put him in position to witness one of the seminal events of the war.

56 *Peoria Daily Transcript,* March 19, 1863.

CHAPTER 12

An Army on the Move

By late March, Grant knew he could wait no longer to take action. His attempts to find a water route around Vicksburg had failed. Remaining in the disease-ridden camps in Louisiana was not an option for the Army of the Tennessee. Neither was returning to Memphis, which would have been an admission of defeat. Grant's only viable course of action left was to march his men down the western bank of the Mississippi, using roads running along the top of the natural levees. The roads had been impassable earlier in the year, but had opened up once water levels dropped. It was not an ideal route. According to one description, the levees looked like "several dozen horseshoes that someone had carelessly tossed on the ground, sometimes touching one another at odd angles, sometimes separated."[1]

The plan was for Grant's army, with McClernand's corps in the lead, to advance south along this route, working their way along the paths, slogging through water when necessary, and sometimes being ferried across channels that cut across the roads. Once he got his men south of Vicksburg, Grant needed to transport them across the Mississippi River and strike inland to find an approach to the city from the east that avoided the bluffs and swampland surrounding it. The 17th Illinois (McPherson's corps), remained behind.

One noted historian of the campaign wrote, Grant's plan was "full of dangers and risks. Failure in this venture would entail little less than total

---

1   Woodworth, *Nothing But Victory*, 315-316.

Ulysses Grant, depicting him with the two stars of a major general, a promotion he received in February of 1862. It is possible that the image was given to Senator John Lindsay when he visited Grant in April of 1863. The image is from E & H. T. Anthony, 501 Broadway, New York City. *Author*

destruction. If it succeeded, however, the gains would be complete and decisive." In the end, Grant hoped the military risks would be less than the political risks of languishing in Louisiana or withdrawing his army north and admitting defeat.[2]

Despite the condition of the roads, Grant's troops made a successful march, and the canals the Yankees had dug provided one benefit for the army: The flooded countryside protected the army's right flank as it moved along the levees. Grant's gamble paid off. He now had men in position south of Vicksburg, at New Carthage, Louisiana. The next part of his plan was a real unknown. Troop transports had to get down the river to carry his men across to the Mississippi side. To get there, however, the vessels had to run the gauntlet of artillery protecting Vicksburg, something long thought to be virtually impossible.[3]

Commander David D. Porter put together a flotilla of eight gunboats and three transports loaded with supplies for the Union troops at New Carthage. The transports were piled with hay and bales of cotton to provide additional protection from enemy fire. On the evening of April 16, Porter ran his little fleet downriver past Vicksburg. Fortunately for the Union, many of the Confederate officers in charge of the artillery were occupied at a party, which gave Porter

---

2   Edwin Cole Bearss, *The Vicksburg Campaign: Grant Strikes A Fatal Blow* (Dayton, OH, 1985, 1991), 21.

3   Shea and Winschel, *Vicksburg is the Key* 90-91; Giambrone, *Illustrated Guide to the Vicksburg Campaign*, 45; Shea and Winschel, *Vicksburg is the Key*, 91-93.

precious time for his ships to steam downriver before the Rebels opened fire. Although the Confederates still managed to fire more than 500 rounds, only one transport and a coal barge failed to successfully make the journey. Kate Stone, the Louisiana woman who wrote of Union troops pillaging her home, watched as the guns from Vicksburg lit up the sky that night.[4]

Senator Lindsay, who was part of Governor Yates' entourage, watched the spectacle from Grant's headquarters ship *Von Phul*. Lindsay later wrote of arriving on board *Von Phul* with Yates. "We found our way up through a dark passage and when we reached the cabin there was a gentleman seated at the head of a long table with a lamp burning before him," he recalled. "He was an ordinary looking personage—apparently in deep study—and smoking a clay pipe." Lindsay was surprised to discover this "ordinary" man was General Grant, as "all form grand ideals of distinguished military generals." Grant, though, was "without one particle of ostentatious vanity or fuss and feathers."[5]

Governor Yates asked General Grant how he would like to travel downriver on one of the transports. The army commander replied, "if he was a soldier in the ranks and required to face the danger he would move himself by a sense of duty to his country. But while in the command of an army if he would place himself in such peril—when others were willing to take this post of danger—he would be looking for a request from the War Department to send in his resignation."[6]

Lindsay described Porter's flotilla moving past them in the darkness "with the upper decks but faintly outlined looking like phantom boats floating upon some dark mysterious sea." The senator and the others watched as the fleet proceeded one by one down the river. "Soon, as if by magic touch, the whole 8 miles of batteries sprang into lurid flames flooding hill city river and forest with the brilliant light of that noon day sun." Lindsay could see the Confederate artillery crews outlined on the shore, and described how "hundreds of strange weird beings moved to and fro all along the shore with torches in their hands as if ministering to the wrath of the infernal. Vast dense clouds of smoke now arose—rolled up over city and hill—and forming into towering columns all along the Eastern sky—and burnished into intense brilliancy by the reflection

4 Ibid., 98-99; Ural, *Don't Hurry Me Down to Hades*, 118.

5 From an unpaginated account written by Senator John Lindsay, in the collection of the author.

6 Ibid.

of the lurid flames all along the shore." After Porter's successful run, Lindsay recalled that Grant "showed no exultation or joy over his triumph but was apparently more silent and thoughtful."[7]

Lindsay also noted that he heard that evening that everyone who sailed under the Vicksburg guns that evening were volunteers, drawn by lot. "A boy 18 years of age drew what he called a prize—a position on one of the transports. He was offered $100 for his prize, the young hero refused it, and lived to tell the story of his peril in defence of his country. I thought when I looked at these floating tombs their courage was more than mortal," he continued. "Protected by a frail wooden boat and some cotton bales—against 8 miles of batteries of the heaviest guns in the northern or southern army. Had such cool manly courage ever been equaled-surely it was never surpassed."[8]

Six days later, six additional transports made the run. Five of the transports, though damaged, survived the trip. Grant now had the means to ferry his men across the Mississippi below Vicksburg. Over the next few weeks, the remainder of Grant's army, first McPherson's corps and then Sherman's command, used the overland route to reach New Carthage, and from there were either ferried or marched overland farther south to the town of Hard Times, Louisiana.

Grant made one unsuccessful attempt to cross the river to Grand Gulf, before finding an alternative landing site farther south. On April 30, Grant's men crossed the river and landed at Bruinsburg, Mississippi. At that time, it was the greatest amphibious operation in American history. Grant now had his troops south of Vicksburg on the Mississippi side of the river, and the Confederates were not there to throw back his advance.[9]

Over the next 17 days, Grant's troops pushed inland, meeting and defeating Confederates at Port Gibson, Raymond, Jackson, Champion Hill, and Big Black River Bridge, finally penning John Pemberton and his garrison inside Vicksburg's sprawling defenses. The 17th Illinois, part of John D. Stevenson's brigade in John Logan's division, McPherson's corps, did not arrive in Mississippi in time to take part in these important battles. Instead, the regiment remained behind in Grand Gulf until May 14, unloading supply ships and

---

7   Ibid.

8   Ibid.

9   Shea and Winschel, *Vicksburg is the Key*, 106-108.

assisting the wounded sent back from the Mississippi battlefields. The regiment did not catch up to its division until May 17. They may have missed the sharp fights leading to the gates of Vicksburg, but they would not miss the struggle for the city itself.

Jennie to Josiah

Peoria, April 27th 1863
Capt J. Moore

My Dear Friend,

I thought "some person" had almost forgotten how wearily the hours go by when no message comes from the dear one. Yes I think three weeks entirely too <u>long</u> a time to wait for a letter. I hope it wont happen so again. Now remember dear friend, remember how "lonesome" <u>Jennie</u> is with <u>thee</u> so far away. Tis true I have my home and friends, yet while the one who is dearer than all these is absent. I cant but feel sad and lonely. I received your dear <u>missive</u> of the 13th inst this morning. I was much pleased to hear of the welfare of our dear wanderer. Oh that he could give us a "Roll" some "pleasant evening". Wouldnt we have a chat over "old times" I think they are not forgotten. I hope they may be soon again realized.

I presume you have seen father ere this. The last we heard from him he was in Memphis. I think they intend stoping at Providence on their way down. We miss father so much it doesnt seem like home with him away. Andie was better the last time we heard from him. I do wish he could come home with father. Oh this cruel war will there ever be an end to it—I dont believe we will ever have peace again. Although the coming of the negroes does give us a slight ray of hope. I should like to see a Regt of them on dress parade.

I do think it too bad Mr. Tom Currie putting temptation in your way by sending you "old bourbon" Thats just the way persons commence, by drinking "<u>native wine</u>" <u>then</u> they must have something stronger. Tom and Sarah were out on last Friday. Tom was home from the store on account of having a very bad cold. He thought if he came into the country it would cure him. he is very anxious to have Sarah go East this summer he is afraid if she doesnt take Willie away from Peoria during the warm weather that he will get sick, and poor Sarah thinks if she goes without her dear husband then she will be so homesick. I really pity her. I'm glad I

never get homesick. I think it very foolish for persons to be this afflicted. What do
you think?

Well my dearest friend what shall I say to interest <u>thee</u>. Oh if I could only
speak instead of writing. how happy I would be. It seems as though my heart were
always saying, <u>Come home</u> dear wanderer come, and yet it calls in vain. days weeks
and months pass slowly away and still this <u>loved one</u> cometh not.

So Lt. McClanahan did get home as well as "somebody" else. I think he truly
deserved it for being so faithful.

Well dearest friend I <u>see</u> you are looking weary so I'll not write any more to
night. I would that it were more worthy your reading. but please take this will for
the deed, like a dear good boy with this hope I will give thee a kind good night kiss.
Remember and <u>write soon</u> too.

Jennie

Senator Lindsay caught up with his son Andie in camp. According to
Andie's captain, J. M. McCulloch, on or about April 25 the senator "came to see
him while we were on the march to a point below Vicksburg. He found him
very weak and told him he could get him discharged but the boy was plucky and
refused but accepted a detail in the Commissary Dept." Andie's change in
assignment was effective April 26, 1863, by order of General Grant.

Senator Lindsay or Governor Yates may have used their time with Grant to
request the transfer. That same month Grant told visitor Frederick Law
Olmsted (one of the founders of the U.S. Sanitary Commission and later a
noted designer) that he was continually besieged by Midwestern governors with
requests. According to Olmsted, Grant described Yates as "an amiable and
weak man [who] seemed to think it his business to help any citizen of Illinois to
anything he wanted." The barrage of requests from Yates were "all written in
the most earnest tone of personal and official anxiety,' said Grant, 'yet there are
so many of them, they can't mean anything." Yates probably thought he could
turn Lindsay into an ally—or at least neutralize him—by providing assistance to
his son. As we will see in Jennie's letter from May 5, Lindsay was successful in
bringing Andie home to recuperate. He remained home for two or three
months. Captain McCulloch, who was captured by the Confederates in April
1864 and held until the war's end, claimed Andie became ill while at Young's

Point early in 1863, although Andie later wrote that he fell sick while on detached service from the company.[10]

Josiah to Senator Lindsay

Grand Gulf Miss
May 14th 1863
Hon J. T. Lindsay,

Dear Friend,

Your kind favor of the 3rd inst and posted at Cairo Ills, came duly to hand to day and contents noted. I was pleased to hear of your safe arrival at Cairo tho I regretted your having to leave Providence so prematurely, but it was a necessity, I am much obliged for your kind profer in assisting me with the Gov, tho at present there is not much prospect of an opening. I saw the Gov. since coming here he was quite unwell and by this time I think has returned. our Regt. was detained here on post duty but is now about to march to the front to report to Gen Stephenson of Logan's Div, Logan had hard fighting yesterday he took Raymond repulsed the rebels and took 300 prisoners. he had about 80 killed & wounded the enemy lost heavily. our army is progressing nobly some of our troops expected to reach Jackson today where there is every prospect of a large battle Just now a gun boat arrives that reports fighting the last two days at Port Hudson.[11]

Various rumors come from the Potomac. some seem rather disastrous the last is that Stoneman[12] with his cavalry had reached and captured Richmond, but

---

10 Simpson, *The Civil War: The Third Year*, 114-115; Pension records, James A Lindsay, National Archives.

11 Port Hudson was another stronghold on the Mississippi River more than 100 miles farther south just above Baton Rouge, Louisiana. It was under the command of Maj. Gen. Franklin Gardner and besieged by Maj. Gen. Nathaniel Banks, whose 48-day siege of Port Hudson would prove the longest real siege of the entire war. Gardner surrendered after Vicksburg fell. See Larry Hewitt, *Port Hudson: Confederate Bastion on the Mississippi* (Baton Rouge, LA, 1994).

12 This is a reference to Maj. Gen. George Stoneman, the head of Joe Hooker's cavalry in the Army of the Potomac. Stoneman's raid was a large cavalry operation in mid-April before the

nothing is believed we are prepared for the worst, as we never expect much from that part.

The weather here is beautiful and Providence seems to favor us in every manner possible. Where God is for us we need not fear opposition.

But as the train is about to start I must close. I hope Andie is well and has had ere, this the pleasure of once more seeing the folks at home.

Remember me to Mrs Lindsay, Miss Jennie and all engrossing friends.

Yours truly

Josiah Moore

Josiah's comments about Lindsay assisting him with the governor, and the lack of openings, suggest Lindsay was trying to secure a promotion for Josiah, and even perhaps the colonelcy of another Illinois regiment. Although he would serve for three years, Josiah never rose higher than his initial rank of captain. Not every captain was promoted, but Josiah was educated and officially recognized at Shiloh for his exemplary conduct under fire. It is possible that Josiah expressed strong abolitionist views to others, or echoed the views about John Brown he had expressed in writing back in 1859. The Democratic party was dominant within the 17th Illinois, as the political maneuvering to fill the colonelcy after Shiloh aptly demonstrated. Josiah's views, assuming others were aware of them, may not have been well received and may have hampered any promotions.[13]

There may have been opportunities for Josiah to seek an appointment in one of the new black regiments. Other men from the 17th, including Abraham Ryan, had done just that. However, that probably would have required Josiah to spend additional time in the service, and he may have already decided not to remain past his initial three-year enlistment.

---

opening of the Chancellorsville campaign. It was intended (and failed) to cut Lee's communications to force him to call back, not capture the Confederate capital.

13 Ramold, *Across the Divide*, 67.

Josiah to Jennie

Grand Gulf Miss.
May 14th 1863
Miss Jennie E. Lindsay,

"My Dear Friend"

Another sweet respite permits the "wanderer" to commune with the "dear absent one."

Your dear epistle of the 27th ult. came duly to hand and is now on my desk. would that the writer were present, then, this fair sheet would be laid aside for that fairer one, "sweeter, dearer, far." Your kind missive was rec,d three or four days since and just about two hours after mailing my last in which I believe I betrayed some signs of being a little lonesome. but it was too late for correction, however the brighter day quickly succeeded the darker morning. and as I was just then about to embark on an expedition , it made the duty much lighter to have news from my dear Jennie.

Our Regt. went down the river 15 miles by boat landed and marched out 4 miles to the Hospt,l where were kept the wounded of the first battle at this place. we found them doing very well, of course it was a sad sight, there were about 300 in all, and dear Lady you can have some idea of a chivalrous villa when I tell you that this 300 wounded men was quite well accommodated in the first & second stories the 3rd being still occupied by the natives consisting of the owner, who by the way is a widow lady and two others, also widows—quite a trinity for one habitation! well I think they are having quite a singular time of it down south here, I am so sorry. perhaps I am a little interested. our business was to move the wounded up to this point but when we got about half to the boat and order came for us to return quickly to the Gulf as the rebels intended making a raid, but they did not come. we are still doing duty at this post, but now have marching orders and will probably start tomorrow, so dear lady you will perhaps hear from me next at Jackson.

I had, today, a letter from Mr. Lindsay dated at Cairo on the 3rd inst I was glad to hear that thus far he arrived safely, also that Andie had a prospect of visiting home, so ere this, no doubt, there has been one happy meeting and I am sure that none can wish you a more happy good cheer than your humble sr'vt I wish my father would come and take me home I am so backward you know that I dont like to go of myself among strangers.

Well never mind my dear Jennie, hope still lingers with her sweet solace that through the kind favor of a divine protector there will be another "happy meeting" of course the fortune of cruel Mars may defer this happy time and I would not excite any hopes that might be frustrated, but I assure you that it is no pleasure to be separated from one so sincerely lived, and I anxiously look for our national affairs to take such a turn as will not only result in an honorable adjustment of national troubles but also allow friends to return to loved ones at home.

My health is still quite good. I was pleased to hear that dear Jennie "never got homesick," i.e. when speaking of Mrs Currie. But dearest friend you look tired of this long letter, so wishing you a full participation in all the joys that makes life worth living or heaven worth gaining I will give thee a kind goodbye kiss.

With most sincere regards, as ever
J. Moore

P.S. I enclose one secesh post stamp so that dear Jennie can write to her little secesh friend now dont forget. good bye. J.M.

When Josiah expressed his strong desire to return to Jennie after what he cynically calls "an honorable adjustment of national troubles," we can assume this "adjustment" included restoration of the Union, but once again he remained silent on the issue of abolition. Either Josiah had modified the strong sentiments he expressed in 1859 when he wrote of the hanging of John Brown, or he was again avoiding the subject because of Jennie's father. Just a few weeks prior he certainly expressed an opinion on arming blacks.

Jennie to Josiah

Peoria May 5th 1863
Capt J. Moore,

My Dear Friend,

This is such a lovely evening. Oh how I do wish some one was here to help me enjoy the beautiful moonlight. I cant tell you how pretty everything looks. The fruit trees are all in blossom and by the bright light of the moon all nature looks peaceful and happy yet the heart sighs for a kindred spirit to commune with in this quiet hour.

Your kind letter of the 21st inst was received on last Saturday. You can imagine what a dear welcome missive it was. Oh that I could have such a one every day, or which would be almost as pleasant to see the writer. That would indeed be "joy beyond measure". When will the days grow bright again dearest friend. I sometimes get impatient for their return.

So you've seen my dear old father. Well I envy you both. Poor me hath eyes and yet can not see thee. We are looking for father home the last of this week. I do hope we will not be disappointed if he brings Andie with him. Wont there be joy in this household. You better come and see what happiness he will bring. Cant you come too please. Jennie wants to see you ever so much, and just think youve been gone four months. Oh I wish you would get real home sick then perhaps you would come. I think you would enjoy being here this month every thing looks so beautiful. quite an improvement on last winter at the time you were in Peoria you could now go into the country without any trouble, and find the folks at home too, just try wont you?

I went to Sarah Curries yesterday after Church. I am not in the habit of visiting on Sunday, but you know what a pleader Sarah is then I couldnt think of depriving her the pleasure of my company.

Tuesday morning: Well dear friend I dident think last evening when I commenced this letter what a pleasant interruption I would have. I suppose you have already quesed who the interrupter was. Andie gave us quite a surprise. We did not think of looking for them until the last of the week, but I assure he was none the less welcome for coming sooner. I could scarcely beleave it was him. I thought it as dream, but as he is still here this morning it has become a reality. he left father in Cairo, we look for him this evening.

Andie said he saw you a minute Oh how I did wish you had come to then Jennie would of been happy.

Andie will be with us about a week he will then go to Memphis. I think he looks so badly, but as he is at home now I think he will get better.

Well dearest friend I guess I will have to say farewell for a short time. You know we now have a soldier boy with us and he is waiting for me to go down town with him. Yes dont think dear friend because we have one with us we have no thoughts for another. Oh no he to is kindly rememberered would that he were with us in person, with the fond hope of seeing him soon. I will now bid thee dearest friend good bye.

Jennie
Please write soon

Josiah would soon have a good deal to write about in his next series of letters to Jennie.

"A Miserable Business"

AFTER successes at Port Gibson, Raymond, Champion Hill, Jackson, and finally Big Black River Bridge, Grant and the Union Army of the Tennessee had bottled up John Pemberton's Rebel army inside Vicksburg's expansive defenses. The Union encirclement of the river city also cut the Southern Railroad of Mississippi line, depriving Pemberton's army and Vicksburg's civilians of military supplies, food, and ready reinforcement.[1]

Grant's actions had been assisted by the dash of Col. Benjamin Grierson's column of cavalry, which had departed La Grange on April 17 and cut its way through Mississippi and Louisiana. The cavalry tore up railroad track, cut telegraph lines, and made its way back to Union lines at Baton Rouge. Grierson's Raid distracted Pemberton's attention away from Grant as he began his inland campaign against Vicksburg.[2]

The now-dependable supply route provided by the Mississippi River made it easier to maintain the Army of the Tennessee, which had largely lived off the land during its inland thrust. However, the army would still suffer from a number of deprivations as well as the stifling heat of a Mississippi summer while it invested the embattled Confederate garrison.

Grant's 50,000-man army would eventually form a 12-mile ring around Vicksburg. Whether early in the campaign or weeks later, the men in blue felt

---

1 McPherson, *Battle Cry of Freedom*, 629-631.

2 Hicken, *Illinois in the Civil War*, 155.

little comfort gazing at the imposing defenses of Vicksburg. Even today, the intervening 150 years have done little to dull the overpowering presence of the fortifications. Grass, shrubs, and trees barely conceal the ugly scars cut into the land by the men who built the Vicksburg line, and the trenches dug by those seeking to pierce the defenses. The distance between the Union and Confederate lines shrank with each passing day, as the Union engineers inched their way closer and closer, tightening Grant's grip on the city.

A staff officer in McPherson's corps, which included the 17th Illinois, described what the Union army faced. "The approaches to this position were frightful—enough to appall the stoutest heart," he affirmed. "A long line of high, rugged, irregular bluffs clearly cut against the sky, crowned with cannon which peered ominously from embrasures to the right and left as far as the eye can see. Lines of heavy rifle-pits, surmounted with head logs, ran along the bluffs, connecting with the fort, and filled with veteran infantry."[3]

Once he had driven Pemberton's 30,000 men inside the Confederate lines, Grant decided to move quickly to complete his victory while his opponent was off balance. He knew Confederate president Jefferson Davis would not sit idly by and let Vicksburg fall without a fight, and that Davis was already cobbling together an "Army of Relief" to move against Grant's rear. This command, now under Gen. Joseph Johnston, posed a real danger to Grant, especially if Johnston was able to combine his army with Pemberton's command. The existence of this threat in his rear convinced Grant that he did not have the time to engage in siege operations against Pemberton. He would have to take the city by assault. That meant the men of the Army of the Tennessee had hard fighting in their immediate future.[4]

Outside Vicksburg, the 17th Illinois caught up with the other regiments of its new brigade under Brig. Gen. John D. Stevenson. Stevenson was a lawyer, former legislator, and a veteran of the Mexican War who had started his Civil War service as the colonel of the 7th Missouri. In 1861, Stevenson's 7th

---

3   Bruce Catton, *Grant Moves South*, 450.

4   Shea and Winschel, *Vicksburg is the Key*, 167-170. None of the troops for Johnston's Army of Relief would come from Lee's Army of Northern Virginia. In early May Lee won a decisive victory over the Army of the Potomac at Chancellorsville. After convincing Davis that an invasion of the North was the best way for Lee to help Pemberton, Lee moved north into Pennsylvania, an offensive that created near-panic in cities such as Washington, Baltimore, Harrisburg, and Philadelphia. His move ended in disaster at Gettysburg (July 1-3) and did not help Pemberton in any meaningful way. Coddington, *Gettysburg Campaign*, 5-6.

Missouri was known as the "Missouri Irish Brigade" and demonstrated it was willing to fight anyone—Rebel or Yankee. A soldier of the 13th Illinois, writing of the 7th's arrival in camp in August 1861, reported, "It is said there are 800 men, and the first day they came here there were 900 fights." Writing about Stevenson, another observer noted, "He is a person of much talent, but a grumbler. He was one of the oldest colonels in the volunteer service, but because he had always been an anti-slavery man all the others were promoted before him. This is still one of his grounds for discontent. . . . Thus all the world will not go to suit him." The 7th Missouri remained part of Stevenson's brigade, along with the 8th and 81st Illinois, the 32nd Ohio, and Josiah's 17th Illinois.[5]

McPherson's troops occupied the center of the Union line roughly opposite the Confederate strongpoints of the 3rd Louisiana Redan and the Great Redoubt, where the Jackson Road crossed into the enemy defensive line. William Sherman's XV Corps was deployed on McPherson's right and held a line running north all the way to the Mississippi River. John McClernand's XIII Corps held the left flank.

Determined to take the city immediately, Grant launched his first assault against the Vicksburg defenses on May 19. He ordered Sherman to attack a heavily fortified position northeast of the city known as the Stockade Redan. At 2:00 p.m., Sherman's troops lined up along what would turn out to be an appropriately named route: Graveyard Road. Despite outstanding bravery and good fighting, the effort failed miserably. Sherman lost 942 men, killed, wounded, and missing. Confederate losses were perhaps 200.[6]

Though the attack did not come close to success, Grant decided to expand the effort with a more general assault by all three of his corps. Over the next two days the Federals inched their lines closer to the Vicksburg fortifications. On the evening of May 21, the army received orders to make the attack the next morning at 10:00 a.m. Union artillery would pound the Rebel lines prior to the attack. Grant ordered that only skirmishers and sharpshooters would be allowed to fire their weapons on the approach, and that all others would advance with their bayonets fixed but not stop to fire.

Stevenson's brigade assaulted the Great Redoubt on May 22, the most impressive fortification on the entire battlefield. The bastion sat astride the

---

5   Boatner, *Civil War Dictionary*, 798; Kaiser, *Letters from the Front*, 151; Robert Girardi, *The Civil War Generals* (Minneapolis, MN 2013), 172.

6   Shea and Winschel, *Vicksburg is the Key*, 146-147.

Jackson Road, a main artery connecting Vicksburg with the state capital at Jackson. At its tallest point the fortification measured 21 feet. To further impede a Yankee assault, at the base of the fort the Confederates had cut a ditch 14 feet deep and eight feet wide. Troops from Louisiana, the 21st and portions of the 22nd regiments, garrisoned the fort, which was also directly supported by three artillery pieces.[7]

When he heard the attack plan, William Alexander, George Smith's "bunkmate for a year," replied, "George, if we go into the fight tomorrow I will be killed." Alexander was 26 years old and a farmer who had signed the company's muster sheet immediately after Smith. His bunkmate admitted feeling the same premonition, but "prayed to God and promised him that if spared I would serve Him the rest of my life."[8]

Others in the regiment had similar forebodings. Men took the opportunity the evening before the attack to write letters home. They handed the letters, along with other personal effects, such as photographs and rings, to the unit's cooks, who would send the articles to the families if the soldier fell in battle.[9]

Union artillery bombarded the Confederate strongpoints throughout the night of May 21 and into the daylight hours of the 22nd. Stevenson, meanwhile, moved his troops up to within 200 yards of the Rebel lines into a sheltered ravine. "We drove in the enemy outposts at an early hour then held an advanced position until the storming column was formed," recalled Smith.[10]

Most assaults during the period of the Civil War used linear tactics, meaning the assaulting troops lined up in ranks, like a wave designed to roll over opposing lines, and move forward. For this attack, however, Stevenson formed his men into columns, deeper than they were wide. He placed the 7th Missouri and 81st Illinois on the right of the formation, with the 8th Illinois and 32nd Ohio on the left. Josiah and the men of the 17th were deployed in front as skirmishers, moving and shooting at the Confederate line to force the defenders to keep their heads down and make it more difficult for the gray artillerymen to work their pieces against the attacking columns. Major Frank Peats commanded the 17th in the absence of Lt. Col. Smith, who had been

---

7 Woodworth, *Nothing but Victory*, 407-412; Drawings of the defenses in the collection of Vicksburg National Military Park.

8 Smith, *History of the 17th Illinois*.

9 Hicken, *Illinois in the Civil War*, 169.

10 OR 24, pt. 1, 719-720; Smith, *History of the 17th Illinois*.

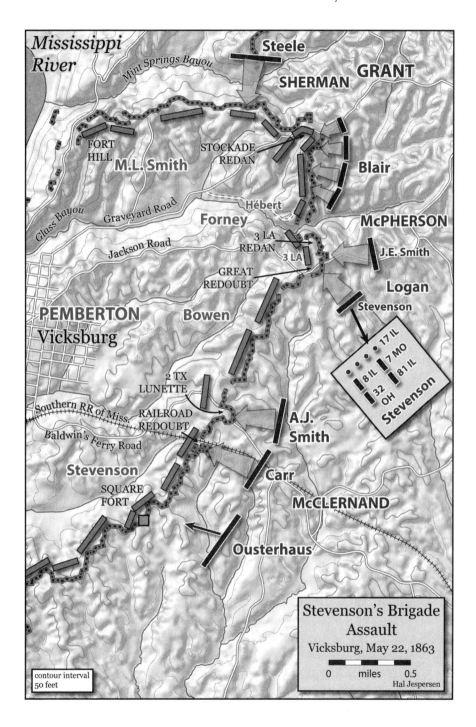

**Stevenson's Brigade
Assault**
Vicksburg, May 22, 1863

0   miles   0.5
Hal Jespersen

contour interval
50 feet

commanding the regiment in the absence of Col. Addison Norton, who was in a Louisiana hospital. About 30 or 40 of Stevenson's men carried ladders to climb the steep earthen walls and get into the works.[11]

For one of the first times in military history, members of the attacking forces synchronized their watches so all the assaulting columns would move at the same time. The Union assault began promptly at 10:00 a.m. In Stevenson's brigade, the 17th made the initial advance, followed by the other four regiments. Josiah commanded the right wing of the thinly deployed regiment. William McClanahan of Josiah's Company F, now promoted to lieutenant, led skirmishers in front of the 17th's advance. In his report, The enemy, wrote Stevenson, opened with their artillery, "literally sweeping down officers and men." Iron and lead struck down six successive color bearers of the flag of the 7th Missouri.[12]

Making matters worse, the fire from some of the Union guns supporting the assault fell short of the enemy lines. Acting Sgt. Frank Smith of the 17th's Company C claimed that shrapnel from Capt. Samuel DeGolyer's battery of Michigan artillery wounded several men in the attacking column. "You can imagine that our yells back at DeGollyer's were not honey sweet," he added.[13]

The columns stormed forward to the base of the Rebel fortification. The Irish of the 7th Missouri planted their green flag with its Irish harp in the ditch. Above them fluttered a nearly identical flag, held by Confederates of Irish heritage also from Missouri. One of the Confederates opposing Stevenson's brigade was Capt. David Todd, President Lincoln's brother-in-law.[14]

Stevenson's men reached the base of the Rebel fortifications only to discover, to their horror, that the ladders carried forward to climb into the fort were too short. Unable to scale the steep and tall walls the attackers huddled at the base of the Great Redoubt, understandably reluctant to retreat across the open field that was now being inundated with artillery iron and small arms fire. Some found that huddling against the walls of the fortification kept them out of the line of fire—until Confederates inside the fort began rolling hand grenades into the ditch, where they exploded among the throngs crowded against the

11 Ed Bearss, "The Fall of Vicksburg," in *Civil War Times Magazine* (July 2006), 25.

12 Monmouth College, *Oracle*, 39-40; OR 24, PT. 1, 719-720.

13 Letter from Frank Smith in the possession of the Vicksburg National Military Park.

14 Woodworth, *Nothing but Victory*, 414.

walls. Finally, with the 17th Illinois providing cover, the survivors of Stevenson's brigade withdrew across the killing fields to where they had begun the attack. Both George Smith and William Alexander survived the attack.[15]

At 3:00 p.m., while the men of the 17th were being relieved by other troops, a Confederate bullet fulfilled Alexander's deadly premonition. According to Josiah, Alexander "was shot in the left lower jaw—the ball entering in the upper lip and passing out under the ear. He was carried off the field alive but died immediately." Smith recalled that he missed the call to retire and was not present for roll call. The man sent to relieve him was killed immediately.[16]

General Stevenson commended the regiment for "services rendered in protecting their comrades in the advance and . . . the hot fire poured into the enemy as the column retired." The men had shed much blood for no gain. Four of the brigade's officers and 30 enlisted men were killed, along with 15 officers and 230 enlisted men wounded, all in about half an hour. "Oh it is a miserable business," lamented a member of the 8th Illinois. "It is an almost if not entirely human impossibility to take this fort from this side." Three men of the 17th, including Alexander, were killed, and 22 others wounded. There is no reliable record on the number of Confederate casualties.[17]

Sergeant Duncan's log entry of the next day was as mournful as it was brief. "Last night berried Will Alexander and Thos. Nelson." Thomas Nelson, a recruit who had joined the unit in October 1862, was a native of Nova Scotia. He was married and had enlisted at the age of 28, but missed the fights at Fredericktown, Donelson, and Shiloh. The Vicksburg assaults were his first real battles. Nelson was shot through the left temple and died instantly. "He rested his head on his knee and remained in this position," observed Josiah.[18]

15 Shea and Winschel, *Vicksburg is the Key*, 150; Woodworth, *Nothing but Victory*, 439; *OR* 24, pt. 1, 719-720.

16 Letter from Josiah Moore in the June 12, 1863 edition of the *Monmouth Atlas*; Smith, *History of the 17th*.

17 Woodworth, *Nothing but Victory*, 414; Bearss, *The Vicksburg Campaign: Unvexed to the Sea*, 822. Other attacks were made all along the lines, but none succeeded. Union casualties were reported as 502 killed, 2,550 wounded, and nearly 150 missing, roughly equally divided between the three corps. Rebel losses are unknown, but probably did not exceed 500. Peats, who had led regiment in the failed effort, told his wife that he blamed the failure on the "want of cooperation among the general officers." In that same letter, Peats noted that Smith returned to command that same day. Letter from Frank Peats to wife, May 28th, 1863

18 Illinois Civil War Muster and Descriptive Rolls Database; Letter from Josiah Moore in the June 12, 1863 edition of the Monmouth *Atlas*.

The 77th Illinois, absent Andie Lindsay, attacked another fortification on May 22 called the Railroad Redoubt. The regiment was part of the line commanded by General McClernand, under whom the 17th had fought at Fort Donelson and Shiloh. Although the Union troops pushed near the top of the redoubt, they were ultimately as unsuccessful as the rest of the Federal assaults. The 77th Illinois lost heavily, with 130 men were killed or wounded.[19]

The assault effectively marked the end of McClernand's time with the Army of the Tennessee. During the battle, McClernand claimed he was on the verge of a breakthrough and requested reinforcements. He mismanaged the additional troops sent to him, and afterward made disparaging remarks about other troops and officers not under his command. The targets of his vitriol included Grant himself. McClernand's behavior added to the bad blood that already existed between he and his commander, and Grant took the opportunity to relieve him on June 18.[20]

Frank Peats had served under McClernand at Shiloh and had an equally bad opinion of that officer. McClernand, Peats wrote his wife, was "the most intensely selfish man I ever knew." He added that he "has a violent temper which he does not try to control, vindictive and overbearing makes him insolent to his peers and abusive to his subordinates." Peats also expressed concern for McClernand's young wife, who had accompanied her husband throughout the campaign, complete with baggage and servants. "I am afraid under present circumstances his retirement will not prove conducive to domestic felicity," he added, "for he is very irritable and his connubial abilities are not very fascinating."[21]

After the May 22 assault, Grant had no choice but to resort to siege operations in an effort to "outcamp the enemy." He had Vicksburg surrounded and would now see how long the Rebel garrison could last. The men of the Army of the Tennessee "went to work on the defenses and approaches with a will," wrote Grant. The boys from Warren County, Illinois, dug into the earth around Warren County, Mississippi, as a deadly game of sharpshooting replaced frontal assaults. There was no respite for men on either side, either from enemy lead and iron or from the unrelenting Mississippi weather. The

---

19 Hicken, *Illinois in the Civil War*, 172-174.

20 Woodworth, *Nothing but Victory*, 431-433.

21 Simpson, *Ulysses S. Grant*, 189; Letter from Frank Peats to his wife, June 24, 1863.

men of the 17th Illinois would be without any kind of shelter until the city surrendered.[22]

A few days after the fight of May 22, Union troops spotted a white flag over the Confederate parapet. Hopes soared that the end was at hand. Unfortunately for the tired, dirty, and hungry men on both sides, it was not to be. Pemberton's men could simply no longer stand the stench of the unburied Union soldiers who had perished in the fighting and still lay unburied beneath the walls where they fell. Pemberton wanted a truce to bury the bodies.[23]

---

22 Grant, *Personal Memoirs*, 532; Pension papers of Robert Duncan, NARA.

23 Shea and Winschel, *Vicksburg is the Key*, 151. Grant was still concerned with the Confederate Army of Relief forming around Jackson and Canton in his rear under General Johnston. A pair of divisions were allocated to cover his rear and protect against any surprise attack. As the siege dragged on, Grant was reinforced by the IX Corps under Maj. Gen. John Parke, which was assigned to also keep Johnston at bay. Sherman was put in overall command of the effort, and Brig. Gen. Frederick Steele replaced him at the head of XV Corps. Johnston delayed moving too long and complained that he did not have enough men to make a difference. After some preliminary movements in late June, too late to do anything of substance, Pemberton surrendered on July 4. For more information, see Jim Woodrick, *Civil War Siege of Jackson, Mississippi* (Arcadia Publishing, 2016).

CHAPTER 14

The Death of a "Worthy Son"

 May 30, Josiah wrote to Jennie for the first time since the bloody failed May 22 assault.

Josiah to Jennie

Vicksburg Battle Field
May 30th 1863
Miss Jennie E. Lindsay

Esteemed Lady,

This is such a lovely moonlight evening Oh how I do wish that some one could help me enjoy its balmy southron breezes! But you say that your evening looked so peaceful. what a contrast I believe I would prefer the wish of dear Jennie—a cooler climate and warmer hearts would be much more desirable.

Well my dear friend you last dear letter of the 5th inst. came to hand as we were just leaving Grand Gulf. I believe I wrote then that you might expect my next from Jackson Miss. But as you see it is Vicksburg and ere this I presume you have heard of the muss that we have raised out here in the woods. well the row is still progressing and as yet I see little signs of settlement.

We have had some hard fighting but as yet have only succeeded in driving the rebels within their works. this is the 12th day of the battle, however for several days the rebels have not dared to show themselves not even to fire a cannon, once and awhile a sharp shooter creeps up and fires at our men but this is all they dare venture. some of our men hold positions within 50 yds of the rebel forts but their works are so strong that it is hardly possible to scale them. our forces made a charge on the 22nd inst but only a few reached the inside and they had to retire immediately. my Co. lost 2 killed & 4 or 5 wounded during the charge, I believe it was the hottest fire that we have ever met. during rest of our time since our arrival we have been engaged as skirmishers and have not lost very heavily.

One of our best men was killed on the 28th his name was John B. Stephenson.[1] For the past year he has been acting as assistant Srgn. he was one of my Co. and none will be more sadly lamented. he was beloved by all. but death loves a shining mark. Oh what an unspeakable weight of guilt must forever rest on the vile perpetrators of this rebellion. eternity will be too short for their punishment. the eternal fires of perdition must strive in vain to effect the calous heart of that incarnate fiend so lost for time and eternity as to plunge a nation such as ours into such a cruel civil war. but justice cannot sleep forever. and I hope that when this strife is over our nation may come forth as gold from the refiners furnace—true the fire is strong enough, and I believe that when we are properly chastised and return in humility to acknowledge that God whose anger we have provoked, that all will be well. then and not till then will we enjoy peace and all its blessings. But dear friend you will please excuse this sermonizing. At present I can give but few items that would interest you. I presume you've heard of the more than probable death of Col. Cromwell.[2] that will be sad news to his family. I saw him a few days before.

I think our hardest fighting is over here, I think the rebels will not dare to come out and must surrender when their provision gives out. we just lie round now and if one shows himself shoot at him. strange past time! but such is war.

1   Sergeant John Stephenson was the Monmouth physician who enlisted during the patriotic fervor of April 1861. The manner of his death makes it clear just how lethal sharpshooting was along the lines.

2   Col. John Cromwell commanded the 47th Illinois and was killed at the Battle of Jackson on May 16. www.ilsos.gov/genealogy/CivilWarController.

Well you have at last seen that dear "soldier boy" I am so glad, for I know how happy it would make dear Jennie. I almost envy him. but it is sweet to know that another is "kindly remembered."

But I fear I am imposing too much on good nature so my dearest friend I must bid you adieu for a short time, for I am looking every day for one of those dear little messengers that serve so much to cheer the heart. with implicit trust in that God who ever careth for us. I bid thee a kind good night. tho cannons round me roar may dearest Jennie sweetly sleep, a kiss.

J. Moore

P.S. My next shall be from Vicksburg. you'l see goodnight. I write this on a cartridge box and under the shade of some bushes I have not been in a tent for over a month. Goodbye J.M.

Sharpshooting continued to exact a heavy toll, and Stephenson's death provoked in Josiah not just tremendous sorrow but an intense anger at those he believed were "the vile perpetrators of this rebellion." This letter marked what might be labeled the "high-water mark" of Josiah's enmity against the South, or at least against those he blamed for the conflict.

Just as he had after the death of Clark Kendall at Fort Donelson, Josiah undertook the difficult task of breaking the news to the Stephenson family back home in Illinois. Josiah wrote his letter on May 29 (the day before his missive to Jennie) and mailed it to Stephenson's father. It was a long letter as far as such things go, for Josiah had a lot to say. The letter was subsequently published in the June 12, 1863, edition of the Monmouth *Atlas*:

Vicksburg Battle-Field
May 29th, 1863
Samuel Stephenson, Esq.

Dear Friend:

With feelings of the deepest sorrow I now seat myself on the battlefield to make a sad record—the death of your most worthy son John B. Stephenson. He was killed yesterday, at 2:30 pm by a rifle ball passing through the head, close behind the ear. He died instantly.

Our regiment occupied the position of sharp-shooters, and was posted from within 150 to 200 yards from the rebel fort. The Dr. was the only regimental physician present, the others being absent, two on detail and the third sick. As at all other times, the Doctor was close by where his duty called him.

During the day, the rebel gunners became very troublesome, and several of our cannon opened on them. While this fire was progressing, the Dr. and another left the Hospital Station—ten rods in rear of the regiment—and went to the front to see the effect of our guns on the rebel works, and after remaining here awhile was about to leave, but just as he turned round the death-blow came. He never spoke. He was not with our company when killed—he was in the quarters of company C.

The news came to me immediately, and Mc[3] and I went and found him and carried him back. We had a coffin made, and I procured a bushel of salt to preserve the body; so that I think he will be easily removed. We buried him on the field a short distance below where he fell, and close along side of two others of our lamented comrades, William Alexander and Thomas M. Nelson who were killed on the 22nd inst. The board that marks the grave is the lid of a cartridge box and marked "Dr. John B. Stephenson, Co F, 17th Ill. Vol. Infantry. May 28th 1863."

After the fall of Vicksburg, I think there will be no trouble in moving the body, should you wish it; but at present it would be very difficult to do anything. I think, however, that with the blessing of God on the means at our disposal, the fall of the infernal city is not far distant. Our army is in good spirits, and though this is the eleventh day of the battle, yet the troops seem more buoyant than ever. But I need not detain you, the news is already too sad. May the God of grace prepare [next sentence is illegible] . . . *dence from an All Wise Jehovah. No news ever came to me so unexpected,* [next sentence is illegible] . . . *than the Dr. I do not say half. To know him was to love him. He was extremely kind and obliging, and ever attentive to duty; and the regiment had the highest confidence in his professional ability. He is mourned by all yet we trust that our loss is his unspeakable gain.*

3   "Mc" is Lt. William McClanahan of Josiah's Company F.

I have taken charge of some of his personal items, and shall keep them subject to your request, or until I get an opportunity to send them home.

You have our highest sympathies. May a kind heavenly parent give us all grace to prepare to meet where all tears shall be wiped away.

The rebels have only fired a few shots from their cannon in 4 or 5 days. I think they are afraid to bring their guns to bear on our line of artillery. Their forts, though formidable, are badly breached but I think the rebels will submit to a siege before surrendering.

A most terrible cannonading has been kept up mostly all day by our guns. I do not yet know of a single reply from the rebel guns except sharp shooters, who have at this point killed and wounded one: 1st Capt. Rodgers, commander of McAllister's Battery, and 2nd, De Goylin, Commander of a Michigan Battery.[4]

Adieu, J. Moore

There is an interesting difference between this letter and the one Josiah sent to the Kendall family. His prior letter focused almost solely on the sympathy he felt for them. This one, however, explains the military progress of the campaign against the city. Perhaps Josiah was seeking to assure the Stephensons that their son's death was not in vain, and they could expect military success and the restoration of the Union. Josiah might have intended his words as a rebuttal to the Peace Democrats, for whom he and many others in the 17th expressed such strong distaste. As he did for the Kendall family, Josiah also expressed his strong belief in heavenly redemption.

The same edition of the *Atlas* printed a letter written to Maggie, Stephenson's sister, from Lt. William McClanahan. McClanahan had cut a lock of Stephenson's hair and removed a ring from his finger, which he gave to Josiah to send home to the family.

Some succor, at least, came the 17th's way. On May 27, Addison Norton, the regiment's colonel who was still at Young's Point suffering from a disability, wrote Frank Peats that he had purchased a barrel of whiskey for the men, which "if properly used will be beneficial." Norton sent the letter via Lt. Col. Smith, who had recently returned to lead the unit in Norton's absence. Norton hinted

---

4   "DeGoylin" is Capt. Samuel DeGolyer whose guns had mistakenly injured some of the men of the 17th Illinois during the May 22 assault.

Henry H. Penniman served as assistant surgeon of the 17th Illinois. He signed the disability certificate and discharge for James Earp after the latter's injury at Fredericktown. Penniman would go on to become the surgeon for the 5th U.S. Colored Artillery. The image is inscribed on the back: "To Capt. Josiah Moore with the regards of the original."

Author

in the letter that Smith was somehow lacking as a commander. He also encouraged Peats to convince the brigade commander, John Stevenson, to have Smith detailed "as picket officer or detached in some way until after the final result." Norton would resign his commission on July 9, 1863.[5]

The spartan living conditions endured by the men did not mean a shortage of alcohol. "Drinking is abundant in the army," Henry Penniman, the assistant surgeon of the 17th Illinois, wrote to his wife in June, "though this is luxury denied at these situations except to officers." He continued: "By liquor, time is killed, spirits supported, care dismissed, and thought drowned. Indeed I had no idea how dreadful are morals in the army. I will explain these matters to you. Every other man will get drunk if he can and every officer is frequently drunk. General John A. L____is stupidly drunk, report says, every night; and officers follow suit generally."[6]

---

5   Letter from Addison Norton to Frank Peats, May 27, 1863.

6   Division commander John Alexander Logan, like McClernand, was a Democratic political general from Illinois. He had fought in the Mexican War and served in both the state legislature and the U.S. Congress and risen through the ranks from colonel of the 31st Illinois to his present position. One soldier described Logan as having "black oily hair, and a long drooping black oily mustache." "Don't he look savage," observed a captured Rebel when he saw Logan. As Penniman noted, the general also enjoyed his drink. During the Vicksburg siege, he was

Penniman's interesting letter also noted Stephenson's passing —"We had a fine young man killed out of our hospital mess"— but he had a dim view of most of the men of the regiment, and observed the negative effect Stephenson's death had on his comrades. "[I]t is dreadful to see how much worse a mess or squad will become after one of their number is killed," he explained. "The balance, some nine or ten, are more profane, more trifling, more reckless, more everything that indicates a worse condition of heart than before."

Penniman had an aversion to the common soldier even before he entered the service. "I have never mingled, you know, with the lower dregs of society, and, every day, the associations are painful," he confessed to his wife. "It is dreadful and disgusting. Profanity is universal—often, and generally common oaths—sometimes dreadfully severe and heaven-daring in its tone." He tried to set a good example, he explained, but such actions were like "going among swine with pearls, and showing the brutes clean garments." He ended up just making "an occasional remark" and setting a "strict example in all I say and do." The doctor also complained that all the men wanted to do was "to play cards, to drink, to eat, to run around, to do anything that will hinder the serious thoughts of eternity." He tried to converse with two people in the regiment "reputed to be religious," he added. "One is not agreeable, and the other I tried in vain to draw into some very general religious talk [but] it was no use."[7]

It is possible that Josiah was one of the two "reputed to be religious." If so, Josiah may have rejected Penniman's attempts to socialize because he found his disdain for the men of the 17th Illinois simply insufferable.

Jennie to Josiah

Peoria May 26th 1863
My Dear Friend,

Your most welcome letter of the 7th inst arrived in due time. I was very glad to hear from the dear absent one. The long looked for General has at last arrived. He

---

once observed sitting in only his hat, shirt, and boots, playing a violin while some freed slaves danced around him, all of them downing copious amounts of whiskey. He was also a capable combat officer. Boatner, *Civil War Dictionary*, 486-487; Hughes, *The Battle of Belmont: Grant Strikes South*, 18; Hicken, *Illinois in the Civil War*, 10, 157.

7 Blaisdell, *Civil War Letters*, 128-130.

came on last Wednesday. We find him very pleasant and interesting so much so that I find my self wishing every day that some one were present to help share the pleasure of hearing so many good men express their thoughts.

Andie is still with us he has been home just three weeks he intended returning a week ago but Capt Wilson came home just the day before he intended starting, and said he need not go back for a month if he did not feel better. But Andie has improved so much he doesnt look like the same boy he did when he came home. father said he believe he commenced improving the day after he left the Regt. poor boy the thought of getting home was enough to make him feel better. he often says he can hardly realize that he is at home it seemed to him while he was sick that he would never get home. I believe you met Capt Wilson while you were in Peoria last winter. he has given Andie a place and says he will take good care of him. he talked of leaving on next Friday but I hope he will not go until next week. We want to keep Andie as long as we can it is so pleasant to have him home. I think it most time our other "soldier boy" were coming home, dont you think so.

Good Morning, May 27th

Well dearest friend it seems as though this epistle were destined to linger with me. I have made several attempts to send it forth. yet I am always interrupted. You will have to blame this General Assembly for the delay. We have so many friends here and you know they must be entertained and it is very pleasant to do so yet it occupies all the time. Oh how I do wish you could be here. You know we love to have the dear one share all our pleasure. at least I do, and I believe it right to judge others by our selves.

I received your missive of the 14th ult, on last evening. I can assure you dear friend it gave joy unto the heart that misses thee so sadly. I feel so anxious about the loved one now amid the scene of strife and bloodshed. Yet I trust God will preserve him in the hour of danger.

We have had great rejoicing over the late victories in the West. We feel proud of our brave western soldiers truly you have done nobly. The last report we had was that Grant had taken Vicksburg. I hope it may be true.

Capt Wilson was out on last evening he intends leaving on next Monday for Memphis where he has been ordered to report. he does not know where he will be *sent to from there, so Andie wil have to go yet he will not have so hard a time as he had while with the Regt. Capt says he will give him an easy place.*

I've not yet received those "little secesh articles" you speak of probably they prefer not to come North. Well dearest friend I know you are tired but then if you will stay away you will have to be afflicted by such poor little scribbles. I will send thee my dear friend a good morning kiss.

Write soon

Jennie

The report Jennie heard about Grant taking Vicksburg was premature, although the Army of the Tennessee was daily tightening its grip on the city. Throughout the month of June its guns pounded the trapped Rebels. By the end of the siege, the fleet's gunboats had fired 22,000 shells into Vicksburg. The artillery shells killed both civilians and soldiers alike. Although the number of civilian casualties is unknown, one estimate is that the prolonged shelling killed 20 women. To escape the projectiles, citizens dug more than 500 caves into the sides of Vicksburg's hills. One Vicksburg resident described her new abode as having three rooms and a six-foot entrance covered by a cloth "door." On one side of the entry "foyer" was a bedroom, with a dressing room on the other. The only room in which people could stand upright was the entrance room.

In addition to enduring the shelling, the city suffered from a lack of food. Hungry soldiers and civilians were eventually forced to consume dogs, cats, horses, and even rats. At least two babies were born during the siege. Someone maintained a sense of ironic humor and named one of the children William Siege Green.[8]

Meanwhile, Gen. Joseph Johnston and his Confederate Army of Relief lurked somewhere east of Vicksburg around Jackson. Johnston, however, showed little inclination about launching an offensive. As a precaution, however, Grant had Sherman create an exterior line to guard against any assault from the east. Even though the combined forces of his army and Pemberton's

---

8 Faust, *This Republic of Suffering*, 137; Marten, *Civil War America*, 46; Winschel, *Triumph and Defeat*, 154.

outnumbered Grant's in May, Johnston could never seem to find the right circumstances to initiate an attack.[9]

The siege dragged on into June. Both sides lacked suitable shelter and remained largely exposed to the elements. The 47 days the Union soldiers spent without tents left a lasting impression on them. "The sun was scorching hot— we shall never forget the fearful hard rains which we had to expose ourselves in," Sergeant Duncan wrote. The lack of clean water also posed a real problem. "The water does not agree with the men," one soldier complained. "A good many of them are complaining with the diareah." "We are camped under a hill side to shelter us from the Rebel shells,' wrote an Iowa soldier in McPherson's corps. "the discharge of small arms is almost constant along the line."[10]

Grant's men dug zig-zag trenches that reached in places to within just five yards of the Confederate fortifications by the end of June. In many places the two sides were so close that the "dirt from the two trenches blended together," observed one of the trapped Rebels. According to one estimate, Grant's army dug more than 60,000 linear feet of excavations. The digging also included attempts to tunnel under the Confederate earthworks, pack the tunnels with gunpowder, and blow up the strong points along with their defenders. On June 25, the first attempt to do this ended with more loss of life, but no change in the defensive positions.[11]

Sometimes the digging itself was as lethal as enemy bullets. Henry Pressly of Josiah's company died on June 4 when the sides of the trench in which he was digging collapsed. Pressly, an Ohio-born accountant, was the son of William Pressly, a leading Monmouth citizen who had founded the Warren County Library and funded a professorship at the college. Henry was 23 years old at the time of his enlistment in 1861. Sergeant Duncan claimed more would have died in the accident had they not been out of the trench getting a whiskey ration—perhaps from the barrel recently sent by Addison Norton. Pressly, who abstained from alcohol, had remained behind to keep digging. According to Duncan, Pressly was buried next to Stephenson and the men killed in the May

9   Shea and Winschel, *Vicksburg is the Key*, 167-169.

10 Pension Records of Robert Duncan, NARA; Brooks Simpson, *The Civil War: The Third Year*, 239, 265.

11 Giambrone, *Illustrated Guide to the Vicksburg Campaign*, 86; Shea and Winschel, *Vicksburg is the Key*, 158-160.

22 assault, "each buried in coffins and salt thron about them in order to preserve the remains."[12]

Josiah to Jennie

Vicksburg Battle Field Miss
June 10th 1863 11 A.M.

My Dear Jennie,

Another moment of sweet delight permits the "soldier boy" to commune with his dear friend. How joyous a world of "sunshine and shade"! Yes, dear Jennie, as the deep gloom of midnight seems only to lend enchantment to the starry world, so through all the smoke and carnage of battle my dear friend ever appears the guiding star—the same dear lovely one—ever present from the sweet recollections of a happy past when through evenings of sweet associations we were wont to live as tho' the trials, troubles and sorrows of a sinful world were only fancied or imaginary—Ah cruel indeed would seem the hand that would break such a spell, tho it is scarcely meet that the subjects of King Immanuel should be found complaining, but I trust that the darker night is far spent and the dawn of the brighter day is near at hand.

Your kind and welcome remembrance of the "26th & 27th" ult came to hand on yesterday. I was pleased to hear of your good health and your being so much delighted with the opportunity of entertaining such good company as the "General"—indeed I would not think strange—such notable personages are generaly very fascinating, at first I was almost disposed to feel—Oh not jealous a little envious but you can imagine how displeased I was with myself when on reading a little farther I learned how anxious dear Jennie was to have the "absent one" to share the pleasures and advantages of such an occasion, so now my dear friend you will please excuse my little selfishness I only plead as a palliation the term "absent one" were this removed then I should not complain. aint that fair?

---

12 Duncan, company log; Monmouth College, *Oracle*, 60.

I hope dear friend that you may have a very pleasant and interesting time during the Synodical Session. I used to enjoy such occasions very much, but if I remember right the ladies used to have quite busy work at such times. am I mistaken? and hence I have often thought that if the ladies did have any enjoyment on such occasions it must consist in making others happy, but tho I would not have my dear Jennie "weary in well doing" yet she must not work too hard else some one else will not be pleased.

Well dear lady I am much obliged to you for your congratulations of our Western troops on their successes, for they are almost without a parallel in the history of war. I wish, however, I could join you in your rejoicings over the fall of the ill fated Vicksburg but I fear that news was rather premature I write this within 400 yds of the rebel works and if I raise my head a little too high a rebel bullet immediately tunes its harp, so that I think there must be a mistake, but I trust and believe that with the blessing of God on the means now at our disposal the fall of the city may be put at not distant date.

Our Regt, was on duty day before yesterday and as on such occasions we take position within from 50 to 150 yds of the rebel forts, I proposed a conference with the rebels so after night a little I met two of them half way and shook hands and had quite a chat. Strange work aint it? after shooting at each other all day—they belonged to the 38th Miss., one a native the other a Norwegian.[13] I believe I could have easily persuaded the latter to leave his "chivalrous friends" but the former kept a close watch. They talked quite hopeful of their ultimate success, tho they admitted that their rations were scarce we only talked over general news, but we parted as we had met, as tho we were friends, tho we were again firing at each other in less than half an hour.

13 The 38th Mississippi Infantry was part of Brig. Gen. Louis Hébert's brigade, Maj. Gen. John Forney's division, Lt. Gen. John C. Pemberton's Army of Mississippi. The 38th Mississippi began its service with the Confederate army in 1862, but had yet to leave its home state, having fought in the battles of Corinth and Iuka before being sent to Vicksburg in late 1862. Although none of the companies were recruited in Warren County (where Vicksburg was located), many were from nearby counties. During the assaults of May 19 and 22, the 38th Mississippi was positioned closer to the river (between the 3rd Louisiana Redan and the Stockade Redan), so it did not participate in the fight that bloodied the 17th Illinois. Sometime in early June, the 38th Mississippi was shifted opposite Josiah's regiment. Website of the Mississippi Sons of Confederate Veterans: www.mississippiscv.org/MS_Units/38th_MS_Inf.htm.

I went within about 20 yds, last night, of the rebel fort in our front our men are digging a causeway and through it we can advance almost close to the works without being noticed. to say the least the rebels are very closely hemmed in and they scarcely venture to show themselves any more. our artillery now plays on them from every point of our lines and I wonder how anything can live under the fierceness of the fire. they use but little artillery.

Since I last wrote I believe I had but one accident in my Co.—Henry K. Pressly he was killed on the 4th inst by the caving of a bank, while helping to excavate a pit for a Magazine over a tun of earth fell on him, poor fellow it was sad news for us all and no less so will it be for his folks at Monmouth. he was an only son. he was a noble soldier and most exemplary christian. thus the entire 4 killed from my Co since our arrival here were among the very best men, men whose moral worth made them dear to all who knew them. sad indeed is such a sacrifice but not less sad than the object is great and it is to be hoped that after establishing for the second time our liberties, American freemen may rule in the fear of God.

Well dear lady it seems strange that that little article has not yet come to hand. I expressed it from Millikens Bend May 1st and addressed the box to "T.L. Currie Esq. Peoria Ills," if the agent was honest I cant see where the mistake could occur. the box contained a little basket for you and a fan for Mrs Currie. their value was not of so much importance as the curiosity. perhaps Mr. Currie could look them up yet. I was so spited that I did not have them at the boat to send them with Andie when he was going home. that was my intention but I missed it.

Now my dearest friend I presume you are glad that this paper has given out so I shall not tease you longer. this is to pay you for your last two days letter. but I don't care if you write every day. I would rather you would write. Hoping that this may find thee in good health as it leaves me "I will now give thee my dear friend a good evening (kiss)."

J. Moore
P.S. When you say "I think it most time our other "soldier boy" were coming home" you spoke the sentiments of another but at present dear Jennie there seems to little prospect of such a bright day tho' I hope always for the best of course that is to get to see you know goodbye. J.M.

Josiah's account about meeting men of the 38th Mississippi between the lines is well corroborated. Another member of the 17th, Lt. George Buck of Company K, was an eyewitness and wrote about the same encounter and mentioned Josiah by name: "Capt Moore of Co. F met one half way the last day we were out sharpshooting in the night and had a long talk with him. They do not get beef anymore and their mills are burned and so they live on parched corn and molasses." Such interactions tended to ease the hatred between the sides. One Union soldier who had the chance to meet his counterpart in the trenches in Vicksburg wrote that "if the settlement of this war was left to the Enlisted men of both sides we would soon go home."[14]

One soldier of the 38th Mississippi that Josiah might have met between the lines was Capt. John Jones of Company D. Jones was 26 years old. A lawyer before the war, he graduated first in the class of 1856 from the University of Mississippi. Like Josiah, Jones wrote of these nocturnal social activities between the warring sides. "On the right of my regiment the Federal lines were about one hundred yards down the hill, and every night 'Johnnie' and 'Yank' would call a truce and meet between the lines in friendly intercourse, and thus the 38th and the 17th Illinois became good friends," he explained. "On parting the 'boys' would shake hands and caution each other, in all seriousness, to 'keep heads down after daylight,' when they would shoot at each other's heads with the eagerness of sportsmen." As on other parts of the battlefield where the Union lines burrowed close to the Rebel defenses, Jones wrote that eventually the 17th Illinois and the 38th Mississippi shared "a common breastwork."[15]

The fraternization in the evening did not end the deadly work the next day. Sometimes soldiers threw hand grenades into their opponents' trenches. "It had the appearance of a ball game," wrote the Rebel Jones, "only the players never caught the balls but fled from them." One day a Union soldier tossed a dead rattlesnake into the Confederate lines. More sympathetic soldiers would sometimes throw a cracker and politely inquire about their opponents' condition.[16]

14 Letter in the collection of the Old Court House Museum in Vicksburg; Mitchell, *Civil War Soldiers*, 37.

15 J. H. Jones, *The Rank and File at Vicksburg*, in Publications of the Mississippi Historical Society Vol VII ed by Franklin L. Riley (Oxford MS 1903), 23.

16 www.mississippiscv.org/MS_Units/38th_MS_Inf.htm.Ibid., 23.

Sharpshooting was another deadly game that Josiah mentioned in his June 10 letter. Dr. Penniman said he and the other two members of the regimental medical staff slept together in an eight-foot-square tent pitched under the side of a hill to avoid the threat of Rebel sharpshooters. However, Captain Jones of the 38th Mississippi claimed his men had the worst of it. Since the Confederate lines were higher than the Yankee lines, the Rebels were silhouetted against the sky whenever they rose above a parapet or poked a rifle through the firing ports, while the Federals were almost impossible to spot. Jones found out later that the Yankees would "get the range of one of our ports and lash the gun securely, so as to preserve it." The Federals would then wait patiently until "a hole was darkened by a Confederate head, the trigger was pulled and a bullet was put through it with unfailing accuracy." Jones quickly learned that using the gun ports "meant instant death." One Yankee sharpshooter killed Jones's brother, who was also a member of the 38th Mississippi. He was only 19 when he died.[17]

Others in the 38th Mississippi observed how their war had become rather mundane. "The same old routine of shelling and sharpshooters still continues," wrote William Faulk, a captain in the 38th. "We can do nothing during the day but eat and sleep, and but little to eat and that very common." Faulk recalled how Union sharpshooters claimed at least one man from the 38th on three consecutive days that June. Others followed throughout the month. Like many of his counterparts in blue, Faulk typically would give "thanks to Almighty God" for those days when there were no fatalities.[18]

A sharpshooter also claimed a unique participant in the battle when a Union bullet struck "Douglas," a camel kept by the 43rd Mississippi as a pet. There was no time for sentimentality, though. Once Douglas was dead, hungry Confederates carved him up for dinner.[19]

---

17 *Ibid.*, 24-25. *Biographical and Historical Memoirs of Mississippi,* Vol 1 (Chicago, IL1891), 1055.

18 Blog: Mississippians in the Confederate Army, Post dated June 14, 2012: www.mississipi confederates.wordpress.com.

19 Mobile *Daily Register,* March 23, 1860, pg. 1 col 7; Michael Sorenson, *A Most Curious Corps,* in *Military Images Magazine,* Vol. XXVII, Number 5, (March/April 2006), 16-17; J. W. Cook, *"Old Douglas":The Camel Burden Bearer,* in *Confederate Veteran Magazine,* Volume 11, 494. According to available evidence, Douglas the camel arrived in the country as part of an agricultural experiment, and his owner gave him to the 43rd Mississippi's colonel. In the late 1850s the U.S Army, under the direction of then-Secretary of War Jefferson Davis, established the United States Camel Corps, a short-lived experiment to use camels as pack animals southwestern desert. Douglas was not part of that endeavor.

The 17th Illinois was occupied on skirmish-line duty during all of those long and deadly weeks, withstanding almost constant sniping and the pounding of cannon from both sides. According to one source, by early June the 17th was responsible for having fired 100,000 rounds since the siege's beginning. Dr. Penniman described life for the men of the 17th during this period this way:

> Marching and countermarching, fighting, watching, and digging, with hot weather, dry and excessively dusty roads and fields, miserable camping—places on the ground, and great scarcity of water—and what we dig for is unhealthy, with very great excess of noxious chemical compounds—short diet, sleepless nights, dirty clothes, absence of tents, distance of wagons, and much confusion among these countless hills, all have aided in rendering the troops debilitated, and most decidedly uncomfortable.

According to Penniman, the regiment rotated into the front line every fourth day. The men would advance at 3:00 a.m. and relieve the previous regiment in the rifle pits. They would remain in that advanced position for 24 hours, until their relief arrived. During their time on the front line, the men had to endure the broiling Mississippi summer sun, poor water—and torments from other residents of the state. "The ground here is full of all sorts of insects," complained Penniman. This included the usual scourge of the soldier—body lice. Infestations of these tiny insects overcame all attempts by soldiers to defeat them. Even when the men kept themselves clean, close proximity to lice-ridden comrades allowed quick transmission from one body to another. At times, lice colonies became so large that they looked like "a blanket crawling over grass and tree trunks."[20]

Major Peats wrote to his wife that it would be "incredible were I to enumerate the number of narrow escapes from death that transpire us." Once, a 30-pound shell landed near Peats' tent and scattered his mess equipment but did "no further damage but to demoralise my cook." Penniman added that he had "three bullets scatter the dust near me, in quick succession, while walking over a part of one of our roads exposed to view of these rebels." And of course, he added almost unnecessarily, he had "dressed many a dreadful shell wound."[21]

---

20 Frank Peats letter to wife, May 28, 1863; Blaisdell, *Civil War Letters,* 122, 126-128; Adams, *Living Hell,* 47.

21 Frank Peats letter to wife, June 24, 1863; Blaisdell, *Civil War Letters,* 123, 127.

Jennie to Josiah

Peoria June 11 1863
Capt. Josiah Moore,
Dear Friend

Your dear epistle of the 30th inst came last evening just in time to chase away one of those blue spirits that seek to intrude its self upon our lonely hours. Yet how quickly it flies away at the approach of the joyous message from the dear one.

You dont know how lonesome we are now father and Andie both gone at the same time they left about a week ago. We have not heard from Andie yet, we are looking for a letter every day and are very anxious to hear as he was not so well when he left home. You dear soldier boys are the cause of a great deal of anxiety by the folks at home.

Well dear friend I do hope you may write your next letter from Vicksburg. I will begin to look for you home after that famous city has been captured, now please dont disappoint me. I'll promise not to go to Chicago if you will only come.

I hope that report about Col Cromwell will prove untrue. it is hard to know what to believe we hear so many such reports.

We are having very pleasant weather now though rather cool for June.

Peoria seems quite deserted since the General Assembly adjourned the members seemed to be very well pleased with their visit to peoria and well they may for they were treated almost as well as the 17th Regt men while here. (Well dearest friend what shall I write to interest thee. Oh that this might be laid aside for another pleasanter medium. Oh that I could speak with thee in place of sending such a miserable little scribble. I know none but a generous heart could pass the many imperfections by.)

Sen. Ross passed through Peoria several days ago on his way home.

We are looking anxiously and almost impatiently every day to hear of Vicksburg being in our possession the opinion seems to be that if we get Vicksburg the rebellion is at an end in the west. I hope it will be so, yet I've almost feared to look for such an event ever to be realized. Surely we deserve Gods wrath to be poured out upon us for as a nation we have gone sadly astray forgetting all the while to whom we should give honor and praise, in time of trouble God shows us how weak we are in our own strength He leads us to feel our utter dependence on him. Our only hope in the present is that God will come and save us, we know that all his promises are sure.

Well dearest friend I see you are weary. I will not impose on good nature any longer but will just bid thee a kind farewell for a short time hoping soon to hear glad tidings from the dear one who is kept in kindly rememberance by.

Jennie

P.S. Please write soon and often, dont forget that someone gets lonesome. JEL good bye.

Jennie to Josiah

Peoria June 22nd 1863

My Dearest Friend,

Twilight shadows have just faded into night, so the heart retires in gloomy sorrow to ponder over the dreary present. This pen hath not power to tell thee, dear "wanderer" how I long for thy presence this evening. Alone all alone with naught save this fair sheet for a companion. Silently it sympathizes. Its voice hath no music to greet the listening ear. Yet it grows precious as I think whose dear eyes are to gaze, upon it. Oh I envy thee little messenger.

Father Mother and brother Johnnie left home a week ago to make Maggie a visit. George's mother is spending the summer with them so Maggie couldent think of coming home, but mother must come and see her. So gone, she has and left poor me all alone, to keep house so any cares are many. I fear the weight of them will effect my health or perhaps mother will discover on her return that the house has suffered more than I. Well we look for them home next week and I'm sure they will be welcome. As Willie says to me last evening Oh Jennie isent it awful lonesome without Mother, yes our mother dear is sadly missed. I can realize what home is without a mother.

I'm going down to Mattie Cutlers tomorrow to [illegible] her to come and stay with me this week. I've not seen her for nearly a month, I like to have her visit me she is such good company.

Capt Ryan brought us a letter from Andie he had just arrived in Memphis when he wrote he says he is now getting well. I am so glad to hear of his health improving it is so hard to have the dear boy sick away from home. Capt Wilson may go to Vicksburg. I'm curious to know where they will be sent too. We are looking daily for a letter from Andie. he will know when he writes again.

You said my dear friend your next letter would be written from Vicksburg. how I wish I could receive a letter from you written from that City. Yet I trust you will not defer writing until you are inside its walls. I should almost despair hearing from thee. I wish you could write often if it is but alive. I feel so anxious about you. perhaps I'm asking to much yet I hope the pleasure of hearing from you will plead an excuse.

I fear dearest friend this letter will prove rather uninteresting. I have no news to write you so I tell you about this not very interesting self, but perhaps you will say a poor subject is better than none. Well I will no longer impose on good nature but will say unto thee dearest one fare the well. accept if thou will a good night kiss.

Jennie E. Lindsay
Please dont forget to write soon. J.E.L.

"We Enjoyed Our Fourth of July Hugely"

THE grinding, grueling, deadly siege carried on into July. Though Vicksburg had not yet fallen, it was only a matter of time. The Confederate troops and civilians clung to the hope that Joseph Johnston would rescue the beleaguered city, but their optimism waned with each passing day. "Joseph E. Johnston was our angel of deliverance in those days of siege, but alas! We were never even to touch the hem of his robe," observed one of Vicksburg's civilians.[1]

With no apparent hope of relief from Johnston, supplies dwindling, and starvation and disease rampant, virtually everyone in the city realized Vicksburg's days were numbered. General Pemberton briefly entertained the notion of breaking through the Union lines so his army could live to fight another day (something General Johnston had encouraged him to do), but the physical condition of his men and animals made any such effort impossible. As confirmation, Pemberton received a communication late in June signed by "Many Soldiers" that read, "If you can't feed us, you had better surrender us, horrible as the idea is, then suffer this noble army to disgrace themselves by desertion." By July 2, Pemberton made his decision. He informed his commanders that he intended to surrender the garrison on July 4, apparently

---

1 Giambrone, *Illustrated Guide to the Vicksburg Campaign*, 89.

hoping that patriotic feeling among their foes would lead to more favorable capitulation terms.[2]

On July 3, a mounted detail that included Brig. Gen. John Bowen, one of Pemberton's best generals, rode out of the city under a white flag. The party hoped to negotiate terms of surrender, but Grant's reply ended that hope. As he had at Fort Donelson, he demanded unconditional surrender. Bowen left unsatisfied. Sporadic firing occurred until 3:00 p.m., when another white flag appeared. This time Pemberton himself rode out to meet with Grant. Pemberton trotted on horseback out the Jackson Road, where Grant and his staff awaited. The commanders met just outside the lines of Logan's division, not far from the 17th Illinois, which gave the men of the regiment an excellent view of the historic proceedings. After a few curt and awkward exchanges between the two opposing generals, their respective staffs discussed details of the capitulation. Unable to reach a resolution that afternoon, Grant promised Pemberton his final terms would arrive that evening.[3]

In the end, Grant relented a bit and agreed to parole the Confederates in Vicksburg, meaning the soldiers would swear not to take up arms again until properly exchanged with Union prisoners. This would keep Grant from having to detail critically needed troops to guard the almost 30,000 men who would fall into his hands. Grant also hoped that many of the fatigued and dispirited enemy soldiers would simply return to their homes and stay there. To further pressure Pemberton, Grant instructed pickets posted near the enemy lines to let the Confederates know that Grant was offering them a chance to go home. This, he reasoned, would create a clamor within the Rebel army for Pemberton to accept the terms.[4]

Pemberton, of course, had no choice but to accept Grant's offer, and he did so after midnight on July 4. The official time of the surrender was set for 10:00 a.m. on the 87th anniversary of the day recognized as the start of American independence. That morning, numerous white flags went up over the Vicksburg defenses and Confederates "came pouring over their works and stacked their arms," recalled Frank Peats. Loud cheers reverberated along miles of elated Union lines. "We enjoyed our fourth of July hugely," was how Peats

---

2 Shea and Winschel, *Vicksburg is the Key*, 170-173.

3 Woodworth, *Nothing But Victory*, 449;. Shea and Winschel, *Vicksburg is the Key*, 173-178; Frank Peats letter to wife, July 5, 1863.

4 Shea and Winschel, *Vicksburg is the Key*, 177.

put it. Officially speaking, the people of Vicksburg would not celebrate the Fourth of July again until 1945, just as the Second World War was winding down.[5]

The long siege was over. Vicksburg belonged to the Yankees, and the Mississippi River was now flowed "unvexed to the sea." Pemberton surrendered nearly 30,000 men, the largest surrender of Americans in the nation's history. The Yankees also confiscated 172 pieces of artillery, 38,000 rounds of artillery ammunition, 58,000 pounds of black powder, 50,000 firearms, and 600,000 rounds of small arms ammunition.[6]

Josiah to Jennie

"Vicksburg" Miss.
July 6th 1863

My Dearest Friend,

As you see the storm has passed and through the mercy of my heavenly protector my life and health are still preserved for which I hope I am truly thankfull and it is now with feelings of the highest pleasure that I once again come as it were to speak with the "dear one" at home.

Ah! Yes, I almost hear her say in a half suspicious manner—near time to speak with one who is claimed to be so highly regarded as to be ever held in constant remembrance—so indeed my dear Jennie does it appear, but it is not because you were forgotten; neither because I intended to make good what I said when I intimated that my next should be from "Vicksburg" tho such items are not by any means disagreeable when coinciding without the sacrifice of interests equaly as clear, but my dear Jane Elizabeth was not written to, because for several days before the surrender we were kept almost constantly on duty, each of your last two dearest little messengers came to hand while I was in the rifle pits, and one of them

---

5 Peats letter to wife, July 5, 1863; Gordon Cotton and Jeff Giambrone, *Vicksburg and the War* (Gretna, MS 2004) 153.

6 Shea and Winschel, *Vicksburg is the Key*, 178. The surrender not only ended the suffering of Vicksburg's military garrison and the civilians but prevented more bloodshed among the Federals. If Pemberton refused the surrender terms, Grant was prepared to mount another frontal assault on the defenses on July 6. Woodworth, *Nothing But Victory*, 447.

I had to read by a very dim light—It dont do to make too much light near where rebels are, they shoot so—but such letters must be read, and I think none were ever more highly appreciated, especially your last of the 22nd ult—Oh Jennie I think it one of the sweetest letters you have ever written indeed it seems the very counterpart of its dear author and tho I knew it was cruel yet I almost felt pleased to learn that that dear lovely writer was "all alone"—a partner in adversity—for you know dear lady that we are sympathetic beings and then I believe that my dearest friend could never write such a letter unless under the inspiration of that bright genus which seems to draw nearer as a dark and "dreary world" recedes—I wish I could see you just now for I think you would be more lovely than ever—the star gets more beautiful as the darker hours gather round. it is now almost six months since the sad parting of two dear friends—that evening is still present—the time is past and it seems to have gone as a dream tho it seemed an age ahead. now then what do you think of the next ten months?[7] can they fly as swiftly? Oh I think I must have another furlough. Well I didn't think. perhaps my dear Jennie could get a "leave of absence". Wouldn't that do as well? I presume it would be only necessary to secede.

Well my dearest friend as you are aware this great City fell on the "fourth" hadn,t we a big 4th yes the greatest ever I had or was ever had in these United States. you no doubt have heard the particulars of the surrender. the rebel troops are here yet tho they are being paroled as quickly as possible. Genr,l Grant did not wish to incur the expense of sending so many North as he says to be sent back immediately exchanged and ready to fight, but he paroles them here each takes his parole and starts for home and many of them say that they are done fighting for the rebelion in the West and will never return also a great many of the rebel troops are from West of the Miss river and when they once get over there, farewell to Pemberton's great army only about 18,000 now but they lost very heavily scarcely a Regt. but had from 50 to 100 killed we had no idea that we killed so many—never did I see worse used up men—never did I think that I could feel sympathy for a rebel but when a poor fellow that has been living for several days on "mule meat" comes up like a child and begs for even a piece of "hard cracker" and when he gets it seems as thankful as tho he had received a treasure, I could not treat him coldly.

---

7   The ten months are a reference to to the length of time Josiah had left in his three-year enlistment..

We had 1000 lbs extra on hand and I just divided them among about 3 Regts. and I never saw more thankful men they have the privilege of the entire works and our boys and them associate very freely and our boys have treated them so that I believe one half are almost converted. they say they never dreamed of such treatment from an enemy and seem quite overcome, but my dearest friend hoping that you will forgive this delay on account of the scircumstances and that this may find you well. I by leave to return your good night kiss with interest wishing to borrow again.

as ever, goodnight J. Moore

P.S. I shall write again soon tho please dont forget that some one will be lonesome if his beloved friend remains silent very long a week is too long, now Jennie aint it? I think so, dont forget goodnight J.M

* * *

News of Vicksburg's fall led to wild celebrations throughout the North. Frank Peats' wife wrote about one in Rockford, Illinois. "A hundred cannon were fired," she reported, "large bonfires were made . . . the old torches of the wide awakes[8] were hunted up and the people formed a torch light procession Our streets sang with national airs." The exchange of letters between Peats and his wife was noteworthy for another reason. Bessie Peats had received Frank's letter of July 5 and responded by July 9—a clear demonstration of the Mississippi River's importance for rapid transport of all kinds of goods, including letters.

But before the book was closed on the siege, the 17th Illinois and the 38th Mississippi suffered tragic events on July 4. As the surrendering Confederates lined up in front of their fortifications, others gathered weapons that had been left in the trenches by the dead and wounded. One gun was still loaded with buckshot. The weapon accidentally discharged, and the projectiles struck Mississippian Samuel Miller. According to one of Miller's comrades, the unfortunate soldier "turned around and inquired who did it, and never again uttered a word. He began to fall, and I saw the blood beginning to flow from his

---

8 The Wide Awakes was an association of young Republican supporters who would march in oil cloths and carry torches. David Donald, *Lincoln* (New York, NY, 1995), 254.

mouth. We held him and soon life was extinct." "There was something peculiarly pathetic in such a death," wrote Captain Jones, "and it touched deeply the grim soldiers who witnessed it. To have survived the dangers and horrors of the siege to die thus, how pitiful?"[9]

As if to balance the ledger, a similar misfortune struck the 17th. A handful of soldiers, thinking they were committing a harmless prank, rolled an unexploded shell into a mess tent. Henry Brown of Company E was drinking coffee inside when the shell exploded. A large piece of shrapnel struck Brown in the back and mortally wounded him. "The hardest part to bear was that it was the 4th of July morning and only a couple of hours before the rebs marched out and stacked arms," wrote one of Brown's friends. "He saw the fight through without knowing it and died at the moment of victory."[10]

Pemberton later claimed that he surrendered, not for lack of food or ammunition, but because his men were suffering too greatly from exposure. Yet by the end of the siege, Confederate soldiers were receiving only a handful of rice and peas as a daily ration, so finding food for them now became paramount. Once more, the 17th Illinois helped out the 38th Mississippi. "On the night of the 3rd no rations were sent to us, and it was not until the evening of the 4th that General Grant supplied us," recounted Captain Jones. "A fast of forty eight hours in our already starved condition made us ravenous. Our friends of the 17th Illinois fraternized with the 38th and aided us greatly by many acts of kindness. They would go out to their sutler's tent with the greenbacks we had borrowed from their dead comrades and purchase food for us, and doubtless many a starving 'Reb' felt that his life was thus saved."[11]

Jones also told a story of a lieutenant, perhaps from the 17th, who offered to give him the "trash" in his haversack. For Jones, those two pounds of ginger snaps and butter crackers were "luxuries I had not seen in three years." The hungry Confederate quickly gobbled up the offering. "Could we meet, how gladly would I kill a fatted calf and prepare a feast for him, but I am sure it could never equal the luxury of the repast he afforded," admitted Jones.[12]

9   Cotton and Giambrone, *Vicksburg and the War*, 105; Jones, *The Rank and File at Vicksburg*, 30.

10 Phil Rayburn, "Three Galesburg Men in the Civil War," Www.thezephyronline.com/wellsbros.htm.

11 Winschel, *Triumph and Defeat*, 149; A sutler was a private contractor who traveled with the army and sold a wide variety of goods to the soldiers.

12 Jones, *The Rank and File at Vicksburg*. 30-31.

General Logan's division, including John D. Stevenson's brigade and the 17th Illinois, was ordered to lead the Yankee approach into Vicksburg. The men started for the city about noon, just two hours after the surrender. A member of the 32nd Ohio, another regiment in Stevenson's brigade, reported passing thousands of their former foes who were "very much down in the mouth. They said they had their last ration that morning." He saw few civilians, but the ones he spotted "looked sad. I think they hid in their homes to keep from being seen."[13]

The bands of the victorious troops played as they marched into town. They reached downtown Vicksburg around 2:00 p.m. A member of the 33rd Illinois Infantry saw "rebel officers and Union officers riding together . . . both so drunk they could hardly sit on their horses." He also noted "the women were the most upset. They passed by . . . heads held high but with tears in their eyes."[14]

According to Josiah, General Grant warned his men not to show any "sound or sign of exultation . . . over the fallen foe." By all indications, the overwhelming majority of the Union troops obeyed the order. Not only did the victorious soldiers share their food with the starving men of the Vicksburg garrison, but a Confederate noted the Union men were also "respectful and considerate. No insolence of manner, and but little offensive taunting." Another agreed, stating, "No word of exultation was uttered to irritate the feelings of the prisoners. On the contrary, every sentinel who came upon post brought haversacks filled with provisions, which he would give to some famished Southerner, with the remark, 'Here, reb, I know you are starved nearly to death.'"[15]

Once Joe Johnston received word that Pemberton had surrendered his Vicksburg army, he withdrew his Army of Relief back to the capital at Jackson. Grant ordered Sherman to pursue, and on the evening of July 16, Johnston abandoned the state capital without a fight. While Sherman's men were dealing with Johnston, the 17th Illinois and the other troops of the Army of the Tennessee remained at Vicksburg. They now had to make the transition from siege to occupation. By the spring of 1864, black troops, raised as a result of

13 Woodworth, *Nothing But Victory*, 451.

14 Edwin C. Bearss, *The Vicksburg Campaign: Unvexed To The Sea* (Dayton, OH, 1985), 1296

15 From a memorial address given at Woodhull, Iowa by Josiah Moore on August 8, 1885. In collection of author; Woodworth, *Nothing But Victory*, 454.

President Lincoln's order, made up about one-half the force garrisoning Vicksburg.[16]

*   *   *

Jennie to Josiah

Peoria June 29th 1863

My Dear Friend

The present moment suggests a quiet little chat with thee. I trust my dearest friend you will have patience to listen for a little while. Your welcome letter of the 10th inst arrived several days ago, having just mailed one to you the day before receiving it I thought you might not be pleased to have another missive so soon hence the delay in not answering your last dearest letter. how much pleasure it gave. I was feeling so lonely I can well say blessed be letters when coming from the hand of the loved one.

Mattie Cutler came out on Wednesday and staid with me until Saturday evening we had a real pleasant time. I felt a little lonesome after she left but it will be all right this evening for Mother dear is coming home I think when I get her home I'll not leave her go away again. if Maggie wants to see her she will have to come home now dont you think that fair? thats just what I think. Poor George would not be half so lonely as I am.

That little "secesh article" came to hand on Saturday. I presume it came to the express office some weeks ago. They are very careless about delivering packages. The little "basket" is very pretty and doubly interesting from having been made by the hand of a secesh lady. please accept my thanks for the dear little gift. I must tell you my dear friend I'm very partial to one "lone star" and sad is my heart when I can not see it. Oh that it might be always present that would indeed be joy. The past would then be forgotten in the happy present.

---

16 Bearss, *The Vicksburg Campaign*, 1279; Grant, *Personal Memoirs*, 576; Jeff Giambrone, *To Die By the Flag Rather Than Disgrace It, Black Mississippians in the Union Army*, March 30, 2012 blog.

The rebels are having quite a merry time in Pennsylvania.[17] isent it too hard it does seem as though the eastern troops can not accomplish anything there must be a great wrong somewhere but it certainly is not for a lack of bravery among the soldiers. The west present a more hopeful picture, and if Vicksburg falls we may indeed look for that brighter day. How sad it must be for you to lose such good men from your Co. The influence of such persons is so much needed among the many careless ones yet it is a great consolation to know that they were better prepared to obey the call than the wicked ones. Capt Ryan while here gave me a rather sad picture to look upon he said the last time he saw you were putting one of your men in a box. Oh I did feel so sorry for you I knew it was a sad office for you.[18]

Well my dearest friend you have been such a quiet good boy while I've been talking with you. so I'll not ask your kind attention longer but will say farewell for a short time. May God ever love thee and preserve thee from danger is the earnest prayer of one who kindly remembers the dear absent one.
Yours truly,

Jennie
P.S. I do hope you will "tease" me with another dear missive soon it gives me great happiness to be thus teased. Please don't forget.
Jennie sends you a good bye (kiss) J.E.L.

The city's surrender was a traumatic event for the residents of Vicksburg. When the campaign began, citizens and soldiers alike fervently believed that God would deliver them from the Yankees. "God being on our side we will assuredly gain the victory," wrote one Confederate officer in March 1863. Just two months later, food had become more important than victory for the beleaguered city. The change in fortune made Southerners wonder why they had incurred God's wrath. In the North, Vicksburg's surrender on the day that celebrated the nation's birth was taken as evidence that God favored the Union.

17 A reference to Robert E. Lee's second invasion of the North. Following his victory against Maj. Gen. Joseph Hooker at Chancellorsville, Virginia, in early May, Lee moved west into the Valley and then north into Pennsylvania. On June 28, Maj. Gen. George Gordon Meade replaced Hooker as commander of the Army of the Potomac. The two armies met for three days of battle (July 1 through July 3) at Gettysburg, where Meade repulsed Lee's assaults and won the first clear cut, large-scale victory of the war in the Eastern Theater.

18 This was probably Henry Pressly, who had been killed the previous month in the collapsing trench.

Vicksburg's fall on July 4 was not just a patriotic commemoration, it was also a moral and religious one. As one historian put it, for the people of both sides, "faith offered consolation but also provided set explanations for victory or defeat, ways for both understanding and coping with the vicissitudes of war."[19]

Jennie's negative view of the Union forces in the Eastern Theater was indicative of widespread sectional rivalries. In many cases, Western troops viewed the Easterners as "bandbox" soldiers, hardly up to the rigors the men of the Western theater were forced to endure. Troops in the East routinely disparaged their Western counterparts as more a backwoods rabble than a disciplined fighting force. Senior military leaders felt this tension as well. Writing about the Grand Review in May 1865, when the Eastern and Western armies marched in triumph through Washington, D. C., General Sherman would note, "Many good people, up to that time, had looked upon our Westerners as a sort of mob."[20]

Josiah to Jennie

Vicksburg Miss
July 9, 1863
Miss Jennie,

My dear friend,
    Permit me the honor of presenting you a copy of the Vicksburg Illustrated. tho my preference is decidedly for "northern pictures" tho I very much envy this now i.e. its privileges.

With the compliments of, yours as ever
J. Moore

P.S. Genl. Logan's Div. has been left at this post, which is very fortunate for us. all the other troops started at the time of the surrender in pursuit of Johnston, and news just now comes that 5000 prisoners are on their way in here, if that is so the

---

19 Boatner, *Civil War Dictionary*, 331-339; Manning, *What This Cruel War Was Over*, 115; Rable, *God's Almost Chosen Peoples*, 264-265.

20 Wiley, *The Life of Billy Yank*, 321-322; William T. Sherman, *Personal Memoirs of William T. Sherman* (New York, NY, 1890), 378.

rebels are used up in this part, for Port Hudson cant stand long.[21] I presume we will
yet have to go East, however I think nothing better ever happened in the East for if
they let Lee's army ever return they should have their country laid waste but Lee
had better be carefull or he will arrouse An old Pa ductch.[22] J.M.

Three days after this letter, Addison Norton, the 17th Illinois's colonel, resigned July 5 (effective July 9). He received a surgeon's certificate of disability due to "Adema left leg, the sequel of a fracture of the tibia received May 4 1862 and also of an ulcer of the great toe of the left foot." Norton claimed, "I have a family of small children," and that his wife was ill. His resignation left the regiment in the hands of Lt. Col. Smith.[23]

Jennie to Josiah

Peoria July 24th 1863
My Dear Friend

> The "Storm" has indeed passed and we have great reason to be thankfull for
> what our Western Army have accomplished. We are beginning to believe the
> rebellion is about at an end in the West. You well might have a "big" 4th" when it
> brought to such a happy event as the fall of Vicksburg. We had a very quiet fourth
> in Peoria, but when we received the news from Vicksburg it seemed like the 4th of
> July a few years ago.
>   I received your letter of 6th inst just four weeks from the day I received the one
> of the 16th of June. That wasent long was it? to wait for a word from the "dear
> one" Well when 3 weeks passed and no message came I then ceased to look for a
> letter. I thought by your not writing you were surely on your way home but alas I
> was doomed to be sadly disappointed, now why dont you come. I do want to see you
> Oh ever so much. I was so glad when I saw through the papers that Gen. Logans

21 Josiah was right. Port Hudson. The last Confederate strongpoint on the Mississippi River surrendered on July 9 after a real seven-week siege, the longest in American history. After Vicksburg, Port Hudson, and Gettysburg, people on both sides of the Mason Dixon Line began to realize the course of the war was turning decidedly in favor of the North. Shea and Winschel, *Vicksburg is the Key*, 203.

22 Josiah and his comrades had not yet received news that Lee had been defeated six days earlier at Gettysburg.

23 Military and pension records of Addison Norton in NARA.

Div. were left in Vicksburg. I thought my dear friend would surely get a furlough then, and so I looked for Somebody but that dear somebody did not come. You ask, what I think of the next ten months[24] *they now look like so many years. I think that you will be just a real naughty boy if you dont come home before that time. I know your Mother will think so too and you know dearest friend it is always right to try to please her. Just to think of not seeing the dear loved one for ten months. O it must not be they would indeed be long long weary months.*

George and Maggie and Mr. Louck and family came down on Friday evening. George had to leave home on business and Maggie thought it a good time to make us a visit. I told her I wished he would have to go away often so we would have her home but she thought it was awful cruel for me to wish such a thing. She is just as full of mischief as ever. You see dear friend there is not much chance for me to be "alone all alone" at the present time. yet with all around me I feel lonesome for the one dearer than all is absent. Oh why cant those bright days of the past return to us soon again. If you could only come home now how happy we would be. The thought of the next "ten months" would be lost in the happy present. I can scarcely write anything but Come home for it seems to be the one wish always present. Well dearest friend I am just now hoping you will have to read this miserable scribble by a "very dim light" I am sorry it's such a poor return for your dear missive. I received your copy of the "Vicksburg Illustrated" it looks a little like hard times in Vicksburg. Your letter was dated three days before the note which accompanied the paper yet I received them at the same time. Well my dear friend I shall not try your patience longer but will bid you a kind good night hoping to see or hear from you soon.

Yours as ever

Jennie E. Lindsay
P.S. George and Maggie wish to be remembered to you. J.E.L.

Josiah to Jennie

Vicksburg Miss
9 P.M. July 28th 1863

---

24 Jennie's reference to the "next ten months" was a response to the same term used in Josiah's July 6 letter. It refers to the length of time he had left in his military service. Josiah's three-year enlistment was scheduled to end in May 1864.

Well My Dear Jennie,

How fares my dearest friend this lonely evening? I hope very well.

You will please excuse my partiality for this little "secesh relic[25] *tho I almost envy it now! dont you? however I hope its wayward work is over and that it may now engage in a more noble business than the bearer of little secesh messages. O dear I am ashamed to write a letter on such paper, but if it pleased the taste of the southern chivalry I presume that we Northron "mud sills" should say thy will be done. Still if it dont suit Jennie why I can write another on white peoples paper—wont that do?*

Now then I have just come to renew that "quiet little chat". O dear Jennie you cant imagine how lonesome I am this evening so much so that after tattoo had sounded I could not go to rest till I should have a few moments sweet converse with the "beloved one" far away—Your dear welcome letter of the 30th ult only came to hand on yesterday about a month on the way. O how anxiously I looked for it. I could not imagine what had happened—I had a letter from Mrs Currie by Capt Ryan forwarded from Helena and I thought you might have sent one too by him and it had been miscarried. indeed I did not know what to think, tho there was one poor "soldier boy" that felt very much as tho he had lost his "best friend."

But marks on the envelope made the explanation, it had been sent by mistake to the 19th Ills which being in Rosecrans Dept. you can gain some idea of its travels it came all right and seemed to be well cared for—not opened like lost letters often are.

Shall I not soon have the pleasure of another dear message from my dearest Jennie I think it is near time. you must not send any more so far around and you need not fear my being "not pleased" by two coming about the same time—I scarcely even think of the time for when I am alone and as we are now not busy, it affords not a little consolation to reread and ponder over the dear words of the "loved one" who tho far distant is ever present on memories brightest page. Now dear Jennie you will please not forget this, tho I know you will not feel as lonely on the return of your dear Mother yet you know how it is to be left all alone.

I am glad those little articles had come to hand I had about concluded that they had been captured by the wrong party I am glad however that the "lone star" has been more fortunate i.e. in being captured by the right one. this you know my

---

25 The "secesh relic" is the piece of very crude brown paper upon which the letter was written. This is likely something Josiah found after he entered Vicksburg.

dear lady is a very important item in warfare. I hope that I am worthy of your very high compliment my dear Jennie, and I hope that I truly apreciate the favor of enjoying the sincere regard of such a dear friend whose presence seems as tho it would be happiness itself. but my dear friend while it is sad that such a cruel space must separate us yet we have reason for thankfulness to that God who thus far has preserved our lives as dear to him from all the ills and dangers of a sinful world. How many bleeding sorrow stricken hearts have been made since we first met?—parted never to meet below only in sad remembrance—our meetings have been joyous and partings tho sad yet not bereft of hope,s brighter rays—indeed the anticipated joy of meeting one so dearly beloved almost seems as thos it would compensate for parting sorrows, tho if it could be avoided I can asure you my dear Jennie my part of the experiment should be found wanting.

But I must tell you my late troubles. I have lost Lieut McClanahan.[26] *He resigned on the 24th and went home he had been speaking of resigning for some time but I did not think of him going so soon. He resigned on account of his Father's death—he required some strong plea of that kind so as to succeed. he goes home an honorable faithful and worthy soldier we had been tried friends and I will very much miss him not even having another officer in the company—he will no doubt call at Peoria on his way home, tho I think he now goes by way of Ohio for a partner. aint he sensible? so now you see poor me is left all alone. now Jennie wont you please remember this. I shall.*

Andie was out to see me a few days since he is quite well he anticipated a few days rest while Capt Wilson took a trip to New Orleans.

As I said I had a letter from Mrs Currie a few days since and shall answer it soon. How does she like "southron airs"?—she mentioned about receiving the fan and about you being in then at their house they have gone to her fathers she says to live.

We are still staying in the suburbs of Vicksburg tho I hear some talk of moving but as yet hear of no place designated indeed we may stay all summer.

---

26 Lieutenant William McClanahan was one of the Monmouth students who had joined the company at its formation. After William's father, John McClanahan, had been mortally wounded earlier in the year at Fort Donelson, William resigned on July 24, 1863, to return home and assist his family. He would reenlist in May 1864 and commissioned captain of Company A, 138th Illinois Infantry. Monmouth College, *Oracle*, 39. Company F suffered both Lieutenant McClanahan's resignation that July and its last wartime death. William Voris, the man who had attempted to steady the skittish men of the 53rd Ohio at the battle of Shiloh, died of disease at the Union hospital at Milliken's Bend. Duncan, Company log; Military records of William Voris in NARA.

Most of our troops have returned from Jackson we did not go out there Logan thot his troops had done enough.[27]

Johnston got a way and made a pretty good escape after all our troops pursued a short distance but he out ran them and got away so we are not in much danger now of being surrounded indeed I think that the rebellion has played out in the West. never again can they get hold of the Miss. I am trying to make Grant believe that the war is about over in the West when I think I have this nearly accomplished I shall ask him to let me go home. wouldnt that be taking the advantage of him?

But I fear that I have not only "teased" but very much wearied my very dear friend with too long a letter. So hoping to hear from you very soon and that this may find you in good health. I now bid thee my dearest friend "good night" sweet dreams.

as ever J. Moore

a goodnight kiss to dear Jennie

P.S. I cannot make this a complete secesh rig for want of an envelope but a union will do as that will finaly comprehend all anyhow—perhaps even some "little secesh" also. I'll go now, goodbye—only for a very short while. J.M.

Jennie to Josiah

Peoria Aug 11th 1863
My Dearest Friend

Oh what joy it would be to gaze upon the face of one so dearly remembered. How my heart prays for that happy meeting. Sometimes that bright day looks so far away that I almost despair of ever seeing it realized. I do hope you can persuade Grant to leave you come home soon for what is the use of you staying now I think you have done your share in fighting. Is he generous enough to give your place to

---

27 Occupation duty had its own perils. On July 25, John Rook, a soldier in the 17th's Company A, was killed by the accidental explosion of a shell while serving on outpost duty. Military service file of John Rook, NARA.

some one else just think of the many men now at home who are anxiously awaiting an opportunity to serve their country, but alas there is no place for them, for the very reason that you soldiers will persist in staying until peace be restored. Now I do think that very unkind and selfish surely all ought to have a chance to prove their love for their country by offering their life as a sacrifice. Now my very dear friend I trust you will think of this.

Poor boy, I can imagine how much you will miss Lieut McClanahan. I am real sorry for your sake that he resigned it must have been very pleasant to have a good companion one in whom you could trust. Well I think you will have to resign to. Oh how I wish you could.

Your dear welcome missive of the 28th ult came to hand on yesterday. I was just beginning to feel a little mite cross at you when nearly six weeks had passed and no answer to my letter of the 30th inst. But I had no idea of it taking such a journey. I shall now expect to hear from you very often, as you say you are not very busy. Now please dont forget.

Maggie and George left us on Saturday evening, it seems so lonely without them. I tried to persuade Maggie to stay all Summer but it was no use. Mr Currie went with them to Chicago to see Walter he was on his way home and was taken sick at the Sherman [The back page of this letter is illegible].

Josiah to Jennie

Vicksburg, Miss
August 14th, 1863

My dearest Jennie,

I hope that you are well this pleasant evening. I must tell you of the very happy surprise occasioned by you last dear epistle of the 24th ult. I rec'd it when about going to supper but not recognizing anything familiar in the outer style I put it, with some others, by, for a more convenient season, so supper being over, I sat down to look over my letters—several were opened and hastily glanced at, and then came one and it was opened in about the same indifferent manner as the others—But see the contents! There, is the dear familiar handwrite of a dearest friend—Could it be so? I expected a message from the dear one but such is a daily expectation—nor could I feel persuaded of the fact till I had seen the signature—when confidence was immediately restored and sweet joyous memories quickly recalled. Whether or not you intended such a ruse, I can assure you dear friend that you succeeded most admirably, but the humble subscriber has only to say in the words of the "Old Reader" "Try, Try again."

Well dear Jennie I must congratulate you on being not "all alone" tho I presume that Maggie would not thank me for such a compliment since it is so much at her expense—I can almost imagine what times she and dear Jennie will have—each one beset on sportively plaguing the other, but tho Maggie may be as "mischievous as ever" yet I have no fears but what her more sedate and quiet sister will keep up her own side. "Smooth water" they say "runs deep". Yet what a happy scene, the sweet mirthful and innocent asociation of two dear loving sisters? What more noble, more heavenly? And tho I may be deprived of the pleasure of being even a casual observer yet I rejoice to know that amid the carnage of war and ruins of society there still remain "unbroken ties"—sacred and undisturbed by the grim Destroyer and that the one ever dear to me is among that happy number.

Now Jennie please accept my thanks for your kind concern for my dear mother[28]—and if I am a "naughty-boy" I assure you it will be no fault of mine for I think I shall try and see the "dear loved one" even before the expiration of the "ten months"—only nine now but as yet dear friend I have no idea of how soon, of course I would not say for certain and then be compelled to disappoint my beloved lady—but I believe that I have never in all my life felt more lonsome than since the fall of this place. I constantly find my self wishing for the presence of one without whom life is only a dreary waste—spent without an object, but dear lady perhaps I should not presume too much. Yet I flatter my self that my regard for you has not been formed by the impulse of the moment, from a partial friendship it has grown stronger and stronger till thy presence seems as tho it would be happiness itself, and I have reason to believe that my dear friend has not been wholly indifferent to this high esteem, for O what a source of joy those dear missives have been—each seems to set forth the sweet and noble disposition of their beloved author , yes beloved, Jennie you have well said "blessed be letters." Would that I could repay such noble worth "but I trust I shall shortly see thee and then we shall speak face to face."

I was not a little surprised yesterday on calling on the 77th to hear that Andie had gone home. He had been to see me and said that he would come and stay a few days while Capt. Wilson was away on business but I presume the captain

---

28 Josiah's reference to Jennie's concern for his mother is likely related to the death of Josiah's father on August 10, 1863. Josiah was unable to return home for the funeral.

concluded to go home and take Andie along, so you will have the pleasure of seeing him again.

I hear some talk of our Div. going to Memphis but as yet nothing certain. My health is quite good and with my best wishers that this may find thee in joy and peace, I bid my beloved Jennie a kind goodnight.
As ever

J. Moore

P.S. With your pleasure, please remember me with sincere regard to my very kind host and hostess—George and Maggie, tell Maggie that I would not wish George to leave her only just as often as you would want her to come and see you, aint that fair? Please write soon, now goodbye sweet sleep pleasant dreams J.M.

After the near-constant skirmishing and anxiety of the campaign, Josiah acknowledged that this quiet period had aggravated his feelings of loneliness and his longing to return home. There is a noted absence in his letter of the vitriolic language Josiah used to describe his Rebel opponents after the death of John Stephenson. It could be that his deep sorrow over Stephenson's death had subsided a bit over time. It is also quite possible that Josiah's many interactions with Confederate soldiers made him see his enemies in an entirely different light. It was not uncommon for the hatred on both sides to ease after personal encounters. One Union soldier who had been captured in 1862 was amazed to learn that Confederates were as devoted to the same religious faith as he was. He said there was "nothing so discouraging as the evident sincerity of those he was among in their prayers." An officer of the 59th Illinois noted his surprise when "last night we heard one preacher preaching in the Rebel lines and another preaching in our lines" and realized the prayers and petitions were the same.

While in occupied Vicksburg, members of the 20th Illinois, the regiment that had created riots and drunken binges less than two years earlier, wrote that they attended the local Methodist church, "which was sometimes presided over by our Army Chaplain, and sometimes by their regular pastor, a southern man." Even President Lincoln noted the same conundrum in 1862 when he noted, "Each party claims to act in accordance with the will of God." However, the president did not let that fact weaken his resolve. "Both may be, and one must be, wrong. God cannot be for and against the same thing at the same time. In

Robert W. Rogers was a private in
Company F of the 17th Illinois.
This image was taken by Barr &
Young, which is clearly stamped on
the lower-front of the photograph.
D. P. Barr and J. W. Young was one of
the first photography companies
to set up shop after the capture
of Vicksburg.

Author

the present civil war it is quite
possible that God's purpose is
something different from the
purpose of either party."[29]

The second paragraph of
Josiah's letter, in which he
referred to the happy reunion of
the two sisters, provides another
indication of the war's disparate
impacts. While towns like Peoria
remained physically unscathed,
Josiah participated in the
destruction that had created such
misery for Vicksburg's civilians.

Robert M. Campbell served as a
corporal in Company F of the 17th
Illinois, and later a captain in the 47th
U.S. Colored Troops. This image was
also taken by Barr and Young in
Vicksburg. *Author*

29 Woodworth, *While God is Marching On*, 199, 200.

Sanford A. Kingsbury was the chaplain of the 17th Illinois. This image was taken by Capitol Gallery in Springfield, Illinois.
Abraham Lincoln Presidential Library and Museum

Josiah to Jennie

Vicksburg, Miss
9 P.M. August 21/63

My Dearest Jennie,

I hope is well this evening. I just come to bid her "goodbye"—I hope for only a short time however.
Our Brig'd starts tomorrow on a ten days scout west of the Mississippi.
For several days I've looked anxiously for a dear message from my dearest friend but as yet none has come but I shall expect one on my return—I know my beloved friend will not disappoint me.
I shall not detain her longer for she begins to look sleepy I know she will excuse this abrupt interruption but I could not leave without a short call.
So while I'd gently steal away, those dear lips I'll kiss and say—Goodnight my own dear Jennie.
Sweet sleep pleasant dreams and joy be ever thine is the bright hope of yours as ever.

J. Moore

The "ten day scout" Josiah mentioned was an expedition under Brig. Gen. Stevenson to Monroe, Louisiana. Although Henry Bush of Company D mentioned taking part in the same reconnaissance, the *Official Records* do not list the 17th as a participant. This is likely the same expedition Grant authorized to go into the countryside and find former slaves who could be pressed into service as Union soldiers. In August 1863, Grant wrote to Lincoln that he gave the arming of blacks his "hearty support" and that, along with the Emancipation Proclamation, it was "the heaviest blow yet given the Confederacy." That was an interesting statement coming from the man who captured Vicksburg—certainly a heavy blow against the Rebels—and a man who had once owned a slave. Given that he had freed his slave rather than sell him, it could be that Grant was ambivalent about the institution. A week after his letter to Lincoln, Grant wrote to his friend and political patron Elihu Washburne, a Congressman from Illinois: "Slavery is already dead and cannot be resurrected. I never was an Abolitionist, not even what could be called anti-slavery, but I try to judge farely & honestly and it become patent to my mind early in the rebellion that the North & South could never live at peace with each other except as one nation, and that without slavery."[30]

As Grant came to the realization that emancipation was a weapon to "punish slaveholders, weaken the Confederacy and protect the Union from future internal strife," so did more of his soldiers, and even those who held racist views. One conservative Democrat in a Missouri unit told his wife in December 1863 that it was pointless to debate emancipation because "slavery is already dead and buried." As the war continued, the desire to end slavery grew among the men of the Yankee army. As occupiers in slaveholding areas, soldiers personally witnessed how the loss of slave labor affected the South's ability to make war. The fall of Vicksburg alone sent tens of thousands of former slaves streaming into the city. One female plantation owner said her entire region became "almost depopulated of negroes." Even in areas the Union armies had yet to reach, rumors of a Yankee presence had a striking impact on the slaves. They often slowed their work or ceased working altogether. Some slaves threatened their soon-to-be-former masters, knowing that Yankees and the promise of freedom were nearby. When one slave refused an order he simply said, "Mr Paxton, I want to tell you that that thing is played out."[31]

An increase in religious feeling also swept through both Yankee and Confederate camps in the fall of 1863. In June, during the Vicksburg siege, Harold Penniman, the assistant surgeon of the 17th Illinois, observed a lack of notice paid to Sunday. "Sabbaths come and go unheeded, no difference; same

30 Diary of Henry Bush, Co. D 17th Illinois, Regimental files F-278, Vicksburg National Military Park; Simpson, *The Civil War: The Third Year*, 488, 500-501.

31 Gallagher, *The Union War*, 2, 143; Levine, *The Fall of the House of Dixie*, 155-158.

cannonading, same duties, and all," he complained. "It is a fact, that the blessed Sabbath has passed more than once, and I did not know it." Now, perhaps due to the unprecedented death and destruction caused by the war, there was a significant surge in religious feeling among soldiers on both sides and in all theaters of operation. This movement came to be known as the "Great Revival of 1863." In Northern camps, the fact that more soldiers had come to see slavery as a moral threat that "angered God" might have spurred the revival.[32]

For some soldiers, embracing religion could have been a way to push back against the amoral influences of army life, or a means of saving their souls after a campaign of killing, stealing, and destruction. A similar passion had swept army camps the previous fall and winter, so the explanation could simply be that soldiers alleviated the boredom of winter camp by turning to religion. However, combat seemed to make men more devout, and it was common for soldiers to credit God for keeping them safe.[33]

Other men remained immune to the Great Revival. Many scoffed at the need to observe the Sabbath or even recognize God. A member of the 8th Illinois wrote that he "couldn't imagine the soul of a soldier who had died in the defense of his country being consigned to an orthodox hell."[34]

Although combat seemed to make men more inclined to look to God, not all could find Him. One young soldier on his deathbed, encouraged by a chaplain to come to Jesus, moaned piteously, "He is not here, He is not here." Nonetheless, those men who wanted to avail themselves of religious service could, although their less devout comrades might commence "gambling and cursing within earshot of a Sunday service."[35]

The men also had to deal with the uneven quality of the military chaplains. The soldier gave many religious men high marks, particularly if they shared the deprivations of campaigning and followed the men into battle. Not all were held in such high regard. General George Meade, the curmudgeonly head of the Army of the Potomac, divided the army's chaplains into two camps: those who "do nothing" and those who "make themselves obnoxious by interfering in matters they have no business with." Even Penniman, the assistant surgeon of

---

32 Blaisdell, *Civil War Letters*, 130; Manning, *What This Cruel Was Over*, 119.

33 Woodworth, *While God Is Marching On*, 190, 193, 196-197, 214; Rable, *God's Almost Chosen People*, 306.

34 Ibid.,189, 259.

35 Ibid., 176, 204-207. Woodworth, *While God Is Marching On*, 182, 190.

the 17th, grumbled about the regiment's religious leaders. "The chaplains are of little account, and generally keep regimental post-offices; attend to such light duties, and, so far as I learn, are discouraged in endeavoring to reform abuses. Our regiment," he added, "has had not chaplain for nearly a year. From all I can learn, his acquaintance had but little or no confidence in his piety."[36]

Josiah made no mention in his letters of any revivalist events in the 17th's camp, or anywhere else for that matter. It could be that Josiah, who received a leave to return home and was absent from late September 1863 until almost January 1864, simply missed these activities. However, it could also be that the spiritualism of the Great Revival never reached the 17th Illinois or surrounding units. In many camps, North and South, Sunday continued to be just another day.[37]

*   *   *

Jennie to Josiah

Peoria Sept 3rd 1863

My own dear Friend,

I've just come to answer your kind "good bye." These two little words bring to my heart a feeling of loneliness. Somebody has gone. I know it must be so, yet I get very impatient sometimes because I cannot see thee.

I suppose you have returned ere this as your "ten days" had passed before I received your "good bye" of the 21st. I would I could hear of your coming in place of going. The time seems so long, to look forward to the next nine months O dear it seems like ages. It must not be so Surely dear friend thou canst "steal awhile away."

We paid "Camp Mather" a visit on yesterday. The grounds are beginning to look like old times again they are making great preparation for the coming fair. While there the place recalled to my mind the happy past, and with the thought of the dreary present I could not help repeating Come again bright days of hope and pleasure gone.

---

36 Woodworth, While God Is Marching On, 154-158; Rable, *God's Almost Chosen Peoples*, 118; Blaisdell, *Civil War Letters*, 128.

37 Woodworth, *While God is Marching On*, 188.

Well dearest friend I see you are getting real sleepy so I'll not tease the dear one any longer with a good night kiss I will say unto thee, my own dear friend farewell for a short time.

Jennie

Josiah was granted a 20-day leave to return home, effective September 28 through October 18. He stopped in Peoria first to visit Jennie and then took sick at some point soon thereafter. The illness prevented him from rejoining his regiment at the appointed time, and he was listed absent without leave from October 18 through December 24. While he was gone, the regiment participated on an expedition from Vicksburg to Monroe, Louisiana, and had a skirmish at Bogue Chitto Creek on October 17.[38]

It was typical for soldiers on leave to feel conflicted. Josiah clearly had a burning desire to get back to Peoria to see Jennie, and to travel home to see his family. However, as the man charged with overseeing the welfare of the men of Company F, he probably thought about them just as often and felt the pull to return to them.[39]

Josiah to Jennie

Galena Ills Oct. 12th 63
DeSoto House

My dearest Jennie,

As you see I've almost reached home but not quite able yet tho I expect to try in a few days. I reached here on the 7th inst after a severe trip of ten days during which I was sick all the time. This has been my first day to be up a little since my arrival but I think the fever is broken and I shall soon recover, I shall soon try and go home as the Dr thinks there is the best place to cure my voice.

I think I shall not be able to move round much before 2 weeks.

38 Dyer, *Compendium*, 783.

39 James McPherson, *For Cause and Comrades*, 87.

But dear Jennie I shall not detain you longer with my poor scrible at this time it is only to give some idea of my whereabouts and I hope to hear from you soon my address will be Hanover Ills for two weeks at least I think.

Hoping that this may find thee dearest friend in good health I bid thee a kind goodnight.

As ever yours,
J. Moore

P.S. Please write. J.M.

Jennie to Josiah

Peoria Oct 17th 1863

My Dearest Friend,

Never before had I been so anxious to hear from you as at the present time, so I need not tell you dear friend what relief your dear missive of the 12th inst brought to mind, although it gave me sorrow to hear of your long illness. I was so glad to know that you had a at last arrived so near home. I've been real unhappy ever since I received your letter of the 23rd ult. I was so afraid you would not be able to leave Vicksburg, but you are now with the dear ones at home and you know good care will add greatly to you recovery. Poor dear boy, you surely have had a hard time, but I hope all will soon be well again.

Andie leaves us on Monday next for Vicksburg. Although his health is very good I almost dread to see him leave for fear of his getting sick again. Yet I suppose I ought to remember, "Sufficient unto the day is the evil thereof." I think there are but few persons who keep this in mind, for it seems a part of human nature to honour trouble.

George paid us a short visit on Tuesday. He left us real provoked because I would'ent go home with him so he tried to get Mother to promise to let me spend the winter with them. They plead they are so lonesome it is so pleasant to be with all the dear ones so I scarcely know how to decide the question.

Well dearest friend I know you are tired of this scribble so I'll not detain you any longer but may we not hope, my beloved friend to have you with us soon. We would try to take good care of our dear invalid wont you trust us? How I wish you would. Please let me hear from you soon, as I shall be very anxious about you. Hoping this may find thee in better health. I now bid my beloved friend a kind good night.

As ever yours,
Jennie

P.S. I think dear friend this poor little scribble hath great reason to cry out pardon, yet to well it knows it pleads its cause to a humane judge. Good bye J.E.L.

Josiah to Jennie

"Home" Hanover Ills.
Nov. 3rd 1863

My dear Jennie,

   Another happy moment permits me to commune with the dear one; it seems like a long time since I wrote the last and still longer seems the time when I had hoped of laying aside this dull medium, but even the subjects of hope are sometimes disappointed.
   I need not tell you how welcome your dear missive of the 17th ult. was. I rather fear that I proved a barrier to your "Chicago visit"—if so I am sorry that any persons should be disappointed on my account, since my wanderings are so uncertain at present; but I think George should be satisfied when he got one. What do you think Jennie?
   Well dear lady you perhaps will think strange that I am keeping so quiet and that I've not been moving round—and I must say it is no fault of mine. It may be that I am lazy only such disposition never troubles me. But I've been having a renewal of my sickness. The fever returned worse than ever last week and tho broken now I feel not very brave. I am trying to march round some but think I've forgotten how tho I may learn. I cannot talk very much yet and hence you know I would be in a bad condition to wage war with the ladies, unless I could get some on my side.
   I am in hopes however that as I get stronger my voice will improve. The drs can't do much in such business.

I expected to be able to move ere this but it seems almost as distant as ever now. I would like if I could just go part of the way perhaps then I'd not be in such a hurry. I would almost like to comply with dear Jennie's request but fear that my mother would not like to see a sick boy go away—well I can go when I'm well wont that do?

Hoping that this may find beloved Jennie in the enjoyment of good health surrounded by the love and friendship of good and dear friends.
I remain as ever

J. Moore

P.S. I think I shall not leave here before the last of next week or the 14th inst. A letter comes in 3 days so if convenient dear Jennie please write. O much oblige, Yours J.M.

While Josiah and Jennie exchanged letters during his illness, a story in the Peoria paper highlighted Senator Lindsay's political difficulties. On November 3, the *Daily Transcript* took obvious delight in reporting on another exchange between former law partners Lindsay and Colonel Ingersoll. The senator was taking Ingersoll to task for abandoning democracy and going over to abolitionism. "Don't talk to me about democracy," retorted Ingersoll. "I was a democrat in 1856 when you was a Black Abolitionist. I was a democrat when you helped dress young ladies in black and put them in a procession to represent 'Bleeding Kansas.' If the Republican party ever had anything to do to bring on this war, you had your share in it, and no man is so contemptible as he who gets into a scrape and then runs away and abuses him for what he himself is guilty." The *Daily Transcript* concluded, "Lindsay was silenced."[40]

Ingersoll's rebuke of Lindsay is a good example of the increasing disdain in which the members of the military held the Peace Democrats. Contempt for those who wanted "peace at any cost" united the men in the ranks, whether they were abolitionists, emancipationists, anti-black, or even longtime Democrats such as Ingersoll.[41]

In July 1863, New York City was rocked by violent uprisings over the implementation of the draft. Rioters burned, looted, and even killed, taking

---

40 Peoria *Daily Transcript*, November 3, 1863.

41 Ramold, *Across the Divide*, 115.

particular aim at the city's black residents. New York was not an altogether unlikely site for such an event. The city had a high population of both poor and immigrants who adamantly opposed the draft, and its business leaders and elected officials remained concerned over the war's impact on their commerce with the South. The violence of 1863 did not end until Union soldiers were brought into the city and fired volleys into the mobs. More than 300 people died in the strife.[42]

Far from being horrified at the government action, the army strongly supported the violent end to the riots. In the eyes of the soldiers, the rioters were traitors, not innocent citizens, and their actions helped prolong the war. When soldiers heard about people back home sowing seeds of discontent, they looked forward to delivering retribution to those who were hurting the war effort. Sometimes the presence of soldiers home on leave precipitated brawls, including an incident in Charleston, Illinois, in March 1864. Rather than apologize for these domestic skirmishes, the soldiers rationalized their behavior. They felt they were the ones who knew what was necessary to win the war, and they needed the full support of those at home.[43]

Compounding the distress over the "fire in the rear" were widespread reports of Copperhead-driven conspiracies in the North. One reported scheme involved an attempt to free Confederate prisoners in Illinois and arm them for an advance on the state government in Springfield. In Columbia County, Pennsylvania, a Union officer was shot to death when authorities moved against an area known as the "Fishing Creek Confederacy," where it was believed deserters, Copperheads, and anti-abolitionists had congregated. The army rounded up more than 40 people, tried them, and then shipped them off to Fort Mifflin in Philadelphia. Certainly, many on the home front understood the soldiers' frustration and attempted to offer support. A Methodist clergyman declared, "Those at the front kill rattle snakes, we at home must kill copperheads."[44]

The Confederacy faced its own internal divisions. Pro-Union sentiment was strong in parts of Georgia, northern Alabama, and eastern Tennessee. The

---

42 McPherson, *Battle Cry of Freedom*, 609-611; Stashower, *The Hour of Peril*, 203; Adams, *Living Hell*, 32.

43 Ramold, *Across the Divide*, 12, 15, 128-134, 140-141.

44 *Ibid.*, 131; Jonathan W. White, Remembering the Fishing Creek Confederacy, *Pennsylvania Heritage Magazine*, (Summer 2014), 6-13; Rable, *God's Almost Chosen Peoples*, 231, 232.

western counties of Virginia ultimately split off and formed the new state of West Virginia in 1863. A North Carolina trooper wrote to a friend in August 1863 and advised him to "get up a company and go to Raleigh" to kill the editor of the local newspaper because he had "come out in favor of the old union." In Mississippi, Confederate veterans, deserters, and freed slaves in Jones County rose up in armed insurrection against the Confederate authorities, and even tried to create their own government. In general, though, government opposition was more sporadic and less organized there than that in the North, perhaps because the South lacked a political focus like the Peace Democrats. The presence of Union troops in large parts of the Confederacy also helped unify Southerners against a common threat.[45]

As the fall 1863 elections approached, the rank and file in the Union armies watched the political developments on the home front with some trepidation. They remembered well the Copperhead gains in 1862. Men who had never followed election campaigns began taking a keen interest in political affairs back home, particularly those from Ohio, where the infamous Clement Vallandigham was running for governor. When the election results showed a resounding defeat for the chief Copperhead, men from all states rejoiced. Ninety-five percent of Ohio's military men voted for Vallandigham's opponent.[46]

* * *

Jennie to Josiah

Peoria Nov 7th 1863

My Dear Friend,

As you say, I did indeed think it very strange not to hear from you. Sometimes I thought you might be coming soon therefore deferred writing. But when days

---

45 McPherson, *Battle Cry of Freedom*, 297-304; Sally Jenkins and John Stauffer, *The State of Jones: The Small Southern County That Seceded From The Confederacy* (New York, NY 2010), 2-5. Letter from A. A. Bethune to G. W. Graham, August 12, 1863. Used with permission of Mary E. Stuart Perrin.

46 Ramold, *Across the Divide*, 136-137, 143-146; Weber, *Copperheads*, 121.

numbered into weeks and still no words either verbal or written came to cheer the weary hours passed in uncertainty. I fear Hope had almost faded into doubt yet your dear missive of the 3rd inst chased all the clouds away and hope once again brightens the present.

This is such a beautiful day how I wish you were here to help me enjoy it remember dearest friend I am looking for such a pleasure soon now please dont disappoint me.

Sarah Currie left on Tuesday for Chicago. She intends staying with Maggie until the last of next week, that is if she dont get homesick.

Well dear friend the thought of talking with you soon almost puts to flight the idea of writing, yet I wanted to tell you to be sure and come next week. Do take good care of your self for somebody is very anxious to have the dear one well again. I will give you the news when we meet. Go with many kind wishes for thee, my dearest friend. I will say good bye.

I remain as ever yours,

Jennie E. Lindsay

Josiah to Jennie

"Home", Hanover Ills Nov. 24th 1863

My Dear Jennie,

You will no doubt think strange that I still write from "Home"—but so it is—indeed it is a very pleasant place but I scarcely seem inclined to leave it, tho I think it realy seems high time. I have fixed on several times to move but disappointment that bane of earthly sorrows still denied the right.

I think, I can soon travel, now however, and I shall try to move a little. I am gaining strength pretty fast but my voice does not keep pace, tho it has improved some. I think this cold climate is not good for it. I must have a warmer.

Your dear letter of the 7th inst. came duly to hand and I could have replied sooner but at one time I thought to dispence with such reply, as I intended to leave this week but when the time came I had to travel to bed and hence my disappointment, so dear Jennie you will please excuse my delay.

If all is well I have now calculated on next week—tho I expect I shall go by way of Monmouth and perhaps spend a few days. I will write you again when I leave here.

If you were here now we might have a good sleigh-ride as quite a snow fell today, but of course it will be just as good at Peoria—indeed you may be even now enjoying its pleasures. But I must go to sleep and dream of more happy times—this is already tedious.

So dearest Jennie wishing you good health, happy dreams with sweet sleep, and in the joyous anticipation of an immediate and happy meeting I remain as ever Your affectionate friend

J. Moore

Josiah to Jennie

Cairo Ills
Dec. 20th 1863

My dear Jennie,

Having a little spare time I devote it to sending you a few lines ere I leave the pale of civilization, thos it is not long since it was my painful task to use those thrilling words "goodbye" yet I can scarcely think that they are past.

I reached the train in due time and took passage for Cairo, but had to stop at ElPasso till about night i.e. from noon. The day was pretty cold and you may be sure I [illegible] fell into the temptation of Lot,s wife—many a lingering look was cast toward the dear happy days of the past week when with the beloved one all seemed joyous as a [illegible]. I spent the night on the cars arriving here about 8 a.m. Saturday. I was much surprised to find no snow this of course recalled our sleighride—still there is a pretty sharp frost. You will ask why I am locating at Cairo. Well dear Jennie I might have gotten a more desirable place but so it is and I cant better it. Very few boats are now mooring. I do not expect one till evening. This makes "time fly" very slowly but I must make the best of it—last sabbath was unpleasant outside—how sadly are the times reversed. This is all sunshine without but dark and lonely within. I shall try however and live not so much in the present—i.e. only stay here.

I shall write again on reaching V—till then and ever, with sweet memories of the happy past and brighter anticipation of a brighter future, with the best wishes of a devoted and loving friend I again bid my beloved Jennie a kind adieu.

J. Moore
P.S. Please excuse a hasty scrible goodbye J.M.

Josiah finally rejoined his regiment on Christmas Day. Lieutenant Colonel Smith, writing to Major Peats who was back in Illinois on a recruiting mission, reported that Josiah's health "is not good but much better than when you saw him."[47]

One of the members of the 17th Illinois reported on how the men were faring with occupation duty. "Usual routine of camp duty and a small amount of drill intermixed is about all we have to do," he said, although he did add, "Vicksburg is full of women now."[48]

In his letter a year earlier on October 7, 1862, Josiah had informed Jennie, "Find enclosed a secesh letter I got it among some secesh baggage at Iuka." On November 23, 1863, the Peoria *Daily Transcript* published a "secesh letter picked up by one of our boys." It may well be that this letter, from a wife to her husband in the Confederate army, is the one Josiah mentioned. Even if it is not, it offers a fascinating, heartfelt glimpse into the suffering war also brings to the folks at home:

Seat yourself down to let you know that we hain't had nothing to eat! The cows is got so they don't give no milk. Since you and the three boys were conscripted I've had to see to everything. I have to go barefooted all the time. My feet is full of sores and splinters. I close by saying we are sick and hellish mad. I remain your slavish wife until death which hain't fur off without a great change!

SS Tynne
PS I hain't in humor to write.
PS How can I write when I hain't got nothing to eat? Sis Boone is dead and I am glad of it.

---

47 Letter from Lt. Colonel Frank Smith to Frank Peats, February 2, 1864. Peats collection.

48 Letter from Wes Hull to Frank Peats, December 13, 1863. Peats collection.

1864 CHAPTER 16

"O Such Destruction"

Ulysses S. Grant was moving up, and that meant the Army of the Tennessee would have a new commander.

The 17th Illinois had served under Grant almost from its inception. He was elevated to command of the Military Division of the Mississippi in September 1863, and just six months later, in March of 1864, Grant was promoted to lieutenant general (the first person to hold that rank since George Washington) and given command of all the Northern armies. Lincoln was disappointed in George Meade's failure to destroy Lee's Virginia army after Gettysburg, and knew Henry Halleck was simply out of his depth in the field and behind a desk trying to run the giant war effort. The president watched the rise of Grant in the West and believed he was the man who could oversee not only the defeat of Lee, but the coordinated destruction of the entire Confederacy and bring an end to the war. William T. Sherman moved up into Grant's former spot as the head of the Military Division of the Mississippi, and James McPherson took the reins of the Army of the Tennessee.[1]

William Tecumseh Sherman was an 1840 graduate of the United States Military Academy. Stationed in California during the Mexican War, he had missed the fighting and afterward left the army to go into business. He became the superintendent of a military academy in Louisiana in 1859 (subsequently Louisiana State University), but resigned when the sectional troubles reared

---

1 McPherson, *Battle Cry of Freedom*, 718-719; Woodworth, *Nothing But Victory*, 460, 490-491.

their head. For a time he was in limbo, but he rejoined the army as a colonel in May 1861 and fought as a brigade commander at Bull Run that July before being transferred to the Western Theater, where he acquired a reputation for emotional instability. It was not until he linked up with General Grant that Sherman enjoyed real success in the field. He and Grant understood one another, and Sherman quickly became one of Grant's most loyal supporters, and visa versa.[2]

After the rather uneventful six months following the capitulation of Vicksburg, Sherman was concerned about the condition of the men garrisoning the city. He cited a "general relaxation of effort," along with a surfeit of soldiers taking leaves, furloughs, and discharges. In many ways, this lull was typical of the war. Battles were vicious and deadly, but active campaigning was also relatively infrequent. Campaigning usually ended in the late fall when cold weather set in, and did not resume until the following spring when the snow melted and the ground dried out. Men looked for various diversions during this interlude, and during the intervals between marching and fighting. Some read, some enjoyed chess and other board games, and others played music. Many soldiers turned to gambling to pass time. "I declared to keep from playing cards while acting of a Solider I hope and pray to God to assist me in my intentions and be my guide through this terrible for sure war," recorded Robert Duncan in his company log. Many men recalled and wrote about the cards and other gambling materials they had tossed or spotted along the side of the road on the march to battle. Few wanted to have those materials found on their bodies if they were killed in a fight.[3]

Josiah witnessed the same signs of relaxation in the men of the 17th Illinois noted by Sherman. Josiah returned to the regiment on Christmas Day to find "the old 17th . . . basking in the sunlight of their own grandeur and greatness as they gently mused on the prospects of being soon filled up by recruits." He returned just in time to experience Christmas in Vicksburg. Lieutenant Colonel Smith, the regiment's commander, recalled that the Union garrison enjoyed the holiday, and the 17th regiment had "the fewest men drunk" because the command was deployed on picket duty. It was, recorded Smith, "a perfect hell

---

2   Boatner, *Civil War Dictionary*, 750-751.

3   Sherman, *Personal Memoirs of Gen. W.T. Sherman*, 362; Woodworth, *Nothing But Victory*, 460; Bell Irvin Wiley and Horst D. Milhollen, *They Who Fought Here* (New York, NY, 1959), 144-154. Blog, *Mississippians in the Confederate Army*.

downtown that day, everybody was drunk officers, soldiers, citizens, civilians, negroes, and women."[4]

Josiah continued corresponding with Jennie from Vicksburg. Sadly, none of her letters from 1864 have survived. We know she continued to write to Josiah because he referred to her letters in those he penned to her in return. Perhaps he destroyed them in case he was captured because he didn't want them to fall into enemy hands. Or, they may have been lost on the way home, or destroyed in another manner. Unfortunately, we will likely never know.[5]

Josiah to Jennie

Miss J. E Lindsay
Peoria Ills
Vicksburg, Miss.
Jan. 9th 1864[6]

My beloved friend,

    Another happy opportunity affords the dear privilege of [illegible] *my "weekly"—"dear privilege" indeed as it seems the only and best substitute for the more desirable – but my dear Jennie, something seems to be wanting , not only is the loved one absent, but, for many long and weary days, no word of happy cheer has come to greet our lonely "soldier boy"—no dear message has yet come to cheer the lonely hours—Well I presume I must "learn to labor and to wait"—our Southron mail has been very irregular, but perhaps not more, than that going North. tho I believe this is my fourth since leaving the City I shall expect to hear from thee dearest Jennie pretty soon however, and then more often—now Jennie please don't forget—else these four months will seem very long—very true, you may say, for they have a long subject. Ah, yes, but nature deals in opposites.*

4   Letter from Josiah Moore to Frank Peats January 3, 1864. Peats Collection; Letter from Lt. Col. Smith to Frank Peats December 29, 1863. Peats Collection.

5   Hess, "Tell Me What the Sensations Are," 123.

6   Josiah misdated this letter 1864.

Josiah Moore and others in the field? This remarkable image, which seems to show one man reading or preaching to five others, appeared in *Military Images* magazine (Vol. XXV, No. 3, November/December 2003), and is from an album of images of the 7th Indiana Cavalry. The subjects are identified, left to right, as follows: "W. Watts, C. P. Phelps, General McConnell, R. H. Harvig, W. L. Ashe, and Captain Moore." "McConnell" is brevet Brig. Gen. John McConnell of the 5th Illinois Cavalry. No other identified individual with the surname "Moore" attached to these units resemble the "Moore" in this photo. The "Moore" depicted here is also quite tall, and Josiah was 6'4". In addition, the facial resemblance to Josiah, and his postwar career as a preacher, makes it highly likely that this is Josiah reading scripture around the time of the Meridian campaign. *John Sickles*

Andie was to see me yesterday. he still seems to enjoy his good health. I also saw him again, at the "festival" of our "Union Literary Asociation"[7] on last evening, where we had a very pleasant time i.e. considering the barbaric surroundings, we had quite a good supper—our guests consisted of society members & invited friends (soldiers) a few Southron females and Northern ladies a few of whom were old acquaintances, of course it is very cheering to see "white—folks" so far South—

---

7   Josiah makes no specific mention of any kind of religious fervor sweeping the camps, but the Union Literary Association could have been some type of religious endeavor, or some kind of intellectual convocation. Unfortunately, I could not find anything further about it.

there are now quite a number of young ladies, from the North, here employed as teachers of contrabands, they seem very well pleased with their work and say they succeed far beyond expectations, one of the young ladies teaches the soldiers of the Regt.

The weather has been quite cool for some time, tho no snow—I presume there is glorious sleighing up North—We have not all "gone in" as Veterans yet, tho some Regts have been caught pretty severely—the old 17th is not so rash.

My health still improves a little, but O how much better could I but hear "good news" from my dearest Jennie yet hoping soon to enjoy this dear favor, I bid her now a kind good night—with best wishes for many joyous days.
I am as ever yours . . . a kiss.

J. Moore

Josiah to Jennie

Miss J. E Lindsay
Peoria Ills
Vicksburg, Miss.
Jan. 16th 1864

My dear Jennie,

Tho no kind message has yet arrived from the loved one I have resolved to try again, and while seated by my desk tho [illegible] rather [illegible] I feel as tho a "kindred spirit" sympathizes.

About two hours after writing my last we rec,d "marching orders"—Our Brgd went aboard of boats early sabbath morning (sabbath you know is the day) to go in pursuit of rebels who had blockaded the river 150 miles above. We started but like all sabbath day work, the expedition proved a bore. The weather was quite cold, the boats were crowded the men were much exposed, there was much ice running in the river and it took us about 4 days to go about 120 miles. So as you may easily imagine, when we arrived the bird had taken the wings of the morning and flown far hence and we found "all quiet on the Potomac."

The "rebs" had succeeded in crossing 2500 stand of arms to the Ark shore and got them safely away West into the interior before our arrival. we caught a couple of their pickets—returned covered all over with glory and honor and mud, and reached the city of the hills about noon yesterday—so [illegible] *it be.*[8]

In my last I spoke of having no orders to move so I may say now but we may get here before sabbath yet—as with the soldier so with the christian it behooves him to be always ready.

Now my dearest friend just imagine how disappointed somebody was on his return on yesterday and still no joyous salutation from thee—almost a month since the sad adieu was given and yet all is still as the mid—night hour. It is now about 9 P.M., a cool balmy air floats gently round, gay Luna marches proudly through a starry world and casts a gentle smile on loved nature's calm repose—one remains unchained and awaits the smiles of a brighter light. now dearest Jennie don't forget that your soldier boy is away from home. goodnight sweet sleep and happy dreams with the best wishes of your devoted friend as ever.

J. Moore

Josiah to Jennie

Vicksburg Miss.
Jan 30th 1864

My beloved friend,

Your evening's chat is welcomed—yes, thrice welcome! and tho a substitute may now obtrude I would not promise the dear reader an equal amount of pleasure—Oh my dear Jennie why did you wait so long? over one month—yes and a half to that, from we parted till I first heard from you—You may believe I had numerous visitants—by way of conjectures as to what had happened—sometimes I thought you might be sick, then again that you were delaying for mischief, or worse still, quit altogether—so you see I had plenty to think about, and not a very pleasant time either. But your dear message of the 16th inst dispelled all clouds

---

8   The foray Josiah described was the January 10-16, 1864, expedition to Sunnyside Landing, Arkansas, to counter Confederate guerillas harassing shipping on the Mississippi River. The 17th Illinois was part of a force that included the 81st and 124th Illinois, the 7th Missouri, and the 8th Ohio Artillery. The force left on the January 10, found little or nothing, and returned to Vicksburg on the 16th after suffering no casualties. Dyer, *Compendium*, Vol II, 784.

and fears, tho I had so set myself to the hard task of learning to wait, that I scarcely realized, for a time, that the spell was broken.

I was glad to hear that you were well, tho a little surprised at your promotion—indeed I can almost pardon your silence, since you had something more useful to do, perhaps you think kitchen girls have the best chance of getting married. how is that Jennie? I wish I could help you i.e. about the time meals are ready—O dear I think I could stay in the kitchen all the time—I could try—O I must tell you my dream—On the eve of receiving your letter I drempt of being in your house and in quite a hurry to see someone. I left the parlor and near the back door of the hall I met Mrs. Lindsay, just spoke, and was about to pass on, when she spoke and said she supposed I wanted to see Jennie who was just then in the dining room, I thot I took about one step and would see you in an instant—when I—waked—O how disappointed I felt—such a sudden transition I could hardly credit it—But you will notice, Jennie, that I was going towards the kitchen—perfectly, willing to share its honors—when you get tired, only about half do the work and then they will release you—I know I should not dictate anything bad, but you need not remember it. I wish you much success, only take good care of your dear self, aint it too bad jennie that kitchen girls get married and leave people to work for themselves—aint they foolish? I think so.

Well my dear Jennie you must spare some time this evening and leave the old kitchen of this world for the more spacious halls of joyous friendship, where the memories of the past cluster round in sweet delight, and where friends were wont to meet as they would meet again, to enjoy the happy association of happy friends, tho here I only stay, I dont live here, I mostly live over those dear times when two selfish little individuals used to arrogate the idea that the population of this world was in the aggregate, two, but as you say another month has past and the brighter moment draws nearer. so it does—our 4th month is now on the wane but even this seems long, poor little creature how lonesome you must now be, after George and Maggie have gone. I am real sorry you did not get to go along but of course you could not feel right to leave the dear folks at home. You can tell Maggie I am glad she got caught in a snow drift, because she called me naughty. O you asked if I took my medicine—Well I took it but it was not as good as what Jennie gave—it lacked the charm of the giver. Now my dearest Jennie you must not wait so long again, please dont? Cant you let me hear from you once a week—if you do I will not forget "Saturday" so with the best wishes of yours as ever I gently steal away with my goodnight kiss.

J.

Please write me a very long letter and please your—goodnight   J.

> *I almost forget to tell you—I did not write last Saturday, the mail came late in the evening I waited to hear from it expecting a letter surely but dear me it came not—so I did not feel very well and went to bed—I was not well but I believe a letter would have cured me, so you aint done giving medicine yet—goodnight my dearest Jennie sweet—J.M.*
>
> *I saw Andie a few days since he still keeps very well, I have been very busy since my return and now there is an expedition afoot, a large one.[9] I do not know however whether or not I'll go I dont like to risk my health now, tho I'd like to be along. J.*

The large expedition Josiah mentioned in closing referred to a plan being drawn up by Sherman. He was concerned about Rebel forces left in Mississippi and Louisiana that threatened shipping on the river, and also wanted to eliminate the rail transportation center at Meridian, Mississippi, about 135 miles east of Vicksburg. "When men take up arms to resist a Rightful Authority we are compelled to use a like force, because all reason and argument cease when arms are resorted to," reasoned Sherman. "When the provisions, forage, horses, mules, wagons, etc are used by our enemy it is clearly our duty & Right to take them also; because otherwise they might be used against us. In like manner all houses left vacant by an inimical people are clearly our Right, and such as are needed as Storehouses, Hospitals, & Quarters."[10]

Sherman also issued instructions for his men to leave women, children, and other non-combatants alone unless any of them "comes out into the public streets & creates disorder." In that case, they should be "punished, restrained, or banished." Sherman also directed that anyone communicating with "parties in hostility" were to be treated as "spies & can be punished according to Law with death or minor punishment." His directive foretold anguish and destruction for a wide swath of people in that part of Mississippi.[11]

Sherman moved out of Vicksburg on February 3 with about 20,000 men in two infantry corps screened by a force of cavalry. Because he wanted to travel

---

9   Sherman's forthcoming Meridian Campaign, February 3-28, 1864, in which the 17th Illinois would participate.

10   Woodworth, *Nothing But Victory*, 479; Marszalek, *Sherman, A Soldier's Passion for Order*, 238.

11   Simpson, *The Civil War: The Third Year*, 687-688.

quickly with sufficient supplies for the expedition, he reserved the wagons for food and ammunition and instructed his men, including officers, to leave behind all their tents and baggage. That caused a lot of complaining. "There is a considerable swearing going on among the officers to think they can not take any tents or baggage " admitted the 17th's commander Smith. The cold and blustery conditions were not ideal for camping in the open. Sergeant Duncan, the 17th's company clerk, reported that at one point during the campaign the men had to deal with "a half inch of ice."[12]

The 17th Illinois was now part of Jasper Maltby's brigade and, along with the 8th and 30th Illinois and 7th Missouri, formed part of the right wing (XVII Corps) of Sherman's advance. Steven Hurlbut's XVI Corps formed the left wing. Josiah was supposed to remain behind because of his health, but he talked his way into participating.[13]

James McPherson's men moved through the capital at Jackson, where "plantation houses and homes were burned and nearly one-half of" the town destroyed, and then on through Brandon, Morton, Hillsborough, and Decatur before reaching Meridian. The people of Jackson, observed Duncan, were "getting their so-called southern rights I suppose." Sherman ordered the destruction of the arsenal, storehouses, and any other structure that might serve to assist the Confederate army. Some civilian structures, such as houses and retail establishments, were also torched. "Sherman's army left fire and famine in its track," wrote one Yankee soldier. "The country was one lurid blaze of fire; burning cotton gins and deserted buildings were seen on every hand. I regret to say it but oft times habitations were burned down over the heads of occupants, but not by order."[14]

The 17th, along with many other units of the force, destroyed rail lines including the Southern Railroad of Mississippi and the Mobile and Ohio by

12 Letter from Lt. Col Smith to Frank Peats February 2, 1864; Marszalek, *Sherman, A Soldier's Passion for Order,* 253; Letter from Lt. Col Smith to Frank Peats, February 2, 1864.

13 Jasper A. Maltby, an Ohio native, businessman, and gunsmith, enlisted in the 45th Illinois and became its lieutenant colonel. He was a good officer with the unlucky attribute of attracting enemy metal. He was first wounded in the Mexican War, again by two musket balls through his thighs and above his elbow at Fort Donelson, and struck in the head and side by flying timber from the explosion of a mine at Vicksburg that crushed his ribs and caused severe internal injuries from which he never fully recovered. Maltby, whose brother was a Confederate captain, would later serve as Vicksburg's military mayor. He died there on December 12, 1867. Welsh, *Military Histories of Union Generals,* 219.

14 *Sherman's Forgotten Campaign,* 190.

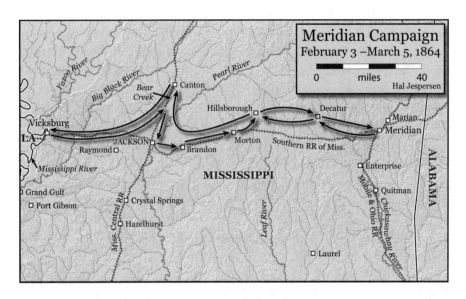

removing the rails, placing them over a fire hot enough to soften the metal, and wrapping them around a tree or pole. The soldiers called the result "Sherman's neckties."[15]

A woman from Meridian offered the civilian perspective in a letter to her mother that somehow found its way into the pages of the *New York Times* in March 1864: "Our store was burned to the ground and so was another of our new houses," she wrote. "My two milch cows were killed, and every one in the town; and for eight or ten miles around all cattle and horses. . . . The railroad is torn up, both up and down for miles and all the ties burned and the iron bent and destroyed. O such destruction! I do not believe you or anyone else would know the place. There's not a fence in Meridian. I have not one rail left."[16]

When the expedition ended, Sherman reported, "Meridian, with its depots, store—houses, arsenal, hospitals, offices, hotels, and cantonments no longer exists." We drove the enemy "out of Mississippi," exclaimed Sherman, "destroyed the only remaining railroads in the state, the only roads by which he could maintain any army in Mississippi threatening to our forces on the main river. We subsisted our army and animals chiefly on his stores, brought away

---

15 William Lorimer paper, Vicksburg NMP; Duncan, Company log; Margie Riddle Bearss, *Sherman's Forgotten Campaign: The Meridian Expedition* (Baltimore, MD, 1987), 174-190. Woodworth, *Nothing But Victory*, 484.

16 Ibid., 305.

Brigadier General Jasper A. Maltby, a former officer in the 45th Illinois Infantry, was badly wounded at both Fort Donelson and again at Vicksburg, and later promoted to brigadier general in August of 1863. Maltby led the brigade in which Josiah and the 17th Illinois served during the Meridian Campaign. After the war, he was appointed military mayor of Vicksburg, but he never fully recovered from his wounds and died there on December 12, 1867. *Author*

about 400 prisoners and full 5,000 Negroes, about 1,000 white refugees, about 3,000 animals (horses, mules, oxen) and any quantity of wagons and vehicles." One of the participants also reported that "pork seemed plenty as the woods were full of razor back hogs."[17]

Thousands of former slaves—"negro men, women, and children of all ages and with all their belongings that could carry with them lined the flanks of our army front to rear . . . all having the inspiration they were now a free people"— followed the army column back to Vicksburg. One historian described the Meridian Campaign as "military emancipation at high tide." It has been estimated that some 5,000 slaves emancipated by Sherman's men trailed their liberators to freedom—a number that would double later that year when Sherman marched from Atlanta to Savannah. During the Meridian campaign, a Union soldier had called out to one young former slave, "Where you going to, youngster?" "I'm gui-in to glory, master," came the reply. However, given the desolate nature of the ground over which both Sherman's men and the newly freed slaves moved, it was hunger and starvation, and not glory, that permeated all ranks.[18]

17 OR 32, pt. 1, 176; Lorimer paper; Bearss, *Sherman's Forgotten Campaign*, 192.

18 James Oakes, October 23, 2013 lecture at Dickinson College, Carlisle, PA; Lorimer paper; Woodworth, *Nothing But Victory*, 486-487; Oakes, *Freedom National*, 374.

The men returned to Vicksburg on March 3. After 30 days spent living outdoors, their uniforms were in rags and "one man in every five or six was barefoot." Maltby's and the two other brigades of the division covered 27 miles on the final day and "double-quicked" the final eight miles into Vicksburg.[19]

Confederate authorities assessed the severe damage to the Southern Railroad, the line destroyed by the 17th Illinois and the other units of Maltby's brigade. The report read: "Between Jackson and Meridian—4 bridges entirely destroyed, aggregate length 950 feet; 47 bridges entirely destroyed aggregate length 3,248 feet; 4 miles of track torn up, iron badly burned and bent, and most of the cross ties burned. Five thousand cross ties will be required, 300 bars of iron, and 500,000 feet of bridge timbers to complete the work." Other rail lines to and from Meridian suffered as much, or worse.[20]

In his official report, McPherson wrote that his men had marched 360 miles and destroyed 55 miles of railroad, along with 53 railroad bridges and culverts and more than 6,000 feet of trestle work. In addition, the expedition destroyed 19 locomotives and 28 rail cars. Mortimer D. Leggett's division, which included Maltby's brigade and the 17th Illinois, claimed credit for 24 of those 55 miles of track, 52 of the 53 bridges, and 4,000 feet of the trestle work.[21]

The XVII Corps lost 13 men killed, one officer and 36 enlisted men wounded, and one officer and 103 men captured or missing. According to George Smith, seven members of the 17th Illinois were captured while on a foraging expedition. Silas Warren of Company F and Lt. Edmund Ryan of Company A were reported among the missing.[22]

While the Meridian expedition does not rank as one of the war's (or Sherman's) greatest achievements, it did provide the Union with a dress rehearsal of sorts for the more notable (or notorious) effort by Sherman later in 1864 when he cut the heart out of Georgia on his March to the Sea from Atlanta to Savannah on the Atlantic coast. The Meridian expedition taught Sherman lessons he would use on his later march. The Meridian experiment demonstrated that the central portions of Southern states lacked a strong military presence, and that his foot soldiers could live off the land by raiding

19 Woodworth, *Nothing But Victory*, 487.

20 Bearss, *Sherman's Forgotten Campaign*, 242.

21 *OR* 32, pt. 1, 213 and 225.

22 Letter from John Griffin to Frank Peats, April 20, 1865.

field and taking what was needed from citizens. That knowledge became pivotal for the success of the March to the Sea.

* * *

Josiah to Jennie

Vicksburg Miss
March 5th, 1864

My Beloved Friend,

> *The long expected and happy opportunity again affords the lonely "soldier boy" sweet converse with his dear dear Jennie—Thrice joyous eve.*
> *Our famous raid was concluded on yesterday when by a forced march of 26 miles we reached our City of the hills.*
> *When at Canton 60 miles distant I wrote a hasty scrible by firelight and sent by a messenger coming in on special business, if you rec'd it, all right Jennie, but if not it is not much loss for it was realy too rough to be seen in civilization. I addressed it the same as this, having rec'd yours of Jan, 25 just before starting, in which you spoke of soon visiting Chicago—On my arrival yesterday I found to my great joy two of those dear missives that "cheer the heart"—you cannot imagine how I longed to realize the happy event—each lingering day seemed like an age— but "hope deferred" was "pleasure obtained", tho to have met the author would have been "joy beyond measure", but such a "happy day" would be too much in this barbarous clime—enough, to hope that the day is not far distant when such a happy event may be realized beyond the frowns of "grim visaged war."*
> *Our raid was quite prosperous tho we lost several men, but we drove the rebels at every point—our principle work consisted in destroying R. Roads of which we disabled about 500 miles, thus destroying all rebel communications within 150 miles of this place. My health tho rather slim on starting improved so that it was never better than now, I believe even a "slow sleigh—ride" would not hurt me, i.e. my dear Jennie being along. O dear, there I wouldn't care how slowly, providing a termination would be likely to separate.*

I was glad dear Jennie to hear of your prospective Chicago visit and hope that you have ere this arrived in safety, to find George & Maggie well and to enjoy yourself as ardently as he who loves—What will you now.[23]

My best regards to George & Maggie, I can almost envy the happy trinity. O I forget three is no company—Well my dear dear Jennie I hope necessity may not soon again cause such a blank in our communications. With best wishes of your loving friend I bid thee dear Jennie a kind goodnight. J. Moore—a kiss goodnight.

Please write often and I can assure you dear Jennie that if "sweet Saturday eve" is not improved it shall be no fault of this humble subscriber. yours.J. M.

Unfortunately, Josiah did not write about the destruction and confiscation of civilian property he certainly witnessed on the Meridian raid, so his thoughts on that activity will forever remain unknown. Large numbers of former slaves accompanied the Union troops back to Vicksburg, something else he did not include in his letter home to Jennie.

Josiah to Jennie

Vicksburg Miss,
March 12, 1864 "Saturday"

My Dearly Beloved,

Another joyous evening returns with all its joyous memories and not less pleasant duties.

Your dearest of the dear little messenger of the 20ult came duly to hand and my dear, dear Jennie I need not tell you how it was read and reread, for should I make the attempt this pen, would fail, its love "lingers with me still"—O my dear Jennie I can scarcely feel myself worthy of such pure and holy regard, to merit such seems too much for such as I, yet it is no dream—I feel as tho I have already realized the truth and reality of such affection and tho poor the return, yet could you but read this heart, dearest Jennie, you could see how supremely it loves thee—no rival can there be found—If I be "king", there can be but one queen, and

---

23 Approximately three lines of text were deliberately cut from the letter at this point.

that, my own dearest Jennie. Yet, O dear, Jennie is not here, dear loved one, how sad and lonely seems the darkening world—"happiness" can never be found so far from thee. Yet soon will the day break be dawning, there, O there! the pleasures of you will blossom once more and we'll all meet again in the morning.

I was so sorry to hear of your illness—yet pleased to learn of its short duration—Indeed I think that your idea of taking sick just to test the good qualities of Maggie's nursing is rather amusing. I think I shall tell Maggie sometime of your mischief—and then, O dear, you propose that if I was there you would have me take your medicine—Why Jennie aint you ashamed? Why if I were there, I would not let either George or Maggie nurse you, how would that suit you? O well, my dearest, I think I should be there about that time.

I was very glad indeed to hear of your safe arrival and that you found all well, you seem very much amused with Maggie's skating, tho I presume, not more than myself. O Jennie why did you not tell me that dream of Maggies, some of her jokes I presume—I guess she saw your letter. Well dearest I will promise to pardon that "poor scribling" as you insist on naming it, only let me have at least one dear letter from my dearest Jennie once a week, and if remembering "Saturdays" will prevent dear Jennie being sick—then dear Jennie shall not be sick any more—now aint that fair?

Well I fear my darling is being wearied so I will not detain longer. Only tell Maggie that she must let you be when you are writing.

Hoping that this may find my dearest love in good health enjoying the love and association of good and dear friends, I again bid thee a kind goodnight—as short while. As ever,

J. Moore

P.S. How long do you intend remaining in Chicago, Jennie? If you remain some time could I not, improve the address. I have only guessed at it but hope you may get my letters all right. As above J.M. My goodnight kiss, Sweet dreams.

Josiah to Jennie

Vicksburg Miss. Mar. 19 1864
Sat. eve.

My dear Jennie,

In the absence of my "weekly visitor" I must speak with the dear original, whom tho cruel space may separate, yet imagination pictures the more pleasing reality—two months is not too much to anticipate, Jennie dearest, is it? I know that even this seems an age, yet what of it, if "hope defferred is pleasure obtained."

Well dearest, I have not been doing very much this week, unless, as you say, and you know dear Jennie's words cannot be forgotten, I have been "living a sort of dream life." I have been writing most of the time, making out our Muster & Pay Rolls, and tho you may say, why what has that to do with our evening chat? Well you see that name, exquisite because of asociations, "Peoria Ills," occurs on the rolls very often. and never without the recalling of some joyous moment of the past.

Perhaps you may chide me for allowing my mind to wander so from my business. yes, but, dearest, might there not be allowed some difference of opinion on what is "my business"? This granted, my business continues good, I shall continue to think of thee amid the sweetest memories of the day and not less will be my joy to know that one does miss me at home, yes beloved friend I believe I can appreciate full well your meaning, where you contrast your "own quiet home life" with the more stirring scenes of the Queen City—the glitter and show of the outer world, afford but little enchantment, when there is nothing among them that we can call ours—O but I didn't intend to tease you my dear by telling my experience—Please excuse, or, give me a kiss—now I am going, goodbye—

Dear Jennie, how do you do? none better I hope, I have not had a letter from you this week. Well dearest when these two months are over, then, then if you dont write, I'll go where writing will be. O dear, I dont know—a humbug I guess, the only bug word I can remember—I have not reenlisted yet.[24] Dont much like the idea of going into such large crowd, would prefer a more select company, think I know where there is one. O yes, I see I have tired you out my dear, aint you pleased to see this sheet so nearly full? well when next Sat. comes there again comes another sweet opportunity—in the mean time I bid thee, beloved Jennie, a kind good night.

Yours ever

J. Moore

---

24 Josiah and the original men of the 17th Illinois were sworn into Federal service in May 1861 for a three-year term, so their original enlistments were approaching an end. It appears as though Josiah had not yet decided to reenlist, or perhaps he was teasing Jennie by hinting he might sign up again.

Jane Elizabeth good night sweet dreams & sweet kiss goodbye, only a short time tho. J.M.

Andie was to see me this week he looks very well indeed, it seems like home to see him, enough to know he is Jennie's friend—good bye. J.M.

Josiah to Jennie

Vicksburg Miss. March 26, 1864
"Sat eve"

Beloved friend,

Another weary week has gone with all its joys & sorrows, yet the dear absent one is silent. All is hushed and still, yet she is unheard from. I have been looking very anxiously all week, dear Jennie, for the dear little message of love, that which Jennie alone can send.

Well my dear Jennie, I hope all is well, but you cannot imagine how anxious I feel when over three weeks pass without bringing any remembrance from my dearest Jennie.—my letters may not reach you and hence you may justly think me very indifferent, or you may be unwell and cannot write—or again you may be unwell and do not wish to write and create anxiety—But I hope my dearest that nothing of this is so. O I would not, I could not be so cruel as to give thee my dearest darling, one moments pain by seeming indifference—no indeed, my dear, no pangs shall ever thus pierce my dear Jennie's loving heart, a love too sacred, too pure, to be coldly treated, a love more desirable to be possessed than all earthly treasures, yes, my dear you are my "happiness", and with thee alone it can be enjoyed— separation from thee is only endurable, in hope of the brighter day, and that day is slowly approaching, yet O how tardily it seems to linger by the way. But it has pleased a kind Providence to preserve thus far and to him still I look for the happy end, less than two months of our time now to serve—and then Jennie I'm coming for a kiss—well I guess so. I aint going to travel 1000 miles for nothing, you'll see if I do, I've not forgotten, tho I may be out of practice. I can soon learn however, dont you think so?

Well my dearest , I've teased you long enough, so if you will pardon me, I will give you a good night kiss, but I forgot, now my dear Jennie unless you write soon. I must have more than one kiss on my return—so now you know the consequence of your failure, no backing out—Well now dearest I must bid you another goodnight, as oft before, hoping soon to realize thy gentle "goodnight kiss" in reality I remain as ever yours.

J. Moore

Josiah to Jennie

Vicksburg Miss. April 2, 1864
My Beloved Friend:

Your dear letter of the 18ult. has been for several days the welcome companion of your humble servant—its joys and sorrows are mine—days of anxious care and watching tell but too plainly what was the matter, but as the brighter day has its cloud and shade, so I hope that ere this my dear Jennie may have fully recovered. In my last I expressed fears that your ill health was keeping back those thrice welcome little visitants—yes, too true. Yet had you tried me I think I could have pardoned all their "little failings"—even tho they had been "blue" letters. Indeed I think you must have been very lonely during that "four weeks" of silence, for tho well, I had my dark experience quite to hearts content, and you are not alone in tribulation. I think, myself, dear Jennie that I was a little "naughty" but for your sake I try and be good now. I only wish I were with you till I would get that scolding—just think of me being so abused—well I'm coming for my share pretty soon, so you must be prepared.

Well dearest you wished me not to say anything about me—just think what a trouble you are to me and now I must think of you, for I must think of somebody. I cannot must not think of me. Well dearest friend I believe I can spend my time very joyfully thinking of you. I want no better subject. I believe I can imagine how "selfish" you've been thinking of your "soldier boy"—Yes my dear Jennie I fear you do think too much, for tho it gives great pleasure to know that I am missed by the dear one at home, and tho I would not have her forget me, yet I must say that little self would forego the pleasure of a kind remembrance if such a relief will only restore the loved one to health and vigor. I know that you do indulge in too much anxiety, and now especialy when unwell I know it cant be good—and in about two months from now if your Mother dont know you just tell me, wont you please.

It troubles me to know that you have been so unwell since your arrival in C—I fear that close city life is not as congenial as our quiet country home, tho I would *have expected different—as I think Maggie could keep you always stirring or in some exercise, not to say mischief, O no—but I hope that all may yet be well.*

My health still continues quite good. I have plenty to eat and plenty to do and I believe could feel happy did I know that you were also happy—I saw Andie a few days since he is now with another man and I think has a chance to stay some time here. he is very well. Troops are moving from here North every day. We have been expecting to go along but no orders as yet there is some idea now that as our time is so nearly out we may remain here till discharged.[25]

Hoping to hear from you often and that this may find you fully recovered I bid you my dear darling a kind good night.

Yours, J. Moore

Josiah to Jennie

Vicksburg Miss
Apr 9/64 "Sat. eve"

Beloved Friend,

Sweet indeed is the evening that, in its weekly course, returns with joyous memories of the past—a seeming foretaste of better things to come—when this dull medium shall only remain as the relic of the weary waiting hours of the anxious past. But Time with noiseless step is speeding quickly away—another week nearer. I hope, the meeting of dear friends, when it shall again be my happy privilege of meeting one long loved and esteemed as the dearest of the dear—I hope she is well this evening—enjoying good health and the sweet society of near and dear friends, nor yet forgetting that a distant one claims a kind remembrance from his dearly beloved Jennie.

It is 9 P.M. and I've just been viewing the fairy form of the delicate Luna sinking quietly down to rest, seemingly far, far away in the distant North— perhaps to watch with gentle care the sweet slumber of my dear darling Jane Elizabeth, or by a passing smile recall the brighter day when evening shades grew

---

25 Based on this, it appears Josiah decided not to reenlist. Jennie's ill health could have been the reason why he made that decision.

brighter as they gathered round—I dont intend that such fine mellow moonlight evenings shall very long tease me in my loneliness—how long? well—a month & half—O aint that a long time! I think some days long enough now to cut up for a year. I can only write you six letters more. Now what do you think my dearest? Will that be enough—perhaps too many?

But I have been tormenting you all evening and perhaps my dear is not well tho I hope better. I would not be so cruel as to cause thee dearest one moments sorrow, but to know that thou art happy is happiness enough for me. My health continues excellent, for which I hope I am truly thankful to Him from whom all our blessings flow. Andie was to see me this week. He is quite well. He spoke of coming out tomorrow. I presume you are aware that our present prospects are to stay here our time out. Mostly all other troops are gone. So now dearest darling I shall expect to hear from thee often. Beloved good night, a kiss.

Yours, J. Moore

The substance of this letter and the others sent during this period of the war (the Vicksburg occupation) reflect a more subdued lifestyle in anticipation of returning home. Josiah's last letter especially paints a relaxed and almost bucolic portrait of camp life. His mention of "Luna" surely conjured up for Jennie a mental image of the moon hanging over the encampment, smoke rising from campfires, and the men talking, laughing, reading, or writing letters home. Earlier in the war, Josiah's letters usually brimmed with military matters, often in anticipation of great martial deeds to come, or they described the fate of he and his comrades after a major battle. He fully realized that after the Meridian Campaign, there was little fighting left to do in the region, and he was preoccupied with the prospect of returning home.[26]

Josiah to Jennie

Vicksburg Miss. Apr. 16 1864
9 Sat. Eve

---

26 Unlike the letters Josiah wrote during active campaigns, the letters penned from and around Vicksburg are remarkably consistent, even down to their physical attributes. Each was written on the same type of lined paper, and almost every one begins on the same line of the first page.

My beloved Friend,

You will perhaps think this rather a late hour, and that I've encroached a little too much on sweet sat. eve—the more than sacred time of my own dear loving Jennie, this may be so, yet Ive still reserved the sweet stilly hour for thee—did I say reserved? Well my love, that is hardly correct either. I had better said stole a few hours to fix up my business for the week—yes "stole a few hours" from thee dearest—i.e. I tried to do some work and think of thee also—I mostly prefer to leave the work out—Children you know like to have the sweetest first—You need not fear. My indulging in that "practice", however that you mention—the subjects in this vicinity don't exactly suit my taste—rather different from that to which I've been used. And Jennie I believe I would rather not change now. I know many seem to think that if they live in Rome, they must do as Rome does—very nice Philosophy—yet I would prefer the love of one, a love that has no measuring value here below—a love than which all other earthly joys fade in the distance—the love of my own dearly beloved Jennie is enough for me—I only hope I may be made worthy of it.

Well dearest I have now two of those dear messages of love. I cannot find words to express the joy they brought but as the "span of separation" seems to narrow, each dear message seems more like the beloved author. O dear I envy them so much—that of the 8 inst came today—only a week since it left my love—but I hope soon to meet thee dearest—not to receive the parting kiss—no, no, I could not again leave my love, she has become too near and dear to me.

I congratulate you on your happy visit and wish you much joy on your return to our own dear home.

As yet I do not know when we may go up the river, but please write often I shall get word in time to let you know of our leaving.

As ever thine, beloved good night   J. Moore

A good night kiss to my dearest, I would send thee many, but I trust to bring them, shortly myself. Till then I shall "practice" none—what few I have, I keep for one—Dearest goodnight J.M.

Josiah's comments regarding the apperance of other women may well be in response to an inquiry from Jennie about whether he was attracted to any of the female inhabitants in the area. Her inquiry may have been prompted by the writings of people like Robert Bunting, a Texas chaplain who spread lies about widespread marriages between white troops and slave women. Bunting claimed the weddings took place in the homes of the brides' former masters, and that afterward, the homes were ransacked. While there was certainly some socialization, and even marriages, between Southern women and occupying Yankee troops, there is no evidence of widespread fraternization between soldiers and slaves. However, such stories motivated the men in the Rebel armies to keep fighting and preserve their Southern social structure.[27]

Josiah to Jennie

Vicksburg Miss.
April 23, 1864

My dearly beloved,

Another week "nearer to thee", yet not without its "hopes and fears"—need I recount them? or shall I tease my darling with them?—Well I believe she loves romance, but this is reality—at least quite enough for your humble subscriber. When I last wrote you dearest I little dreampt, that ere I should again enjoy the happy privilege of holding sweet converse with thee, I should again run the gauntlet for Libby[28]—yes I did—just so—enough for me at least—Our Regt. started to Yazoo City, 60 miles N.E. of here, on the 18 inst in Company with 2 Colored Regts & some Cavalry—when we had gone about 40 miles we were brought to a very sudden halt by a heavy artillery fire in front. we prepared to fall back but found the enemy in our rear also, and from all account either party too many for us—well we must get out—the country quite rough and covered with timber with few roads, but we at last discovered our track leading to the Yazoo River (10 miles distant) as yet unoccupied by the enemy so after some skirmishing we gained this road and reached the river with but small loss—here we were to meet the gun boats but they did not come for nearly a day. During this time the enemy kept a short distance off being rather afraid to attack while we were in a temporary fortification but we dare not go out. Two gun boats came and some

---

27 Mitchell, *Vacant Chair*, 130-131; Manning, *What This Cruel War Was Over*, 109-111.

28 Josiah's reference to running the "gauntlet for Libby" is a reference to the notorious Libby Prison in Richmond, Virginia, a common destination for captured Union officers.

provisions, this was very joyful news indeed. the boats tried to run to the city (Yazoo) 18 miles but failed. The rebels had erected such heavy batteries. One boat ran past but could not return. The rebs were geting reinforced so we had to send for help also, we could not advance—but during this time the rebs at 3 P.M. yesterday made a combined attack on the boat that run above, and was alone, and captured her—so there we were in a fix—we must get back or surrender, the latter we could not do, so we loaded our baggage on transports, that came up, during last night and left before day this morning. I presume the rebs did not discover our leaving so we got away pretty quietly after all—but we consider our escape as rather narrow—We arrived at 5 P.M. this evening after spending 5 days of about as exciting a time as we have ever as yet spent in the service—I dont want it more so however, tho I feel as tho we have great reason to thank Heaven's King for our safe return.[29]

At 12 O clock last night I took my Co, out to watch the rebs while the boats were being loaded. I got a little lonesome—so I took from my pocket book a letter and read it by moonlight—How sweetly sounded those dear words "my own dear love"? May I say they are from my dearly beloved Jennie—may I be worthy of them—they are a treasure—O dear I wish I could lay aside this pen and greet thee darling in a happy meeting, but I must wait a few more days long days, but I scribbled a long letter and I fear not very interesting to my dearest but I know her sweet disposition to overlook little faults on such occasions—so hoping to hear from thee my beloved Jennie, very soon—I bid thee a short adieu, Yours truly.

J. Moore

P.S. Much love and many kisses to thee dearest. J.M.

Josiah to Jennie

Vicksburg Miss
April 30 1864   Sat Eve

---

29   While the *Official Records* mention the actions that Josiah described, no mention is made that any portion of the 17th Illinois was engaged. However, Janet Hewitt, ed., *The Supplement to the Official Records of the Union and Confederate Armies*, 100 vols. (Wendell, 1994-2001), vol. 9, 256-257, describes the action much as Josiah did. The captured gunboat was probably the USS *Petrel*. Rebel cavalry captured it when it was tied up along the river bank. OR 32, pt. 1, 674-675.

My darling Jennie,

With mingled joy and sorrow I improve the ever joyous opportunity of spending the evening with thee dearest—joy, that time makes some progress and thus advances the "brighter day," Joy to have the sweet privilege of again perusing one of those dear messages, such as none but my dearly beloved can write—thrice welcome! nothing dearer, only my beloved darling—yet it was not without a thrill of sadness that I learned of my being unhappy or unwell, I had hoped that a return to "sweet home" and friends most dear, would be a truly happy event for my darling—yet she complains of being so lonely—well I think there is one that can fully sympathize with thee dearest, one whose joys and sorrows would be thine— one who loves thee too dearly to learn with indifference that a single pang of sorrow should ever disturb thy kind and loving heart or cause that sweet genial spirit a moments sadness—yet my beloved amid cloud and storm there is still a bright sunlight beyond, so for thee my brightest hopes still linger near—yes you must be "well" when I "come home"—or will you dearest claim that it is your turn now since I had my turn last winter—well recollect you made me take medicine last winter—Oh dear I think I could take medicine again, out of such a kind hand—But I hope that there may be no necessity for anything like this. I hope to be well, and see thee as I have seen thee before, when life seemed a pleasure—when that sweet genial spirit made thee a friend most dear. one whose very remembrance is happiness itself—what then must thy presence be?

Well I have only to write four letters more, at least I hope so, aint I kind? Would that all could be laid aside even now for the more joyous meeting, but as the Poet says I presume we must "learn to labor and to wait." As yet I have no definite idea of when we may be relieved, tho not till about the 24 of May after which we have to go to Springfield to be mustered out and settle our accounts—My Brother wrote me a few days since that he had got home from college and he wanted me to come home directly—he wanted to see me before he returned—what does my Jennie think? Pretty strong claims—I do not know, but I think he can wait a little while—they will think more of me if I linger a little by the way—aint that a pretty good notion? I think so—Oh dear it seems as tho I would rather spend one minute with thee my beloved darling than a month any where else, even tho home is dear also.—yet there is one dearer than all besides—and that is the house of the heart. I may wander far or near yet the heart returns in sweet delight to the one it loves—and I hope to come with it soon. till then dearest may heaven's sweetest blessings make thee happy.

My health is quite good since my return from the late March—I think we have made our last trip—and as the time of our Return home draws near, I cannot but regret to leave the work unfinished, tho by the blessing of God I still hope to see it prosper till crowned with a glorious peace.

Your dearest letter the 18 inst came yesterday. I am sorry that you did not get my letter before leaving Chicago. I dont know how it failed to reach you as did the others, as I most invariably mail all my letters on Monday—but I hope that such disappointments may soon cease—My darling Jennie goodnight sweet dreams a kiss to thee

J. Moore—

Dearest please write soon. write a long letter, I never tire reading your letters please try me   good bye soon to meet again, a Kiss. J. M.

Josiah to Jennie

Vicksburg Miss
May 7 1864 Sat. Eve

My Darling Jennie,

I hope I may ever prove myself worthy of the "trust" so kindly committed to my care, dear darling one, you need not fear my forgetting this evening—that would be forgetting happiness itself—and you know I am a little too selfish for that—no indeed I could not so forget thee—tho I must acknowledge that I have been forgetting thee, for some time, tho I believe the kind heart of my beloved darling will pardon the mistake—if such—I hope I may ever be worthy of the love of one whose very principle seems to be love itself—a love that has grown brighter and purer as clouds and sadness gathered round—a love without which life itself would be a burden—a love only possessed by my beloved darling Jennie, my "happiness."

Well dearest I need not tell you that your sweetest message of the 27 ult came yesterday—its every word seemed to breath the spirit of their beloved author— indeed I've not done much but read over its "sweet words" since, and not "sleepy" yet, tho I had a sweet dream over them last night—I believe it would almost pay to stay here just for the sake of getting such sweet letters—no I guess not, just for variety—I believe I should prefer a "sweet kiss" once and awhile—will I say all the time? Yes—but only such as darling Jennie can give—in this I would not prefer variety—Well sweetest, I was much rejoiced to hear you speak of being so well, if my writing serves to cheer that dear loving heart, in the least, rest asured no effort of your beloved shall be wanting, nor would I forget the evening "kiss" tho darling I hope soon to be able to present such in person—yes indeed my dear when that "three years of weary waiting is ended" our meeting I think will be "joy beyond measure"—a full realization that "hope deferred is pleasure obtained"—tho I must say that to me the "deferred" part has presented but little to fascinate.

Well as it is becoming late I had better not detain thee darling friend much longer—only 2 more to write, so I hope—then I shall see if Thomas has any trouble with Willie—He must not tease you too much then, else I shall come in for a share, that I may be ever worthy of thy love giving as I do my heart to thee, my beloved darling Jennie with highest hopes I kiss thee another goodnight, sweet dreams.

Yours as ever

J. Moore

P.S. We have moved camp lately a little farther from town since which time I've not seen Andie, but he was well when I last saw him—I am glad he escaped the perils of the Red River Expedition.[30] Several of the 77th have fallen, and among the rest Lt. Col. Webb who I suppose will be much lamented in Peoria—such is war— But I bid thee goodnight and a kiss to make thee better. J.M.

Josiah to Jennie

Vicksburg Miss May 14 1864
"Sat. eve" 8. P.M.

---

30 The Red River Campaign (March 10 to Mary 22, 1864) was a combined-arms Union effort under Maj. Gen. Nathaniel Banks to capture Alabama and parts of Louisiana. The series of battles and skirmishes that ensued along the Red River in Louisiana failed miserably, and nearly cost the North the entire fleet of Union gunboats when most of them were temporarily trapped when the water level fell. For more information, see Gary Joiner, *One Damn Blunder from Beginning to End: The Red River Campaign of 1864* (Rowman & Littlefield Publishers, 2003).

My darling Jennie,

A few more days and I hope to lay aside this tardy, but long cherished medium, I have many things to write but I would not use paper or ink, as I trust to come to you shortly, that we may speak as in days of "Auld lang signe"—I feel very well indeed this evening and I have many reasons, any one of which I think should arouse even the most despondent.

1st It is ever a pleasure to hold sweet converse, even by pen & ink with, my beloved Jennie.

2nd My health continues very good, a blessing for which, I trust I am truly thankful to Him who is a present help in every time of need.

3rd The anticipation of very soon being able to realize the joy of that oft repeted verse "Hope deferred is pleasure obtained" sends home a thrill of sweeetest Joy only to be excelled by the more "happy day."

4th Nor can I forget the bright prospects that a kind Providence is now presenting to our dear country in the triumph of the cause that is Just.—our news up to the present represents the movements of Grant's army as successful beyond all expectation—we hope the best—I had felt a little "blue" for some time over the course of events, but if reports are correct—Grant—by the blessing of God is about to retrieve all losses[31]—What do you think, Jennie, I proposed to " go in" again for 90 days providing I could get a Regt. but I guess I can't, so I won't go—you aint angry are you my dearest?—if so I must have a kiss.[32]

As yet we have no intimation of when we may go up the river, mostly all the troops have gone out from here to engage the attention of the enemy, have, while Grant & Sherman operate elsewhere, so we cannot leave till these troops return, tho we expect them every day now, and, think that we will leave here by the middle

31 Grant made his headquarters in the field instead of in DC, and accompanied General Meade and the Army of the Potomac against Lee's army. Grant's grinding Overland Campaign began in early May 1864 in the Wilderness, and moved around Lee's flank, By the middle of May (at the time of Josiah's letter), both armies were locked in a bloody duel around Spotsylvania Court House. Sherman, meanwhile, was leading a combined force of three armies against Joseph E. Johnston's Rebel Army of Tennessee .in North Georgia. By this time Sherman had flanked Johnston off Rocky Face Ridge and was fighting the Rebels around Resaca. Katcher, *The Civil War Day by Day*, 128-130.

32 Earlier letters indicated that Senator Lindsay was attempting to get Josiah a promotion. Josiah's reference to "go in again" may relate to yet another attempt by the senator to help Josiah, but there was no regiment for him to command (or serve in) for such a brief period, or the transfer would required a much longer enlistment requirement.

of next week at the farthest, So, as it requires over 6 days for a letter to reach me, it will be uncertain sending a letter after the 16 inst—with kindest wishes and brightest hopes, I again bid thee my own dearly beloved darling Jennie, "goodnight," a kiss.

Your loving friend as ever,

J. Moore

    P.S. My paper gives out too soon. I shall not use it much longer for its naughtiness aint that a good plan dearest?—O I forgot to tell you that I saw Andie yesterday. he had a letter from Mr. Lindsay. he is not very well he has the chills and fever slightly—i.e. he keeps around but looks rather thin—I wish he could go home with us, but I presume he cant get away again. "good night" my love J.M.

Despite the horrors of war Josiah had witnessed, his faith in God remained unchanged. Like many men of his age, he credited the Lord for the success of Grant and Sherman had thus far achieved. For people like Josiah, "religious conviction has produced a providential narrative of the war," noted one historian who also said that faith gave "the bloodshed some higher and presumably nobler purpose." As it was with Josiah, religious faith among large numbers of Americans remained strong and allowed Northerners to continue on despite the continued carnage at places like the Wilderness, Spotsylvania, and other fights that would spill the blood of sons, husbands, and fathers until the spring of 1865. People "imagined death as redemptive, holding out the possibility of eternal bliss, and aestheticizing battlefield deaths." Many like Josiah continued to believe in a loving God that controlled their destiny and that of the country. By May 1864, Josiah felt he had a pretty clear view of his destiny.[33]

---

33 Rable, *God's Almost Chosen Peoples*, 9; Clarke, *War Stories*, 4-5.

Home

As the terms of enlistment for the three-year regiments approached their end, members were offered an opportunity to reenlist until and serve until the end of the war. Those who did got 30-day furloughs, and regiments in which most of the men reenlisted would be thereafter known as "veteran" units.[1]

Many soldiers declined to reenlist. As one Michigan veteran put it, "After serving three years for our country cannot we go home, satisfied that we have done our share toward putting down the rebellion, and let those who stayed at home come and give their time as long; the country is as dear to them as us?" A Massachusetts man expressed similar sentiments. "I shall not re-enlist, and my reasons are first, I have no desire to monopolize all the patriotism there is, but am willing to give others a chance. My second reason," he continued, "is that after I have served three years my duty to my country has been performed and my next duty is at home with my family." If the promise of a furlough and an enhanced unit designation did not do the trick, plying men with alcohol sometimes got them to extend their time in army. Even this ploy had its limits. "Lager beer," joked one soldier, "has nearly lost its veteran Power."[2]

---

1 Woodworth, *Nothing But Victory*, 488.

2 Bruce Catton, *A Stillness At Appomattox* (New York, NY, 1953), 34-35; Manning, *What This Cruel War Was Over*, 149-150.

Another who decided against further fighting was young artilleryman Willie Shepherd, who had written of his horror at seeing the battlefield at Shiloh. "I have done my duty to my Country, I hope faithfully," he explained, "and as there are so many, many thousands that have not served, & who can, just as well as I, it is not, in my mind, my duty to reenlist." Perhaps to Willie's chagrin, one of those who stepped up to take his place was his brother Freddy.[3]

Those opposed to reenlisting believed they were free to simply complete their three-year term and return home as men "free in conscience." A common sentiment of the 1861 veterans was, "For three years we have done all this; go thou and do likewise." There is little indication that those in the 17th Illinois who opted not to reenlist had any concern that they would be viewed as abandoning the fight, although Josiah, in his April 30, 1864, letter home to Jennie, certainly experienced a least a pang of regret in this regard.[4]

About one-half of all Union soldiers who had joined in 1861 reenlisted. That was not the case in the 17th Illinois, where Josiah and most of his comrades declined. Josiah's health issues played a part in his decision. The opening shots at Fredericktown, the bitter cold, the horrific cannonade and assault at Fort Donelson, the carnage of Shiloh, the bloody initial charge at Vicksburg followed by squalid and deadly siege conditions—together with all the other hardships and events—had long ago ended any romantic notions of war he had once held. The men of the 17th had seen their share of death and suffering. Just six of those who had enlisted with Josiah in Company F in April 1861 decided to reenlist. They, along with replacement troops who had joined the regiment, were transferred to the 8th Illinois, which would go on to fight under General Sherman through the Atlanta campaign and then on to the March to the Sea and into the Carolinas. On May 19, the departing men from Company F boarded a steamer for the long trip home up the Mississippi River.

From the date of enlistment in 1861 to June 1864, Josiah's Company F lost 14 men: eight killed or mortally wounded, five from disease and one man, Pvt. Jeremiah Deckert, to murder; nine others were wounded. By war's end, the 17th Illinois's losses as a whole would be three officers and 71 enlisted men killed or mortally wounded, and one officer and 71 enlisted men died of disease.[5]

---

3   Ural, *Don't Hurry Me Down To Hades*, 157.

4   Linderman, *Embattled Courage*, 263.

5   Private Jeremiah Deckert deserted while assigned to an artillery battery and was found dead in Memphis in March 1863. An officer noted on Deckert's official record, "None too soon."

*   *   *

Josiah to Jennie

Camp Butler Springfield Ills
May 26, 1864 8 P.M.

My darling Jennie,

Tho you have no doubt heard of us being on our way home, yet I presume you will be anxious to learn of our whereabouts.

Well dearest we are here—and O dear how I wish I could say there—but I hope soon to realize the bright reality—tho as yet I have no definite idea of how soon we may be able to get away from here. You can scarcely imagine, dearest, how slowly the wheels of time roll round and yet it almost seems like a dream to look forward with the certainty of soon enjoying the sweet smiles and happy asociation of one so long admired and ardently loved-yet it is a reality-hope look on the brightest side-to remember thee gives me ever my happiest moments, what will it then be to enjoy the pleasure of being with thee? Yes darling I am coming, coming to kiss away the tear of sorrow and cheer that dear loving heart that has loved so long and waited with such anxious solicitude-but I hope that I may be ever worthy of such a dear loving friend.

Well darling I need not detain I hope soon to lay aside this tardy medium- I have many things to say but I would not use pen & ink-I would enjoy the happier feast by waiting a few days- We came here on yesterday morning and I think we will not be ready to leave till about Monday if we are longer detained, I shall write to thee dearest Jennie that you may know.

I saw Andie as I left V[icksburg]. I was sorry for him poor fellow for I know he would have liked to come home-but he counts the time and reconciles himself to his work-he does not look quite as well as he had been tho he did not complain much.

Well beloved I have almost written a full letter and not said much either but you know I never tire. so please excuse.

Your true and loving friend, J. Moore

Sweet dreams and a kind good night to thee ever near ever dear and never forgotten again goodnight sweet dreams and a kiss to my beloved. J.M.

The men of the 17th were officially mustered out of service June 4, 1864. Before this took place, they were informed that a mistake had been made in 1861 and that they had never been properly mustered into service. After three years in the army, the 17th Illinois was officially sworn into service and then promptly mustered out. Before he ended his term, Josiah owed one final debt to the military and was charged $5.10 for "one fife, one inkstand, and fifty cap letters."[6]

No one from the 17th wrote much of their farewells to the men with whom they had served for three years. They joined the army to protect their homes and the Union, but came to realize they were also fighting for one another. Most soldiers were concerned about being exposed as a coward and word about that getting home, but they also wanted to have their comrades present on either side of them. One Union soldier who wrote about leaving his three tent mates at the end of his enlistment referred them "our family." "There was a sadness deep in our hearts in this parting hour," wrote a man from New York of his muster-out. "We boys had been together for three years; we had formed close friendships. . . . [W]e had borne danger, hardship, and privation alike. . . . So it was hard to separate and say goodbye, one with the other; but we shook hands all around, and laughed and seemed to make merry, while our hearts were heavy and our eyes ready to shed tears." Sergeant Robert Duncan, Josiah's company clerk, noted in the final entry in the official log of Company F that "the 17th is all on their way rejoicing." Duncan tarried a bit in Springfield to see some friends training for their upcoming military service, and ended the final log entry by stating that he was taken by two friends to an "ice cream saloon" where he was treated to "oysters, cigars and L.B."[7]

Unlike the men who remained in the service until war's end, those who returned before final surrenders received little if any public celebration. It might have seemed almost disrespectful to conduct major celebrations when men were still dying by the thousands on the war's several fronts. A loving greeting from family and friends, and perhaps a mention in the local newspaper, was about all the men of the 17th could expect.[8]

6   Illinois Adjutant General Report; Military Record of Josiah Moore. NARA.

7   Mitchell, *The Vacant Chair,* 158; James Robertson, Neil Kagan, ed., *The Untold Civil War: Exploring the Human Side of War* (Washington, DC 2011), 148; Duncan, company log. L.B. almost certainly stands for lager beer.

8   James Marten, *Sing Not War* (Chapel Hill, NC, 2011), 34.

Josiah to Jennie

Hanover Ills
"Home" June 20, 64 7 A.M.

My Darling,

I presume ere this can reach you, we can sympathize—each being lost—tho there is such a thing as the "lost is found"—some consolation in the lone hour.

Well my dear I have at last had the pleasure of greeting the "old folks at home"—where I found all well-except my sister and one of my brothers who are absent on a visit.

After leaving you on Friday I made the train in good time and reached Monmouth about 11 A.M.—staid a few hours and left at 8 P.M. and reached Galena at 7 A.M. on Saturday June 18-took a birds eye (turtle dove) view of the City, met some of my cousins, from the country, who brought me home, which I reached on Saturday evening at 7 P.M. -I went to church yesterday- saw a good many friends-tho one was absent.

Well dearest I presume I must tell you about when I can "work my way around"—next week of course. I think I can reach Peoria about Tuesday on my way to M.

I regret not having an opportunity of speaking with Mr. Lindsay before leaving but I shall send him a few lines now, and when I call on my way down, I can then speak to him.[9]

Now beloved please excuse this hasty letter, my brother is now waiting to take me to the P.O. 4 miles distant from which the Mail leaves at 10 A.M. so now my dearest little "turtle dove" I bid thee a kind adieu for a few days only.
My kindest regards to Maggie and all the friends, tho dont let them see this-it is too hastily written.

Yours J.M.

---

9 Josiah's comment about his regret in not speaking with Mr. Lindsay almost certainly referred to his intention to ask for Jennie's hand in marriage.

EPILOGUE

Thereafter

THE war dragged on for another year after most of the men of the 17th Illinois returned home. Ulysses S. Grant continued his campaign in the East Theater against Lee's Army of Northern Virginia, trapping the Rebels against the cities of Petersburg and Richmond in what would become a quasi-siege of nine long and bloody months. The almost incessant fighting from May 1864 to the following spring paid off in early April 1865 when Lee's army was driven out of its entrenchments and surrendered at Appomattox Court House, Virginia.[1]

General Sherman, Grant's trusted lieutenant in the Western Theater, broke the South's back with his campaign to take Atlanta in 1864. In a series of masterful maneuvers, he flanked Joseph Johnston and the Army of the Tennessee all the way south to the gates of Atlanta, where Johnston was sacked by President Davis. Corps commander John Bell Hood was elevated to command with the understanding that he would assume the offensive. Hood's attacks could not alter the Union tide of victory, however, and Atlanta fell in early September. That November, Sherman took some 60,000 men and cut a swath of destruction eastward across Georgia and captured Savannah on December 22, 1864, which he offered to President Lincoln as a Christmas present. Sherman's victory in Georgia and the securing of the Shenandoah Valley by Maj. Gen. Phil Sheridan earned Lincoln a second term when he won

---

1 McPherson, *Battle Cry of Freedom*, 733-735.

reelection in November 1864 with strong support from the men in the field—despite the fact that his opponent, George McClellan, was the former beloved commander the Army of the Potomac.[2]

Sherman continued his campaign in the spring of 1865, driving north into the Carolinas until Johnston, back in command of a cobbled-together army, surrendered in North Carolina shortly after Lee capitulated at Appomattox. Confederate president Jefferson Davis was captured in Georgia on May 10, and the remaining Rebel armies put down their arms shortly thereafter. Northern jubilation over the end of the war was dimmed by the April 14 assassination of Lincoln at Ford's Theater by actor John Wilkes Booth.[3]

The Union had been restored, but it had taken four long years and had cost, according to the latest research, upwards of 700,000 dead—a number equal to all the dead suffered by America in all of her wars from the American Revolution through Vietnam; hundreds of thousands more were maimed. By way of comparison, a soldier had a one-in-four chance of dying during the Civil War, but a 1-in-126 chance during the Korean War. Two percent of the 1860 population of the United States died in uniform. Today, that would be the equivalent of about 6,500,000 people.[4]

Soon after hostilities ended, the nation sought a return to normalcy. At the end of the war, the Union army numbered more than one million men. In keeping with the American aversion to large standing armies, one year later Congress fixed the size of the Regular Army at 54,302. In 1876 that number was further reduced to about 27,000 men, even though ongoing conflicts with Indians required a standing military force in the West.[5]

Despite some lingering hostility toward men who had remained home instead of actively supporting the war effort, the men largely put aside their differences with those in their communities after the Union victory. However, the motivation that drove men to enlist, the concept of "Union," remained strong. Secretary of State William Seward talked about "Their great work is the preservation of the Union and in that, the saving of popular government for the world." The preservation of the country always remained the paramount goal.

---

2 Sherman, *Personal Memoirs*, Part II, 231; Boatner, *Civil War Dictionary*, 323-324; McPherson, *Battle Cry of Freedom*, 804-805.

3 Ibid., 853-854.

4 Ibid., 854; Adams, *Living Hell*, 11-12

5 Gallagher, *The Union War*, 124-125; Ramold, *Across the Divide*, 169.

When General John Logan, in whose division Josiah served at Vicksburg, gave his farewell address to the Army of the Tennessee in 1865, he told his men, "You pledged your brave hearts and brawny arms to the Government of your fathers," and said that those efforts "won for your country renewed respect and power at home and abroad."[6]

More than a decade later, Ulysses Grant, who had by this time served two terms as president of the United States, explained, "What saved the Union, was the coming forward of the young men of the nation. They came from their homes and fields, as they did in the time of the Revolution, giving everything to the country. To their devotion we owe the salvation of the Union. The humblest soldier who carried a musket is entitled to as much credit for the results of the war as those who were in command. So long as our young men are animated by this spirit there will be no fear for the Union."[7]

The soldiers may have saved the Union, but returning home was much more difficult than many imagined. "Killing was once again homicide, foraging was again theft, and incendiarism arson," wrote one historian. "Even language was a problem: camp talk had to be cleaned up." A Confederate wrote of similar concerns: "How can we get interested in farming or working in a store or warehouse when we have been interested day and night for years in keeping alive, whipping the invaders, and preparing for another fight?" For large numbers of these veterans, homecoming was, as one writer described it, "a task as onerous and demanding as any military campaign."[8]

Many returning troops disliked talking about the war and their roles in it. Some believed that speaking of the killing, foraging, and the destruction of civilian property they were forced to do would make them look immoral. Others simply wanted to put the memories of the carnage behind them. Outsiders interpreted the silence as heroic modesty. Others might call it an effort at self-preservation.[9]

Near the end of the war, Charles Morey, a man in the 2nd Vermont, reflected on what he had seen in army life—the killing, theft and destruction of

---

6   Gallagher, *The Union War*, 1-2, 27.

7   Ibid., 161-162.

8   Linderman, *Embattled Courage*, 267; James McPherson, *The Untold Civil War*, 148; Brian Matthew Jordan, *Marching Home: Union Veterans and Their Unending Civil War* (New York, 2014), 3.

9   Linderman, *Embattled Courage*, 266-271.

public property. "Society will not own the rude soldier when he comes back," explained Morey, "but turn a cold shoulder to him because he has become hardened by scenes of bloodshed and carnage." Morey held out hope, writing that "there are feelings, tender feelings, down deep in the soldier's breast, which when moved will prove that all that is good is not quite dead." Morey never had the opportunity to demonstrate to family and friends that those feelings still existed within him. He died in April 1865, just one week before the end of the war in the East.[10]

Many on the home front were indeed wary of the hardened returning veterans. Some civilians believed the soldiers' experiences made them unfit for polite society; that the changes wrought by the war "raised the specter of disorientation, disrespect for authority, and criminality." "There is no disguising it, boys, the people are afraid of us," claimed a New Hampshire veteran Many employers refused to hire veterans because he believed they could "do nothing hereafter for a living but fight."[11]

One veteran observed that many of the former soldiers were "homeless, friendless wanderers" because of their feelings of displacement and inability to be hired. Even a man as celebrated as Joshua Chamberlain, a hero of Gettysburg, was accused by his wife of physical and emotional abuse. Alcohol abuse, perhaps started or accelerated in the service, plagued many veterans seeking to wash away the killing fields from their minds. Many feared for their future, for the three or four years they had spent in the service were years they could have dedicated to acquiring an education or learning a trade.[12]

One of Josiah's former comrades endured his own mental hell even before leaving the service. Edmund Robbins, the soldier from the 17th Illinois who had written of the degradations visited on civilians in Tennessee during the occupation in 1862, went on to become an officer with the 53rd U.S. Colored Troops. In October 1864, he had sent home a dispiriting letter to his parents that is worth reproducing almost in full:

Vicksburg, Miss
Oct. 8th 1864

10 Edward Alexander, "And Then We Kill," *Hallowed Ground*, Civil War Trust, Volume 14, #4 (Winter 2013), 30-31.

11 Jordan, *Marching Home*, 43, 54.

12 Marten, *Sing Not War*, 53-54, 101; Jordan, *Marching Home*, 43-44, 54; Adams, *Living Hell*, 211.

My dear father & mother

. . . At this present time I am most acutely despondent though more composed than yesterday. I have been about three weeks with a working party of the regiment in the woods near the Yazoo River getting out shingles and came back to camp last Saturday. I was most miserable, dissatisfied with myself and though assured, I had no cause for such feelings. Still could not divest my self of them.

I believe if I was clear of the army once more, I would come home and work on the farm where if I could not be free from such ideas I would at least be free from observation. You understand how I feel. There are but a few who can appreciate it in the least, and that makes association irksome and even painful You ask what I am going to do. This state of mind makes me undecided and vacillating.

You say of course come home, but what good will twenty days do If I could stay a few months, and work and study, and visit I should no doubt be benefited I see no prospect of such a thing unless my superiors become as dissatisfied with me as I am with my self, in which case I sometimes think I never should see home again. Now you see I am adding to your anxiety and to your care and why do you wish me to write under such circumstances? . . . . My opinion is that I shall not come home this winter. But if my superiors ever think as ill of me as I do of my self I may if I am released from the army honorably.

I rejoice with you in the cheering news from the Army and Navy. If I was at home I should vote the second time for Old Abe. . . . At the present time I am rather a miserable fellow but hoping that the writing of this letter will give some relief from the twinges of conscience at least on letters unanswered. I remain as ever your affectionate son.

E. C. D. Robbins

P.S. J. A. Griffin arrived here in Sept. and has entered on his duties and is getting along finely. I think he will make a fine officer with a little experience.

Just one week after writing his letter, Robbins committed suicide. The John A. Griffin mentioned at the end of the letter had already left the 17th Illinois to take a position as an officer with the 53rd USCT. Griffin left a graphic description of Robbins' final moments: "[He] first took a piece of tent rope and made a noose of it then, as if to be sure, passed that down, and after putting cartridges in his blouse pockets, caps in his vest pockets and loading his piece

John A. Griffin was a private in Company D of the 17th Illinois before being promoted to lieutenant and finally captain in the 53rd U.S. Colored Troops. Griffin wrote about the tragic death of Edmund Robbins. The back of the photo is inscribed, "To my mother." Someone else added, "probably sent from Vicksburg in 1866." *ALPLM*

(an old musket) put the muzzle in his mouth holding it there with his left hand while with his right he put it off with the ramrod."[13]

Few if any studied the mental health of the returning soldiers, a field that was still in its infancy, although newspapers reported numerous incidents that clearly demonstrated something had changed in many of them. There were thousands of Union veterans who moved from town to town after the war, tortured in their sleep by "dreams of war and fighting." A matron at the Illinois Soldiers' and Sailors' Home spoke of one afflicted veteran who fought "his battles over again." The former soldier, she explained, "fought the rebels all day, tearing his bed and clothes until exhausted." An Iowa soldier was similarly afflicted. A survivor of Shiloh, the Hawkeye was unable to shake the effects of that bloodbath and spoke of it like an illness: "I have had Shiloh since the sixth day of April 1862."

Today we understand that these men were suffering from post-traumatic stress disorder, or PTSD. Earlier in the 20th century, it was referred to as simply "shell shock," and during the Civil War period, "nostalgia"—a gentle way of saying the instabilities were simply the effect of a prolonged absence from home and a longing for family. About four in ten Vietnam War veterans suffered some level of psychological stress from their service. It is not unreasonable to assume this applied to a similar percentage of Civil War soldiers, particularly

13 Letter from John Griffin to Frank Peats, April 20, 1865.

since these men commonly served with family, friends, and co-workers and often saw them killed in horrific ways.[14]

Soldiers, of course, suffered physical as well as emotional maladies from wounds, poor diet, accidents, and prolonged exposure to the elements. According to some estimates, Civil War veterans were 56 times more likely to suffer from chronic diarrhea and dysentery as well as elevated levels of heart problems. According to one study, 93 percent of men younger than 18 at the time of their enlistment developed physical ailments linked to battlefield trauma. One was a veteran who contacted Frank Peats in 1884 to ask his assistance in getting a disability pension. "At times in my suffering I have been tempted to take my life," he explained. Edmund Robbins was not alone in his sufferering.[15]

*   *   *

By all accounts Josiah emerged relatively unscathed from the clutches of war. He moved quickly to return to a normal life and fulfill the desire he had nourished since that day in the spring of 1861 when he first met Jennie. On July 1, 1864, just days after the end of his military service, he and Jennie married at the Lindsay home in Peoria. Josiah wore his captain's uniform. Reverend Isaac S. Mahan, Jennie's uncle, performed the service. According to family records, the couple honeymooned in Minnesota.

Josiah and Jennie suffered another separation when Josiah left in September 1864 to finish his undergraduate studies at Monmouth. He was there when he heard that news of Lincoln's assassination on April 14. "The sad news of yesterday has made me feel as I never did before—it seems as tho I must be dreaming," he wrote Jennie just two days later. "[T]he news of the President's assassination so shocked me that I could do but little. . . . Hoping that God may remove the cloud from our weeping land and that even good may be brought out of the present mysterious dispensation of his providence." In a postscript, Josiah added that when he attended a religious service, "The house

14 Ramold, *Across the Divide,* 9; Adams, *Living Hell,* 151; Jordan, *Marching Home,* 82, 189 Marten, *Sing Not War,* 10, 86-90.

15 Ibid., 86-87; Letter from Anton Coon to Frank Peats, April 18, 1884. Peats collection; Jordan, *Marching Home,* 189.

Josiah Moore, in a photo taken in 1864 on his honeymoon in Minnesota (Whitney's Gallery #2 in St. Paul.). Compare the haggard and exhausted appearance of him in this photo with his 1861 image. *Author*

Jennie Lindsay on April 6, 1865. The photo includes the inscription, "My army companion Josiah Moore and now my companion "in arms" sweeter far." The photo was taken by A. Hesler, Chicago, IL. photo. *David and Liz Djupe*

was filled as I never saw it before—the audience seemed very much affected—a deep sad feeling seems to pervade every breast."[16]

Josiah was still at the school when other returning veterans arrived after the war's end. The Monmouth College *Oracle*, a magazine published by the college in 1911 on the fiftieth anniversary of the war, made a note of the men who enlisted in 1862 and returned in 1865:

> *Tongue can not tell nor heart feel the joy at their coming. They had opened up to four million black people the opportunity to make the best of themselves and revealed the perpetuating power of republican institutions. . . . Social receptions were given them. They were feasted and dined. Public entertainments were arranged . . . with all the luxuries and delicacies of the season. Bells were rung and the nights made glorious with brilliant fire works.[17]*

Unlike so much writing of the time, which usually focused on how the men had saved the Union, the publication explicitly took note of the emancipation work the men from Monmouth had so nobly performed. The *Oracle* also took note of another impact of the war: Many of the men who had returned from the war and were now attending the college did so with permanently damaged bodies. "The empty sleeve and the resounding crutch on the conscious floor," continued the *Oracle* editorial told too plainly the story of their sacrifice."[18]

Josiah continued at the school until June 1867, received a master's degree, and remained to complete seminary studies. Except for brief visits to Monmouth, Jennie remained in Peoria until June 1867.[19]

An 1865 article in the *Atlantic Monthly* pointed out the real value that women like Jennie played in winning the war. They provided "so many bonds of love and kindness to bind the soldier to his home, and to keep him always a loyal citizen. If our army is . . . more pure, more clement, more patriotic than

16 April 16, 1865 letter from Josiah Moore to Jennie Lindsay Moore.

17 Monmouth College *Oracle*, Volume XV, No 34, May 30, 1911, 12. Though Josiah made no comment in any of his letters to Jennie, one has to wonder whether he compared the attention given to the soldiers at war's end with the subdued reception the men of the 17th Illinois received when they returned in 1864 after their three-year terms were over.

18 Monmouth College, *Oracle*, 12; Clarke, *War Stories*, 147. More than 22,000 men and boys of the Union army had suffered the loss of at least one limb. Their compensation was a $15 per month pension.

19 From letters in the collection of the author.

other armies, if our soldier is everywhere and always a true-hearted citizen it is because the army and soldier have not been cast off from public sympathy, but cherished and bound to every free institution and every peaceful association by golden cords of love." Women, explained one historian, "had saved the republic from militarism's corrupting potential: despondency on one hand and brutality on the other." During the war, men were "fighting to protect republican democracy," while women worked "to preserve republican virtues." While the men were fighting against the South, their women back home were helping them resist the temptations of camp and army life and the threats they posed to the "moral person."[20]

Veterans spent the first few years after the war trying to forget the horrors they endured at places such like Fort Donelson, Shiloh, Fredericksburg, Gettysburg, Vicksburg, and Cold Harbor. They tried to put their military lives behind them. Few glamorized their martial deeds. John Logan was a key figure behind the formation of the Grand Army of the Republic, a veterans' group formed to celebrate their service. Even ten years after the war, however, the GAR contained but 30,000 members—just two percent of the North's surviving veterans. The situation in the South at that time was similar.[21]

The American desire to forget the war sometimes manifested itself in unfortunate ways. During the 1870s, soldiers on leave from combat against the Indians on the plains or in the southwest were sometimes treated with disrespect and outright insults. Joshua Chamberlain, who became president of Bowdoin College in Brunswick, Maine, faced a revolt by students when he attempted to infuse discipline and personal growth through military drill. In what had to be particularly galling for Josiah given his affinity for the Presbyterian faith, the United Presbytery of Keokuk, Iowa, declared the GAR to be "inconsistent with the principles of the United Presbyterian Church" because of its "unworthy and dangerous" officers, "extra judicial oaths," "secretive meetings," and its "selfishness."[22]

A short history of the 17th Illinois, penned by Josiah in 1868 for one of the unit's reunions, demonstrates the resistance to romanticizing the war. Rather than a soaring ode to the regiment's heroics, or a testimony to its role in saving

---

20   Clarke, *War Stories*, 85.

21   Linderman, *Embattled Courage*, 266-297; Boatner, 487.

22   Linderman, *Embattled Courage*, 273-274; Jordan, *Marching Home*, 160.

the Union, his account consists of nothing more than a simple recitation of dates and places of the 17th's movements and dispositions. Perhaps in an acknowledgment of this aversion to remembering, Josiah noted in the margins of the paper that he hadn't had time to present the work. We do know that many former comrades of the 17th tried as best they could to remain in contact with each other, and that Josiah attended a number of reunions.[23]

By 1880, things had begun to change. Interest in the war grew, fueled by both Northern and Southern veterans who found solidarity through their shared experiences. Participation at reunions and other events increased, as did the popularity of related souvenir items. Some of this resurgence came from a renewed respect for the U.S. Army and the war it was fighting on the Western frontier. Accounts from that time describing the war on the plains used some of the same language that had lauded the character of the 1861 volunteer. By 1883, the GAR had grown to 146,000 members, and at its peak in 1890 the organization boasted a roster of 428,000. The view of the war as a terrible evil was supplanted by stories of martial glory being repeated in veterans' halls, camps, and reunions across the country. While the war might have made men "brutal," it also made them "strong" and better able to endure the world's trials. One Union veteran told a group of young people that they needed to remember "how grandly" their fathers and grandfathers had died in the war. Like many others, Josiah increased his participation in GAR activities. In 1890, he served as the state chaplain of the Illinois branch.[24]

As this positive view of the war predominated, the men of the 17th Illinois had less difficulty speaking publicly about their experiences. During one convocation with his former comrades, Josiah had an interesting incident connected to his encounter with the teamster back in May of 1862 on the approach to Corinth when he had pulled the man from the wagon and pinned him to the ground with his knee. On May 30, 1883, Josiah was asked to deliver a "War Reminiscence" at a "Camp Fire Sociable" at Whitmore's Hall in Woodhull, Illinois. Also on the program was Rev. W. S. McClanahan, Josiah's

---

23 Moore, *History of the 17th*; Invitation to Frank Peats.

24 Linderman, *Embattled Courage*, 275-277, 292- 294, 297; Marten, *Sing Not War*, 153. Civil War service almost became a prerequisite for high public office, with participation in the war looked upon as "an important mark of merit." Having served and survived became all important. Except for Grover Cleveland, every nineteenth-century president after Andrew Johnson (who had succeeded Lincoln) served in some military capacity. Eric Foner and John A. Garrity, eds. *The Readers Companion to American History* (Boston, MA 1991), 191, 864.

former lieutenant in the 17th. McClanahan, who witnessed the incident with the teamster, told the story to the assembled crowd. As it turned out, the former quartermaster was in the audience that evening, and the next day Josiah received a note from the man along with a dollar bill "for giving command on your knees."[25]

As the passing of time changed the nation's view of the war, former adversaries began to fraternize. Yanks and Rebs marched together and sat around the campfires at reunions. They had shared something unique, and they had survived. Black soldiers who had played such an important part in the war were largely excluded from these gatherings. It's ironic that the blue and gray veterans drew closer together, while the black veterans who had fought for the Union were increasingly marginalized in the postwar narrative.[26]

Josiah and the men who had shared that dark period in American history continued on with their lives. Andie Lindsay had remained in Vicksburg until December 1864, and his record lists him as a deserter for the months of September and October "while on detached service." He rejoined his unit in New Orleans and an order from General Thomas Sherman[27] restored him to the active rolls of the regiment with no penalty. Andie was detailed to the quartermaster department on April 10, 1865, and mustered out of the service on July 10. He must have liked New Orleans, because he returned to the city shortly after the war. He traveled back to Peoria and married a woman named Helen Jewell, but divorced in 1880. Single again, Andie moved to Nebraska, where he continued to be plagued by malaria, which had dogged him throughout his Civil War service. He was granted a pension of $4.00 per month in 1882, and it gradually increased to $24 per month. He spent time in and out of hospitals before he died in January 1913. Jennie's brother remained a staunch Democrat throughout his life.[28]

William Lindsay, Jennie's other brother, enlisted in the 53rd Illinois in late 1864. He survived the war and was mustered out of service in July of 1865. Jennie's sister Maggie, who had provided much companionship during the

---

25 Document in possession of author.

26 Linderman, *Embattled Courage*, 278; Clarke, *War Stories*, 184.

27 General Thomas Sherman was not closely related to William T. Sherman, although some contemporaries mistakenly believed they were brothers.

28 Boatner, *Civil War Dictionary*, 750; *Compendium of History, Reminiscence and Biograph of Nebraska* (Chicago, IL 1912), 1060; Military and Pension files of Andrew Lindsay.

John T. Lindsay, father of Jennie Lindsay, from late 1800's. *Author*

difficult war years, died in June 1865 and was buried in Peoria. She was just 25 years old.[29]

Jennie's father John Lindsay, who so tormented Unionists in Illinois, served two terms in the state senate. His views of the war softened as the North's fortunes improved. By the end of his public service, he suffered significant hearing loss and, with that, his ability to make a living. He and his wife Sarah moved to Nebraska with Andie, where Sarah died in 1885. Her remains were taken back home to Peoria. John lived until 1906 and was buried in Nebraska.[30]

29 Report of the Illinois Adjutant General.

30 Ibid.

Robert Ingersoll, the Democrat and one-time law partner of John Lindsay, whose clashes with Lindsay provided much fodder for the Peoria *Daily Transcript* during the war, was discharged from the service, returned home, and became a prominent member of the Republican Party. He served for a time as the attorney general for Illinois. Despite being the son of a minister, he became a leader in the agnostic movement and is typically acclaimed as the most famous American orator of the last part of the nineteenth century. One newspaper columnist described him as "the most famous American you never heard of." He was an acquaintance of the rich and powerful and delivered the eulogy at the funeral of the poet Walt Whitman. He died in 1899.[31]

Frank Peats was mustered out in June 1864 and returned home to Bessie, whom he had married in November 1861. Frank became the sheriff of Winnebago County, Illinois. After two years of suffering with stomach cancer, he passed away in 1895. Bessie died in 1917.[32]

Robert Duncan, the sergeant in Josiah's company who recorded most of the company's daily activities and was wounded at Shiloh, left the army in 1864 along with most of the company. In his application for a pension, Duncan stated that he was of sound body when he entered the army but was afflicted with chronic diarrhea, which began in 1861 and continued for years after his discharge. (He later suffered from "hemiplegia," or paralysis of one side of the body due to a stroke he suffered in 1884.) In 1868, Duncan married Mary Alice Dalzall and the couple moved to Iowa, where they had three children. He divorced Alice with a filing in the state of Nebraska in 1884 and married Ella Goodshaw just a week later. Alice was not aware of the divorce until she applied for a widow's pension after Robert's death in 1906. In her legal filings, Alice claimed she left Robert in Iowa due to a business failing and returned to Illinois so her family could help support her and her children. At some point, Robert moved to Nebraska and filed for divorce, claiming that Alice had abandoned him. Alice's claim for a widow's pension was denied. Robert Duncan's remains lie in the Monmouth Cemetery.[33]

---

31 Website of pbs.org. Website of the Council for Secular Humanism. John Kelly, "Robert Ingersoll, the 'Great Agnostic'", *Washington Post*, August 11, 2012.

32 From material contained in Peats collection and pension records for Frank Peats and Bessie Peats in National Archives.

33 Pension records of Robert Duncan. NARA.

James Earp, who was shot during the 17th Illinois' first real battle at Fort Donelson and discharged from the service because of the wound, moved around a good deal after the war. By 1881 James was in Tombstone, Arizona, along with his more famous brothers, Wyatt, Virgil, and Morgan. He was managing a saloon and gambling house on October 26 when his brothers engaged in the famous gunfight at the O.K. Corral. James's disability was perhaps the reason he did not participate in the firefight with his brothers that day.[34]

Captain James Jones of the 38th Mississippi, who buried a brother at Vicksburg and wrote of fraternizing with members of the 17th Illinois, rose to become the colonel of the regiment. Two more of his brothers, one just 17 years old, died in fighting in 1864 at Harrisburg, Mississippi, a fight in which Jones himself was severely wounded. James survived the war and was elected to both the Mississippi house and senate, and later served as the state's lieutenant governor. Tragedy continued to follow the former Confederate officer after the war when his only two children, a boy and a girl, died very young. Jones lived a long life and passed away in 1911. There is a monument to him on the Vicksburg battlefield, placed there by his family shortly after he died. It is near the spot where Jones and the men of the 38th Mississippi endured the long weeks of siege opposite Josiah and the men of the 17th Illinois.[35]

Following completion of his studies, Josiah entered a new service—the service of the Lord. For almost three decades he served a series of Presbyterian congregations throughout Illinois in El Paso, Macomb, Canton, Peoria, Woodhull, and Kewanee. He also spent a brief period as a missionary in Missouri. Josiah and Jennie had six children: Margaret (born June 3, 1865), Jennie (born on October 9, 1867), Jessie Maggie (born on July 4, 1871, and died the same year), Jessie Rogers (born March 12, 1873, and died that August), Charles (born August 28, 1874), and Herbert (born August 17, 1876. Herbert would become president of Lake Forest College north of Chicago).

As the years went by, Josiah, like other veterans, witnessed the passing of many of the men with whom he had fought. William S. McClanahan, Josiah's lieutenant until the death of his father in battle caused him to resign, died in

34 Guinn, The Last Gunfight, 207, 233.

35 Biographical and Historical Memoirs of Mississippi, 1055; Giambrone, Illustrated Guide to the Vicksburg Campaign, 239; Letter from Jones to Joe Pendleton in Pendleton's pension file, Texas State Archives. Courtesy of Jeff Giambrone.

Cabinet photo of Josiah Moore as chaplain of the Illinois Grand Army of the Republic (G.A.R.) Josiah served as chaplain in 1890. *Author*

June 1888. He had returned to school, become a preacher in March 1864, and reenlisted as a captain in another Illinois regiment that May. He was discharged later that year, returned to religious service, and fathered eight children, two of whom died in childhood. Josiah praised McClanahan in the *Oracle* as a soldier who "seldom missed one of the many marches and skirmishes that occurred almost daily. . . . [A]mid all these scenes of danger and bloody strife he bore the part of a true hero, inspiring all around him to deeds of noblest daring."[36]

As he advanced in years, the health issues Josiah had suffered during the war worsened. In August 1890 he applied for a pension under the terms of the Pension Act of June 27, 1890, citing physical problems due to "Varicose veins in left leg, and throat trouble, the latter contracted in the army" after he spent one month with no shelter during the Vicksburg siege. His request was denied. These health issues forced his retirement from active ministry in 1893, and Josiah and Jennie moved to Lake Forest, Illinois. In 1896, Josiah, now 62 years old, applied for total disability due to "cardiac asthma" that caused him to "suffer day and night." He was granted a pension of $6 per month. Despite his maladies, he remained active in GAR activities and served as the commander of the organization's Lake Forest Post. In January 1896 he was still six feet three inches tall and weighed 198 pounds.

Josiah died on February 9, 1897, and was buried in Springdale Cemetery in Peoria—Jennie's home town, the place where Josiah's military service began in earnest, and where the couple had first met. Various Illinois papers, including

36 Monmouth College, *Oracle*, 39-40.

Reunion photo of 17th Illinois Infantry, taken on August 28, 1889, at Sylvan Park in Peoria. Josiah is in the last row, third from the left. The "lady-major" Belle Reynolds is in the front row, fourth from the left. Robert Campbell, who served in Josiah's company, is in the front row, third from the left. *David and Liz Djupe*

Josiah Moore and family. Josiah and Jennie are seated in the front. The children, left to right: Charles, Jennie, Margaret, and Herbert. Based on the ages of the children, this photo was taken sometime in the 1890s. *Paul Djupe*

those in Galena, Peoria, Woodhull, and Canton, reported his death. In addition to Jennie and the children, he was survived by two brothers and two sisters. Coincidentally, Josiah's death arrived at the very peak of interest in the Civil War.[37]

Josiah's pall bearers included two former members of the 17th Illinois, Robert Campbell and George Bush. Campbell had left the 17th in 1863 to take an appointment as an officer in one of the new black regiments. Another former member of the regiment, Thomas Stephenson, conducted the service.

A brown leather book, with "In Memoriam, Josiah Moore" embossed on the cover, was prepared shortly after his passing. Inside are various recollections of Josiah, including newspaper articles, a ribbon from one of the 17th's reunions, and mementoes of his education, which Jennie or the children attached to the pages. The invaluable book also includes numerous letters and

37 Marten, *Sing Not War*, 147.

David Djupe, Josiah's and Jennie's great-grandson, with his wife Liz. According to family legend, the love seat pictured here is the one on which Josiah proposed to Jennie. David passed away in October 2015. *Author*

telegrams sent to Jennie and her children by Josiah's friends and wartime comrades.[38]

One of the letters in the book was from Abraham Ryan, who was serving as the president of the Savings, Investment and Trust Company in East Orange, New Jersey. "I remember his talents, his bravery, his manly bearing in all his actions, the love and respect that his men, his fellow soldiers and officers bore him," Ryan wrote of Josiah. "A purer, more upright man I never knew." Ryan died in 1903 and is buried in Falmouth, Massachusetts.

Leonard Ross, the former colonel of the 17th Illinois, sent a communication to Jennie dated April 9, 1897:

> *Capt. Moore was my ideal man and soldier. . . . For the soldierly bearing and high moral standing attained by the 17th Reg't Ill. Vol. Inf'y in the civil war it was*

---

38 All of this is in the possession of the author.

*indebted to no one person more than to Capt. Moore. From our first meeting in
Peoria in May 1861, we were friends, and without a cloud or a shadow we so
continued till the day of his death. I loved him as a brother, and can well
understand the extent of your great loss. I too, am no stranger to the sorrows of
bereavement. Within the last 18 months it has been my sad lot to part with wife,
brother and sister. The friends and relatives on the other side of the River far
outnumber those remaining here. If this life were all—if there was no hope beyond
the grave—how sad, indeed, would be our lot. In this your great sorrow accept for
yourself and family my sincere sympathy and condolence; and please say to your
sons that I hope and trust they will spare no efforts to become as good, true, manly
and grand men as their honored father.*

*Wishing that our Heavenly Father may watch over you and yours and guide
and direct all your ways, I am very truly.*

Your friend,
Leonard F. Ross

Ross himself died just four years after writing this message, and was buried in
Lewistown, Illinois.[39]

At his death, Josiah had an estate valued at about $13,000, including notes
and the home in Lake Forest. Jennie lived off the estate and a widow's pension
of $12 per month until 1900, when many of the investments failed and her
children took her in. Her income declined from $130 in 1897 to $60 in 1899.
Jennie died in October 1924. She is buried in suburban Chicago. No one knows
why Josiah and Jennie, who were so devoted to each other during their mortal
lives, are buried so many miles apart.[40]

39 Boatner, *Civil War Dictionary*, 709; Illinois, www.findagrave.com.
40 Pension file of Josiah Moore. NARA.

2016 APPENDIX 1

An Interview with Gene Barr,
author of *A Civil War Captain and His Lady*

SB: Thanks for talking with us today Mr. Barr. How did you come to write your book on this topic?

GB: Thank you. I acquired this collection of 75 letters some years ago, found the story utterly fascinating, and I thought it would make a good book.

SB: How specifically did you find out about Josiah's letters?

GB: I acquired the letters from a business colleague who had inherited them a few years prior. He knew of my interest in this period of American history, and asked me to help him dispose of them. After I quickly perused them, I decided, with the encouragement of a good friend, to acquire them. It became apparent that if the letters were sold, the collection would be broken up and the story of these two individuals would never be told.

SB: What was it about the collection that convinced you of its worth?

GB: It became clear very quickly that this was a correspondence between a Union Civil War officer (Josiah Moore) and a woman (Jennie Lindsay) he had met before leaving for war. The letters documented their courtship over a period of three years. There are a large number of publications that reproduce soldier letters, but that is because it was easier for families back home to keep them in good condition. However, it was much more difficult for a soldier at the front enduring the rigors of campaigning to keep letters from the home front, so having correspondence from both individuals, as well a few from other family members, is very rare.

SB: Did anything leap out when you first read the letters?

GB: Lots of things. First, it was obvious both of the individuals were very literate and their letters were full of details of army life, battle, politics, religion, life on the home front, the course of the war, and so forth. So many letters from this period dwell on the very mundane. Now of course there is some of the mundane here as well, but that is the exception and not the rule.

SB: Did you transcribe the letters yourself?

GB: I did. I personally keyed in each of the 75 wartime letters (there are a number of postwar letters as well) and then detemined how this touching story fit into the climate of the period.

SB: What was it like to read so many private letters between two young people like this?

GB: Reading the letters was a fascinating trip back in time. Because there are so many, I was able to better understand the personalities of both Josiah and Jennie. The rarity of having access to something like this, together with the extraordinary detail in these letters, gave me the impetus to put their personal story into the larger context of the time in book form.

SB: Can you give me some examples?

GB: Sure. For example, Josiah wrote quite a bit about his regiments, the 17th Illinois Infantry and its battles at Pittsburg Landing—Shiloh—Fort Donelson, and the initial fighting at Vicksburg and the siege that followed, three of the big battles in which he was engaged. This is fascinating unpublished material, and Jennie's replies from the home front added real historical value. But that is just the beginning. The letters also discuss their belief in God, their evolving views of blacks and slavery, the causes of the war, and so forth . . .

SB: And Jennie's father added a twist to the story . . .

GB: When I discovered that Jennie's father was a prominent member of the Peoria, Illinois community—he had served in the Illinois House of Representatives prior to the war and then was elected to the state senate as a Democrat in 1862—the political aspects of the letters took on an entirely new view. And her father, John Lindsay, went on to become one of the best-known Peace Democrats while his daughter is courting a Union soldier whose views did not fully match his own.

SB: Was there anything difficult about writing A Civil War Captain and His Lady?

GB: Reading the letters was often a challenge. It wasn't simply that in some cases the ink had faded or words were illegible, but the language was a bit stilted and the quirks in punctuation often made it difficult to follow. And I kept nearly all the original punctuation and quirks, changing only very little for readability issues. It became less of a challenge as I got into the rhythm of their writing patterns. Another thing to overcome was the lack of information on the 17th Illinois Infantry. There is very little about this regiment. I did find some unpublished material on the 17th, and it helped that I was able to connect with David Djupe, the great-grandson of Josiah and Jennie, who lived in the Chicago area. He provided a wealth of information on Josiah and Jennie and other family members.

SB: What was it like connecting with Josiah and Jennie's great-grandson?

GB: After reading all of the letters between Josiah and Jennie, it was great to meet David and his wife Liz. Having a tangible connection with the descendants of the people I had "met" through their correspondence was amazing. David had a significant amount of background information on the family and he was more than willing to share it with me. In fact, the photos of Josiah and Jennie in the book were provided by Dave, along with other photos we used. Dave is keenly interested in history and both he and his wife have done extensive research on their family. His enthusiasm about this project, about sharing the story of Josiah and Jennie with others, was a great encouragement for me.

SB: How did you decide to footnote the letters?

GB: That was tough and a balance had to be found. It is easy to overdue that, and if you do then the footnotes overwhelm the main material. I tried to identify the people mentioned, and the units and events, and keep a light fingerprint throughout. This isn't a history about the 17th Illinois, but a presentation of the letters of a pair of Civil War-era lovers engulfed in a civil war.

SB: Let's talk about that last point. Why did you want to reveal the role of a soldier's sweetheart?

GB: I thought it would be illustrative to present a real old fashioned 19th century courtship—rituals and all. Jennie's letters gave me the opportunity to show the role of women on the home front, how it differed among classes and regions, and document the importance of how letters from home encouraged those at the front and kept up the morale of the men in the ranks. Of course negative comments from home could hurt morale—and there are examples of that in this book. As I mentioned earlier, a few publications include letters between a husband serving in the military and his wife at home, but letters that document an evolving courtship are rare, especially in this number.

SB: Should we have a spoiler alert and talk about what happened to Jennie and Josiah after the war? Was there an after?

GB: Well, readers will have to stop here, if they haven't read the book! Josiah does survive the war. He marries Jennie, is ordained a Presbyterian minister, and they raise a family. One of the more fascinating aspects of this story is the postwar period experienced by people like Josiah. It was enlightening to see how these veterans and our country moved forward after four years of fratricide that saw 600,000 or 700,000 Americans die. These vets faced many of the same physical, mental, and spiritual challenges faced by our fighting men and women today. They suffered extensively from PTSD, and a lot of that is documented in the book, including suicide. It was also noteworthy to discover how the view of the war changed among Americans in the decades after it ended and the hurdles faced by those who had been enslaved. It is all here.

SB: We should mention that this previously unpublished material on the 17th Illinois is entirely contained within the war's Western Theater.

GB: It's certainly no secret that the Eastern Theater has received significantly more attention for a number of reasons. There are exponentially more books and articles on the battles and campaigns of Virginia, Maryland, and Pennsylvania, than those fought in Mississippi, Tennessee, and Georgia. The material I acquired and discovered in my research not only brings new information to light on conflicts such as Fort Donelson, Shiloh, Vicksburg, but also Josiah's first skirmish at Fredericktown, a variety of smaller expeditions in which he and his regiment participated, and the fascinating if nearly bloodless Meridian Campaign in early 1864—which was really a trial run for Sherman's March to the Sea. *A Civil War Captain and His Lady* also delves into the Midwestern home front and the politics of states, in this case Illinois, where partisanship threatened to seriously disrupt the war effort.

SB: Thank you for talking with us today, Gene.

GB: You're welcome.

Bibliography

Newspapers

Peoria *Daily Transcript* (Peoria, IL)

Monmouth *Atlas* (Monmouth, IL)

Philadelphia *Inquirer* (Philadelphia, PA)

Washington Post (Washington, DC)

Archival Sources

Abraham Lincoln Presidential Library, Springfield, IL

    Campbell, Robert M. *Brief History of the 17th Regiment Illinois Volunteer Infantry*

    Vanauken, Abram Papers: Vanauken, A. J. To the Beat of the Long Roll: The Diary of A. J. Vanauken, Company K, 17th Regt Ill Vol., 1861-1863

    Smith, George O. A Brief History of the 17th Illinois Volunteer Regiment

Bradley University Library

    May, George. "Democratic Political Tradition in Peoria County to 1900," Master's thesis.

Gene Barr Collection

    Moore, Josiah, *History of the 17th Illinois*

    Original Muster Sheet for Company F, 17th Illinois

    Photos, and Memorandum Book

Illinois State Archives, Springfield, IL

    Regimental papers of the 17th Illinois Infantry

Knox College Library

Colville, Robert. Jottings from the 17th

Lake County Discovery Museum, Wauconda, IL

Peats, Frank Papers

Mary Elizabeth Perrin and Family

A. A. Bethune Letter, 5th North Carolina Cavalry

Monmouth College, Monmouth Illinois, Department of History

William Urban, Paper on William P. Rupp

National Archives

Claycomb, Murry. Military Service File and Court Martial Records

Deckert, Jeremiah. Military Service File

Duncan, Robert. Military Service File and Pension Records

Earp, James. Military Service File and Pension Records

Lindsay, James A. Military Service File and Pension Records

Moore, Josiah. Military Service File and Pension Records

Norton, Addison. Military Service File

Oelert, Ferdinand. Court Martial Records

Peats, Frank. Military Service File and Pension Records

Pressley, Henry. Military Service File

Robbins, Edmund. Military Service File

Rook, John. Military Service File

Ryan, Abraham H. Military Service File and Pension Records

Old Court House Museum, Vicksburg, MS

Buck, George Letter

Peoria Historical Society

Barnett, Rockwell, *Peoria in Civil War Days*, February 20, 1956

Texas State Archives

Jones, J. H. Letter to Joe Pendleton

Vicksburg National Military Park

Bush, Henry Diary

Lorimar, William Paper

Smith, Frank. Letter

Warren County, IL Historical Society

Duncan, Robert. Company Log of the 17th Illinois, Company F

Government Publications

The War of the Rebellion: *A Compilation of the Official Records of the Union and Confederate Armies.* Washington, DC: Government Printing Office, 1880-1901.

Book, Magazines, Periodicals, and Circulars

Adams, Michael C. C. *Living Hell: The Dark Side of the Civil War.* Baltimore, MD, 2014.

Alexander, Edward. "And Then We Kill," *Hallowed Ground*, Volume 14, #4, Winter 2013.

Aley, Ginette and J. L. Anderson. *Union Heartland: The Midwestern Home Front During the Civil War.* Carbondale, IL, 2013.

————. "Inescapable Realities: Rural Midwestern Women and Families during the Civil War," in Aley and Anderson, *Union Heartland.*

Allen, Stacy. "Shiloh," *Blue and Gray Magazine*, Volume XIV Issue 3.

Atkinson, Rick. *Day of Battle.* New York, NY, 2007.

David F. Bastian. *Grant's Canal: The Union's Attempt to Bypass Vicksburg.* Shippensburg, PA, 1995.

Bateman, Newton, et al. *Historical Encyclopedia of Illinois and History of Peoria County*, Vol 2, Chicago and Peoria, 1902.

Bearss, Edwin. "The Fall of Vicksburg," *Civil War Times Magazine*, July 2006.

————. *The Vicksburg Campaign* (3 vols.) Dayton, Ohio 1985.

Bearss, Margie, *Sherman's Forgotten Campaign: The Meridian Expedition.* Baltimore, MD, 1987

Biographical and Historical Memoirs of Mississippi, Vol I. Chicago, IL, 1891.

Blaisdell, Bob, ed, *Civil War Letters: From Home, Camp, and Battlefield.* Mineola, NY, 2012.

Boatner, Mark M. *The Civil War Dictionary.* New York, 1959.

Boritt, Gabor, ed. *Why The Civil War Came.* New York/Oxford, 1996.

Brands, H. W. *The Man Who Saved the Union: Ulysses Grant in War and Peace.* New York, 2012.

Bryner, Cloyd. *Bugle Echoes: The Story of the Illinois 47th.* . Springfield, IL, 1905.

Buell, General Don Carlos. *In Battles and Leaders of the Civil War.* Century Series, Vol 1 No 4, April 16, 1894, New York, 1894.

Catton, Bruce. *Grant Moves South.* Boston Toronto, 1960.

————. *A Stillness at Appomattox.* New York, 1953.

Cedere, David. "Carrying the Home Front to War: Soldiers, Race, and New England Culture during the Civil War," in Cimbala and Miller, ed. *Union Soldiers and the Northern Home Front.* New York, 2002.

Cimbala, Paul A and Randall Miller. *Union Soldiers and the Northern Home Front.* New York, 2002.

Circular and Catalogue of the Officers and Students of Monmouth College. Monmouth, Illinois 1861.

Clarke, Frances M. War Stories: *Suffering and Sacrifice in the Civil War North*. Chicago, 2011.

Coddington, Edwin B. *The Gettysburg Campaign: A Study in Command*. New York, 1968.

Cotton, Gordon and Jeff Giambrone. *Vicksburg and the War*. Gretna, MS, 2004.

Cunningham, O. Edward, Gary D. Joiner and Timothy B. Smith, ed. *Shiloh and the Western Campaign of 1862*. New York, 2007.

Connolly, S. J. *The Oxford Companion to American History*. Oxford, 1998.

Cooling, Benjamin. "Forts Henry and Donelson." *Blue and Gray Magazine*, Volume IX, Issue 3, 1992.

Dickson, Paul. *War Slang*. New York, 1994.

Donald, David. *Lincoln*. New York, 1995.

Dyer, Frederick H. *Compendium of the War of the Rebellion*. New York, 1959.

East, Ernest E. *Abraham Lincoln Sees Peoria: An Historical and Pictorial Record of Seventeen Visits From 1832 to 1858*. Peoria, IL 1939.

Faust, Drew Gilpin. *This Republic of Suffering: Death and the American Civil War*. New York, 2008.

———. "Ours as Well as Men," in James McPherson and William J. Cooper, eds. *Writing the Civil War*. Columbia, SC, 1998.

Foner, Eric and Garraty, John A., eds. *The Reader's Companion to American History*. Boston, 1991.

Force, M. F. *Campaigns of the Civil War: From Fort Henry to Corinth*. New Jersey, 1881.

Gallagher, Gary. *The Union War*. Cambridge, MA, 2011.

Garrison, Webb. *The Encyclopedia of Civil War Usage*. Nashville, TN, 2001.

Giambrone, Jeff. *Illustrated Guide to the Vicksburg Campaign*. Gretna, MS, 2011.

Giesberg, Judith. *Army at Home: Women and the Civil War on the Northern Home Front*. Chapel Hill, NC, 2009.

Goodheart, Adam. *1861: The Civil War Awakening*. New York, 2011.

Grant, Ulysses S. *Personal Memoirs of U.S. Grant*. New York, 1885.

Greenberg, Amy S. *A Wicked War*. New York, 2012.

Groom, Winston. *Shiloh 1862*. Washington, DC, 2012.

Guinn, Jeff. *The Last Gunfight*. New York, 2011.

Hess, Earl J. *Braxton Bragg: The Most Hated General of the Confederacy*. Chapel Hill, 2016.

———. "Tell Me What the Sensations Are': The Northern Home Front Learns about Combat," in Cimbala and Miller, eds., *Union Soldiers and the Northern Home Front*. New York, 2002.

Hewitt, Janet, ed., *Supplement to the Official Records of the Union and Confederate Armies*. 100 vols. Wendell, NC., 1994-2001

Hicken, Victor. *Illinois in the Civil War*. Urbana and Chicago, IL, 1966.

History of McDonough County, Illinois. Springfield, IL 1885.

Hogan, David J. et al. *Irish American Chronicle*. Lincolnwood, IL, 2009.

Holt, Michael F. *The Fate of Their Country*. New York, 2004.

Hughes, Nathaniel Chears. *The Battle of Belmont: Grant Strikes South*. Chapel Hill, NC, 1991

Hurt, R. Douglas, "Agricultural Power of the Midwest," in Aley and Anderson, eds. *Union Heartland: The Midwestern Home Front During the Civil War*. Carbondale, IL, 2013.

Jobe, James. "The Battles for Forts Henry and Donelson." *Blue and Gray Magazine*, Volume XXVIII, Number 4, 2011.

Jones, J. H. "The Rank and File at Vicksburg." *Mississippi Historical Society*, Vol VII. Oxford, MS, 1903.

Jordan, Brian Matthew. *Marching Home: Union Veterans and Their Unending Civil War*. New York/London, 2014.

Kaiser, Leo. "Letters from the Front." *Journal of the Illinois Historical Society*, Volume LVI, Number 2, Summer 1963.

Katcher, Philip. *The Civil War Day by Day*. New York, 2010.

Kellogg, Mary E. *Army Life of an Illinois Soldier: Letters and Diaries of the late Charles W. Wills*. Washington, DC, 1906.

Lehrman, Lewis E. *Lincoln at Peoria: The Turning Point*. Mechanicsburg, PA. 2008.

Leslie, Frank. *The Soldier in Our Civil War*. New York & Atlanta, GA, 1893.

Levine, Bruce. *The Fall of the House of Dixie*. New York, 2013.

Linderman, Gerald. *Embattled Courage: The Experience of Combat in the American Civil War*. New York, 1987.

Manning, Chandra. *What This Cruel War Was Over*. New York, 2007.

Marten, James. *Civil War America: Voices from the Home Front*. New York, 2003.

———. *Sing Not War*. Chapel Hill, NC 2011.

Marvel, William. *Lincoln's Darkest Year: The War in 1862*. Boston/New York, 2008.

———. *The Great Task Remaining*. New York, 2010.

Marszalek, John F. *Sherman, A Soldier's Passion for Order*. New York, 1993.

May, George. *Students History of Peoria County, Illinois*. Galesburg, IL, 1968.

Mayer, Daniel and Jeffrey Rankin. *A Thousand Hearts Devotion: A History of Monmouth College*. Monmouth Illinois, 2002.

McClintock, Megan, "The Impact of the Civil War on Nineteenth Century Marriages," in Paul Cimbala and Randall Miller, eds. *Northern Home Front*. New York, 2002.

McClintock, Russell. *Lincoln and the Decision for War*. Chapel Hill, NC, 2008.

McPherson, James M. *Battle Cry of Freedom: The Civil War Era*. New York, Oxford, 1988.

———. *Tried by War: Abraham Lincoln as Commander in Chief*. New York, 2008.

———. *For Cause and Comrades: Why Men Fought in the Civil War*. New York, Oxford, 1997.

McPherson, James M. and William J. Cooper. *Writing the Civil War*. Columbia, SC, 1998.

Mitchell, Reid. *Civil War Soldiers*. New York, 1988.

———. *The Vacant Chair: The Northern Soldier Leaves Home*. New York/Oxford, 1993.

Monmouth College. *Oracle*, Volume XV Number 34, Monmouth, Illinois, 1911.

Moses, John. *Illinois Historical and Statistical*, Vol II. Chicago, 1892.

Mujic, Julie. "Ours Is The Harder Lot," in Ginette Aley and J. L. Anderson, eds. *Union Heartland: The Midwestern Home Front During the Civil War*. Carbondale, IL, 2013.

Murnane, James H. and Murnane, Peadar. *At the Ford of the Birches*. Monaghan, Ireland 1991.

Musgrave, Jon. "Welcome to New Egypt!" *American Weekend Magazine*, January 6, 1996.

Nortrup, Jack. "Richard Yates: A Personal Glimpse of the Illinois' Soldiers Friend." *Journal of the Illinois State Historical Society Volume*, LVI, Number 2, Summer 1963.

Oakes, James. *Freedom National: The Destruction of Slavery*. New York, London, 2013.

Rable, George C. *God's Almost Chosen People: A Religious History of the Civil War*. Chapel Hill, NC, 2010.

Ramold, Steven J. *Across the Divide: Union Soldiers View the Northern Home Front*. New York and London, 2013.

Richard, Patricia L. "Listen Ladies One and All: Union Soldiers Yearn for the Society of Their Fair Cousins of the North." Paul A. Cimbala and Randall M. Miller, eds. *Union Soldiers and the Northern Home Front*, New York, NY, 2002.

Robertson, James, edited by Neil Kagan. *The Untold Civil War: Exploring the Human Side of War*. Washington, DC, 2011.

Shea, William L. and Terrence J. Winschel. *Vicksburg is the Key*. Lincoln, NE, 2003.

Sherman, William T. *Personal Memoirs of Gen W. T. Sherman*. New York, 1892.

Silber, Nina. *Daughters of the Union: Northern Women Fight the Civil War*. Cambridge, MA and London, England, 2005.

Simpson, Brooks D. *Ulysses S. Grant: Triumph over Adversity, 1822-1865*. New York, 2000.

———. *The Civil War: The Third Year Told by Those Who Lived It*. New York, 2013.

Stashower, Daniel. *The Hour of Peril*. New York, 2013.

Summers, Mark Wahlgren. "The North and the Coming of the Civil War." Gabor Boritt, ed. *Why the Civil War Came*. New York/Oxford 1996.

Tuttle, Lori. "Major Belle Reynolds of Peoria." *Illinois History: A Magazine for Young People*, February 1994.

Ural, Susannah J. *Don't Hurry Me Down to Hades: The Civil War in the Words of Those Who Lived It*. London, 2013.

———. "Monmouth College in the Civil War," Journal of the Illinois State Historical Society, 2 1978.

Wagner, Margaret E., Gary W. Gallagher, and Paul Finkelman, eds. *The Library of Congress Civil War Desk Reference*. New York, 2002.

Wallace, Lew, *Battles and Leaders of the Civil War. People's Pictorial Edition, Part III*. The Century Series, Vol 1 Number 3, April 9, 1894, Century Co.

Walton, William, ed. *The Letters of Edwin Weller from Antietam to Atlanta*. New York, 1980.

Weber, Jennifer L. *Copperheads: The Rise and Fall of Lincoln's Opponents in the North*. New York, 2006.

Welsh, Jack D., M.D. *Medical Histories of Union Generals*. Kent, OH., 1996.

Welcher, Frank J. *The Union Army 1861-1865: Organization and Operations*, 2 vols. Bloomington and Indianapolis IN, 1993.

White, Jonathan W. "Remembering the Fishing Creek Confederacy," *Pennsylvania Heritage: a Quarterly of the Pennsylvania Historical and Museum Commission and the Pennsylvania Heritage Foundation*, Volume XL, No3, Summer 2014.

White, Ronald. *A. Lincoln, A Biography*. New York, 2009.

Wiley, Bell I. *The Life of Billy Yank*. New York, 1951.

Wiley, Bell I and Horst D. Milhollen. *They Who Fought Here*. New York, 1959.

Williams, T. Harry. *Lincoln and His Generals*. New York, 1952.

Wilson, James Grant. *Biographical Sketches of Illinois Officers Engaged in the War Against the Rebellion of 1861*. Chicago, 1862.

Winschel, Terrence J. *Triumph and Defeat: The Vicksburg Campaign*, Vol. 1. New York, 1994.

Woodworth, Steven. *Nothing But Victory: The Army of the Tennessee 1861-1865*. New York, 2005.

———. *While God is Marching On: The Religious World of Civil War Soldiers*. Lawrence, KS, 2001.

Internet Sources

www.civilwar.illinoisgenweb.org/reg_html/index.html. (Rosters from the Illinois Adjutant General Report)

www.ilsos.gov/isaveterans/civilMusterSearch.do. (Illinois Civil War Muster and Descriptive Rolls Database)

www.thezephyr.com/wellsbros.htm. (Rayburn, Philip, *Three Galesburg Men in the Civil War*, Zephyr Online, February 1, 2000)

www.tnvacation.com/civil-war/place/288/la-grange-union-supply-base/ (La Grange, TN.)

www.lagrangetn.com/chronology.htm. (LaGrange, TN.)

www.knox.edu/about/we-are-knox/our-history.html (Site for Knox College, Galesburg, IL.)

www.eureka.edu/discover/our-history/ (Site for Eureka College, Eureka, IL.)

www.findagrave.com (Illinois Find a Grave website)

Index

About the Author

Gene Barr is the president and CEO of the Pennsylvania Chamber of Business and Industry, the largest broad-based business advocacy group in the state. He has spent more than forty years in the political and government affairs world, including more than twelve years with a Fortune 100 energy company.

Gene has a bachelor's degree in political science from St. Joseph's University in Philadelphia. He is a board member and former chair of the National Civil War Museum in Harrisburg, Pennsylvania, and spent many years engaged in Civil War living history events. A father of three, he lives with his wife Mary in Mechanicsburg. *A Civil War Captain and His Lady* is his first book.